Contrasts in Punishment

D1319023

Why do some modern societies punish their offenders differently to others? Why are some more punitive and others more tolerant in their approach to offending, and how can these differences be explained? Based on extensive historical analysis and fieldwork in the penal systems of England, Australia and New Zealand on the one hand, and Finland, Norway and Sweden on the other, this book seeks to address these underlying questions.

The book argues that the penal differences that currently exist between these two clusters of societies emanate from their early nineteenth-century social arrangements. The Anglophone societies were dominated by exclusionary values systems, in contrast to the more inclusionary values of the Nordic. The development of their penal programmes over this two-hundred-year period, including the much earlier demise of the death penalty in the Nordic countries and the significant differences between the respective prison rates and prison conditions of the two clusters, reflects the continuing influence of these values. Indeed, in the early twenty-first century these differences have become even more pronounced.

John Pratt and Anna Eriksson offer a unique contribution to the growing importance of comparative research in the history and sociology of punishment. This book will be of interest to those studying criminology, sociology, punishment, prison and penal policy, as well as professionals working in prisons or in the area of penal policy across the six societies that feature in the book.

John Pratt is Professor of Criminology at Victoria University of Wellington, New Zealand. From 2009–2012 he was also a Royal Society of New Zealand James Cook Research Fellow in Social Science, and from 2010–2011 he was a Fellow of the Straus Institute for Advanced Studies of Law and Justice at New York University. He has published extensively in the areas of the history and sociology of punishment and comparative penology. In 2009 he was awarded the prestigious Radzinowicz Prize by the Editorial Board of the *British Journal of Criminology*.

Anna Eriksson is a Senior Lecturer in Criminology at Monash University, Melbourne, Australia. In 2009 she was awarded the New Scholar Prize by the Australian and New Zealand Society of Criminology for best publication, and in 2012 was the recipient of one of only two Australian Research Councils Awards for early career researchers in criminology, funding a three-year study on comparative punishment between Australia and Sweden.

Routledge frontiers of criminal justice

Contrasts in Punishment

An explanation of Anglophone
excess and Nordic exceptionalism

John Pratt and Anna Eriksson

LONDON AND NEW YORK

First published 2013
by Routledge
2 Park Square, Milton Park, Abingdon, Oxon, OX14 4RN

Simultaneously published in the USA and Canada
by Routledge
711 Third Avenue, New York, NY 10017

Routledge is an imprint of the Taylor & Francis Group, an informa business

British Library Cataloguing in Publication Data
A catalogue record for this book is available from the British Library

Library of Congress Cataloging-in-Publication Data
Pratt, John, 1949–
Contrasts in punishment: an explanation of Anglophone excess and Nordic
exceptionalism/John Pratt and Anna Eriksson. – 1st ed.
    p. cm. – (Routledge frontiers of criminal justice; 7)
   Includes bibliographical references.
  1. Punishment–Scandinavia–History. 2. Punishment–English-speaking
countries–History. 3. Criminal justice, Administration of
Scandinavia–History. 4. Criminal justice, Administration of–English-
speaking countries–History. I. Eriksson, Anna. II. Title.
HV9960.S34P73 2012
364.60917'521–dc23   2012023376

ISBN13: 978–0–415–52473–5 (hbk)
ISBN13: 978–0–415–65690–0 (pbk)
ISBN13: 978–0–203–09611–6 (ebk)

Typeset in Times New Roman
by Swales & Willis Ltd, Exeter, Devon

For Isabella

I murmured that I had no shoes; then I met a man who had no feet.
– old Persian proverb

Contents

Illustrations

Figures

Tables

Preface

This book developed almost by accident, with some lucky breaks and happy coincidences along the way, rather than being the product of some carefully worked out plan that was then rewarded with a generous research budget. It grew from an opportunity that occurred towards the end of 2003, when my employers, Victoria University of Wellington, announced that there was money available for seeding research – but with the caveat that it had to be spent by the end of the year, otherwise it would be lost. At that time, New Zealand's Labour-led coalition government had copied Tony Blair's utterly specious promise to be 'tough on crime, tough on the causes of crime'. The inevitable consequences were a dramatically increasing prison population and, thus, overcrowded prisons, amidst a frenetic and usually uninformed public discourse on law and order. It was at this point that the idea suddenly came to me – although I then had very little idea of what it would actually involve – that I would like to do research on *low imprisonment* societies: how had they managed to avoid the fiasco that was taking place in New Zealand and similar Anglophone societies? Accordingly, I put in what proved to be a successful bid for some of the funding. This then allowed me, at very short notice, to undertake a European tour that lasted one month, during the course of which I visited a number of countries, including Denmark, Finland, Norway and Sweden (although not Iceland, which simply seemed too remote and too much of a 'special case' because of its population size). I spent a few days in each country, visiting one or two prisons in each and having discussions with academics and civil servants.

Nils Christie, at the Institute of Criminology, University of Oslo, whom I already knew, arranged my trip to Norway, and also provided me with contact people in the other Nordic countries, particularly Henrik Tham at the Department of Criminology, University of Stockholm, and Tapio Lappi-Seppälä at the National Research Institute of Legal Policy in Helsinki. It was the interest and encouragement of these three gentlemen, in particular, that made it possible for the Nordic research to develop as it did. I also recognized early on that, to maximise the value of any research that I undertook, it was going to be important to look at *clusters of societies*: this would have much more sociological impact and validity than a study of one small modern society (as most of those with low imprisonment rates seem to be). In these respects, the Nordic countries were the most obvious choice. Furthermore, there were no *immediate* language difficulties since just about everybody spoke excellent English in these countries.

In addition, through Henrik Tham and Jukka Kekkonen (another pivotal Nordic figure for me) in the Faculty of Law, University of Helsinki, I was offered Teaching Fellowships for 2006 that included free accommodation and an honorarium. This would mean that fieldwork in Sweden and Finland would mainly be self-financing. It was also clear, though, that I would need institutional support in each host country, in terms of having a community of interested others to whom I could turn for guidance, introductions, etc. At that time, criminology at the University of Copenhagen was in the process of reorganization; in contrast, there was a lively research community at the Institute of Criminology in Oslo (a member had also asked me on arrival, 'Why have you come here? Nothing ever happens here', which, after all the law and order 'noise' in New Zealand, was exactly what I wanted to hear). Hence, the selections of Norway (a visit funded by my university's research and study leave allowance and a travel grant from the Scandinavian Research Council for Criminology), Finland and Sweden for the Nordic research. Most regrettably, I had to decline the offer of a subsequent Fellowship at the University of Copenhagen, which Flemming Balvig was able to secure for me, after I decided – thankfully – that that the study of *three* low imprisonment societies was sufficient for the purposes of this research.

A two-part article, based on this research, appeared in the *British Journal of Criminology* in 2008 (the editor, Pat Carlen, had very helpfully suggested that I split my otherwise too lengthy manuscript in this way before submission). These papers concentrated mainly on post-1940s Nordic developments, because this was the period for which English documentation was mostly available. The Anglophone countries, in effect, were silent comparators at this point. Thereafter, I had an important decision to make. Instead of signing off at this juncture, I chose to take the research further and to turn it into a more specific explanation of the penal contrasts between the Nordic and Anglophone societies. More fieldwork in the former was undertaken in 2008–2009 with the assistance of two more Teaching Fellowships, another Scandinavian Research Council for Criminology travel grant and funding from Victoria University. More significantly, however, it was imperative that I now started to mine previously untranslated Nordic documentation to advance the analysis. Fortunately, this did not then depend on my own attempts to learn Swedish since, in 2008, I serendipitously met the joint author of this book, Dr Anna Eriksson, based at Monash University, at a conference in Perth, Western Australia, and I was able to recruit her to the project. Swedish herself, and fluent in Norwegian and Danish as well, she was, amongst other things, able to take charge of the vast majority of the Nordic translations and provide guidance on Nordic society as a whole, as the comparative project that the research had now become began to take shape. Without this contribution from her, it would simply have been impossible for this book to have been written.

At much the same time that Anna began work with me, in 2009 I was awarded a Royal Society of New Zealand (RSNZ) James Cook Research Fellowship in Social Science (with thanks to John Morrow and Pat Carlen for their letters of support). This took me out of university teaching and administration and allowed me to concentrate specifically on this research, as well as providing some limited funding for the Anglophone fieldwork: the logic for the three societies that were selected for this purpose – England, New Zealand and Australia – is explained in the Introduction. More good fortune then followed: I was invited to take up a Fellowship at the Straus Institute for Advanced Studies of Law and Justice at New York University for the 2010–2011 academic year. In the company of eight other 'Punishment Fellows', a group convened by David Garland who also chaired the workshop sessions that we had, this proved to be a providential experience. I am very grateful to the RSNZ for temporarily suspending the Cook Fellowship so that I could spend the year there, and for then allowing it to resume. This meant that from July 2009 to June 2012, when the manuscript was completed, I lived continuously, if not always harmoniously, with this project.

The book builds on and embellishes ideas and materials set out in my 2008 *British Journal of Criminology* articles, 'Scandinavian exceptionalism in an era of penal excess, parts I and II'; 'Penal excess and penal exceptionalism: Welfare and imprisonment in Anglophone and Scandinavian societies', in Adam Crawford (2011) (ed.), *International and Comparative Criminal Justice and Urban Governance*, Cambridge University Press; and, with Anna Eriksson, 'Scandinavian exceptionalism in penal policy', in the *Nordisk Tidsskrift for Kriminalvidenskab* (2009); 'Mr Larsson is walking out again: The origins and development of Scandinavian prison policy', *Australian and New Zealand Journal of Criminology* (2010); 'In defence of Scandinavian exceptionalism', in Jane Dullum and Thomas Ugelvik's (2011) *Penal Exceptionalism?*, Routledge; and 'Penal policy and the social democratic image of Society', in Kerry Carrington, *et al.* (eds) (2012) *Crime Justice and Social Democracy*, Palgrave Macmillan.

I would like to thank everyone who took the time to have discussions about penal policy in their country with me as the fieldwork was undertaken; similarly, all the prison staff and inmates at the penal institutions that were visited for their helpfulness; and Lars Krantz for facilitating these visits in Sweden; similarly, Jonas Uchermann in Norway, Esa Vesterbacka and Jarmo Littunen in Finland; the New Zealand Department of Corrections; Luke Grant in New South Wales; and in England, Alison Liebling who introduced me to Alan Scott and Eileen Fenerty-Lyons at North West Prisons, and they then very kindly arranged visits for me. I am also grateful to Magnus Hörnqvist, Hanns von Hofer, Roddy Nilsson, Yngve Hammerlin, David Brown, Mark Finnane, Paul Morris, Ragnar Kristoffersen, Allan Brodie, Wayne Morrison, Melanie Nolan, Philip Stenning, Russell Smandych, and Karen Harrison for their advice, assistance and encouragement as the project took shape. I would particularly like to thank Nicola Lacey, who read an early version of the whole manuscript and provided very helpful directions and suggestions, as well as David Green, Thomas Ugelvik, Per-Åke Nylander, David Riley and Charles Sedgwick, who read and commented on individual chapters. I would also like to thank Thomas Ugelvik and Jane Dullum for organizing conferences at the University of Oslo in 2009 and 2010 that allowed me to present the ideas behind the *British Journal of Criminology* articles to Nordic audiences. Thanks are also due to Thomas Sutton and Nicola Hartley at Routledge for their support and encouragement. A succession of Victoria University of Wellington research grants allowed me to hire as research assistants/translators Carin Lennesiö, Kimberley Gustavsson and Leonard Swahn in Sweden, and Line Marie Sørsdal, Linda Gulli and Silje Finstad in Norway. Ilse Lehtimaja translated a large amount of Finnish language documentation. In addition, I was able to hire Craig Carpenter and Swati Bhim in Wellington. Anne Holland worked for me throughout this period and also formatted the manuscript, prepared the tables and figures and collated the bibliography. Thanks are due to my daughter Isabella and dog Suzie for being themselves. I am greatly indebted to Anna Chang for her tolerance, forbearance and encouragement. The end product, of course, remains the responsibility of myself and Anna Eriksson.

John Pratt
Institute of Criminology
Victoria University of Wellington
New Zealand
June 2012

Introduction

Two prisons, two kinds of societies

A feature article in *Time* magazine (May 2010: 18) carried the headline, 'Norway Builds the World's Most Humane Prison'. It went on to state that the King of Norway had formally opened Halden prison (see Figure 0.1), accompanied by a chorus of 30 men and women, each wearing a blue [prison officer] uniform, who gave a 'spirited rendition of "We Are the World"'. The prison's amenities included 'a sound studio, jogging trails and a freestanding two-bedroom house where inmates can host their families during overnight visits'. Furthermore, 'the air isn't tinged with the smell of sweat and urine. Instead, the scent of orange sorbet emanates from the "kitchen laboratory" where inmates take cooking courses.' The prison was designed so that it 'looks as much like the outside world as possible', its architect explained. To avoid an institutional atmosphere, 'exteriors are not concrete but made of bricks, galvanized steel and larch; the buildings seem to have grown organically from the woodlands'. While there is 'one obvious sign of incarceration – a six metre concrete security wall along the prison's perimeter – trees obscure it and its top has been rounded off "so it isn't too hostile"'. Within the prison, the reporter noted that 'the cells rival well-appointed college dorm rooms, with their flatscreen TVs and minifridges. Designers chose long vertical windows because they let in more sunlight . . . every 10 to 12 cells share a living room and kitchen. With their stainless steel countertops, wraparound sofas and birch coloured coffee tables, they resemble IKEA showrooms . . . Prison guards don't carry guns . . . and they routinely eat meals and play sports with inmates.'

Different prison arrangements were reported in New Zealand's *Sunday Star Times* (21 June 2009: 1) under the headline 'Inmates Told: Build Your Own Jail Cells'. Here, the report continued, 'prisoners could be forced to build their own jail cells from shipping containers to cope with a "dangerously high" prison population that is expected to spill over in six months. It is the latest of the government's hardline "tough on crime" measures.' Opening the unit, the Corrections Minister stated that using prisoners to build their own cells was 'a great idea'. The cells would be 'spartan but humane and clean. . . prisoners need to learn construction skills so they can earn their keep and frankly, it's a lot better than being locked up all day in a cell . . . the shipping containers would provide a better standard of housing than some of the country's older prisons'. A 78-bed unit opened a year later, consisting of 13 twelve-metre-long containers, each of which had been converted into three cells (see Figure 0.2). Each of the cells (six metres by three metres) accommodates two men. Justifying these measures, the Corrections Minister informed her audience of journalists that '[these] are actually prison cells at the end of the day. They are not a holiday camp, even though there is an outside space and they are very humane . . . crime is voluntary. If people want to commit crimes, there is going to be a response and the response may well be prison' (*AM*, abc.net.au, 5 June 2010).

Two episodes in contemporary prison development from two modern societies, each representing very different ways of thinking about punishment. In the first, the investment in what is acclaimed as humane prison design in Norway is celebrated by prison management, staff, and the highest state authorities. All the usual indicators of prison existence have been variously camouflaged, hidden or removed. No expense has been spared, it seems, to make this prison look 'as much like the outside world as possible'. The symbolic importance of a prison of this nature for the country as a whole, not just the prison service, is recognized by the presence of the Norwegian monarch at the opening ceremony – here was a country, it seemed to say, that responds to lawbreakers with humanity and tolerance, and is proud of this. In contrast, the report from New Zealand indicates that *every expense* has been cut back as far as possible.

Traditional methods of prison construction have thus been bypassed as the shipping containers are converted into cells, using cheap prison labour – at around a maximum of $NZ30 per week, prisoner wages in this country are negligible –

Figure 0.1 Halden Prison, Norway. Photograph: Statsbygg, Norway.

Figure 0.2 Shipping containers that were to be converted into prison cells in New Zealand's latest prison building scheme to address overcrowding. Photograph: Greenbiz.com.

for this purpose. Here was a country, it seemed to say, that liked to boast of the severity of its response to crime: the plans for the new unit were thus one part of a broader package of 'tough on crime' measures (which, at that time, included 'removing parole eligibility for the worst repeat violent offenders, allowing the cars of illegal street racers to be crushed and the seizure of the assets and profits of gangs . . . [and tightening] prison release conditions for serious child sex-offenders'). There was no head of state to open the unit – what happened in these nether reaches of New Zealand society was not a matter with which dignitaries should concern themselves; nor was there any choir of guards to hymn in proclamation. Instead, the Minister of Corrections took the opportunity to justify the initiative to the media from the perspective of her political party. At pains to point out the absence of anything that could be considered a luxury, it was the 'spartan' nature of this initiative that was celebrated. There was no attempt to disguise these aspects of the unit, save for the throwaway remark that what it offered was preferable to some of the existing New Zealand prisons. Ultimately, her message was that *prison cells*, and nothing more, were being built. By definition, this meant that expectations about their design and format should be determined by the proviso that their accommodation should not be – could not be – raised above the lowest level of tolerable human existence in this society. If inmates subsequently found such conditions intolerable, then the solution was in their own hands: give up crime, or continue to live in these bleak surrounds.

Two very different ways, then, of thinking about punishment. However, these differences are not just specific to two small societies that sit at opposite ends of the earth. Instead, as will be set out in more detail in Chapter 1 (Understanding Differences in Punishment), each example is typical of the different ways it has become possible to think about punishment in *the clusters of societies* to which these two countries belong: the Nordic countries, on the one hand (Finland, Norway and Sweden, for the purposes of this research), and a particular group of Anglophone countries, known as 'the White Commonwealth' (England, New Zealand and Australia, with specific emphasis on the state of New South Wales,[1] for the purposes of this research) on the other. Thus, as regards the remarks about 'the world's most humane prison' and the prison units made from shipping containers, it would be possible to find similar reports to these, or variations on the themes in them, in each of the other societies in the respective clusters to which Norway and New Zealand belong. What we would be most unlikely to find, however, is any cross-cluster transference. Shipping container cells are not part of any aspect of Nordic prison arrangements; in just the same way, it would be inconceivable to find any of these Anglophone countries boasting that they house the world's most humane prison. The purpose of this book is to explain how it has become possible to think so differently about punishment in these two clusters of societies.

Why these societies?

While there are obvious differences between each society in these clusters, *they share important commonalities*: languages, geographical proximity (as regards the Nordic cluster and Australia and New Zealand), histories, political connections, traditions and ancestries. In relation to the Nordic cluster, Finland was part of Sweden until 1809, before becoming an autonomous Grand Duchy of the Russian Empire until 1917, when it was granted independence. The Finnish language has unique characteristics, but the country is officially bilingual (Finnish/Swedish[2]). Norway, from 1521 until 1814, was a Danish territory. Thereafter, until 1905, when it declared its independence, it was unified with Sweden (although this seems to have been of a largely nominal nature: the two countries shared the same monarch and the same foreign policy, but Norway had its own constitution). Its own declaration of independence, after a plebiscite in which 99.5 per cent of the population voted in favour of the dissolution with Sweden, was met with jubilation in Norway and sullen acceptance in Sweden. The Norwegian language is very similar to Swedish, although, during the union with Denmark, the official language had been Danish (which is also similar to Norwegian and Swedish). These societies have similar legal systems, based more on civil, rather than common law, and similar electoral systems based on proportional representation. At the same time, each member of these societies is automatically born into the Lutheran Church that, in the past, provided this region with a remarkably high level of religious homo-geneity. As regards the Anglophone cluster, the imperial bond and colonial ties – and the resulting shared way of thinking and sense of identity – between England, Australia and New Zealand seems to have been particularly strong. The European settlement of Australia and New Zealand, up to the mid-twentieth century in the former, the 1970s in the latter, had been almost exclusively British. At the same time, 'the tyranny of distance' (Blainey, 1966) not only created a close, if sometimes antagonistic, bond between the two remote Southern hemisphere colonies, but also made the ties to Britain all the more insoluble: surrounded, as it were, by 'nothingness' on the one hand, hostile indigenous peoples on the other, the sense of 'Britishness' in all aspects of colonial life gave the settlers a crucial sense of identity. Ward (2001: 2) thus wrote that 'for much of the 20th century Australian political culture was characterized by a deep attachment to the British embrace. London formed the centre of an imperial imagination in which Australia was firmly cast as a loyal outpost of British culture and British civilization.' There is every reason to think that this was even more so in New Zealand. Michael King (2003: 367), one of this country's leading historians, thus quoted its Governor-General's comments from 1924 that 'New Zealanders were "extremely proud" of their British nationality. They claim, in fact, to be even more British than the kin of their Motherland, and that no doubt accounts for the intensely loyal spirit which characterizes the Dominion.'

In these respects, then, we have two clusters of societies that operate within much the same parameters, share much the same way of thinking, and *share much the same ways of punishing their offenders.* As Brodeur (2007: 80) points out, 'clustering countries are joined by geographical, historical and cultural proximity. Figures correlating rates of imprisonment and influencing variables . . . show that these relationships hold as much between clusters of countries as between individual nations.' It also means that generalizations that are made about their penal characteristics carry more weight when they are shown to fit a particular group of societies rather than an individual member of it. But why were these six societies selected in preference to others that could have fitted within each cluster? Obviously, the larger the sample in each cluster, then the stronger the generalizations that can be made about its characteristics. At the same time, though, selection is also determined by pragmatism, especially for multi-society research of this nature. Thus, in relation to the Nordic cluster, it was simply not possible to include Denmark and Iceland for important logistical and financial reasons (see Preface). As regards selection for the Anglophone cluster, the USA was not included because it is a vastly different society from England, New Zealand and Australia in terms of size, history, political structure, race relations, and so on. Although it is a member of the Anglophone world, it is not a member of, and does not share important, unifying characteristics of the White Commonwealth group of nations. But what of Canada, another member of this group? Aside, again, from the logistics and financing that have to be taken into account, there are also good intellectual reasons for not including this country. It seems entirely plausible that colonial ties to England were stronger in New Zealand and Australia than in Canada. For example, Miller (1987: 178) wrote that 'Australians considered they were more truly Britain's children than the Canadians (because of the French Canadians) or South Africans (because of the Afrikaners); only the New Zealanders could claim the same outright familial connection, while Indians and Africans and others within the British Empire could claim nothing but efficient administration'. In fact, Miller is understating Canadian differences. It not only had its constituency of French descendants, which has made it a bilingual society but, in addition, from the late nineteenth century, it attracted high levels of immigration from Eastern Europe. Indeed, in the 1920s and 1930s, immigration from this direction outpaced that from the United Kingdom (Bumsted,

1992: 215) – at a time when Australia and New Zealand still operated an almost exclusively 'British only' migration policy. Over the same period, there was also significant immigration from the United States. In combination, these demographic patterns are likely to have given Canada a rather more heterogeneous identity than the two Antipodean colonies. British settlement might still have been most dominant there but, unlike Australia and New Zealand, ways of thinking about the world were not restricted to British mentalities. Indeed, the economic power of the United States inevitably influenced the development of Canadian markets and culture (Vance, 2009), while it was exclusively Britain that did so in Australia and New Zealand. The subsequent effects of these differences can be seen at all levels of these former colonies. For example, the replication of almost exclusively British sports in Australia and New Zealand, in contrast to those emanating from the USA in Canada; the reluctance of Australia and New Zealand, unlike Canada, to sign the 1931 Statute of Westminster, giving these dominions legislative independence and cutting them loose from the colonial umbilical cord;[3] the way in which the Australian and New Zealand flags still contain British Union Jacks while, in Canada, this was abandoned in 1965 (seemingly with little dissent) in favour of the maple leaf.

This, then, explains the thinking behind, and justifications for, the selections for the two clusters. But this does not mean, of course, that there have been no differences in the past or present in the penal arrangements of the individual societies that were selected. This is immediately apparent when we examine the respective adult imprisonment rates (the research features their adult, not their juvenile, penal systems) from the late nineteenth to the early twenty-first century of these Anglophone and Nordic societies. As Figure 0.3 shows, there has been a generally uniform pattern of development between the Anglophone countries: from particularly high rates at the end of the nineteenth century, they undergo a significant decline to the mid-twentieth, before rising again. Meanwhile, in the Nordic cluster, the rates for Norway and Sweden have been relatively stable throughout the whole period, despite some recent incline. That for Finland, however, rose dramatically in the first half of the twentieth century, as this country became a victim of its own geopolitical history. In the power vacuum caused by the Russian revolution, right and left political factions armed and organized themselves into White and Red Guards, culminating in civil war in 1918. Bloody reprisals followed the victory of the Whites but, from the 1920s to the early 1960s, in addition to dire poverty and an agrarian, rather than an industrial, economy, there was also a profound political silence over these events. This meant that there was no opportunity for healing and reconciliation, and it also meant that Finnish society was, in effect, frozen in time (Kekkonen, 1999). A thawing out only began to occur when this country rejoined the Nordic family of nations in the 1960s. Thereafter, its dramatic decline in imprisonment begins, as its penal programme assumed a more familiar Nordic identity.

What the Finnish divergence indicates is the way in which it is possible for a 'normal level of punishment', under extreme circumstances, to be torn right away from its anchorage, and sent off into uncharted territory. There is no guarantee that the characteristics of punishment will remain fixed and certain in each of these

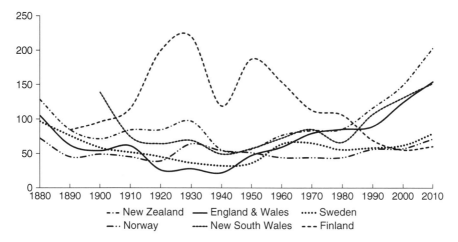

Figure 0.3 Imprisonment rates, 1880–2010 (all six societies).

Sources: New Zealand: New Zealand Yearbook (various); Department of Justice (1981, 1991, 2008). England and Wales: Home Office (2003). New South Wales: Official Yearbook of New South Wales (various); Australian Bureau of Statistics (1982, 2000). Finland: Christie (1968); Falck, von Hofer and Storgaard (2003); Statistics Finland (2012a). Sweden: Christie (1968); Falck, von Hofer and Storgaard (2003). Norway: Christie (1968); Statistics Norway (2012a). All countries: World Prison Brief (2010).

societies. However, the fact that Finland has since made it back to a more familiar harbour illustrates the presence of a longstanding and prevailing sense of shared penal identity within each cluster that, even though it can be disrupted and thrown off course at times, is not erased altogether; an identity that, as eminences such as Fyodor Dostoyevsky, Sir Winston Churchill and Nelson Mandela[4] have suggested, also tells us a great deal about *the kinds of societies that they have been and the kinds of societies they have become.*

1 Understanding differences in punishment

Let us now substantiate, in the first part of this chapter, the differences in punishment between the two clusters of societies that were signposted in the Introduction. The second part of the chapter then introduces and develops the explanatory framework through which these differences can be understood.

Differences in rates of imprisonment

In 2010, Finland had a rate of imprisonment of 60 per 100,000 of population, Norway 71 and Sweden 78. In contrast, the rate of imprisonment in New Zealand was 203 per 100,000 of population, in England 154, and in New South Wales 152 (in Australia as a whole it was 134): rates that, respectively, place them amongst the lowest and highest Western imprisoning societies.[1] But can this measurement be used as a legitimate indicator of punitiveness? There are all kinds of methodological issues and concerns in the way in which imprisonment statistics are produced (are remands in custody included or excluded; are psychiatric institutions for the criminally insane counted or not counted; similarly, in relation to 'young offender' institutions, and so on) that would seem to raise prima facie doubts about such statistics' reliability as a research instrument. It might also be thought that these doubts are then magnified when attempting to compare levels of imprisonment *between different societies*. However, notwithstanding these caveats, imprisonment rates do provide *general pointers to penal trends*, if not totally accurate counts of prison populations, and it is in this context that they have been used in this research. The consistent pattern of imprisonment, from the late nineteenth to the early twenty-first century, that they reveal *within each cluster* (leaving aside Finland) thus raises important analytical questions. For these purposes, as Cavadino and Dignan (2006: 5) note, imprisonment rates are 'often the best [data] available . . . the one[s] most commonly and easily calculated and promulgated on a comparative basis'. At the same time, the validity of imprisonment rates as an indicator of penal difference is strengthened when a second indicator – prison conditions, in this case – seems to confirm their inferences.

Differences in prison conditions

While the two media reports that opened this book may, for obvious reasons, have had their own – and contrasting – measures of hyperbole, the differences in prison conditions between the two clusters were reaffirmed and extended in the fieldwork[2] that was undertaken for this research. This involved visits to 40 prisons (some more than once). These 'tours' lasted between two and four hours, usually in the company of a senior officer. Features of the prison would be explained as it progressed and then, in most cases, there would be further discussions with the governor/manager. On some occasions, it was also possible to have discussions with other prison officers and prison personnel; on others, with prisoners, both individually and in groups. The prisons were selected to give a good cross-section: maximum and minimum security, men's and women's; closed and open, old and new. One of the reasons for conducting the research in this way was that it would be possible to observe *recurring patterns* relating to officer-inmate interaction, dining and visiting arrangements, and various other accoutrements of the material conditions of life that were common to the prisons and prison systems in each cluster.

The differences that then became apparent can be summarized in the following five ways:

- Prison size
- Officer/inmate relations
- Quality of prison life
- Prison officers
- Work and education programmes.

Prison size

Nordic prisons tend to be much smaller than those in the Anglophone countries. It is quite common to find 50- or 60-bed establishments in this region (see Figure 1.1). The logistical consequences are that, despite their much smaller prison populations, the Nordic countries have many more prisons per head of population (see Table 1.1).

These differences in prison size obviously make housing prisoners near their families much more straightforward in the Nordic countries than in the Anglophone.

Table 1.1 Contrasts in prison size

Country	Prison population	Number of penal institutions	Average prison size
England	85147	140	608
New South Wales	11330	35	324
New Zealand	8706	19	458
Finland	3231	35	92
Norway	3446	47	73
Sweden	7286	84	87

Source: World Prison Brief (2010).

It is also clear that prison size is likely to affect staff/inmate relations: the larger the institution, the more likely it is that prison staff and inmates will become more anonymous to each other, mitigating against any sense of solidarity and cohesion or the development of trusting relationships. At the same time, the smaller Nordic institutions are likely to pose less of a threat to local property values and security, a frequent complaint whenever locations are sought for new penal institutions in the Anglophone prison world. Indeed, it seems to be the case that the much smaller Nordic penal institutions become valued community resources rather than objects of widespread antagonism and hostility.

Nonetheless, in recent years, the Anglophone countries have been building progressively larger prisons, both because of the increase in the numbers of people being sent to prison and also as a way of rationalizing and reducing prison costs. In England, this reached its apogee with the plans to build three 'Titan' prisons, holding 2,500 inmates each, in 2007.[3] At the same time, private prisons now constitute some 10 per cent of the total prison stock in England (although there has been no recourse at all to this in the Nordic countries), and are usually justified on the basis that the private sector is not only better able to save money than the public sector but, in addition, the competition it provides is also likely to bring down the costs of public sector prisons.[4]

Officer/inmate relations

There seems to be more routine interaction and less social distance between officers and inmates in the Nordic prisons. Inmates and staff might share the same canteen at mealtimes in some institutions, as well as use first name terms when addressing each other. In Norway, officers knock on the cell door before entering, so that

Figure 1.1 Hamar prison, Norway. The prison has both an open and closed section, with a total of 56 places. Photograph: Statsbygg, Norway.

inmates are not disturbed without prior warning. And maximum security conditions can provide the opportunity for more, not less, interaction between officers and inmates. Thus, at Kumla prison in Sweden, the emphasis on security is rationalized as follows: 'now we are working actively with the prisoners whereas previously we were only monitoring them. Prisoners and staff cook together and we are around when they study or work. We get to know them and how they feel, which also means we can notice early signs of conflict and actively prevent them from escalating by adding more staff or moving prisoners to a different room' (*Dagens Nyheter*, 18 November 2009: 1). Obviously, something other than 'friendship' is being cultivated through such closeness, since these relations are also likely to enhance surveillance and security tasks. Nonetheless, the obligations on Swedish prison officers to undertake counseling and planning with the small groups of inmates for whom they have responsibility seem likely to further reduce social distance and bring about a relatively relaxed atmosphere (Bruhn, Nylander and Lindberg, 2010).

This is not to say, of course, that no such interaction takes place in the Anglophone prisons. While, in New South Wales, staff/inmate relations seemed the most formal, in New Zealand and England relationships were generally relaxed, with both groups on first name terms with each other (although, in New Zealand, there were also occasions when officers addressed inmates as 'Prisoner X', 'Prisoner Y', etc). In England, what is known as the 'decency' agenda has made a significant contribution in recent years to reducing what had previously been the extensive social distance between prisoners and prison staff in that country. Prisoners at Kirkham open prison told us that 'the majority of staff genuinely want to help and want to interact with prisoners'. We were also told several times by staff during the English prison visits that they were 'proud' or 'very proud' of the work they did. However, the position is very different in maximum security areas. Unlike the Swedish example above, personal contact is kept to a minimum; in New Zealand, three officers accompany any movement of an individual prisoner, who must kneel, and face the wall away from them with hands behind his back when they enter the cell. In such prisons in New South Wales, officers are stationed in watchtowers and armed with rifles. There is also an Immediate Action Team that patrols the grounds of these institutions, carrying an array of armaments and dressed in highly militarized fatigues.

Furthermore, whatever the inclinations of the officers themselves in the Anglophone prisons, interaction with inmates is also likely to be greatly restricted by security and budgetary concerns. Broadly speaking, staff/inmate ratios are more favourable in the Nordic countries. For example, in Norway and Sweden there is 1 officer per each 0.8 prisoner; in New South Wales, the ratio is 1:2, and in New Zealand, 1:2.1. One consequence of this is that the great majority of prisoners – virtually all except those in open institutions, and still smaller numbers on 'self-catering' arrangements – in the Anglophone societies eat their meals in their cells, with obvious detrimental consequences in terms of socializing and learning how to live in the company of others without conflict. We were told of one New South Wales and one English prison where officers had tried to instigate weekly lunches but the inmates did not wish to participate. Clearly, with the greater social distances between the two groups that had been part of the institutional history of these establishments, sudden attempts to break this down by one side are likely to be met with caution and suspicion by the other. Again, respect for inmates from staff seems to be more of an institutional feature of Nordic prisons, rather than being dependent on individual officers' discretion. Thus, in most Norwegian prisons, there are weekly meetings between representatives of prisoners and prison officers. There was much less of these arrangements in the Anglophone countries: only in England were these anything like routine.

Quality of prison life

The general 'quality of prison life' – diet, cleanliness, quietness, personal space and visiting arrangements – in both open and closed prisons seems much higher in the Nordic than in the Anglophone prisons. Overcrowding and lack of personal space is much more a feature of the latter. For example, in one New Zealand prison, an institution for 'vulnerable prisoners', the cell is 4 x 2 metres and two inmates have to share this. While there is some cell sharing in the Nordic prisons, particularly in low security facilities where doors are seldom locked and there are large communal areas to compensate, this is an exception to the more general pattern of unshared cells, common rooms and lounge facilities, as well as kitchen areas where inmates can routinely cook light meals. Some prison sections may be fully self catering, including maximum security units. Indeed, while their freedom of movement is much more restricted, maximum security prisoners still enjoy most of the privileges of other inmates. They thus have access to 'conjugal visits' (absolutely prohibited in these Anglophone prison systems), arranged and facilitated by the authorities, in apartments, 'visit rooms' or 'guesthouses' (as at Halden) within the prison grounds. These visits, in which inmates and their family can live together, making their own food, and so on, can last from a few hours to a whole weekend. Where there are no such facilities, as in one small open prison near Helsinki, we were told that inmates were simply allowed home at weekends for these purposes.

In contrast, in the Anglophone countries, what quality of life that there is in the prisons has been, or is in serious danger of being, further eroded by budget cuts and overcrowding. This is particularly gross in English local prisons. At the time of the visit to one such institution in the north-west region, there were 757 inmates when the normal accommodation level should have been 441. At the same time, while the practice of 'slopping out'[5] has now largely come to an end in the Anglophone prisons, it still persists in some. In 2010, there were two New Zealand prisons without in-cell sanitation, nor any means to allow prisoners to leave their cells for ablution purposes during the night. Even so, the provision of toilets in cells built for one person but frequently housing two is a mixed blessing. In England, as one senior civil servant explained to us, the reality of these sanitation arrangements in small cells, particularly when these are shared, is that 'two people are living in a toilet'. The fact that this area may now be curtained, as was seen in a number of the English prisons that were visited, does little to remove the attendant indignities and lack of hygiene. But, again, security, lack of resources, and dilapidated prison buildings prevent prisoners from being able to simply exit their cells for these purposes, as the overwhelming majority of Nordic prisoners are able to do, and where such hygiene issues, and all the indignities raised by them, simply do not exist.

Furthermore, cells and wings in the Nordic prisons are more likely to have furnishings and accoutrements that are of a considerably higher standard than the Anglophone. In Helsinki prison, for example, there are glass tanks containing tropical fish in the library and on some of the wings. The prisoners feed them and clean the tanks. We saw something similar in one English closed prison (the fish tank had been provided by the officers) but we were also told in New Zealand and New South Wales that any such arrangements would be prohibited on the grounds of cost, security ('What if the tanks were smashed and the glass used as a weapon?') and fear of 'public opinion' if the news media ever got to hear of such 'treats'. It was also explained that pool tables were prohibited in a low security New South Wales prison for these reasons. These were available in the English prisons but could only be used under the supervision of officers. And, while there are indeed the 'open spaces' to which the New Zealand Corrections Minister referred (p. 2), these tend to be prohibited areas in the Anglophone prisons, often outside caged walkways or enclosed concrete exercise yards. Even in new prisons, where lounges and common room areas have been factored into the design in these countries, lockdowns or the increasingly restricted association periods make these facilities largely irrelevant.

Prisoners in the Nordic countries, however, are likely to be out of their cells considerably longer than those in the Anglophone systems. In Norwegian closed prisons, lockdown lasts from 8.00 pm (for some higher security prisoners), or 9.00 pm to 7.00 am. In Finland, from 7.00 pm to 6.30 am in the closed prisons. In Sweden, the Corrections [*Kriminalvården*] website states that inmates 'are woken at 7.00 am by a knocking on their door by an officer "to say good morning", which is a small but important aspect of how one treats each [other]'. It goes on to add that lockdown is at 8.00 pm (10.00 pm in the open prisons), explaining that this 'might sound harsh, but many inmates look forward to some peace and quiet . . .. [they] decide when they want to turn off their bedside lamp, and they can contact a staff member if they want to talk for a while in the evening'. In contrast, in New Zealand and New South Wales prisons, the general rule seems to be that there is, in effect, a 16 hour routine lockdown, except for those in lower security classifications. This lasts from 5.00 pm, when inmates take their 'dinner', and breakfast packs for the following morning, to their cells, to 8.00 am when unlocking occurs. There is a further lockdown hour at lunchtime, when this meal is also routinely eaten in the cells. And, while closed prisons in England (except those which are high security) are closer to the Nordic standards – with a 7.30 pm to 8.00 am lockdown – we were regularly told that this was in severe danger as a result of budget cuts. Indeed, in that country, the core working week ends at midday Friday. Prisoners are then, for all intents and purposes, locked down until the following Monday morning. In the closed male prisons in these countries, dining in association barely exists, yet this is *de rigeur* in the Nordic prisons.

Figure 1.2 Laukaa open prison, Finland. Photo supplied by Criminal Sanctions Agency, Finland.

Figure 1.3 Åby open prison, Sweden. Photo: Aren Gharibashvily, Swedish Prison and Probation Service.

Furthermore, a much higher proportion of Nordic prisoners (around 30 per cent) spend their time in open prisons. Here, fences, walls and other barriers are reduced to a minimal level. Sometimes there are none at all (see Figures 1.2 and 1.3).

In some, prisoners are able to lock and unlock their own cell doors. After the prisoners finish work or classes, they are free to walk around the prison grounds and sometimes into the neighbouring communities. As such, many open prisons in this region are more similar to Anglophone 'halfway houses', whereby inmates have regular employment outside the institution, and take part in everyday life outside it, as well. Although English open prisons operate in a broadly similar manner, there are only 10 such institutions, housing about six per cent of the total prison population in this country. There are a small number of similar institutions in New South Wales (also known as afforestation camps), while New Zealand has no genuinely open prisons. Although there are small numbers of inmates who live in low security self-care units, *these remain within the prison complex, with razor wire and security camera surrounds.* At the same time, food servings – one of the most important features of prison life, for inmates – generally seem more varied and generous in the Nordic prisons. The standard Finnish and New Zealand prison menus for 2009, set out in Tables 1.2 and 1.3, provide striking contrasts.

The menu for Finland (the inmates prepare their own food on weekends) seems much less 'institutionalized', not to say substantial, than that for New Zealand. In addition, there are no restrictions[6] placed on 'incidentals' (jam, bread, sauce, etc.). However, the strict measurements of these in the New Zealand menu – 'toast x 2' for breakfast, '15 g of margarine, 35 g of sugar' – are standard practice across the Anglophone prisons. It also contains the supplementary information that 'two slices of bread and 15 g of margarine are supplied with the evening meal when the lockdown period between dinner and breakfast is greater than 14 hours'.

One of the most dramatic features of Anglophone prisons is the reception area for remands or those just sentenced. Here, often in the most squalid, overcrowded and intimidating surrounds, a transformation of the self is expected to take place as the world beyond the prison is shut out and each new reception assumes his or her prisoner identity. They usually arrive *en masse* from the courts, having been chained and shackled in the escort van during the journey. They are then placed in holding cells with groups of others during processing (sometimes lasting for hours). Of these three countries, only in England, it appeared to us, had steps been taken to alleviate this ordeal (as it surely must be, at least for those who have never been in prison before). At Preston, we were told that a night officer introduces himself and gives reassurances to first nighters. Elsewhere, information booklets are given to new receptions. In contrast, the entry to Nordic prisons is likely to be much less dramatic, easing and lessening the transition from free citizen to prisoner. Those sentenced to short prison sentences in Norway and Sweden (although not those on remand, or those sentenced to a prison term for violent or organized crime) are able to avoid such introductions altogether. Instead, they may be given a time within a six-month period when their sentence will start, if they make an application for deferment for various personal reasons. Prospective inmates then make their own way to prison on the appointed day. Ilseng prison in Norway provides instructions

Table 1.2 Prison menu: Finland (2009)

	Breakfast	Lunch	Dinner
Mon	Oatmeal Porridge Bread Margarine Milk	Meat Stew with Dill Potatoes Salad Side Dish	Salmon and Vegetable Soup Pie
Tue	Barley Gruel, Bread Margarine Cheese Tea Sugar	Liver-Vegetable Steak Onion Gravy Potatoes Mashed Lingonberries Salad Side Dish	Sausage and Macaroni Casserole Salad Side Dish
Wed	Yoghurt Bread Margarine Cheese Spread	Minced Meat and Vegetable Soup, Gourmet Porridge/ Date Porridge	Mushroom and Vegetable Casserole, Salad Side Dish
Thu	Rye Porridge Milk Bread Margarine Cheese Spread	Tuna Stew Spaghetti Salad Side Dish	Sailors Steak Salad Side Dish
Fri	Wheat Porridge Milk Bread Margarine Eggs Pie	Chicken Sauce Rice Salad Side Dish	House Meal
Sat	Rice Porridge Bread Margarine Vegetable Tea Sugar	Pepper Meatloaf Potatoes Gravy Salad Side Dish Plum Fool	
Sun	Semolina Pudding Bread Margarine Milk Fruit Cold Cuts Pastry Coffee/Tea Sugar	French Meat Stew Potatoes Salad Side Dish Lingonberry Sour Milk *(this is similar to a* *smoothie)*	

Table 1.3 Prison menu: New Zealand (2009)

	Breakfast	Lunch	Dinner
Mon	Weetbix (x2) Milk (300ml) Toast (x3) Margarine (15g) Spread (20g) Bran (1 dstsp) Tea, Sugar (35g)	Filled Roll (x2) *2 x ham, tomato and coleslaw* Fruit (1 piece) Tea	Braised Sausage Brown Onion Gravy Potatoes, Vegetables (x2) Bread (2 slices), Marg (15g) Fruit (1 piece) Tea, Milk (300ml)
Tue	Ricies (x30g) Milk (300ml) Toast (x3) Margarine (15g) Spread (20g) Bran (1 dstsp) Tea, Sugar (35g)	Sandwich (x3) *1 x cheese and onion* *1 x ham and sauce* *1 x fruit spread* Fruit (1 piece) Tea	Spaghetti Bolognaise Spaghetti Noodles Vegetables (x2) Bread (2 slices), Margarine (15g) Fruit (1 piece) Tea
Wed	Weetbix (x2) Milk (300ml) Toast (x3) Marg (15g) Spread (20g) Bran (1 dstsp) Tea, Sugar (35g)	Filled Roll (x2) *2 x egg, lettuce and mayonnaise* Fruit (1 piece) Tea	Roast Chicken, Gravy Potatoes, Vegetables (x2) Bread (2 slices), Margarine (15g) Fruit (1 piece) Tea, Milk (300ml)
Thu	Ricies (x30g) Milk (300ml) Toast (x3) Margarine (15g) Spread (20g) Bran (1 dstsp) Tea, Sugar (35g)	Sandwich (x3) *1 x creamed corn* *1 x coleslaw and beetroot* *1 x egg and mayonnaise* Fruit (1 piece) Tea	Mince and Cheese Pie Tomato Sauce Potatoes, Vegetables (x2) Bread (2 slices), Margarine (15g) Fruit (1 piece) Tea
Fri	Weetbix (x2) Milk (300ml) Toast (x3) Margarine (15g) Spread (20g) Bran (1 dstsp) Tea, Sugar (35g)	Filled Roll (x2) *1 x luncheon, tomato, lettuce and mayonnaise* *1 x cheese and onion* Fruit (1 piece) Tea	Fish (various preparations) Tomato Sauce Potatoes, Vegetables (x2) Bread (2 slices), Margarine (15g) Fruit (1 piece) Tea, Milk (300ml)
Sat	Ricies (x30g) Milk (300ml) Toast (x3) Margarine (15g) Spread (20g) Bran (1 dstsp) Tea, Sugar (35g)	Sandwich (x3) *2 x cheese and pineapple* *1 x peanut butter* Fruit (1 piece) Tea	Roast Beef, Gravy Potatoes, Vegetables (x2) Bread (2 slices), Margarine (15g) Fruit (1 piece) Tea
Sun	Weetbix (x2) Milk (300ml) Toast (x3) Marg (15g) Spread (20g) Bran (1 dstsp) Tea, Sugar (35g)	Filled Roll (x2) *2 x luncheon, coleslaw cheese & beetroot* Fruit (1 piece) Tea	Beef & Vegetable Curry, Rice, Vegetables (x2) Bread (2 slices), Marg (15g) Fruit (1 piece) Tea

for them on its website,[7] giving details of train and bus services. It then adds that 'the [inmates] may choose whether to use private clothes or borrow clothes from the prison. All inmates will be given the necessary toiletries as needed.' On the day of arrival, the inmate attends a kind of induction class (standard practice in all Norwegian prisons), rather than being left to make sense of their new surrounds as best they can themselves: 'on that evening there is an information meeting for all the [new] inmates that day and a thorough briefing about the prison is given'.

Prison officers

There are significant differences in prison officer culture, recruitment and training. There is much less evidence, for example, of the military origins and traditions of the prison service in the Nordic countries, compared to the Anglophone. In Finland, especially, there are virtually no markings on the officers' uniforms. Indeed, there is evidence of very different expectations of the work and role of prison officers in these societies. This is implicit in the Swedish term for 'prison officer', *fångvårdare*, for which the literal translation is 'prisoner carer'. In Norway, the equivalent term, *fengselbetjent*, means, literally, 'prison servant'. Of course, it could be argued that these mellifluous expressions merely camouflage more sinister intents and purposes. But this then begs the question of why the Swedes and Norwegians should be so sensitive about terminology that is taken for granted in the Anglophone world. Furthermore, the absence of parades, marching, and so on is another clear break from any military ancestry and traditions that, to a degree, are still kept alive in the Anglophone prisons, New South Wales especially. Here, there are likely to be officers' parades at the start of each morning shift in some of the closed prisons. At the same time, it is obvious that the uniform and insignia still carry great emotional and symbolic importance for large sections of the officer body (although a significant minority now work in polo shirts and 'chinos' in New South Wales). More generally, what was also noticeable was the way in which officers in the Anglophone countries would refer to each other as 'Mr', 'Ma'am' or 'Miss' while on duty, as if this formality helped to preserve some sense of hierarchy and structure that public sector reforms and the introduction of flatline career structures have largely stripped away.[8] In contrast, Nordic prison officers all seemed to be on first name terms with one another, whatever their respective levels in the prison service.

These differences in culture are likely to be related to the training the officers receive, as well as the structure of their working environment. In New Zealand, basic training of new recruits takes six weeks, the same as in New South Wales private prisons. Training in the public prisons in New South Wales lasts for 11 weeks. In England, basic training is for eight weeks. In Sweden the training lasts 40 weeks. In Finland, it lasts for one year and in Norway two years. In New South Wales, we were told that the training is a mixture of 'security, case management and special needs'. This includes 'weapons training – some prison officers carry guns. There is also exposure to gas and riots. There is a strong emphasis on ethics, accountability and practical qualifications. We are very supportive of teamwork and training in the culture we want them to have, although this changes depending on which centre they work in. There are strong guidelines around the use of force and video surveillance of incidents.' Similarly, Arnold (2005: 399) writes of prison officer training in England: 'the security aspects of the work are emphasized over and above all else as a critical occupational norm. The need to maintain physical and dynamic security (through relationships) appeared to be intrinsically tied to (and led to) the increase in suspicion, mistrust, vigilance and an overriding concern for their own and others' safety.' Overall, the impression gained during the course of the visits to the Anglophone prisons was of a high regard for practical skills that officers were expected to possess, and the inculcation of an ethos that would foster group cohesion among the officer body. Life skills, it appeared, were more important than educational qualifications. Although, in England, five passes in secondary school fifth-form exams had been part of the eligibility criteria for joining the service, this has been abandoned. There is no stipulation for academic credentials in New South Wales and New Zealand.

In contrast, in Finland, eight per cent of prison officer recruits in 2008 had a university degree; in Sweden, one third of prisoner officer recruits have completed two years of tertiary education; and in Norway the prison service is increasingly becoming a graduate profession. The minimum criteria for entry to the prison service in the latter includes passing the school leaving exam in three subjects (Norwegian, English and Social Studies) and one year's experience of 'working with people', for example, in hospitals, kindergartens or prisons. Here, then, working in prison was seen as much the same as working in any other institution: the prison was not set apart from the rest of society, requiring an altogether different mindset for working there. Indeed, we were told that 30 or 40 per cent of new recruits in Norway are likely to have had experience of working in prison when they apply to join the service. Many law and behavioural science students, for example, work part-time or in vacations as temporary prison officers, an indicator, surely, of the relative lack of stigma associated with such work in this country. In the 2009 intake to the Norwegian prison officer training college, there were 1,680 applicants for 150 places: and this in a country where the rate of unemployment was only two per cent. In other words, there were likely to have been plenty of other career choices for these applicants, yet they chose the prison service. In the Anglophone countries, however, it is only likely to be when unemployment is high that there will be much interest in this occupation. At such times, we were told, 'it's working in Tesco's [a supermarket chain] or working in prisons'. Thus, in New Zealand, a major expansion of the prison estate after 2000 in a healthy economic climate was met by serious recruitment problems, leading to attempts to recruit from the Pacific Islands, South Africa, England and continental Europe (at considerable expense and with limited success).

In contrast to the Anglophone training objectives, we were told that the main goal of Norwegian training is 'to educate people with high moral standards. Ethics and professionalism are important subjects. We want reflexive individuals who think for themselves, their role in society and then on other people. They don't have to know about prisons but they have to be able to reflect on themselves. They study law, criminology, sociology and psychology. Then as their last subject, the officer role. They need to believe that people can change . . . a good prison officer is someone who sees the inmates where they are. They should be able to help prisoners help themselves, but they have to wait and be patient for changes.' There is also, of course, an emphasis on physical security in the training, but what is evident in the above comments is the importance given to the capacity of *the individual officer* to work productively with inmates: their role in the officer group gets nothing like as much attention as in the Anglophone countries. Furthermore, the different gender mixes in the prison staff of the clusters also seem likely to contribute to their differing working cultures and emphases in prison officer training. Broadly speaking, the male/female officer distribution in the Nordic countries is 2:1, while in the Anglophone countries it is 3:1.

Work and education programmes

Inmates in Nordic prisons are more likely to be occupied in work or education than in the Anglophone countries, notwithstanding recent investments and enrolment increases in these facilities in the latter. It is a goal, in the Nordic prisons, that each inmate should be active during the day in either work or education (failure to be so leads to small reductions in their daily allowance). One striking difference in this aspect of prison life is that education is not seen as a remedial extra, as it has been during the history of the Anglophone prison systems – something that illiterates could, in the main, turn their minds to at the end of the working day, even if there was no work for them during the day itself. Instead, it can be an alternative to work. Indeed, one third of the Nordic prison population is involved in educational studies, where tuition is offered up to and including tertiary level. Given, as well, that illiteracy is virtually non-existent in these countries, then the general standard of education delivery is considerably higher than the remedial level that still seems to be the main focus of educational services in the Anglophone prisons; hardly surprising, given that around 50 per cent of their inmates are functionally illiterate. Certainly, there are opportunities for prisoners to study at tertiary level in these countries as well (in their 'free time', we were told) and small numbers are able to make use of these opportunities, but lack of internet access must make this immeasurably more difficult and frustrating than in the outside world. At the same time, the Nordic prison libraries seemed particularly well stocked and equipped, with numerous foreign language volumes to accommodate their non-nationals, something to which the Anglophone prison systems seem barely to have given any thought at all.

As regards payment for work, the overwhelming majority of prisoners in the Anglophone societies earn only a few pounds or dollars per week. The exceptions are the small number of inmates allowed out of prison to work. In New Zealand and New South Wales, combined, there were around 300 such prisoners in 2010. They are paid something like the national minimum wage, for which deductions for 'rent', board and so on are made. Only in the small number of English open prisons does it appear that there is any systematic attempt to have prisoners working beyond the prison itself. But then, given the realities of the job market, and the underskilled and undereducated backgrounds of most prisoners, it was not surprising to hear that 'lots of these [prisoners] were working in charity shops', again being paid nothing more than the minimum wage. While they were, at least, out of prison during the day, there was no sense of any kind of career structure being developed for them. In Finland, however, those working in open prisons are paid 'real wages' for their labour, out of which they pay taxes and 'rent', give money to their family and to their victims, and save for their release. In other words, they are being given the opportunity to participate in the standards and expectation of 'normal life', rather than allow their time to be ordered by the separate standards and values of the prison. Indeed, some Swedish inmates were allowed to continue in the employment they had *before* their prison sentence. At Asptuna open prison near Stockholm, there is a car park for inmates (as there also is at Kirkham open prison in England, it needs to be acknowledged), since some of them commute to work in the city. If they are going to return late, they telephone ahead, and a meal is left out for them on their return. More generally, the allowances for prisoners in closed institutions in the Nordic countries are likely to be several times higher than in the Anglophone, with incidental extras: televisions that are provided free, for example, rather than rented or provided by families, as in the latter.

We also found that work opportunities were increasingly difficult to come by, both for security and economic reasons in the Anglophone countries. In New Zealand, for example, since the mid-1990s, the rule has been that all prison labour must make a profit in order to be justifiable. This brought an end to the cottage industry handicrafts that had previously occupied many inmates during the day, as they made toys, furniture and so on for hospitals and children's homes. The reality in 2010, particularly for those serving short sentences or in low risk categories, was that they were left almost completely to their own devices. In addition, over-crowding pressures inevitably mean that what programmes and work activities there are may be interrupted, as inmates are moved from one institution to another, in the unending task of managing bedspace.

Different pictures of prison life

Of course, we have provided very general pictures here, and in each cluster we acknowledge that we are likely to find exceptions to them. As regards the Nordic prisons, we thus need to be aware that, notwithstanding the vastly superior material conditions of confinement in the institutions, bullying and intimidation still occur. One in eight inmates at Helsinki prison requested to be placed in isolation at some stage of their sentence (Annual Report of the Finnish Prison and Probation Services, 2004). There is an inmate culture in the Nordic prisons, just as there is in the Anglophone countries. Indeed, some of the distinguishing features of these prisons have been turned into local currency by the inmates: the family visits entitlement is something that can be traded or fought over, like cigarettes and phone cards. In Norway, the physical comforts in one open prison for women are remarkable, but this will not ease the distress of those who are mothers of infants. Norwegian prison rules do not allow women sentenced to prison to be accompanied by babies or minors. In addition, conditions for remand prisoners (around one quarter of the prison populations of Norway and Sweden) are considerably more restrictive. Some remandees may even be held in solitary confinement until the time of their trial (for years, in extreme cases). Both Norway and Sweden have been criticized by the European Committee against Torture and Inhumane Treatment for these practices. In Sweden, security has been significantly tightened across all closed prisons in the aftermath of sensational escapes in 2004: the escapees were repeat violent offenders who murdered two police officers during the course of these incidents; guns had also been smuggled into the prison beforehand, with the involvement of organized crime groups, and helicopters were used to facilitate the getaways. In their aftermath, no-fly zones have been in force in the airspace above the maximum institutions in this country, and it now seems that specialist security staff in the prisons are gaining higher status than those performing the traditional 'personal officer' role (Lindberg, Nylander and Bruhn, 2011). At the same time, the new Swedish prison officer uniform – dark blue with crowns on the shoulders – seems designed to reaffirm both the authority and trustworthiness of these officers, after the 2004 escapes.

As regards the Anglophone countries, we need to recognize that, in New Zealand, cultural awareness and sensitivity seems particularly high, and also features strongly in the training of new prison officer recruits. There is also an emphasis on programmes based on Maori culture and ceremony, for Maori inmates who now make up half of that country's prison population (although there is far less emphasis, it seems, in providing them with more mundane opportunities to simply live harmoniously with others). In New South Wales, one is particularly struck by the high level of resourcing for mental health and addiction problems. The Compulsory Drug Treatment Correctional Centre at Parklea was described to us as being 'more like a forensic hospital than a prison. Drugs are treated as a health rather than a crime issue.' In this institution, 'prisoners can be taken out shopping. Lock up is at 7.00 pm or 9.00 pm and they eat in a dining room.' In New Zealand, the Kia Marmara sex offender unit, at a prison near Christchurch, has won international acclaim for its highly successful rehabilitative programmes, and is run very much along the lines of a therapeutic community. Other points to note in the Anglophone countries include the provision of high calibre mother and baby units; special projects that include 'Pups in Prison' (that is, the training and domesticating of guide dogs for the blind); fathers in prison making DVDs of themselves reading books for their children; foreign nationals using DVD messaging to keep in contact with their families; the Wild Life Protection Centre in New South Wales, which employs 12 inmates; and a prisoners' art exhibition in Auckland in 2010. We were also struck by attempts in England and New South Wales (although not New Zealand) to humanize visiting arrangements, within the prevailing security conditions, by providing play areas for children and a cafe, or at least facilities for food and drinks, in the vicinity.

Such developments point to significant attempts by the Anglophone prison authorities to move forward from their histories of squalor, riots, repression, violence from both sides, intimidation and the strikes by prison officers that featured from the 1970s to the 1990s (see, for example, Carrabine, 2004; Sim, 2009). Public sector restructuring in England and New Zealand, and more generous resourcing in New South Wales, has given momentum to this, as has the injection of private prisons (in conjunction with a series of critical official reports, including those from the independent Inspectorate of Prisons, in England, and from the Human Rights Commission and Office of the Ombudsman, in New Zealand). However, it was apparent that, in New South Wales, where there has been much less public sector restructuring, long running tensions and conflicts between state government and prison management, on the one hand, and the prison officers' union, on the other, remain. Both sides are antagonistic towards, and suspicious of, each other. We are still likely to find significant remnants of a militaristic, repressive, prison officer culture. Prison management regularly complain of, and investigate, overtime and sick leave abuse by the officers; meanwhile, officers are suspicious of management's plans for privatization, and complain of cost-saving understaffing.

More generally, institutional arrangements that are the exception, rather than the rule, should not obscure the major structural differences in the respective organization and administration of penal institutions between the two clusters. Essentially, in the Nordic countries, even in the high security units and institutions, prisoners do not become degraded non-citizens with their rights stripped away from them: instead, they retain all their citizens' rights, including the right to vote in elections, education, health services, drug treatment, the rights to work and enjoy holiday entitlements, and so on. This means, for example, that, in Norway and Sweden, education and healthcare services are provided through the respective government departments, rather than Corrections or Justice. As we have seen, while they remain prisoners, they are less likely to be excluded from the rest of society, and shut out of any involvement with it, than in the Anglophone countries. One particularly clear illustration of this occurred in Norway, in the run up to the 2009 general election. A law and order debate was televised from a prison, with the panel featuring the Justice Minister, his Opposition counterpart, and a maximum security prisoner. The debate was reported in *The Guardian* (10 September 2009: 11), as follows: 'In Norway, Prisoners Take Part in TV Debates'. The article continued, 'The primetime show, one of the top debate shows during the election campaign, has caused no outrage in Norway, as it probably would in the UK. There were no headlines expressing shock that inmates could voice their opinions in public debate. Nor was there condemnation of NRK, the Norwegian public broadcaster, for hosting a political debate inside a prison.' Overall, the Nordic prison authorities are committed to the normalization of prison life – making conditions within the prisons compatible with those of the outside world, as far as this is possible. The Norwegian Ministry of Justice and Police White Paper (2008), *Punishment that Works*, reaffirms that 'the normality principle is one of the five pillars on which the activity of Norwegian criminal care works'. In Finland, prisoners' rights are guaranteed in the constitution, under the provisions of the 2002 Prisons Act. The values and goals of the Finnish prison service remain offender-oriented, rather than replete with references to public safety and victims' rights, and include 'safeguarding basic rights and human rights' (Annual Report of the Finnish Prison and Probation Services, 2004: 5).

In the Anglophone jurisdictions, there is a great deal of emphasis on key performance indicators [KPIs] in the annual prison reports. But there is little regard, in these charts and scores, for the effects of the lockdowns, enforced cell sharing, disruptions caused by prisoner transfers, difficulties in visiting arrangements and so on, that are more clear markers of the realities of prison life in these countries. No amount of KPIs can alter the fact that the 16 hour routine lockdown in many of the Anglophone prisons is going to significantly undermine whatever quality of life there is in these institutions. The Nordic prison systems also have their KPIs, but these do not seem to have been allowed to subvert the ethics and morals of prison life in these countries. The purpose of imprisonment, we were told by one Norwegian prison manager, is 'to train offenders how to be ordinary citizens'. Again, in these countries, one is struck by the high levels of trust that seem to exist between prison staff and inmates, and the high levels of self-regulation and norm enforcement: without such attributes, it would simply be impossible for prisons in this region to function as they do. In the Anglophone prisons, however, security has come to assume overwhelming priority (as it is also becoming in the Swedish closed prisons, it must be recognized). Inevitably, in such a risk-averse climate, trust is either undermined or harder to establish. The remarks made to us by a senior officer in a low security establishment in New South Wales exemplify this: 'Don't ever trust a prisoner. Don't ever get close to them.'

At the same time, there not only seem to be much stronger divisions between prisoners and the rest of society in the Anglophone countries, but these also seem to be widening. This is hardly the fault of the prison services in these jurisdictions. Rather, it is a reflection of the level of the (more general) public and political debates about punishment and prisons, in these countries, that then circumscribe prison policy. Even when prison managers are able to point to positive achievements – as with horticultural and farming initiatives in New Zealand in 2010 – these are likely to be challenged or undermined by complaints that productive prison labour, because of its minimal wages, undermines the free market and has to be stopped. Indeed, in these societies, prisoners are reminded of the differences between themselves and free citizens at every level of their existence. They thus have no voting rights.[9] They have no holidays, other than statutory holidays, when they are likely to be locked in their cells for longer than usual. A Radio New Zealand news bulletin, on 25 December 2011, informed listeners that women inmates at one prison would be receiving 'no Christmas services, nor were they being allowed any visitors for security reasons. Priority was given to allowing the guards a day off.' And there is still not the same degree of independent provision of health and education services as in the Nordic countries. Indeed, in New Zealand, these services continue to be provided exclusively by the Department of Corrections. This has particularly important implications in relation to which government department has responsibility for mentally ill prisoners, with regular conflicts between Corrections and the Department of Health, both wishing to absolve themselves of responsibility for this very problematic group. In England, while the National Health Service is now the provider of mental health services in prisons, demand far outstrips supply, meaning that, for many such prisoners, there will be minimal assistance. We were variously told, while visiting the English prisons, that '80 per cent of prisoners have mental health problems and there are *no* facilities here', and that '90 per cent of prisoners have some form of mental health issue'. While the Nordic countries, themselves, have undergone significant deinstitutionalization programmes from the late 1960s, this does not seem to have resulted in the kind of migration of the mentally ill to the prison that has become characteristic of the Anglophone countries (Markström, 2003). At the same time, the Anglophone prisons face challenges that, in many ways, are the unforeseen products of ill thought-out, hasty, government policy. For example, the increasing numbers of prisoners serving indefinite sentences know that their only hope of release is to enrol in 'programmes', only to find that there are never enough places for them on the programmes. In these respects, and notwithstanding the commitment to 'decency' in England, it is as if the prison experience, for many inmates, has become 'tighter and deeper', as one commentator told us; a much more 'intensive experience', in the words of another. Prisoners have to 'actively show compliance', however illogical this might seem when the prison regimes cannot provide them with the wherewithal that the courts and parole board have stipulated they need to demonstrate before they can be considered for release.

Furthermore, prisoners in the Anglophone countries still seem subject to arbitrary and petty rules and procedures that not only affect their daily quality of life but continue to differentiate them from the rest of society. One New Zealand prisoner was, in 2010, thus refused permission to read *The Naked Ape*, by the famous anthropologist Desmond Morris (1967), on the grounds that it contravened the rule that prisoners were not allowed access to pornography. The response of the government in England to European Court of Human Rights (ECHR) rulings is usually to delay, ignore or water down their findings, or to finally accept the decision with bad grace, as if it was symptomatic of baffling EU idiosyncrasy. When, in 2011, after a *2004* ruling by the ECHR, the British government conceded that some prisoners *were* to be given the vote, Prime Minister David Cameron declared himself to be feeling 'physically sick' at this news (*Daily Mail*, 13 April 2011: 2). In other words, there is still an insistence that, not only must those in prison be shut away from the rest of society, but, at the same time, their exclusion, their worthlessness, their shamefulness, their 'difference' must be continually reinforced and emphasized, both to the prisoners themselves, and to the rest of society. Furthermore, we are still likely to find extraordinary levels of squalor and degradation in some Anglophone prisons. The Chief Inspector of Prisons in England maintains that 'you look at the conditions some people are in and what's happening to them and the lack of care they are getting and you think "This is just a disgrace"' (*The Independent*, 6 November 2010: 3).

Overall, just as the variations in imprisonment rates point to substantive (rather than artefactual) differences in punishment, so the contrasts that run right through the respective prison systems of these societies also point to their very different ways of thinking about punishment.

Explaining penal differences

Let us thus return to our initial question – the sociological (rather than any normative) imperative that drives this book – *what is it about these types of societies that can account for their different ways of thinking about punishment?* It is clear that these differences bear little relation to the levels of crime in these societies. If we bracket off inherent difficulties in making such judgements for all kinds of counting, recording and definitional reasons (as with imprisonment rates) then, as Figure 1.4 illustrates, we find that, from 1950 onwards – the point at which police records begin to be compiled with some consistency across these societies, with the exception of New South Wales[10] – there is a high level of symmetry between recorded crime levels.

Crime increased in all these societies for much of this period; from the 1990s it has stabilized or has begun to decline in all of them. However, as was noted in the Introduction, the pattern of imprisonment over the same period shows symmetry *within* the clusters, but not *between* them. As Figure 1.5 illustrates, while imprisonment rates have remained relatively stable in Sweden and Norway, and that for Finland has come down to the same kind of level, the imprisonment rates of the Anglophone societies have, for most of this time, been set on an upward spiral, one that has been accelerating from the 1990s, with the result that the gulf between the imprisonment rates of the two clusters of societies has become considerably wider.

That there is no direct fit between these prison rates and crime rates should come as no surprise. As David Garland (1990: 44) observed, punishment is not merely

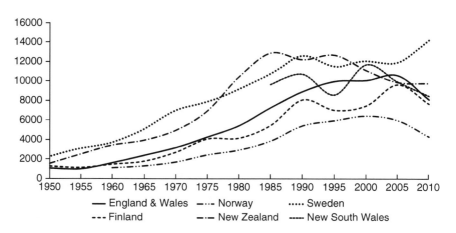

Figure 1.4 Crime rates, 1950–2010 (all six societies).

Sources: England and Wales: Home Office (2012a, 2012b). Norway: Falck, von Hofer and Storgaard (2003); Statistics Norway (2012b). Sweden: Falck, von Hofer and Storgaard (2003); Swedish National Council for Crime Prevention (2012). Finland: Falck, von Hofer and Storgaard (2003); Statistics Finland (2012b). New Zealand: New Zealand Yearbook (various); New Zealand Police (2012). New South Wales: NSW Bureau of Crime Statistics and Research (1990, 2012).

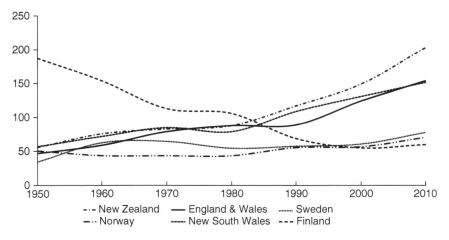

Figure 1.5 Imprisonment rates, 1950–2010 (all six societies).

Sources: New Zealand: New Zealand Yearbook (various); Department of Justice (1981); Ministry of Justice (1991, 2008). England and Wales: Home Office (2003). Sweden: Falck, von Hofer and Storgaard (2003). Norway: Statistics Norway (2012a). New South Wales: Official Yearbook of New South Wales (various); Australian Bureau of Statistics (1982, 2000). Finland: Falck, von Hofer and Storgaard (2003); Statistics Finland (2012a). All countries: World Prison Brief (2010).

a 'utilitarian instrument', the use of which is determined by the quantities of crime being committed in a given society. Instead, it can also be understood as 'an expressive form of moral action . . . a means of conveying a moral message, and of indicating the strength of feeling which lies behind it'. In these respects, it is as if punishment in the Anglophone societies, certainly from the 1990s, has come to carry an excessive, overladen baggage of signs and symbols that are unrelated to the crime rate. Instead, excesses of this kind – both in terms of the extravagant quantities of, and the quality of, punishment to be imposed – perform the function of giving messages of reassurance to anxious and insecure communities: inflammatory speeches are thus made by politicians about the need for more use of imprisonment through longer sentences and curtailment of early release mechanisms; and there are avowals that prisons will no longer resemble 'holiday camps', as with the Minister's comments about the shipping container cells. Such excesses have been characterized by Garland (2005: 814) as being 'a deliberate flouting of the norms of modern and civilized penology, a self conscious choice'. In addition, Ian Loader (2010: 350) suggests that penal excess is associated with 'hyperactivity'; that is, 'the satisfaction of immediate desires by recourse to speed, urgency, indulgence, decisiveness, here and now gratification'. Each exceptional case is treated as the norm, and the laws are rewritten time and again to adjust the entire prison and penal system to the issues raised by the one incident, as if each of these has the potential to make further breaches in the dam of social cohesion that can then only be repaired by recourse to such immediate but continuing repairs. In England, for example, between 1997 and 2008, 53 new Acts were introduced that dealt with crime and punishment: there had been only 42 crime-related Acts in the preceding century. As this has happened, the penal system has been relaid, patched over and rebranded, time and again, with increasingly complex and indigestible ideas and strategies. Thus, the Home Office (2002: 81) White Paper, *Justice for All*, set out its latest plans for an overhaul of the penal system that involved 'a series of new and innovative sentences; a new suspended sentence called Custody Minus; reform of short custodial sentences through the introduction of Custody Plus; a new Intermittent Custody scheme that denies liberty through a custodial sentence served intermittently, for example, at the weekend, but allows the offender to continue working and maintain family ties; and a new special sentence for dangerous sexual or violent offenders'.

These excesses have largely been avoided in the Nordic countries. Law-making usually involves lengthy deliberation in these societies, allowing all the evidence to be digested before arriving at a consensual, rather than polarizing, conclusion. As Jareborg (1995: 99) explained in relation to Sweden, 'a legislative committee typically works for a number of years. All this serves to make the process as rational as possible. The issue is "cooled down" and political difficulties are normally solved within the committee whose members continually consult important persons in their respective political parties.' Similarly, Lappi-Seppälä (2007: 69–70) refers to the revision of the Finnish penal code that commenced in 1972. After four years, 'the Committee ... laid down its principal paper. Again, after four years of preparation a specific Task-Force for criminal law reform was established ... practically all key figures stayed active from the start to the closing of the project (1980–1999) and some remained in the work from their initial start in 1972 till the last official sub-reform in 1999'. At the same time, the use of punishment has been more 'modest' in this region. That is, it has been used with 'restraint, parsimony and dignity' (Loader, 2010: 351). The low rates of imprisonment are a reflection of these characteristics, as is the emphasis on de-stigmatizing the prison experience. Certainly, in recent years, there have been criticisms of this approach to punishment from within these societies, particularly from right-wing populist parties. However, it remains that there has been little by way of departure from existing expectations in the political mainstream. As a consequence, while punishment in the Anglophone societies has come to be characterized by its excesses, punishment in the Nordic societies represents an exception to this trend.

Why is it, though, that punishment performs such different moral actions and conveys different messages in these clusters of societies? In his review of Emile Durkheim's contribution to penal theory, Garland (1990: 75) writes that 'the bonds holding people together and regulating their conduct are always moral bonds, ties of shared sentiment and morality – [but] where moral community is often absent or fragmented ... the role of control and policing is much greater'. By the same token, 'the more authoritative, stable and legitimate the political-moral order, the less need there is for terroristic or force-displaying uses of punishment'. On this basis, the Anglophone levels and intensity of punishment point to the inability of these states to maintain cohesion and social stability from other sources. Excessive levels of punishment become necessary to perform this role, hence the way in which law and order issues have come to feature so prominently in public and political discourse in these societies (Reiner, 2007). But this, of necessity, also means that cohesion and stability can only be achieved by *excluding* significant sections of the population – the rest of the community is united around their exclusion and feels the better for it (Durkheim, 1893/1933). While these excesses have come to play an increasingly central role in the governance of the Anglophone societies (Simon, 2007), it is their *absence* that is striking in the Nordic. Where, then, instead of 'censure, condemnation and reprobation', these signs and symbols convey more muted messages of forbearance, tolerance and restoration, this is indicative of the way in which these states are able to provide social cohesion without needing to attain this through excessive uses of punishment. Indeed, more *inclusionary* social mechanisms are likely to bind these communities together: 'a strong and legitimately established moral order requires only token sanctions to restore itself and deal with violators' (Garland, 1990: 60). Under these circumstances, there is no need for punishment to perform the role it has come to assume in the Anglophone countries.

How is it, then, that these societies have taken on these respective inclusionary and exclusionary characteristics? Various explanations for these differences have been put forward in recent years and have featured:

- *The welfare state.* Drawing on the work of Esping-Andersen (1990), Cavadino and Dignan (2006: 155) argue that there is a strong correlation between penal development and levels of investment in the welfare state. In the 'social democratic model of welfare' in the Nordic countries '[its] ideology, with its emphasis on equality and social solidarity and caring for those at the bottom of society, is likely to see the criminal as a victim of adverse social conditions', thereby making possible low rates of imprisonment and relatively humane prison conditions. In contrast, in the Anglophone countries, with the much more restricted welfare arrangements of the 'liberal' model, 'crime is seen as entirely the responsibility of the offending individual. The social soil is fertile ground for a harsh "law and order ideology"' (ibid.: 24), with attendant consequences for high imprisonment rates and degrading prison conditions.
- *Political economy.* Lacey (2008) argues that the Nordic countries are characterized by co-ordinated market economies, in contrast to the liberal market economies of the Anglophone countries. The extensive welfare programmes of the former need funding that can only be provided from full employment and the taxation this generates, again necessitating low levels of imprisonment to avoid labour wastage. In contrast, the Anglophone societies are able to tolerate higher levels of imprisonment, since welfare benefits are much lower and do not need the taxation generated by full employment to sustain them. Instead, high levels of imprisonment in these societies become affordable ways of managing surplus labour.
- *Political culture.* Nordic politics are marked much more by consensus. With few exceptions, since 1945, parties of both the Left and Right have been committed to maintaining the broad parameters of the Nordic welfare state (Green, 2008; Lacey, 2008). In this region, the social democratic *weltanschauung* has

been the dominant political force. In contrast, politics in the Anglophone countries are more conflictual, with a tradition of majoritarian Conservative governments.

- *The mass media.* As Green (2008) also demonstrates, there are important differences in the structure and content of the mass media in these societies. These are then reflected in the frameworks of knowledge that they construct, and through which crime and punishment issues are understood. Generally speaking, the Nordic media tend to play much more of a public information/ educational role than the Anglophone, which is driven more by sensationalism and scandal, of which crime and punishment have provided a regular supply.

The historical origins of penal excess and penal exceptionalism

Such scholarship tells us a good deal about some of the structural and cultural differences between these clusters, but also leaves important issues unresolved. For example, as regards the welfare state argument, this does not explain *why* the differences in welfare arrangements occurred in these clusters. Nor, in Cavadino and Dignan (2007), is there any significant account of how the supposed linkage between welfare and punishment actually takes place: only a correlation is established.[11] As regards the political economy explanation, the relatively humane conditions in Nordic prisons would seem more problematic than in the above accounts: why, for example, should there be comparatively little social distance in this region between those in prison – most of whom contribute very little to the economic well-being of their country – and those outside? As regards the different approaches taken by the media and the political strength of social democracy in the Nordic region versus that of Conservatism in the Anglophone societies, what is it that has brought about these particular social characteristics?

Matters such as these reflect the way in which contemporary differences in punishment between the different types of modern society are likely to have lengthy historical roots (Whitman, 2003; Lacey, 2006). Indeed, the argument in this book is that the explanation for the current penal differences between the Anglophone and Nordic societies begins in the early nineteenth century, rather than the early twenty-first. Before then, penal affairs were conducted in much the same way in both clusters: they took the form of brutal, spectacular, public executions, and appalling, degrading, prison conditions (see Howard, 1792; Clarke, 1819; Hovde, 1943). Thereafter, however, different ways of seeing and understanding the world, different tolerances, different norms and conventions, different *cultures* – 'all those conceptions and values, categories and distinctions, frameworks of ideas and systems of belief which human beings use to construe their world and render it orderly and meaningful' (Garland 1990: 195) – began to emerge. *Egalitarianism and moderation became two of the central features of Nordic culture, and helped to promote high levels of social inclusion. In contrast, there was more emphasis on individual advancement and division in the Anglophone, which led to higher levels of social exclusion.* At various times along their subsequent routes of development, these values have been moderated and checked, distorted and enhanced, more concentrated in some individual societies within each cluster, less so in others. *Overall, though*, they have continued to provide different ways in which it has been possible to think about the world – and different ways in which it has been possible to think about punishment in each cluster. *At the same time*, rather than the discontinuities and abrupt departures from established modes of thinking that have become such a strong feature of the sociology of punishment in the aftermath of Foucault's (1977) *Discipline and Punish*, it is *the subsequent continuity in penal thought* in the respective clusters of societies – even though, of course, the strategies in which this has been put into effect over this two-hundred-year period have been the subject of considerable change – that provides the analytical framework for this book.

How, then, did these long-term values emerge? As is explained in Chapter 2 (The Production of Cultural Differences), these were brought about by means of a constellation of social forces that began to take effect in the early nineteenth century. Their subsequent effects on the production of these value systems are traced through to the mid-twentieth century, using sources that include official commentaries, reports and enquiries, as well as memoirs, travelogues, literary works and diaries, in the manner that Norbert Elias (1939/1979), the most important scholar on the relationship between the historical development of Western culture and state formation, pursued in his *magnum opus*. As is explained in Chapter 3 (Two Models of Welfare State), these value systems then intersected with these societies' respective models of welfare state, as they came to fruition in the mid-twentieth century. The purpose of this chapter is not to explain *why* the welfare state came into existence but, instead, *how* the two welfare models then institutionalized and gave a materiality to these ways of thinking about the world. In effect, the Nordic model helped to increase solidarity between citizens, and led to high levels of trust between individual citizens and between individuals and the state (Rothstein and Uslaner, 2005). In contrast, although the Anglophone model of welfare provided undoubted, often transformative, benefits, it was nonetheless constrained by its own limitations in bringing about a greater egalitarianism and cohesion. Thereafter, while the Nordic value systems have remained largely in place, notwithstanding the post-1970s restructuring that has taken place right across modern society, those of the Anglophone have become exaggerated and extended, as the restraints that the liberal welfare state had previously been able to place on them have been largely pushed away.

In the last three chapters of the book, we show how these value systems have then provided different frameworks for thinking about punishment. As is shown in Chapter 4 (The Introduction of Modern Penal Arrangements), these came to light, *first*, with the much earlier demise of the death penalty in peacetime[12] in the Nordic societies (for most intents and purposes, by the 1870s). The need for such a dramatic and highly symbolic spectacle of punishment as a way of affirming ruling class power was greatly reduced in these relatively egalitarian, cohesive and homogeneous countries. Characteristics such as these are less likely to favour physically destructive sanctions – as if the values that all members of these societies share are not going to be put at risk by a single act of crime, and do not need to be reinforced and upheld by dramatic penalties. In contrast, in the more stratified, divided and exclusionary Anglophone countries, the death penalty continued to carry great symbolic power: it was thought of as a necessary means of ensuring social order and stability, leading to its retention until the 1960s. *Second*, these differences in thinking about punishment came to light in the way that the modern prison began to perform different moral functions in these societies. During the late nineteenth century, it became a place of terror in the Anglophone societies, and was deliberately advertized as such. As a consequence, prisoners came to be seen as an altogether different species of human being – a species that attracted intense curiosity by virtue of their separation and incarceration in such a fearful place, but one that was simultaneously shunned, excluded, and set apart. In the Nordic countries, however, where Lutheran pastors had a more significant role in prison administration than the Anglophone chaplains, there was considerably more emphasis on education and the performance of productive, rather than afflictive, labour. In such ways, much shorter social distances between prison inmates and the rest of the community began to be established, making their difference seem less pronounced, and their eventual reintegration less problematic.

Chapter 5 (Two Welfare Sanctions) shows how the development of the Nordic 'social democratic welfare sanction', from the end of the nineteenth century to the 1960s, had the effect of simultaneously weaving a more extensive web of regulation around these societies while lessening the intensity and severity of punishment and exclusion. In the Anglophone countries, the 'liberal welfare sanction', over the same period, initially helped to temper the previous emphasis on penal exclusion and introduced a range of restraints on the extent and intensity of punishment. This brought a convergence in prison rates between these clusters by the mid-twentieth-century. This proved to be only temporary, however. As the post-1945 commitment to the liberal welfare state began to weaken in the 1950s and 1960s, so, too, did its ability to build the more extensive solidarity and cohesion of the Nordic societies. Instead, as inequalities and divisions became more pronounced, what inclusionary capabilities the liberal welfare sanction possessed became more limited. As a consequence, the differences in punishment between these clusters of societies widened: Anglophone prison populations began to increase and outstrip the Nordic countries during the 1960s and, while the prison conditions of the latter began to be advertized to the world as shining examples of Western humanity, those in the former became known for their overcrowded, deteriorating, conditions.

In Chapter 6 (Punishment in the Age of Anxiety), we show how, from the 1970s, the cultural values and welfare arrangements of the Nordic countries have, to a large extent, continued to insulate them from much of the Anglophone penal excesses that are to be found in response to the extensive social and economic restructuring of this period. In the ensuing 'age of anxiety', the penal differences between these societies have further widened and have become more extensive. These developments reflect the increasing importance of the role played by punishment in bringing about social cohesion and solidarity in the Anglophone countries. In contrast, the Nordic countries continue to rely on more inclusionary social measures for these purposes, and have no need for such penal excesses.

2 The production of cultural differences

There are two Nordic words that have no direct English equivalent. Literally translated, the Norwegian and Swedish expression *likhet* means equality *and* sameness, the two concepts being indivisible, implying a uniformity in both standards and appearances, or of them 'being the same worth' (Gullenstad, 2002). The nearest English equivalents to the Swedish word *lagom* are phrases such as 'just enough', 'just right' or 'everything in moderation', but these do not adequately recognize the moral force this expression has come to have in Sweden. In that country, *lagom* conveys strong disapproval of anything that suggests over-indulgence, with a simultaneously strong approval of moderation and self-effacement. In such ways, *lagom* and *likhet* have become immensely strong characteristics of Nordic society, signifying as they do an emphasis on egalitarianism and inclusion, as well as the high levels of informal social control that enforce these values, in order to bring about conformity and uniformity, rather than exclusion and division.

That there are no direct English equivalents to these two words also tells us a great deal about the Anglophone societies. There are no direct equivalents because, instead of equality and sameness, there is much more emphasis on individuality and difference; instead of moderation, there is much more emphasis on aggrandizement and self-advancement. In these respects, if the Nordic countries are 'just right' societies, then the Anglophone are 'getting on' societies. Rather than the Nordic values that give importance to egalitarianism, cohesion and the status quo, upward mobility has more value in the Anglophone, particularly because, in these societies, one's standing is very much dependent on one's place in their (more hierarchical) class structures. This is inferred in various English phrases that have no Nordic equivalents: 'keeping up with the Joneses'; 'knowing one's place'; 'looking up to one's betters'. The origins of these different value systems doubtless lie wayback in history, and it may well be that, in the aftermath of social and economic changes in Western society as a whole since the 1970s, they are no longer as visible as was once the case. Nonetheless, from the early nineteenth century, they were given a particular momentum and force through the nexus provided by four particular features of the modern organization of these societies: class structure, degree of homogeneity, the value and function of education, and the role given to the central state in everyday governance. As this occurred, these different value systems fed back into and shaped and reshaped the way in which it became possible to see and understand the world.

Class relations

In the mid-nineteenth century, most land in the Nordic countries was divided into self-sufficient smallholdings that belonged to the *bönder* – independent farmers.[1] This meant that there was no powerful landowning class that lived off the profits of land rented out to agricultural labourers. Norway was the exemplar of this form of social organization. Here, on the death of a landholder, property was shared among all descendants, rather than inherited by the first born, thereby preventing the build-up of large estates. As Crichton (1842: 349) explained, 'the land has been parcelled out into small estates of 40 or 60 acres, affording a competent subsistence, with a moderate share of the elegancies of civilized life; but in no degree supplying the means of luxury, or the accumulation of wealth. The number of proprietors, in proportion to the rest of the population, is perhaps greater than in any other country in Europe. Equally remote from poverty and affluence, and addicted neither to extravagance nor enterprise, they are content to enjoy the simple comforts of their paternal domain.' It was also a matter of necessity to build strong interdependencies in the small rural communities, given the challenges posed by geography, climate and the sparse population – hence, the *dugnad* tradition in this country (similarly, *talkoot* in Finland). Literally, this means 'voluntary community work' but, in practice, it related to a broad range of mutually reciprocated neighbourly activities and support. The Norwegian *bønder* were also politically significant and influential – the 1814 Constitution gave the vote to 45 per cent of the male population, ensuring that these farmers had a potential majority in parliament – indeed, the Farmers' Party maintained a strong political presence throughout the nineteenth and early twentieth century. Although this country retained its monarchy, the nobility was abolished in 1821, with the result being, as the newspaper *Aftonbladet* (1 August 1839: 3) explained, 'there is no court with all its hangers on [in Norway], no arrogant and impoverished nobility with much life at others' expense'.

However, Sweden was then a more stratified society. Here, the nobility maintained their titles and high social status. Laing (1837: 77) thus referred to the 'splendid court' in Stockholm, and noted that 'the Swede has a remarkable fondness for dress; and dresses well, converses well, dances well, has ease and elegance about him . . . this is the influence of a court in a small city'. In reality, though, the Swedish aristocracy had been stripped of most of its land at the end of the seventeenth century. Thereafter, it was redistributed in such a way that the political power of the *bönder* was strengthened in this society, as well. As a consequence, the Swedish nobles did not constitute a ruling elite, detached from the rest of society on large estates. Laing (ibid.: 180, our italics) thus qualified his comments on the court by stating that 'I had formed an erroneous idea of the Swedish nobility. I had imagined they were a rich and splendid class . . . but they are, with few exceptions, extremely poor, living from civil or military employment with small pay. *There are few signs of luxury or opulence in Sweden.*' Indeed, by the mid-nineteenth century 'in the greater part of the country, large properties formed an insignificant minority compared to small freehold farms and holdings . . . *the life and work of the owners of these and their children were so like those of the agricultural labourers that no marked class distinction was available*' (Blomstedt and Book, 1930: 221, our italics). Although universal suffrage was not introduced to Sweden until 1920, the *bönder* still had significant power in the existing structure of government: a four estates diet (two from 1865). Their admission to the *riksdag* (parliament) as a separate estate (alongside the burghers, nobility and clergy) was, in itself, a recognition of their economic and strategic importance (Roberts, 1967: 249). And, as with Norway, the Agrarian or Farmer's Party had an important presence when full democracy was introduced.

In Finland, stability and cohesion in the late nineteenth and early twentieth centuries was under threat from two sources. *First*, land distribution was regulated by a tenancy system, with only about 100,000 privately owned farms (Alestalo and Kuhnle, 1987: 21). Changes from arable to dairy farming, enclosures and growing mechanization during the nineteenth century benefitted yeoman farmers and wealthier tenants at the expense of poorer tenants and landless labourers, who regularly faced dispossession, eviction and poverty. *Second*, Tsarist attempts to 'Russianize' Finland, overriding legislation to the contrary from the fledgling Finnish parliament, led to further instability. The Finnish civil war of 1918 was the product of these destabilizing forces. The subsequent victory of the White Guards over the Red Guards was followed by particularly bloody reprisals. But, at the same time, the idea of a 'free, independent peasantry' (Kekkonen, 1999) gave a strong idoleogical charge to the direction of government policy: it became a symbol of the triumph of the Whites over the Red, Russian-influenced, menace. This was given a material basis with the introduction in 1918 of a more recognizably Nordic form of land distribution. The state was now empowered to buy large estates for subdivision into small farms, and to rent them out as leasehold lands. Legislation in 1922 then allowed uncultivated land to be purchased with state-supported capital. Emerging out of the restructuring of class relations that these measures made possible, the Agrarian Party also became a pivotal player in subsequent coalition governments during the course of the twentieth century.

Overall, then, and despite the differences in the processes associated with it, we find the development of a class structure where the *bønder* and their values were a dominant feature of the social and the political structure of these societies (Stenius, 1997: 165). Indeed, in Norway, this class was idealized. Speaking the local *Landsmal* dialect, as opposed to what was the official Swedish language of this country before independence in 1905, and practising their modest way of life, the *bønder* became the emblem of that country's struggle for national identity and independence. Bjørnstjerne Bjørnson (quoted by Barton, 2003: 104), one of Norway's most renowned nineteenth century literary figures, thus described his work as taking the form of 'a plea on behalf of the peasant . . . we had come to understand that the language of the sagas lived on in our peasants and their way of life was close to that of the sagas. The life of our nation was to be built on our history; and now the peasants were to provide the foundations.' As such, the egalitarianism, uniformity, solidarity and stability that was characteristic of that way of life had become a national characteristic by the beginning of the twentieth century: 'the highest and lowest strata of society are on the whole no farther removed from one another than that there is constant reciprocal action between them, and transition from the one to the other' (*Official Publication for the Paris Exhibition*, 1900: 202). In addition, industrialization, when it arrived in Norway and Sweden in the late nineteenth century (it did not really arrive in Finland until the 1950s), did not lead to urbanization, nor did it disrupt rural life and community. Instead, it was on a relatively small scale, in keeping with the population sizes of these countries (5,000,000 in Sweden in 1900 and 2,240,000 in Norway). The traditions and values of the countryside, and the historical foundations these had provided in the evolution of Norway as an independent nation, were thus able to be maintained,

Figure 2.1 The Nordic ideal: a small cottage or *hytte* in Norway. Note the emphasis on personal space and proximity to nature. Photograph: Dagbladet/Norsk Folkemuseum.

even amongst city dwellers, as they sought what were originally very humble holiday homes in the country (see, for example, Shirer, 1955: 71; Eckstein, 1966: 124). As Figure 2.1 illustrates, these cottages allowed for the celebration of the rural heritage of these countries while simultaneously reaffirming the values of egalitarianism and moderation.

Of course, it is important not to overstate the degree of harmony and cohesion in these societies. Nonetheless, potential conflicts and disunity were likely to be channelled into the existing ways of understanding the world, through the activities of interconnecting and inter-class social movements. These were variously formed by religious revivalists, industrial workers, farmers and temperance supporters during the nineteenth and early twentieth centuries, often in protest at existing social arrangements. Their emphasis remained, though, on egalitarianism, moderation, thrift and sobriety – already existing values that then became further inscribed in these societies, in ways that modified and incorporated dissent rather than repress it. Mead (1968: 167), for example, wrote that the Finnish temperance movement, at the end of the nineteenth century, 'embodied central ideals of Finnish nationalism – it promoted organizations within the sphere of the state, educated people and pursued demand for legislative reforms – it was also rooted in the peasants' own values.'

In the Anglophone countries, however, there were not only more extensive and deeper class differences and divisions but, at the same time, much greater importance was given to individual prosperity and material success, at the expense of egalitarianism and solidarity. And, for the most part, these were also societies that, during the course of the nineteenth century, came to be organized largely around urban values, practices and work routines, rather than those of rural life. In England, industrialization profoundly disrupted rural traditions. In 1801, one in three of the population worked in agriculture; by 1881, this had been reduced to one in eight. The result was a much weaker bond between most of the population and the countryside, those still working on the land and the *gemeinschaft* traditions, obligations and reciprocities of pre-industrial society. As Thompson (1988: 93) observed, 'if the English rustic had the desire to "better himself" he had better leave the land'. Indeed, in the nineteenth century, agricultural workers were the worst paid and worst fed of all manual labourers (Burnett, 1966; Perkin, 1969). Mid-nineteenth-century English literature is thus preoccupied with themes of rural penury and misery, in contrast to the bucolic idealism of Bjørnson's Norway. For example, in his novel *Alton Locke*, Charles Kingsley (1850: 96) describes a rural village as 'a knot of thatched hovels all sinking and leaning every way but the right, the windows patched with paper, the doorways stopped with filth'. Moreover, the class-based nature of land ownership led to vulnerabilities and uncertainties that the more egalitarian Nordic systems of distribution avoided. In George Eliot's (1859/1980: 125, our italics) *Adam Bede*, the grandson of the local squire suddenly announces to a tenant farmer whose family have leased land from this gentry family for generations, that '"I think yours is the prettiest farm on the estate . . . and do you know, if I were going to marry and settle, *I should be tempted to turn you out, and do up this fine old house and turn farmer myself.*" "O, sir," said [the farmer] *rather alarmed,* "you wouldn't like it. As for farming, its putting money into your pocket wi' your right hand and fetching it out wi' your left."'

Certainly, farming and agricultural interests had a strong political influence in the histories of Australia and New Zealand, but there was nothing of the tranquillity and moderation associated with Nordic rural life in such areas in these societies. Indeed, as Australia became the most urbanized society in the world, during the course of the nineteenth century,[2] what lay beyond the cities came to be associated with danger and menace: escaped convicts, bushrangers, hostile Aborigines, lethal wildlife. In these respects, the rural way of life was to be feared rather than romanticized. Similarly, New Zealand: the bush became a place of isolation, a place for misfits and runaways as described in John Mulgan's (1939) novel, *Man Alone*, rather than the setting for some idyllic community life. In effect, then, egalitarian *gemeinschaft* traditions still flourished in the Nordic countries for much of the nineteenth century, but had little purchase in the Anglophone, where the importance of the individual *doing well for themselves*, rising above their status, moving ahead rather than standing still, came to be paramount.

This was reflected in the distribution of political and economic power in the Anglophone countries. Much of this shifted away from the landowners of the pre-modern era towards newly rich industrialists and other *parvenus*. But this did not then mean that the values of the previously dominant landowning class were abandoned or overturned. Their grand properties and lives of leisure remained the ideal to which the newly wealthy could aspire. Hence, the desire of the lawyer and businessman Soames Forsyte, the central figure in John Galsworthy's *The Forsyte Saga* (1922: 71, our italics), to have his own country house notwithstanding that he already owned a substantial property in Knightsbridge in the centre of London. On surveying a prospective sight for a country house, 'something swelled in his breast. *To live here in sight of all this, to be able to point it out to his friends, to talk of it, to possess it.*' Indeed, there was a marked growth in country house building between 1835 and 1889: some 500 were built or remodelled, roughly half of them for newly rich families (Thompson, 1988: 155).

Reviewing these trends, the American poet Ralph Waldo Emerson (1857: 76–7) observed that 'palaces, halls, villas, walled parks all over England rival the splendour of royal estates . . . the hopes of the commoners take the same direction with the interest of the patricians. Every man who becomes rich buys land and does what he can to fortify the nobility, into which he hopes to rise.' In such ways, one's status in England was determined by the extent of one's wealth, extravagance and the ownership of property (see Figure 2.2), rather than any modest consumption and an ability to fit in well with the local community. Indeed, the whole point of buying an English country estate was to demonstrate one's difference from, and superiority to, the rest of the community – 'look at me, look what I have become' – rather than to be at one with it, as reflected in the ownership of *sommarstugor* (summer cottages) in the Nordic countries.

Clearly, though, not everyone could own a stately home. For the vast majority of the emerging bourgeoisie, dreams of the country estate had to be scaled down,

Figure 2.2 The English ideal: Toddington Manor, Toddington, Gloucestershire, built between 1819 and 1840 in Gothic revivalism style. It was owned by Charles Hanbury-Tracy, whose family made their fortune from ironworks during the industrial revolution. Permission granted by English Heritage (2346/66871).

taking the form of suburban villas or multi-storied 'townhouses'. In his *Notes on England*, Hippolyte Taine (1874: 275) observed that 'the city man strives to have his country seat and county surroundings at the outskirts; he feels the necessity of being by himself – of feeling that he is alone, monarch of his family and his servants, of having around him a piece of park or a garden as a relaxation from the artificial life of town and business. Hence have been constructed vast silent streets in which there are no shops, and in which each house, surrounded by a patch of green, is detached and is occupied by a single family.' This also meant that great importance came to be attached to home ownership, as an emblem of one's wealth and social standing. As Emerson (1857: 80) put the matter, 'the English . . . wish neither to command or obey, but to be kings in their own houses'. Similarly, Smith (1915: 1) later wrote that 'no other nation has accepted the home as the foundation of national life to the same degree as England; no other nation esteems the influences of home higher than the English'. In such ways, self-advancement, with wealth and property its key signifiers, rather than the importance given to remaining at the same level as everyone else (as in the Nordic countries), became the driving force of English social life. Binney (1853: 20, our italics), for example, argued that the essentials for a happy life were 'health, cheerfulness, competence, and along with this, *the feeling and consciousness of getting on – of success and advancement*'. As Collier (1909: 158) then explained, 'in England, the prizes are fewer, they are more difficult to win, and they are splendidly rewarded. A really great man in England is rewarded as in no other land, while the failures suffer in proportion.' Beatrice Webb (1926:

13, our italics), the renowned Fabian socialist and social reformer, confirmed in her memoirs that, as a young adult, 'it was the bounden duty of every citizen to better his social status; *to ignore those beneath him, and to aim steadily at the top rung of the social ladder*'.

But it was also important that wealth should free the new English elites, rich from successful investments and the products of industrialization, from having to work, as in the manner of the pre-modern landowners. They would then be able to assume membership of what Collier (1909: 38) referred to as the 'unoccupied classes' or what Ford (1907: 173) termed the 'leisure class'. Such people displayed a confidence and assurance that came from the certain knowledge of the superior social standing that their wealth had given them. The very way they carried themselves, the way they spoke, set them apart (Huizinga, 1958) and provided the etymological basis for expressions, based on these class distinctions, that had 'no equivalent in any language I know. Like "our betters" and "the likes of us" for instance . . . to be happy in England one must be "looked up to" and "well thought of" – more untranslatable phrases!' (Keun, 1935: 160). Furthermore, 'think, too, of the columns, the pages, filled in the newspapers by the doings of the great: where they go, how they look, what they say. Never, in any European country, would the press dare to keep up such a chatter about futile personalities or give so much publicity to such insipid and meaningless figures' (ibid.: 168). Here, then, was a society in which those who stood out in one way or another could find fame, rather than be put in their place for elevating themselves above the rest of the community – and the more they could demonstrate that they lived above the rest of society, the more, it seemed, they gained respect. In the Nordic countries, however, there seems to have been little of such extravagances and fripperies. Travers (1911: 210) wrote that 'so small a remnant of the real "idle classes" now remains in Finland, that there is something quite gallant and pathetic about the efforts of this little band to go on playing when all the rest are at work . . . during the last 20 years one well born family after another has quietly sunk its prefix (*av*) and its intentions are [now] in commerce or public service, while the daughters have learnt to earn their own living as a matter of course'. Here, it was expected that all would work, rather than allow a privileged 'leisure class' to idle away its time with indulgences and extravagances while the rest toiled.

But, if this contrast between class-divided England and the more egalitarian Nordic countries seems clear cut, what of Australia and New Zealand, now known for their egalitarianism, rather than their idle rich? In *New Zealand: A Short History*, James Buller (1880: 142) opined that 'the social disabilities, exclusive caste, the overstrained competition and the stereotyped conventionalism of the Old World have not yet taken root' here. Similarly, Harrop (1935: 270), half a century later, claimed that 'there is an absence of class distinction in its extreme forms in New Zealand'. Furthermore, 'New Zealand boasts not a single millionaire nor any who are starving' (Cowie, 1937: 187). However, while class differences in Australia and New Zealand were not so glaring as those in England, the practices and manners of the English upper classes were deliberately replicated in these countries, from their early years of settlement (Russell, 2002): country estates, followed by inter-

Figure 2.3 Christ's College, New Zealand. Built between 1880 and 1920, and modelled
on the public schools of England. Photograph: Taken by the Steffano Webb
Photographic Studio, Christchurch between 1880 and 1920, and supplied by
the Alexander Turnball Library, National Library of New Zealand.

marriage with other estate owning families; the employment of servants; hunting,
shooting and fishing; attending balls, coming-out dances for debutantes and dinner
parties for the well-to-do; the establishment of fee-paying 'public' (that is, private)
schools for the children of these new elites (see Figures 2.3 and 2.4); the use of
calling cards and elaborate 'introduction' etiquettes.[3]

If anything, these habits and practices became *more* stylized amongst upwardly
mobile colonists. This was because the very isolation and detachment of these
new colonies in the South Pacific was likely to reinforce, indeed petrify, British
attributes at the point of departure from them, rather than loosen ties to what became
known as 'the Old Country' or 'the Motherland'. Settlers took their identity from
Britain because, at that time, neither Australia nor New Zealand could provide the
sense of continuity, familiarity and security to constitute a national identity. They
could only make sense of the circumstances around them by reference back to
Britain and its values (Hartz, 1964). The realities of endless stretches of native bush
were thus reimagined and transformed into more familiar, reassuring landscapes:
'our eyes are refreshed with green, real English green; hedgerows, and plenty of
water and cottages and small houses of every description, surrounded by clumps
and soars of poplars, hawthorn and other English trees; Christchurch nestles all
hidden in English trees, whilst round and about run magnificent roads, shut in on

Figure 2.4 Armidale School, New South Wales, Australia. Established in 1896, it was
also modelled on English public school designs. Photograph: National
Archives, Australia (1949).

either side by hedgerows, gorse, thorne and broom' (Baden Powell, 1872: 12). Their
colonial mentalities oppressed and shut out unfamiliar sights and scenery and the
cultures of what were thought to be the biologically inferior and socially 'primitive'
indigenous peoples of these countries. Indeed, those who came to better themselves
in these two distant colonies tied themselves to the ideal of Imperial Britain and
the respectability and standing this gave them. A New South Wales surgeon thus
claimed, in 1820, that 'the pride and dignified *hauteur* of some of our *ultra*
aristocracy far eclipse the nobility of England' (quoted by Maynard, 1994: 44).
And the ideal of the Canterbury Association in the 1840s was the establishment of
a colonial settlement in New Zealand's South Island that would reproduce 'an
English county with the Cathedral city [Christchurch], its famous University, its
Bishop, its endowed clergy, its ancient aristocracy and its yeoman farmers, its few
necessary tradesmen, its sturdy and loyal labourers' (Purchas, 1903: 32).

However, while the 'bush' or the 'outback' had been ripe for land grabbing by
squatters, or for dubious purchases from the indigenous inhabitants, the power of
the elite class largely came to an end in Australia with the 1850s gold rush, even
though their pretensions lived on until at least the 1920s. As Sherer (1853: 10),
explained, 'all the aristocratic feelings and associations of the old country are at
once annihilated. Plebianism of the rankest and . . . the lowest kind at present dwells

in Australia, and as riches are now becoming the test of a man's position, it is vain to have any pretensions whatever . . . It is not what you were but what you are that is the criterion.' New Zealand, with a view to attracting more immigrants, enacted compulsory purchase legislation at the end of the nineteenth century, allowing smaller land purchases to be made from the great estates that had been established in the early years of settlement. But if, by this point, the egalitarian reputations of these societies had been set in place, immigration to them still presented the opportunity for advancement 'to gain what contemporaries called a "competency" or an "independency", equivalent to the ownership of productive capital, usually landed property' (Fairburn, 1989: 46). In these respects, the egalitarianism in these former British colonies took on a different quality from egalitarianism in the Nordic countries. It provided more equal opportunities for 'getting on' than had been the case in England, with *those working hardest being able to reap the most rewards in terms of the accumulation of fortune, wealth and status. In contrast, in the* likhet *dominated Nordic countries, egalitarianism meant everyone receiving very similar rewards*. I. R. Cooper (1857: 9, our italics) thus wrote, of New Zealand, that 'those who arrive in the colony without capital will, if they enjoy good health, are sober and economical in their personal expenses, and are able and willing to work at any one trade, as farm servants, boatmen, shepherds, or house servants, soon realise a significant capital to invest in land, cattle or sheep, *and thus to render themselves and their children independent*'. As if in proof, home ownership in New Zealand, usually with four to six rooms and one-quarter acre of land attached, increased from 36 to 49 per cent between 1916 and 1926. In Australia, by 1947, home ownership had reached 53.4 per cent of householders, with five rooms per house the norm. What we thus see in these colonial societies, even as they became more markedly egalitarian and less elitist, is a replication of the English values that *elevated* one's status and, in particular, the importance given to property and wealth. In the Nordic countries, however, it was thought that one's occupation should not be allowed to create social distance between oneself and others, and that one's standing should be dependent on contribution to community well-being, rather than level of wealth and prosperity. In these societies, 'one does not talk about work as a way of making a fortune, or that through work one retains the idea of oneself as a creative being . . . *to see that everybody works is the main principle of Nordic societal organization and the force that holds these associations together*' (Stenius, 1997: 164, our italics).

Furthermore, the greater egalitarianism in Nordic class relations was reinforced by the frugality and moderation that the mainly agricultural and under-developed economies of these countries made necessary. As they then became more diversified and industrialized from the late nineteenth century, improvements in living standards were shared across the whole population, rather than concentrated in particularly privileged segments of it. By 1900, about one third of all Swedish families had become members of the consumers' cooperative movement; the king himself was a member. By the 1960s, *Kooperativa Förbundet* had become Scandinavia's largest single enterprise, incorporating businesses such as supermarkets, department stores and restaurants. However, these stores had to be managed on a cash basis, with reserve capital. This meant that 'people were less tempted to buy beyond their means than if instalment buying were a regular practice' (Fleisher, 1956: 320). Again, then, the consumers' cooperatives provided ways of improving living standards, while continuing to emphasize the importance of moderation by controlling spending and making the improvements available to all. The Stockholm Exhibition of 1930, featuring displays of Swedish design and crafts and attracting 4,000,000 visitors, demonstrated that comfort, style, hygiene and cleanliness could be made generally available through mass production, rather than remain the exclusive privilege of the wealthy in exclusive, bespoke manufactures. As *The Times*' correspondent noted (18 June, 1930: 15), 'a very valuable [section of the exhibition] is that of serial, standardized furniture, in which the aims are practicalness, durability and cheapness. It is not easy to be patient with people who look down on such attempts. The great majority of us have to depend upon mass produced furniture, and it is highly important that it should be – as generally here – artistically designed in terms of its production.' In other respects, wage differentials seemed quite small when compared to England (Grimley, 1937; Cole and Smith, 1938). But, at the same time, 'one of the first things that strikes a visitor to Sweden is that in the towns there seems to be no very poor people. There are no beggars, no-one to sell matches, sing or play gramophone records in the streets. There are no children in rags to correspond to the slums of our great [English] cities' (Cole and Smith, 1938: 204). Frugality and moderation, rather than expanse and extravagance, were also striking characteristics of housing provision. In contrast to the emphasis on multi-roomed and gardened property ownership in the Anglophone countries, 'Swedes in the cities live in flats. You will find few families in Sweden occupying a whole house' (Thomas, 1892: 135); 'flats and houses of one room and a kitchen are more common than any other type [in Sweden]. Middle and working class people alike regard all their rooms, often including even the kitchen, as bed-sitting rooms with divan beds and writing desks, and the standard of a separate bedroom for every person and a common living room is rare' (Cole and Smith, 1938: 254); 'differences in the material level of living among the social classes is probably less in Sweden than in any non-Scandinavian European society . . . about three quarters of non-farming Swedish families live in apartments, and while there is certainly variation in size and appointments . . . there is not much variation in quality . . . [and] little class difference in taste in furniture style . . . and little variation in rents', but 'a great deal of mixing of classes' (De Mare, 1952: 219).

These similarities, uniformities and short social distances in the Nordic countries stood in marked contrast to the levels of class separation, division and inequalities in England, in particular, of the Anglophone societies. Here, the shift from rural to urban life had meant that the vagaries and social instability of the industrial revolution were burdens that the poor carried almost exclusively, and became familiar themes in the literature of the period. In *Mary Barton*, Elizabeth Gaskell (1848/1996: 24) wrote that 'large houses are still occupied [in Manchester], while spinners' and weavers' cottages stand empty, because the families that once filled them are obliged to live in rooms or cellars. Carriages still roll along the streets, concerts are still crowded by subscribers, the shops for expensive luxuries still find daily customers, while the workman loiters away his unemployed time in watching these things, and thinking of the pale, uncomplaining wife at home, and the wailing children asking in vain for enough of food.' And as regards the fictional Coketown, in Dickens' (1854/1992: 27) *Hard Times*, where 'the comforts and elegancies of life were made and found their way all over the world', it was 'a town of red brick, or of brick that would have been red if the smoke and ashes had allowed it; but as matters stood it was a town of unnatural red and black like the painted face of a savage. It was a town of machinery and tall chimneys, out of which interminable serpents of smoke trailed themselves for ever and ever, and never got uncoiled.' In contrast to the suburban villas and townhouses of the middle and upper classes, the appalling housing of the poor had been the subject of numerous inquiries and commentaries from the mid-nineteenth century (see, for example, Chadwick, 1843; Second Report of the Royal Sanitary Commission, 1871; Rowntree, 1902). But, after nearly a century of such investigations, Capek (1925: 74) still observed that 'the horrible thing about East London is not what can be seen and smelt, but its unbounded and unredeemable extent. Elsewhere poverty and ugliness exist merely as a rubbish heap between two houses . . . but here are miles and miles of grimy houses, hopeless streets . . . a superfluity of children, gin palaces and Christian shelters.' At the same time, the very organization of public and private space was deliberately designed to keep the classes apart. Taine (1874: 16) thus wrote that England is 'an aristocratic country. At the gate of St James Park is the following notice: "the park-keepers have orders to prevent all beggars from entering the gardens, and all persons in ragged or dirty clothes, or who are not outwardly decent and well-behaved."' On the European continent, British travellers would be annoyed because there were no separate waiting rooms at railway stations for the different classes, which is what they were accustomed to at home (Huizinga, 1958).

Separation was also embedded in the very architecture of the townhouses and villas – the country estates in miniature: 'it is the foremost of all maxims, that however small the establishment, the servants' department shall be separated from the main house, so that what passes on either side of the boundary shall be both invisible and inaudible on the other. The outdoor work of the domestics must not be visible from the house or grounds, or the windows of their offices overlooked. The idea which underlies all this is simple: the family constitute one community, the servants another . . . each class is entitled to shut its door upon the other and be alone' (Kerr, 1865: 567). One of the consequences of these highly regulated and enforced separations was that each class knew very little of the existence of the other, as Faucher (1844) and Mayhew (1851) observed in the mid-nineteenth century. And yet, in Norway, it appears that servants were more likely to be treated as *de facto* family members, rather than kept at a distance as socially inferior employees. The 1868 *Housemaid's Manual* (quoted by Aubert, 1956: 152) thus stated that 'the master and mistress must, if they want to obey the word of the Lord, look out for their servant's welfare, care for them in case of sickness and other accidents, warn them when they see them on off-paths, and on the whole show an affectionate disposition toward them and set a good example, and not load them with more work than their strength permits them to carry'. Indeed, Beckett (1936: 168–9) later wrote that 'Norway is a relatively poor country, and this, added to the absence of aristocracy, tends to a democratic atmosphere. Many a well-born girl, for instance, will take domestic service to relieve the burden on her family; but the family employing her always receive her *en famille*.'

Differences in class relations also produced very different forms of manners and etiquette. Clarke (1823: 662), for example, complained that 'the people of Trondheim – more polished than any other town in Norway – place themselves *without etiquette* at table: everyone sits as he chooses.' There was no respect, then, for hierarchy and status in deciding table placements, much to the distaste of this English visitor. Bowden (1867: 39) was similarly dismayed by the lack of refinement amongst the Norwegian upper classes: 'it is not considered a breach of good manners to put one's knife into one's mouth and you may afterwards help yourself to salt with it.' Thereafter, Rothery (1939: 147, our italics) still found that 'while there is in Oslo a certain amount of formal and diplomatic entertaining, where scrupulous attention is paid to the proper seating of guests, to the etiquette of pouring the wines and serving the food, *such occasions are restricted to a very limited circle*'. English visitors also complained of the lack of deference they received. Laing (1837: 181), for example, suggested that one of the characteristics of the Norwegian lower classes was 'extreme insolence to their superiors. The conduct and deportment of servants is no bad criterion by which to judge the character of the lower orders. More tact is required in Norway in the conduct of superiors towards their dependents . . . The slightest offence towards a menial will occasion the instant oblivion of the kindnesses of years – respect and obligation will alike be forgotten; and the servant will immediately leave his master.' More than a century later, Warbey, *et al*. (1950: 137) similarly found that 'the unabashed freedom of manner of so many Norwegians . . . is usually very charming but it can sometimes be a little disconcerting in waiters and railway porters. They are not brought up to fear the authority of their "betters".' The point, of course, is that in this country, without ingrained class distinctions but with relatively short social distances, codified ways of enforcing differences between respective social stratas and ostentatious displays of deference were redundant.

In England, however, there was a much more elaborate and highly ritualized system of etiquette signs and symbols in existence that determined modes of address, level of acquaintance and social standing. In their instruction manual *The Complete Servant*, Adams and Adams (1825: 20) advised those entering domestic service that 'the grand foundation of your good character must be industry, fidelity to your employers, and an inviolable attachment to truth, both in words and deeds . . . carefully avoid all reproachful, indecent, or even familiar terms in speaking of your master, mistress or superiors . . . the virtue of silence is highly commendable, and will contribute greatly to your ease and prosperity'. Visiting required careful protocols to be followed in the nineteenth century: 'morning calls included the leaving of cards; if left by the lady herself, and not handed in by a footman, the bottom right hand corner was turned up. A married woman left cards on behalf of the husband as well as herself. Some cards had printed on the back, in each corner, a word to indicate the nature or purpose of the call: Felicitations, *Adieu, Affaires'* (Lochhead, 1964: 37). As regards deportment, 'persons do not shake hands when introduced, but simply bow . . . persons meeting at the houses of friends when making afternoon calls need not be introduced to each other, and certainly should not be, unless it is known that such introductions should be mutually agreeable. Nor should persons who have accidentally met in this manner, without being introduced, bow, or in any way express recognition, should they afterwards meet' (Anon., 1871: 42). In contrast, Laing (1837: 109, our italics) remarked of Norway that 'I like the politeness of people towards each other in this country; the putting off of hats or caps when they meet either strangers or friends. *The custom is universal* . . . even the school-boys bow to each other in the streets; such a custom is not to be laughed at, it has a humanising effect. He who had made a bow and received a similar salute is not so likely to launch out into a burst of abuse or violence, even against one who has offended him, as if the previous day had not intervened.' In a society without significant class distinctions, and where everybody had much the same status as everyone else and accorded each other respect on this basis, it was possible to dispense with all the English rituals and protocols for policing social distance and difference.

Degrees of homogeneity

There were also major differences in relation to race and religion, which reinforced the sense of sameness and uniformity in the Nordic countries and the differences and divisions in the Anglophone.

Race

There had been next to no immigration to the Nordic region by the early twentieth century. As Austin (1970: 16) explained, in relation to Sweden, 'Lying so far to the north and having such a severe winter climate, and her soil relatively poor, this country experienced almost no immigration and, over the centuries, very little invasion.' Accordingly, each citizen was likely to seem much the same as any other, not only on account of their economic circumstances but also because of their physical appearance. Outsider groups consisted only of a small number of indigenous Sami people in the far north, a few small Jewish communities and Gypsies – largely invisible for all political purposes. At the same time, the flow of emigration from these countries during the nineteenth and early twentieth centuries, largely because of the intrinsic poverty (Sweden lost 1,000,000 citizens, mainly to the United States, in this way, Finland and Norway 750,000 each), was likely to have acted as a safety valve, ensuring that social tensions were reduced in the struggle over scarce resources, while further reinforcing homogeneity. But, if such levels of racial homogeneity were important features in the development of the Nordic culture of equality and cohesion, did not Australia and New Zealand have similar levels of racial homogeneity amongst their settler populations? Not only was all non-British immigration carefully restricted until at least 1945 (see pp. 4–5), but, at the same time, the majority of British immigrants came from specific areas of that country (see Belich, 1996; Jupp, 2004). And, while the two colonies had very significantly larger indigenous populations than the Nordic countries, new illnesses from contact with Europeans decimated them, to the point where, towards the end of the nineteenth century, it was thought that each indigenous race would simply become extinct. For example, there had been an estimated 300,000 Aborigines in Australia in 1788; a century later there were an estimated 80,000. In addition, Aborigines were firmly shut out of Australian society and were formally regarded as non-citizens until 1967, when a referendum approved of their inclusion in the Australian census for the first time.[4] Meanwhile, in New Zealand, after land wars in the 1860s finally put an end to any sustained resistance to British colonization, the policy was to assimilate the much greater numbers of Maori into settler society, although during this period many Maori, anyway, remained in their traditional communities, largely invisible in the 'Britain of the South Pacific' that was being built around them. In these ways, then, the settlers were able to maintain their well-defined homogeneity – yet it did not lead to the same levels of cohesion and solidarity that it helped to bring about in the Nordic countries. There were three main reasons for this.

First, in both Australia and New Zealand, there was a high level of transience amongst the settler population. While there was common ancestry, there was nothing like the long-established Nordic communities that would allow inter-locking roots and lengthy interdependencies to develop. Indeed, both colonies were marked by dramatic population growth and high levels of population turnover. For example, as regards New South Wales, where the population had grown from 127,000 in 1840 to 1,360,000 by 1900, net migration alone had contributed to 11.1 per cent of this between 1861–1871, and 18 per cent between 1871–1881 and 1881–1891 (*New South Wales Official Yearbook*, 1974: 63). New Zealand experienced similar population growth, from 150,000 in 1860 (two thirds then being Maori) to 815,000 by 1901 (but with the Maori population shrinking to 40,000) and 2,000,000 by 1951. In 1909, for example, '38,650 persons arrived in New Zealand, while 33,931 departed' (*New Zealand Yearbook*, 1910: 270) – something like an eight per cent turnover of the total population of the country in just one year. Indeed, its extreme bursts of immigration and emigration led to highly unstable communities and insubstantial interdependencies within them.

Furthermore, those who did stay tended to move around these new societies, seeking fresh opportunities to better themselves: there was little of the stability and permanence of the Nordic communities. Harris (1847: 67) wrote of Australia that 'it may be as well to notice here a particular characteristic of the free labouring population: it is in a state of constant migration. The man who has a contract job or is a hired servant here this year, probably spends the next at the other end of the country.' This pattern continued for the next half century at least. Sir Timothy Coghlan (1888: 309), in *The Wealth and Progress of New South Wales*, stated that 'the largest increase of population … occurred in 1885, when owing to the depression prevailing in some of the neighbouring colonies, large numbers of adult males flocked to New South Wales … the result of this influx was felt during the following years in the congestion of the local labour market.' Hancock (1930: 270) then reported that 'society in Australia is not yet fixed and formalized. Men do not find it difficult to change their house, or town or class.'

Second, New Zealand, especially, became a very atomized society for much of this period. In part, this was because of the solitary nature of much of the available work – shepherding, gold digging and gum digging, for example. In these respects, while social distances between respective classes in this country certainly became much shorter than in England, horizontal chains of interdependencies were likely to be quite thin and easily fragmented, rather than homogenous and solidaristic. This also led to high levels of fear, suspicion and intolerance of strangers and outsiders, thought keen to take whatever they could from this isolated, fledgling, society, but putting in little themselves before leaving for greener pastures. Vagrants, especially, were demonized (Fairburn, 1989) because of the way in which they challenged the importance of hard work as a means to 'getting on'. Summarizing these attitudes, Lipson (1948: 492) wrote that 'New Zealanders tend to conform to type. The same convictions, prejudices and stock symbols predominate throughout the country. There is not enough internal diversity to produce a clash of opinion . . . the equalitarianism that provides for all within the group can be hostile for those who reject the group standards or who are outside the membership. Free thinkers on religious matters, a handful of oriental residents, refugees from European fascism, advocates of heterodox social theories – all who do not conform are subject to a suspicion and in critical times to a persecution that appears the less justified because these minorities are so utterly impotent.'

Third, Australia's 'mateship' tradition encouraged a multiplicity of shallow and fleeting interdependencies. Mateship (Ward, 1958) was initially a characteristic of relationships – often chance ones, and usually of short duration – that developed in the outback between bushrangers, convicts and labourers. Their circumstances meant that they were temporarily dependent on each other and thus reciprocated favours, gave gestures of goodwill, and so on. They then brought these values to the city and the mateship concept became a feature of Australian society at large.[5] As Harris (1847: 326) pointed out, 'it is a universal feeling that a man ought to be able to trust his mate in everything'. Mateship was organized around egalitarianism, loyalty and friendship with those in one's immediate (working) environment – but with a simultaneous suspicion and disrespect for more removed authority figures. However, by its very nature, Australian mateship was unlikely to bring about the more deeply ingrained solidarity, cohesion and trust that became cultural characteristics of the Nordic countries.

Religion

The virtually 100 per cent religious uniformity[6] in the Nordic countries, the product of automatic membership of the Lutheran Church for all their citizens, at birth, in itself strengthened the intense homogeneity of this region. However, Lutheranism also reinforced its prevalent egalitarian values and level of social cohesion. In its teachings, there is less importance on the Church itself and more on the individual's relationship with God. Salvation could not be granted by priests, as in the Catholic Church but, instead, came about through an individual's own faith and belief in the gospel. To prove they had faith, their knowledge of the Bible would be examined in classes that led up to the ceremony of confirmation. This was a vitally important test to pass, since it was proof not just of an individual's knowledge of God and his works, but, as well, their own trustworthiness, reliability and 'normality' before the rest of the community. We are given an insight to the importance attached to this ceremony by Bjørnson (1882: 65) who, in his novel, *A Happy Lad*, describes a confirmation class waiting for the results of their exam: 'anxiety filled their throats and eyes; they could not see distinctly, neither could they swallow; and this they felt a continual desire to do. One sat reckoning over how much he knew; and although but a few hours before he had discovered that he knew everything, now he found out just as confidently that he knew nothing, not even how to read in a book. Another summed up the list of his sins, from the time he was large enough to remember till now, and he decided that it would not at all be remarkable if the Lord decreed that he should be rejected.'

By the same token, Lutheranism endowed a very particular value to work in these societies. Working diligently was seen as a way of serving God, but one should not try to change from the occupation into which one had been born: to do so would contravene God's laws, since it was God only who assigned each person to their place in the social order (Lipset, 1990). In addition, because God was the only true judge of man, all occupations were of equal spiritual value and dignity: what distinguished one person from another was not their occupation per se, but the way in which their labour was performed. As Luther (1520/1915: 175) had written, 'the first, the noblest, the sublimest of all works is faith in Jesus Christ. It is from this that all other works proceed: they are but the vassals of faith, and receive their efficacy from it alone. If a man feels in his heart the assurance that what he has done is acceptable to God, the work is good, if it were merely the lifting up of a straw; but if he have not this assurance, his work is not good, even should he raise the dead.' Here, then, were a set of beliefs that were locked around these entire socieites, whereby judgmental attitudes to others were proscribed (this was the task of God, not man); where dedication to work brought social stability and cohesion, rather than any ambition for material self-enhancement; and where all were *expected* to work, since the performance of good works was a signifier of God's grace. The English 'leisure classes' could thus have no place in such societies.

The Lutheran Church was also at the centre of village life because of the administrative functions it peformed. As well as providing education and assisting the poor, it presided over all important events and recorded the biographical details of its parishioners: deaths, births (who the parents were, what was their civil status, were the children placed elsewhere, if so, where and with whom) and marriages. The importance it had thus assumed in the administration of everyday life is captured in another of Bjørnson's (1857: 309) novels, *Synnøve Solbakken*, where it is given an almost mystical status: 'in the peasants' mind, the church stands upon a high place and by itself, dedicated to peace, with the solemnity of graves round about, the activity of the service within. It is the only building in the valley upon which he has applied elegance, and its spire therefore reaches a little higher than it seems to reach. Its bells greet from afar his going thither on a clear Sunday morning, and he always lifts his hat to them . . . There is an understanding between him and them which no-one knows.' In the Anglophone societies, however, religious beliefs were much more heterogeneous,[7] with histories of conflict between Catholics and Protestants in each.[8] These were ultimately resolved by the *churches* existing independently of the state. In the Nordic countries, the *church* and state were indivisible. Furthermore, religious beliefs in England were also related to class differences, as Huizinga (1958: 345) pointed out: 'a clergyman of the Church of England, it appeared, was normally a "gentleman", whereas his colleague, who preached in the "chapel" instead of the "church" was not'. And, whereas, in the Nordic countries, pastors were likely to be the children of pastors or from poor families, in England, during the nineteenth century, being appointed to the Anglican clergy became something of a sinecure for second or third sons of the landowning class. Lochhead (1964: 8) wrote that 'throughout the Victorian age [the parson] is more often than not, the cadet of a county family, presented to the family living; a product of public school and university, not of any seminary or theological college'. Thus, in George Eliot's (1859/1980: 113) *Adam Bede*, the Reverend Adolphus Irwine, a 'pluralist' who dines and hunts with the squire and his family, 'was not in these days what is called an "earnest man"; he was fonder of church history than of divinity, and had much more insight into men's characters than their opinions; he was neither laborious, nor obviously self-denying; nor very copious in alms-giving, and his theology was lax. . .[his] recollections of young enthusiasm and ambition were all associated with poetry and ethics that lay aloof from the Bible'. Here, then, rather than helping to bring unity and solidarity, religion was another illustration of the divisions and differences in the Anglophone societies.

The value and function of education

Lutheranism not only helped to bring about the high levels of social cohesion in the Nordic countries; it also put a high value on education. Swedish legislation of 1764 stipulated that no marriage could be celebrated unless both parties had taken communion: but no-one could be admitted to the 'communion table' *if they could not read and had not been instructed in religious study.* As one visitor later acknowledged, 'every Swede must read with the priest before he or she can be admitted to the Lord's table; and every year the priest has to hold a meeting in various parts of his parish, and hear his parishioners read, and examine them in their religion. The peasants here appear to be much more under the eye of their clergymen than in England' ('An Old Bushman', 1865: 81). In such ways, Lutheranism had made literacy accessible to, *and essential* for, all. However, until the early nineteenth century, the intellectual life of Norway had been dominated by Denmark. Laing (1837: 249) thus found that 'a bookseller's shop is a curiosity in Norway . . . Danish books are almost the only books to be had' (Danish at that time, of course, being the official language of Norway). Similarly, Clarke (1823: 510), visiting the Finnish city of Turku, found that 'Books of any kind are seldom seen: there are no booksellers; nor is it possible to meet with a single copy of the work of the few celebrated authors Sweden [sic] has boasted in any of the private houses.' This, though, was because *there were virtually no Finnish books available*: Swedish was then Finland's official language. Thereafter, however, language and literature became expressions of the struggles for national identity in Finland and Norway (see Figure 2.5), generating a literary renaissance. Between 1543 and 1808, only 174 books had been published in Finnish. Between 1809 and 1853, there were another 452; in the next decade, 481 (League of Nations, 1939). The Finnish Literary Society was established in 1845 and the Finnish Artists' Union in 1846, providing classes, prizes, exhibitions and scholarships for young painters to study abroad. In Norway, the importance of the role and place of artists and intellectuals as emblems and icons of national identity was evident in the way in which the death of historian P. A. Munch, at the age of 53, in 1863 was regarded as a 'national disaster'. When nobel prize winner Bjørnstjerne Bjørnson died, aged 73, in Paris in 1910, 'the Norwegian government had his body brought home on board a Norwegian man-of-war. The ship was greeted with a royal salute from the castle as it steamed into Oslo harbour. The mourning which united the whole nation was the best proof how much this poet had meant in the life of the people' (Castberg, 1954: 33).

In Sweden, the establishment of a highly literate society (80 per cent of the population in the eighteenth century) had anyway transformed education into a desirable goal in its own right, rather than simply a means to know God. This country was, thus, particularly susceptible to rationalist thought and Enlightenment values, producing such notable eighteenth-century scholars as Anders Celsius in mathematics and Carl von Linné in botany. Here, too, the national importance of intellectuals and artists was recognized, with foundation scholarships for life made available for them from 1863 through the Swedish Academy. From 1901, the annual awards of Nobel prizes became the most visible sign of the importance placed on intellectual achievement in this country. By the mid-twentieth century, Shirer (1955: 204) noted that 'the writer, the artist, the professor are highly regarded in Sweden. The term "egghead" is unknown.'[9] And Martin (1952: 136) observed that, in Norway, 'respect for academic learning is a very real phenomenon. Professors form an aristocracy . . . in a society which has no aristocracy of blood. It probably had its origins in the village where parson, schoolmaster, doctor and lawyer set the tone.'

Recognition of the broader role of education in modern society had meant that Bible study began to be replaced in schools by subjects such as technology, science, history and languages around the mid-nineteenth century. As this occurred, the state, rather than the church, became the main provider of educational services. Swedish legislation of 1842 stipulated that every parish had to have a school with at least one teacher. Thereafter, the number of teachers increased from 2,785 to 4,241 between 1847 and 1859, while the number of children receiving no education dropped from 22,606 to 7,372. By the 1930s, continuing high levels of investment meant that, 'compared to the United Kingdom, the first and greatest difference [in education] is in the size of classes, a matter on which Sweden is undoubtedly far ahead of this country. While we are struggling vainly for a limitation of the numbers

Figure 2.5 Norway's National Day, 17 May, has become a cause for extensive and jubilant celebrations throughout the country, as can be seen in this undated photograph depicting the 17 May parade at Oslo's main street, Karl Johann. Photograph: Dagbladet/Norsk Folkemuseum.

in elementary classes to 40, and having to endure a large number of classes containing 45–50 children, it is salutary for us to observe that in Sweden the average, in elementary schools, is a little over 30 and that a class of 40 is regarded as a survival from the Dark Ages' (Simon, 1939: 255). In Norway, from 1860, there were provisions for rural school districts, with each to have at least one upper school for advanced education. Provision was also made for qualified teachers and trained inspectors. As regards Finland, elementary education began to be provided by the state from the 1850s, and the first two training colleges for teachers were set up in 1863. Travers (1911: 185, our italics) later noted that 'most elementary school teachers have spent three years in college at the state's expense; and most secondary teachers have been through the university. It would be difficult to find the equivalent of our [English] uncertified elementary teachers in Finland, or our underpaid broken down schoolmasters and schoolmistresses. *You see, both the [Finnish] people and their administrators are convinced of the benefits of education.*' Similarly, Shirer (1955: 397), in the post-war period: 'the position of the public school teacher [in Finland] is rather enviable. Salaries are relatively high and if a teacher is the father of a family he receives extra pay.'

Furthermore, as the school curriculum developed, it reflected a strong anti-elitist strain: 'a characteristic feature of the secondary school in Norway is the relatively small importance which is attached to the classical languages . . . as early as 1869, side by side with the classical line, a modern "line" had been introduced which took the pupil through to a matriculation exam which did not include Latin' (Castberg, 1954: 31). Indeed, the comprehensive state education system largely precluded any private provision. Even 'children of the [Norwegian] royal family attend ordinary schools instead of being taught privately' (ibid.: 27–8). In such ways, education was an extremely important attribute in its own right – it became a means of achieving social advancement, recognition and respect in otherwise relatively egalitarian societies to which all were given access. At the same time, its almost exclusive provision by the state further ensured cohesion and solidarity: nobody would stand outside and above these services in elitist, privately funded, institutions.

However, education was valued in a different way and performed a different function in the Anglophone countries. State education itself was not provided in England until 1870. Thereafter, the school leaving age was steadily raised from 10 to 12 and, post-1945, to 15. Even so, by the early twentieth century, such investment was set at a minimal level (Thompson, 1988). By 1900, 20 per cent of the working class remained illiterate and 55 per cent of schoolteachers had had no formal training (Roberts, 1971). In Australia, a Select Committee of 1860 suggested that half the children aged four to 14 were receiving no education at all. By the end of the nineteenth century, state education consisted of little more than the '"3Rs" [reading, writing and arithmetic], singing and military drill' (Nadal, 1957). At the same time, educational services were dominated by issues of class in all three of these societies, with huge distinctions between the standard of education available for the wealthy, which they would pay for themselves in the public schools, and that for the poor, for whom provision was likely to be from charitable organizations or a very begrudging state. Taine (1874: 122) found that, at Harrow, one of the most elite

English schools, the students had to 'attend classes, lessons, dinner, to enter at an appointed hour in the evening, nothing more; the remainder of the day is their own; it can be spent in their own fashion'. In effect, it was something of a finishing school for those whose class status swiftly elevated them to the upper echelons of government and power, or who would simply join this country's 'leisure class'. He goes on to quote from Thomas Hughes' (1857) novel, *Tom Brown's School Days*, in which Brown explains what he hoped to achieve during his time at another such institution, Rugby School: '"I want to be A1 at cricket and football and all other games . . . I want to carry away just as much Latin and Greek as will take me through Oxford respectably . . . I want to leave behind me the name of a fellow who never bullied a little boy or turned his back on a big one"' (ibid.: 127). In other words, such students were being cultivated to be 'natural' leaders of men, particularly through their prowess on the sports field, which also meant downplaying the importance of academic scholarship and excellence: this could be left to the 'eggheads' of these societies. Nonetheless, in most of the English public schools, a curriculum made up almost entirely of Latin and Greek scholarship perpetuated class distinction in the school curriculum, allowing upper class school students to remain apart from the rest of society and the more vulgar concerns of commerce, industry, engineering and so on.

Meanwhile, those at the bottom received their rudimentary tuition in literacy and numeracy amidst performing 'drill' that would render them suitable to taking orders and keeping in line. In contrast to the healthy, lively, countenances of Tom Brown and his fellow members of the 'First XI' or 'First XV',[10] destitute children and orphans attending 'ragged schools' had 'faces [that] are dull, and not very pleasing, they have a special uniform, blue and grey . . . they were made to line up single file, close up and march before me . . . their faces are disquieting, and resemble those of young prisoners . . . Every one is taught to read, to write, to sing to go through drill' (Taine, 1874: 207). In Coketown school, the factory workers' children were informed that 'you are to be regulated and governed by fact . . . You must discard the word Fancy altogether. You have nothing to do with it. You are not to have, in any object of use or ornament, what would be a contradiction in fact. You don't walk upon flowers in fact; you cannot be allowed to walk upon flowers in carpets. You don't find that foreign birds and butterflies come perch upon your crockery; you cannot be permitted to paint foreign birds and butterflies upon your crockery . . . You never meet with quadrupeds [monkeys] going up and down walls; you must not have quadrupeds represented upon walls. You must use for all these purposes, combinations and modifications (in primary colours) of mathematical figures which are susceptible of proof and demonstration. This is the new discovery. This is fact' (Dickens, 1854/1992: 12). For such students, their education was not a means to social advancement but a form of training that instilled in them a poverty of ambition from which, in conjunction with their material poverty, acceptance of their place at the bottom of the English class hierarchy became all the more straightforward – 'know your place'.

'An Old Bushman' (1865: 119) contrasted these English provisions with those in Sweden, and concluded that 'I like the system of educating youth in Sweden much better . . . in nearly every town there is a public school open to all classes, and peasants are admitted on an equality with gentlemen's sons . . . the salaries are paid by the government which is far more liberal than any other I know, in promoting everything for the good of the country . . . the degrading system of corporal punishment is quite unknown in Swedish schools.' In the Anglophone countries, however, education became another instrument for dividing rather than unifying their populations. Thus, in England, the aim of the Taunton (Schools Inquiry) Commission (1864) was to provide a means of segregation so that '*the lower classes would not be educated above their station nor embarrass the higher [classes] with low company*' (quoted by Perkin, 1969: 301, our italics). Similarly, the views expressed in the New Zealand Education Act 1877: 'children whose vocation is honest work waste in higher schools time which might be better devoted to the learning of a trade' (quoted by Belich, 2001: 130). Meanwhile, the New Zealand gentry had succeeded in 'establishing a small network of secondary schools for their own children. Some were entirely private; most were endowed with land from the public estate, but charged substantial fees for day pupils, even more for boarders . . . *as in England . . . they featured fags,*[11] *prefects, corporal punishments and Arnoldian principals*'[12] (idem, our italics).

A further reason for the limited and fragmented nature of state education in Australia and New Zealand was that the demands of settlement – land clearance, farming, husbandry, pacification of the indigenous populations – were given a much higher priority. This also meant that highly educated people, or those with artistic tendencies, were unwanted immigrants. As Sidney and Sidney (1848: 192) emphasized in their *Australian Handbook*, 'discontented dispositions [had] better stay at home, and so had all the stars of society, wits, diners out, the leading lights of literary circles and of provincial debating societies'. On the other hand, 'as to the class of men who should emigrate, the first is the labourer, with no capital but stout arms and a stout heart. Action is the first great requisite of a colonist: to be able to do anything, to have a talent for making shift.' Similarly, Berry (1879: 59), in his *New Zealand as a Field for Emigration*: 'my fear is, lest lazy or incapable people should imagine that they have heard of a country where the great law about the sweat of the brow is repealed; and where they can succeed without the divinely-established conditions of success. For such to go out will be a calamity . . . in a bustling, prosperous active community, the listless and the lazy speedily go to the wall.' This propensity to put a higher value on physical prowess rather than mental ability remained so in Australia and New Zealand during the nineteenth and the first half of the twentieth centuries. Aughterson (1953: 51) thus referred to 'the intellectual shallowness of Australian society'. As Horne (1965: 17) put the matter in *The Lucky Country*, 'cleverness can be considered un-Australian'. Instead, 'Australians like people to be ordinary' (ibid.: 24). Blainey (1966: 30), too, observed that 'the pursuit of education was seen as snobbery and a way of social advancement that broke up the camaraderies and mateship of workingmen.' Following their visit to New Zealand in the late nineteenth century, Beatrice and Sidney Webb (1959: 25) described it as a 'nondescript place with no intellectual circles'; sport was 'the principal subject of conversation' and young people 'objected to intellectual pursuits'. In these countries, there was no need for highly trained, well-educated, 'specialists' (Fairburn, 1989). Indeed, Northcott (1918: 219) observed that 'employers are negligent in regard to the future supply of efficient skilled labour. They protest that the apprentice is now economically unprofitable, that he is too difficult to control, and too careless of diligence and efficiency.'

The different values and function of education in the two clusters are also seen in relation to higher education. By the early twentieth century, England had seven universities, the same number as Sweden, which had about one seventh of its population. Entry to the Nordic universities was determined by academic ability. Tweedie (1897: 69) wrote of Christiania [Oslo] University that 'it is very liberally open to women'. In these respects, a Nordic university education was never the exclusive prize of already very privileged elites, as it was in the Anglophone countries. Furthermore, there does not seem to have been any elaborate distinctions in the clothing of university students that would then separate them from the rest of the community. At the prestigious Uppsala University in Sweden, 'neither the professors nor the students have any distinctions of dress . . . a student in the streets is not a whit better clad than any working coachmaker or carpenter in England' (Clarke, 1823: 180). And, in Finland, 'only a tiny German cap is worn to distinguish its wearer as a university man' (De Windt, 1901: 117). In contrast, the flamboyant gowns then worn both by Oxford and Cambridge students and their professors affirmed their difference and elite status in England. Indeed, 'this high finishing place of education is for the aristocracy, for the rich, for the minority' (Taine, 1874: 138). But, even then, 'certain poor or low born undergraduates become the toadies [servants] of their noble comrades, who later on will be able to present them with a living . . . in certain colleges the noble undergraduates have a separate table, a particular dress, divers minor privileges' (idem).

Overall, the pursuit of knowledge became commonplace in the Nordic countries through the nineteenth and first half of the twentieth centuries: 'education is very thorough and the result is that Norwegians of all classes are usually well informed' (Tweedie, 1897: 69). Indeed, 'there are libraries on ships, in seamen's homes and in churches. . . the servant girl has a shelf of books in her room and the fisher lad finds a place for a few books in his boat . . . Scientists at the University of Oslo and at the Bergen Museum broadcast their lectures and public school curricula are now being extended to include instructive radio programmes' (Evang, 1957: 113). In Sweden, the *folkhögskolan* (an elementary school that provided training for adults) was a further offshoot of the social movement tradition and, again, affirmed the importance of educational skills to which all should continue to have access: 'every autumn, as the evenings swiftly draw in, some 1,000,000 adult Swedes – one eighth of the entire population – turn out in the cold to flock to adult classes, another aspect of the educational explosion which has deep roots in the Swedish past' (Austin, 1970: 121). At the same time, training and specialization also became important Nordic characteristics, available to all workers: 'Norwegians tend to define in highly specialized terms a remarkable variety of social roles and to recruit men to such roles on the basis of formally acquired qualifications, particularly special schooling. Special functional training is, of course, typical of modern societies, for functionally specific relations play a large role in all of them. But the Norwegians go much farther in this distinction than others: they even insist on specialist schooling for such people as postal or cafeteria workers' (Jenkins, 1968: 223). In such ways, educational achievement and enterprise was something to encourage, something to strive for, a way of winning respect in these otherwise egalitarian societies. One consequence of this was that it became an unquestioned assumption that policymaking should be expert dominated: 'there is enormous respect among Swedes for science, technology and expert opinion. No society in the world utilizes experts and knowledge in the whole process of writing legislation as much as does Sweden' (Tomasson, 1970: 226).

In the Anglophone countries, however, the pursuit of knowledge was much more likely to be regarded as an esoteric, somewhat eccentric, activity practised by dilettantes, and divorced from the concerns and issues of 'the real world'. By the mid-nineteenth century, there were still hardly any free public libraries in England. Collier (1909: 344) complained that 'only in a comparatively few families in the English town is there any continued reading of even such ephemeral literature as [newspapers and magazines]'. Indeed, anti-intellectualism became a strong feature of public discourse. The famed zoologist Thomas Huxley (1880: 137) complained that '"practical" men . . . were of the opinion that science is speculative rubbish; that theory and practice have nothing to do with one another; and that the scientific habit of mind is an impediment, rather than an aid in the conduct of ordinary affairs'. Kingsley (1877: 119), himself both a novelist and philanthropist, had emphasized the importance of *practical skills* – the same skills that had brought many of the industrial entrepreneurs their wealth – rather than those that were merely cerebral: 'they say knowledge is power, and so it is. But the only knowledge which you get is by observation. Many a man is very learned in books, and has read for years and years, and yet he is useless. He knows *about* all sorts of things, but he can't *do* them. When you set him to work he makes a mess of it. He is what is called a pedant: because he has not used his eyes and ears. He has lived in books.' Rather than being celebrated, those with literary or artistic talents were more likely to be treated with suspicion and disdain. Taine (1874: 258–9) thus complained about the cartoons in the satirical magazine *Punch*: 'we all know how in French sketches the artist is raised above the citizen; here, oddly enough, the reverse occurs . . . musicians are represented as salaried monkeys, who come to make a noise in the drawing room. Painters are bearded artisans, unkempt, shabbily dressed, hardly one degree raised above photographers. These are workmen who cannot speak English and who merely form food for ridicule.' In *England: Her People, Polity and Pursuits*, the historian Thomas Escott (1885: 334) argued that such temperaments were indicative of effeminacy and corruption: 'the keen scented, eminently decorous British public perceives a certain aroma of social and moral laxity in the atmosphere of the [artist's] studio, a kind of blended perfume of periodical impecuniosity and much tobacco smoke . . . [T]he popular view of the painter . . . is that the calling which he elects to follow lacks definitiveness of status, and that it is not calculated to promote those serious, methodical habits which form an integral part of the foundations of English society.'

This attitude towards intellectuals was also related to British class structure: the exclusiveness of the universities, for example, that removed such thinkers from the mainstream of society. Thereafter, many remained as 'gentleman scholars', if not employed by the universities, amongst whom, in the late nineteenth century alone, were John Stuart Mill, Charles Darwin, Thomas Huxley, Matthew Arnold, George Bernard Shaw and Robert Browning. Their physical remoteness also emphasized their 'difference' from the rest of society, and frequently made them figures of fun or derision: 'appearances were to be exposed and these men were splendidly eccentric in Victorian society in not keeping them up. They groaned at the thought of formal receptions and preferred to wear rough clothes' (Annan, 1955: 249). Even George Orwell (1941: 160) referred disparagingly to 'the highbrow with his domed forehead and stalk-like neck'. Thus, while intellectuals were expected to have a direct influence on policy development in the Nordic countries, their dislocation from such involvement came to be seen as a defining characteristic of the Anglophone. Arguing against the recruitment of state-employed experts in England, A. V. Dicey (1919: lxxvi), Oxford professor and leading constitutional lawyer, preferred rule by the 'gifted amateur': 'respect for experts ought always to be tempered by constant remembrance that possessors of special knowledge have also their special weaknesses. Rarely indeed does reform come from even the best among professional men.' Similarly, Inge (1926: 102): 'our most influential thinkers and discoverers have rarely been professionals. We are a nation of amateurs in peace and war . . . our great men have had wider interests and more knowledge of the world than can be often found in a university professor.' Indeed, the famous British historian, G. M. Trevelyan (1942: 165) claimed that the history of England was littered with examples of the archetypal 'amateur', such as William Caxton, the inventor of modern printing: 'an early and a noble example of a well known modern type that has done so much for the world, the individualistic Englishman following out his own hobbies with business capacity and trained zeal'. Here, then, thinkers were best left alone rather than recruited to the services of the state.

The role of the central state in everday governance

The impact of the Lutheran Church, the responsibility of which was to facilitate faith rather than give charity, had necessitated that the state administer to the sick and needy. Lutherans rejected the spiritual idealization of poverty and the efficiaciousness of charity that was characteristic of Catholicism: 'voluntary poverty was a form of social parasitism to be punished, not a symbol of spiritual sacrifice to be rewarded' (Witte, 2002: 20). This then put the onus on the state to undertake 'caring work' in the void that the Reformation left. Indeed, an already formidable state bureaucracy in Sweden undertook the first collection of census data in the world, in 1749. Laing (1837: 273, our italics) later noted, with some bemusement, that 'in Sweden there is a department of government for drawing up statistical tables, called the Table Department. Tables on every point respecting the population, property, crops, capital, in short embracing every matter of statistical interest either to government or the political economist, are made out in each parish by the clergyman and the parish writer – a distinct functionary apart from the parish clerk or sexton; and a Table Commission at Stockholm is constantly employed in generalising these local returns and reducing them to tables . . . In any other country, if a public functionary were to ask you how much you sow, how much you reap, what is your capital, what your profits, the inquirer and his commission would be turned out of doors for his impertinence. *Here, people are trained to obedience.*' In effect, what could seem to be the extraordinary extent of state governance to a visitor from England, such as Laing, already seemed, for Swedish citizens, to have become an unremarkable feature of their society. At the same time, the employment of many of the landless nobility in key civil service positions (Laing, 1837) helped to give state organizations additional authority and prestige. A century later, civil servants had become a very highly respected group of workers in Swedish society (Tomasson, 1970).

In addition, state organizations had to play a major role in infrastructural development in these geographically large but sparsely populated countries: 'in times of crisis the state raised loans, which it passed on to industry and commerce. The state was also active in the creation of an institutional apparatus for the provision of credit. Local authorities played an important role in the establishment of local savings banks . . . the state played the main role in the development of the communications network which promoted growth and market integration. The purchase of Sweden's first steamship in 1826 was a state initiative' (Hovde, 1943: 110). In effect, then, there was nothing unusual or undesirable about an enlarged role for the state in these societies: on the contrary, it had become a necessary feature of economic development and social organization. Grimley (1937: 29, our italics) thus observed that 'the question of ownership of public utilities has never been much of an issue [in Norway]. To the great majority of [its] people, it is unthinkable that these should be privately owned and run for the profit of a few . . . *railways were not built for profit. They were built both as an economic and social enterprise, just like you build a highway.*' Post-war reconstruction then necessitated further extensions of state power: 'it was generally conceded that the task of rebuilding Norway's economy after occupation would require collective action under firm state leadership and all political parties were therefore able to agree upon a common programme of economic reconstruction and social reform' (Warbey, *et al.*, 1950: 11).

But the state provided more than infrastructural development. It was able to shape, police, guide and regulate public morality and culture, to bring about what it judged to be the well-being of each individual. Thus, in Norway, '90 per cent of cinemas or movies of Norway are municipally owned . . . there are no privately owned motion picture theatres in Oslo, and there as well as elsewhere in the country, the movie is made into an education factor to a large extent. There is also a state censor of films. You cannot buy time on the state owned radio . . . the radio is an educational factor, and the different speakers discuss objectively all kinds of subjects which tend to enlarge the knowledge of the listener and widen his horizon of human interest' (Grimley, 1937: 29). Alcohol restrictions and prohibition exemplify the deep penetration of the state into everyday life in these societies during this period. Following the campaigning activities of their temperance movements, prohibition was introduced in both Norway (from 1916 to 1927) and Finland (from 1919 to 1932). In Sweden, alcohol purchases were regulated from 1914 to 1955 by the '*motbok* [passbook] system'. That is, 'a passbook is given only to persons who have reached majority age, who possess sufficient income to afford the purchase of alcoholic beverages, and who are known for their temperate mode of life' (Kinberg, 1930: 209). Entry was made of each purchase in the book and, if it was thought that alcohol was being consumed too quickly, the purchaser could be turned away from the state monopoly alcohol outlets (*Systembolaget*). Since the end of prohibition and the *motbok* this remains the only permissable outlet for alcohol sales in Sweden; similarly, the *Vinmonopolet* in Norway and *Alko* shops in Finland.

Such exercises of state power, designed to engineer individual well-being that fitted community expectations and standards, could be both humane and generous on the one hand, yet clumsily insensitive, not to say harshly authoritarian, on the other. Thus, while the state facilitated the extensive development of municipal housing that was made available to all, irrespective of income, those moving into such facilities were subject to high levels of scrutiny and inspection by its bureaucracies: 'it is a house rule that each new tenant must have his possessions disinfected before he moves in so that there will be no danger of vermin' (Childs, 1936: 53). The state introduced sex education to Swedish schools in the 1930s, with a view to ensuring that informed choices could be made regarding family planning and development, rather than allowing this to be ruled by ignorance and myth. However, because it was thought that the mentally retarded were not capable of practicing birth control and would bring large numbers of children into disadvantaged circumstances, the state also assumed the power to prevent them from having any. Swedish legislation in 1935 thus authorized compulsory sterilization for 'legally incompetent' individuals. This was justified by Karl Höjer, Director of the Swedish Poor Relief and Child Welfare Association (1938: 371), on the basis that 'the community having by now assumed main responsibility for care of the feeble minded . . . it is only natural that efforts should be made to prevent an increase in their number'. There were 63,000 such operations up to 1975, the vast majority on women (Broberg and Roll-Hanssen, 1996). In Norway, there were 41,000 between 1934 and 1977. In Finland, there were 1,078 between 1935 and 1955, under legislation allowing this for 'idiots, imbeciles and the insane'. Further legislation in 1950, allowing this to be carried out on eugenic, social or general medical grounds, led to 56,000 more.

The extent and exercise of both formal and informal social controls helped to bring about high levels of conformity and acquiescence to community standards, rather than give encouragement to individual aspirations. Let us go back to Bjørnson's (1882: 65, our italics) confirmation class, waiting for their results, to witness this. One young man had been placed tenth in the class rather than first, even though the exam results had merited the latter. However, the schoolteacher explains to him that 'this, Øyvind, has been a well-merited recompense. *You have not studied from love of your religion, or of your parents; you have studied from vanity.*' Success in this region was not to be an excuse for celebration or pride, where the individual was then elevated beyond the standards or expectations of their community. By the same token, the need to avoid emotional outbursts, the need to avoid ostentation, the need to be seen as similar rather than different, brought with it caution and reserve – *lagom* – in everyday interaction. Clarke (1823: 238) thus noted that 'the Swedes are naturally mild and obliging[,] being rarely provoked to anger, or passionate when disputing with each other'. More emotional outbursts than this were likely to lead to unplanned or ill considered conduct that would shatter the consensus that formed the basis of everyday relationships in these small societies. Undoubtedly, such values could be repressive and stifling. In the late nineteenth century, Henrik Ibsen (quoted by Connery, 1966: 184) complained that 'Norwegians can only agree on one sole point: to drag down what is lofty'. A succession of commentators then variously reported that: 'Sweden is a country where only the mediocre is successful . . . generally speaking, we do not like eccentric or original people, unless they amuse us' (Sundbärg, 1911a: 28); 'the eccentric character in Sweden is rare' (De Mare, 1952: 253); 'nonconformists often have difficulty fitting into Swedish life' (Fleisher, 1967: 342); 'to be different in Sweden is to be burdened with a sense of guilt and to be the worst of failures' (Huntford, 1971: 32). And, despite the cultivation of the creative arts in these societies, luminaries such as Ibsen, August Strindberg and Jean Sibelius spent much of their working lives outside their own countries of Norway, Sweden and Finland.

Yet, out of these pressures to conform, out of the acquiescence to state authority, these societies also seemed able to generate high levels of trust, norm compliance and self-regulation (those same values that have become manifested in their prison systems, particularly the open prisons, in the early twenty-first century). Much emphasis was thus placed on conflict avoidance, and the performance of civic duties and responsibilities that demonstrated the importance of interdependencies, and the need to extend reciprocities towards other members of these societies, rather than out of any deference to or illustration of difference from them. Laing (1837: 159), for example, noticed, in Sweden, that 'the good manners of the people to each other are very striking, and extend lower among the ranks of society in the community than in other countries. There seem none so uncultivated or rude, as not to know and observe among themselves the forms of politeness. The brutality and rough way of talking to and living with each other, characteristic of our lower classes, is not found here . . . there is evidently an uncommon equality of manners among all ranks.' In much the same way, regular references to high levels of hygiene and cleanliness were indicative of the extent of these responsibilities and the readiness to conform to them: 'one thing will strike the stranger on entering a countryhouse here, and that is the scrupulous cleanliness in which the rooms are kept' ('An Old Bushman', 1865: 122). In the 1920s, Gothenburg public gardens were described as 'a dream of delight and colour in summer, while they are so beautifully kept and well ordered that though frequently invaded by festive crowds there appears to be an almost entire lack of that careless abandon that so often impels the British holiday maker to litter even the most pleasant garden with paper bags and food' (Heathcote, 1927: 86). For Simon (1939: 255), 'the Swedes are so orderly and clean that nowhere does one find a dirty or untidy apartment and the flue ventilated lavatories even in the hotels were never objectionable'. Thereafter, the renowned criminologist Torsten Sellin (1948: 14) confirmed that '[Swedish] cities have no slums . . . the visitor is struck by the orderliness and cleanliness of the cities and their recreational facilities for children and adults alike'.

In England, however, the emphasis was much more on self-help rather than state help. A long line of scholars that can be traced from the late eighteenth century to the early twentieth, and which included Adam Smith, Jeremy Bentham, Herbert Spencer, John Stuart Mill and A. V. Dicey, were all of the view that the state should only be allowed minimal intrusion in the lives of its subjects.[13] This would then mean that each citizen would have to take responsibility for the subsequent direction that his or her life took, rather than expect any assistance to this end from the state. Indeed, these ideas were famously popularized in the best-selling writing of Samuel Smiles in the mid- to late-nineteenth century: 'the spirit of self-help is the root of all genuine growth in the individual; and exhibited in the lives of many, constitutes the true course of national vigour and strength. *Help from without is often enfeebling in its effects, but help from within invariably invigorates*' (Smiles, 1859: 1, our italics). State power was thus understood, here, as something debilitating rather than enabling. For example, in *National Life and Character*, C. H. Pearson (1893: 138) claimed that the growth of state power would lead to the decline of 'English adventurousness', the spirit on which the Empire itself had been founded. It thus represented 'an absolute departure from the time honoured English principle of leaving every man to do the best for himself and fare as he may'. As such, the different place and tolerance of state bureaucracies became one of the distinguishing characteristics between England and continental Europe over the course of this period. Dickens (1857), in *Little Dorrit*, for example, satirizes the civil service when he writes of 'the Circumlocution Office', 'the most important department under government'. To become involved with it, though, was like stepping into quicksand: 'numbers of people were lost in the Circumlocution Office. Unfortunates with wrongs, or with projects for the general welfare, who in slow lapse of time and agony had passed safely through other public departments; who, according to rule, had been bullied in this, over-reached by that, and evaded by the other; got referred at last to the Circumlocution Office, and never reappeared in the light of day. Boards sat upon them, secretaries minuted upon them, commissioners gabbled about them, clerks registered, entered, checked, and ticked them off, and they melted away. In short, all the business of the country went through the Circumlocution Office, except the business that never came out of it.' Rather than the state bureaucracies having, as it were, a natural and largely uncontested role in the governance of everyday life, as in the Nordic countries during the nineteenth and first half of the twentieth centuries, it was as if they were at best nothing more than an unnecessary appendage, complicating and obfuscating matters that individuals could – and should – be allowed to accomplish more efficiently and effectively on their own. British travellers in Europe in the late nineteenth century thus took exception to the powers they found invested in continental state officials. One complained that 'surely it is not necessary for government to poke its nose into all private concerns, to have magistrates and police and common councils and commercial councils . . . to control the affairs of the citizens and to protect what is in no need of protection' (quoted by Morgan, 2001: 164). These antipathies to the state and its organizations of government had become cemented into British society by the mid-twentieth century. J. B. Priestley (1934: 389), for example, in *English Journey*, wrote in praise of 'Little England' and against 'red-faced, staring loud-voiced Big Englanders who want to boss everybody about'. Much more preferable to investing state officials with seemingly authoritarian powers, M. Ernest Barker (1947: 554) in *The Character of England*, claimed, was 'the habit of "muddling through" . . . It means that all sorts of men – each in his own way, and each on his own account – are tackling the problems of the moment with every appearance of confusion . . . and yet achieving results which the planner and synthesizer might miss.'

Was this hostility to state power a characteristic of the Anglophone cluster as a whole? In Australia and New Zealand, as in the Nordic countries, the state *had to play* a more central role in infrastructural development. As Siegfried (1914: 54) explained, 'in the early days of a colony there is usually little co-operation between the immigrants; the government is usually the only bond which unites them, and some time is necessary before natural groupings are formed. The government is thus brought by the force of circumstances to perform functions, which in the old countries would lie within the province of private initiative.' However, proposals for any more extensive state intervention in the conduct of everyday life were regarded with scepticism and suspicion (Webb, 1940: 146). Instead, as in England, social advancement through hard work was the expectation: 'a man must perforce be the sole architect of his own fortunes. Industry and energy, enterprise and perseverance pave the pathway to success' (Hay, 1882: 34); and 'it is the hard-worker with small capital who will win in the long run in New Zealand, and to him I commend the colony' (Ashby, 1889: 48). Indeed, across all these Anglophone societies, *the self-made man* making vast fortunes set the example for others to follow, rather than the poor farmers of the Nordic countries. Hence, the central character in Kingsley's (1849: 96, our italics) novel, *Yeast*, is described as having 'carved out his own way through life . . . neither with sword nor pen, but with steam and cotton. . . From a mill owner he grew to coal owner, ship owner, banker, railway director, money lender to kings and princes; and last of all, *as the summit of his ambition, to land-owner*.' Each individual, in effect, was thought to be master of their own fate: 'how a man uses money – makes it, saves it and spends it – is perhaps one of the best tests of practical wisdom . . . some of the finest qualities of human nature are intimately related to the right use of money; such as generosity, honesty, justice and self-sacrifice, as well as the virtues of economy and providence' (Smiles, 1859: 290).

At the same time, though, the importance of self-advancement meant that there was less emphasis on the development of interdependencies and reciprocities than in the Nordic countries. Collier (1909: 32) wrote of 'the grounded horror of interfering in other people's affairs – they avoid the smallest suspicion of even curiosity about one another's affairs or private concerns'. As Maillaud (1945: 27) observed, 'English individualism is undoubtedly the strongest in Europe . . . "not to get involved" is a watchword which one hears time and time gain, whether it is applied to an invitation to lunch or to a sentimental attachment.' Indeed, it was thought that offers of assistance, whether these came from individuals or the state, led only to dependency rather than empowerment. In the late nineteenth century, Jevons (1878: 9) thus claimed that 'there are many good-hearted people who think it is virtuous to give alms to poor people who ask for them, without considering the effect produced upon the people. They see the pleasure of the beggar on getting the alms, but they do not see the after effects, namely that beggars become more numerous than before. Much of the poverty and crime which now exist have been caused by mistaken charity in past times, which has caused a large part of the population to grow up careless, and improvident and idle. Political economy proves that, instead of giving casual ill-considered alms, we should educate people, teach them to work and earn their own livings, and save up something to live upon in old age.' It was to lead to a mindset where there was much less by way of recognition of civic duties and responsibilities than in the Nordic countries. In *England Speaks*, Gibbs (1935: 40), at the height of the depression and mass unemployment, was 'convinced that there are numbers of cases in which the incentive to work is lacking because idleness is subsidised by state relief . . . it will be a tragic thing if the younger crowd are brought up to believe that the state will provide for them, at least on a minimum scale, whether they feel like work or whether they don't'.

By the mid-twentieth century, then, two very different ways of seeing, constructing, understanding and thinking about the world had been set in place. In contrast to the importance given to individual success, and the need to establish barriers of exclusion against the unwanted and the unproductive in the Anglophone countries, we have moderation, reserve, uniformity and inclusion in the Nordic. In contrast to the way in which education was something that the wealthy purchased, but which took the form of disciplinary training for the poor, in the Anglophone countries, in the Nordic it was more readily available to all. Here, intellectual advancement won respect and recognition, while intellectuals in the Anglophone countries were generally regarded as eccentric outsiders – Wood (1958: 162) wrote of a 'suspicion of the expert and an undervaluing of research [in New Zealand]'. In contrast to the way in which advances in state power were to be guarded against in the Anglophone countries, on the basis that this enfeebled the nation's health, this was regarded as an essential means of enriching community well-being in the Nordic countries.

3 Two welfare states

It was at this same mid-twentieth-century point that the respective models of welfare state came into full focus in both clusters of societies. However, rather than their emergence constituting some dramatic break with the previous modes of social organization in these clusters, both were informed by, and then went on to reproduce, their already existing value systems: the emphasis on moderation, egalitarianism and uniformity in the Nordic countries; the emphasis on individual responsibility, suspicion of state authorities and those who looked to them for assistance in the Anglophone. In practical terms, there have come to be great differences in the extent of welfare provisions between the two clusters. In the social democratic welfare model of the Nordic countries, universal benefits are likely to be earnings related (up to 80 per cent replacement value, although on occasions as high as 90 per cent). Education, health and child care are likely to be provided almost exclusively by the state, free of charge or heavily subsidized. Means tested social assistance, however, is available for those who do not qualify for benefits – for example, new school leavers and immigrants yet to establish an employment record in these countries. Because of the extent and scope of this model of welfare, Nordic governments have been committed to maintaining full employment in order to generate the high tax revenue that is needed to fund it. In the liberal model associated with the Anglophone countries, benefits are likely to be means tested and are usually paid only to low income dependants at a flat rate.[1] Welfare services are limited, residual and provisional, with comparatively high levels of use of private education, healthcare, pensions and so on. Anglophone governments, from the end of the 1970s, have been committed to reducing public expenditure and lowering levels of individual taxation.

The first part of this chapter thus addresses how the different value systems of these societies influenced, and were then reinforced by, their respective welfare models, tracing through their development from the mid-nineteenth century to the early twenty-first. The second part examines the effects of post-1970s welfare restructuring, amidst more general social change, on the value systems of these societies and their respective inclusionary and exclusionary characteristics.

The origins and development of the different welfare models

The value systems of these societies informed four episodic features of their development: the extent to which 'less eligibility' should determine social policy; their differing attitudes to state provided security; the dominance of what Castles (1978) referred to as 'the social democratic image of society' in the Nordic[2] countries, against a dominant Conservative image in the Anglophone; and the way in which the relationship between welfare provision and population politics was addressed.

'Less eligibility' and social policy

In England, the Poor Law Commissioners' Report (1834: 335) stated that, when relief was given to the poor, '[their] situation . . . shall not be made really or apparently so eligible as the situation of an independent labourer of the lowest class . . . Every penny bestowed that tends to render the conditions of the pauper more eligible than that of the independent labourer is a bounty on indolence and vice.' To put this into effect, poor law legislation in the same year centralized the administration of relief (thereby restricting local discretion) and insisted that *indoor relief only* should be provided in workhouses that would now be run on the *less eligibility principle* – that conditions in the workhouse should be less favourable than those outside. This was the reason why charities were later not encouraged to provide outdoor assistance in this country. The poor were to be held to account for their miseries and calamities, rather than be given any assistance that would have alleviated them, as if their status was *ipso facto* proof that they had failed Smiles' test of 'practical wisdom'. As *The Economist* (13 May, 1848: 536) explained, misfortune was part of life – it was not the duty of the state to either reduce the risk of it, nor ameliorate it when it occurred: 'suffering and evil are nature's admonitions; they cannot be got rid of; and the impatient attempts of benevolence to banish them from the world by legislation, before benevolence has learnt their object and their end, have always been more productive of evil than good.' To this end, individual parishes were combined into Poor Law Unions, each with their own workhouse, with more than 5,000 built in the next 50 years (this was a particularly English development – labour shortages in Australia and New Zealand over this period had meant that they had no need for this institution). The largest of these institutions might hold 1,000 inmates, although, more typically, around 200 would be accommodated. Nonetheless, 'the union workhouse was in many localities one of the largest and most significant buildings in the area' (Fowler, 2008: 40). For the many thousands[3] committed to it, families were broken up on entrance: there was separate accommodation for children, the elderly, and able bodied men and women. Inside, 'the drab workhouse clothing, deliberately intended to destroy individuality, and the standard workhouse haircut, made paupers instantly recognizable if they went out in public; [they endured] strict hours, compulsory chapel, silent periods, exercise periods, and the largely pointless labour for the fit and not so fit in stone breaking or oakum picking' (Thompson, 1988: 350). In keeping with less eligibility requirements, the diet – consisting, in the main, of carefully measured servings of soup, gruel and bread – was to be 'so regulated as in no case to exceed, in quantity and quality of food, the ordinary diet of any class of able-bodied labourers living within the same district' (Poor Law Commissioners' Report, 1835: 170). Indeed, 'the paupers at Andover Workhouse were so starved during 1845–1846 that they fought each other for the rancid meat on bones they were employed to crush for fertilizer' (Richardson, 2012: 284).

The workhouse became – as had been intended – an instrument of terror for those whose circumstances brought them to it. William Howitt (1838: 131), in his *Rural Life of England*, wrote that 'every poor man's family is liable, on the occurrence of some chance stroke of destitution, to have to their misfortune . . . added the tenfold aggravation of being torn asunder and immured in the separate wards of a poverty prison'. This was what it had become to be poor and desperate in England: the state will keep you alive at a miserable level of human existence if you, in your wretchedness, throw yourself upon its mercy; for such time, though, its Poor Law officials will make sure that your life is one of unending humiliation and misery. Carl af Forsell (1835: 124), a Swedish visitor to England, wondered 'how [such] a wise and sensible nation could have established such preposterous [institutions] . . . if one would want to establish a system which will ruin all sense of independence and morals among the working class, and plant dissatisfaction and anxiety in all other members of society, then the Poor Laws could not be more suitable'. In *Our Mutual Friend*, Dickens (1865: 227) portrayed the workhouse as a more terrifying institution than prison. Betty Higden, fearing the prospect of such internment, cries in desperation, 'Kill me sooner rather than take me there. Throw [my] pretty child under a carthorse's feet and loaded wagon sooner than take him there. Come to us and find us all a-dying, and set light to us where we lie and let us all blaze away with the house into a heap of cinders, sooner than move a corpse there.' There was, though, a reality to such melodrama. Taine (1874: 301–2) observed that 'there is not an able-bodied inmate of [Manchester] workhouse at the moment . . . They prefer to be free and starve . . . The workhouse is regarded as a prison; the poor consider it a point of honour not to go there . . . [where] the human being becomes a machine; he is treated as if he were devoid of feeling, and insulted quite unconsciously.' Despite some minor ameliorations that were put in place towards the end of the nineteenth century,[4] Charles Booth (1894: 330), in *The Aged Poor in England and Wales*, still noted that 'the aversion to the "House" is absolutely universal, and almost any amount of suffering and privations will be endured by the people rather than go into it'. Similarly, Robert Roberts (1971: 21) remembered how, in the early twentieth century, 'workhouse paupers hardly registered as human beings at all . . . able bodied men from some Northern poorhouses worked in public with a large P stamped on the seat of their trousers'. The values of class-divided British society had reduced pity for, or guilt about, those admitted to these institutions: for most, they were simply judged to be victims of their own inadequacies and fecklessness. Although the workhouses were abolished in 1930 (they then became 'public assistance institutions'), they lived on in British society in folk memories, anecdotes and literary representations that provided a legacy of fear and suspicion of the state and its officials amongst those who were dependent[5] on it; and a legacy of distaste and contempt, amongst those who were free from such miseries, for those thought to be so supine and shameless that they turned to the state for assistance.

Even with post-1945 welfare reforms, less eligibility remained embedded in Anglophone social policy. Benefits were to be residual and kept to a flat rate minimum level, in the fear that any enlargement of entitlement would encourage dependency and irresponsibility. The much acclaimed Beveridge Report (1942: 122, our italics) thus explained that 'the flat rate of benefit proposed is intended in itself to be sufficient without further resources *to provide the minimum income needed for subsistence in all normal cases*'. While the 1938 New Zealand Social Security Act had promised 'cradle to the grave security' (Hansard [NZ], 16 August 1938: 341), the subsequent Labour Minister of Justice, A. M. Finlay (1943: 46, our italics), warned that 'the most vital element of social security is undoubtedly its promise of freedom from want ... *[but] nothing not strictly necessary is promised – no frills, no luxuries, no more than healthy subsistence. Freedom from want means not the good life but the bearable life.*' As regards Australia, Mendelsohn (1954: 126, our italics) wrote that 'the unemployed are made to feel that "dole" is not a right but a charitable community donation ... *no firm tradition of community responsibility had been established*'. Here, then, the limits of the liberal welfare state were set in place by the value systems of these societies. The low level of entitlements led to increases in applications for supplementary – but discretionary – assistance. It would still be means tested and, like the workhouse before, was 'destined to leave an indelible mark on popular culture' (Fraser, 2009: 180). Many who were entitled to claim assistance were reluctant to do so because of the way in which this still remained something shameful in these societies – and, at the same time, invited investigation from suspicious state officials (see, for example, Abel Smith and Townsend, 1965; Runciman, 1966). Furthermore, as John Goldthorpe (1968) observed in *The Affluent Worker*, for lower and middle class taxpayers, the new benefits and services were unpopular because they represented 'getting something for nothing', rather than self-advancement through one's own labour.

During the 1970s, there were allegations (never substantiated) that the benefit system in England was so lax and generous that the unemployed, at a time of economic crisis brought about by dramatic rises in oil prices,[6] were able to take European holidays (Deacon, 1978). Thereafter, these suspicions about the welfare 'scrounger', which were always an undercurrent of the means tested nature of the liberal welfare state, have been further accentuated, justifying still more restricted, residual and contingent benefits and entitlements, as if vast numbers of malingerers were hiding among the general body of claimants. In 1997, a form of 'workfare' was introduced in Australia. In New Zealand, emphasis had been given to pressuring single parents with schoolchildren to take low paid or part-time jobs. Under the New Labour governments in Britain, from 1997 to 2010, poverty came to be understood, as it had been in the nineteenth century, more as an issue of *morality* than *material need*. Cabinet Minister Peter Mandelson (1997: 7) thus wrote that 'the people we are concerned about, those in danger of dropping off the end of the ladder of opportunity and becoming disengaged from society, will not have their long term problems addressed by an extra pound a week on their benefits'. There were even suggestions that charities, as in the nineteenth century, should not give material assistance to the poor. The head of the government's Rough Sleepers Unit claimed that 'with soup runs and other kinds of charity help, well-meaning people are spending money servicing the problem on the streets and keeping it there ... It is possible to get "a better sleeping bag on the [streets] than you can buy [in camping shops] ... the homeless should not take their help on the streets when it was on offer inside"' (*BBC News*, 14 November 1999). The onset of 'the global economic crisis' in 2008 then provided Anglophone governments with the opportunity to further penalize welfare beneficiaries by cutting what were thought to be the profligate levels of largesse they received from overblown public expenditure. In England, the Conservative-led coalition government produced a 'three strikes' benefit rule in 2011: the first time an applicant turned down a job or training, they would lose their benefits for three months; the second, for six months; the third, for three years. In these respects, what the liberal welfare state had not been able to dispel, due to its own limitations and restraints, was the longstanding sense of shame and worthlessness associated with the various categories of 'undeserving' claimants in these societies where individuals were meant to make their own way in the world. Hence the sardonic, condescending, message of the Conservative Minister of Work and Pensions, someone near the top of this society, to those near its bottom – would-be beneficiaries – on the abolition of 'the Social Fund' in 2012 (the payment of one-off loans to tide applicants over in an emergency): 'this is not an easy life anymore, chum. I think you're a slacker' (quoted by Toynbee, 2012: 3). *Throughout the development of the liberal welfare state, though, 'being poor' had been looked upon as a sign of personal failure* rather than something that the state should rectify.

The Nordic countries also had poor laws and workhouses, but less eligibility did not impose itself on the development of the social democratic welfare state to anything like the same extent. This is not to say that there was no shame or hardship in being poor and dependent in these societies. However, while every parish, up to the mid-nineteenth century, had to take care of its needy, there seems to have been less pressure to deliberately penalize them. Instead, 'in the old community of the village, indigent and unfortunate neighbours were carried along without sharp or obvious distinctions in status' (Scott, 1988: 340).[7] The variety of outdoor relief practices that were in use to this end included: the collection and distribution of alms: 'in passing along the Swedish roads, the traveller frequently sees a charity box fixed by the wayside ... The poor in Sweden are well provided for, both by these receptacles for casual alms-offerings, and by a regular parish provision' (Conway, 1829: 287); 'boarding out' in return for labour (known as the *laegd* in Norway, *rotegång* in Sweden), whereby 'the homeless and others who are provided with relief in kind from particular farmers are to be furnished with a note setting forth the quantity the individual has to demand of each farm and the time at which they are entitled to demand the same . . . in case the person with whom a pauper has been quartered out does not supply all relief or ill-uses the pauper, they shall be fined, or in the case of ill usage, be imprisoned' (Norwegian Poor Law 1845, s. 26); 'wandering', whereby destitute individuals or families, having lost their farms, moved from district to district, throwing themselves on the mercy of better off relatives;[8] and 'auctioning' of children and the elderly by means of an inverted bidding process in which the lowest bid won: much cheaper than providing institutions for these helpless members of the community, the municipality paid the successful bidder the agreed sum, and the bidder would, in return, board and employ them.

Notwithstanding the humiliation that such practices could cause (see Rahikainen, 2002), the administration of poor relief did not lead to less eligibility based institutionalization. Indeed, in contrast to the deterrent features of the 1834 English Poor Law, mid-nineteenth century Nordic legislation formalized these traditional practices and gave every person *the right to relief* in the district in which they were living or had been born (Swedish Poor Law 1845). Similarly, the Finnish Poor Law (1852) emphasized maintenance according to existing paternalistic responsibilities and social relations: families should take responsibility for their own; employers had to maintain their servants and workers. Entitlements to public support were extended to children, the disabled, the infirm and the insane. Section 9(1) stipulated that the poor, and those in need of temporary support, were expected to earn this by working for the community, yet they were not reduced to performing menial labour in a workhouse. And, while there were 'poorhouses' in existence in some – but by no means all – Nordic communities by the late nineteenth century, these were available when outdoor relief was inadequate, *rather than as a replacement for it*. Sweden, for example, had about 50 such institutions, 'small and urban. None were large workhouses after the English model' (Lammers, 1875: 188). They were not under any centralized administration, nor did they have the deterrent and disciplinary function of the workhouse. Andrews (1877: 6) thus describes Sabbatsberg Poorhouse in Stockholm: 'only its sick and helpless inmates receive full support. The others receive daily food and [a little] money. They furnish their own clothing and bedding. They have a free place to cook their coffee and at the main kitchen can buy cooked food at list rates . . . they must themselves earn the rest for support in or out of the institution. There are 48 inmates who enjoy a pension ranging from four to 130 kronor. There is a very small library, which is much used. A few of the inmates are of noble birth.'

Again, then, there are major distinctions between such institutions and the English less eligibility workhouses: residents wore their own clothes, did their own cooking, kept their own money, worked outside the institution while still living within it and so on. In societies where *likhet* was so prominent and where poverty was widespread, being poor did not carry anything like the stigma and sense of difference that it did in the Anglophone countries. There was, thus, no need for those in the Nordic poor institutions to have their hair shorn, wear clothing that advertized their dependency on the state and so on; nor, for that matter, did state assistance and administration have anything like the negative qualities associated with this in England. Furthermore, that some poorhouse residents were also members of the Swedish nobility is also indicative of the very different standard of living of this class from their English counterparts, as well as the more egalitarian social relations of this region. It was only when late nineteenth century industrialization began to undermine the capability of local communities to absorb the poor through these inclusionary mechanisms that more restrictive poor laws were introduced. Even so, these were directed mainly against the able unemployed (Lindqvist and Marklund, 1995). They were not only in contravention of the Lutheran belief that work was a service to God, but also threatened the stability of the local interdependencies and mutual support systems. In the 1879 Finnish Poor Law, a division was introduced between mandatory care for poor minors, the insane, disabled, chronically sick, old and infirm poor claimants, and discretionary assistance for the unemployed, who would now have to undertake forced labour in workhouses. In Sweden, the state assumed responsibility for the 'defenceless' (*försvarslösa*) – those unable to look after themselves, including many ex-prisoners: 'anyone without a job for more than eight weeks became "defenceless"' before the law and was required to take whatever job offered. It was forbidden to enter a town unless one had a job' (Scott, 1988: 310). In addition to placements in Crown work corps, where they would build roads, canals and so on, workhouses were also introduced for them in Norway and Sweden.

How did the conditions of these institutions compare with those in England? There were similarities in Norway, it seems, particularly the emphasis given to afflictive labour: 'inmates [in Oslo] are employed in various branches of manufacture and domestic industry; at present the chief manufacture carried on is weaving of wool, making various articles of cow hair. Of other employments there may be especially named stone breaking, stone cutting, oakum picking, spinning and knitting. From the workhouse, there is also given work to the poor in the town such as knitting and oakum picking' (Crowe, 1875: 118). Furthermore, 'misbehaviour' could lead to 'correctional punishment' – bread and water diets and/or placement in punishment cells (either complete darkness or constant light). However, in Stockholm, 'at the poorhouses *and* workhouses and charitable institutions the principal kinds of subsistence are rye bread, potatoes, barley-grits and peas. In respect to humanity, cleanliness and economy, the various establishments of Stockholm appear to be well administered' (Andrews, 1877: 10, our italics). In Sweden, then, one form of institutionalization was much the same as any other. Entry to the workhouse was not accompanied by further humiliations that separated out the category of dependants for whom it provided.

But it was not just that the Nordic workhouse held less of the terrors than it did in England. In this region, the workhouse remained *peripheral* to the administration of poor relief, unlike in England, where it became central to it. Workhouses were small and few and far between, and were outnumbered by the less punitive poorhouse (Oslo had eight of the latter, but only one of the former, in the late nineteenth century). As such, relief was more likely to take the form of one of the continuing community traditions – 'the *laegd* accords better with the character and habits of the people, as well as with the material condition of the country . . . to receive a poor guest keeps alive the feeling of voluntary benevolence, and that to do away with the custom makes it a more compulsory affair' (Lammers, 1875: 189) – or in new, non-institutional state initiatives. Blumenberg (1884: 205) referred to 'the establishment of [Swedish] poor-farms [*fattiggårdar*], where relief takers are kept engaged either solely in farming, or in farming combined with other work. The poor-farms have proved to be a great blessing to the country, as well as by urging the poor to contribute to their own living, as by their reduction of the number of people claiming official relief.' Importantly, then, the poor were not to be punished for their poverty, but were to receive assistance intended to lift them out of it. In such ways, the much fainter and more easily erasable imprint of less eligibility in the Nordic countries helped to ensure that universalism, rather than residualism, was better placed to become one of the defining characteristics of the social democratic welfare state, while the state itself became more of a protective, rather than a penalizing, entity. As Swedish Prime Minister Per Albin Hansson explained in the *riksdag* in 1928, its welfare measures would provide a 'people's home' (*folkhemmet*), in which 'the basis . . . is togetherness and common feeling. The good home does not consider anyone as privileged or unappreciated; it knows no special favourites and no stepchildren. There, no-one looks down upon anyone else . . . no-one tries to gain advantage at another's expense, and the stronger do not suppress and plunder the weaker' (quoted by Tilton, 1990: 126). It was to be a building designed to house all, not some cheap, shoddy construction that was the last resort of the worthless. Bolton (1938: 236–7) thus wrote that 'in England, our social services have been generally blighted with Poor Law stigma which has acted as it was meant to do: as a deterrent against people making the fullest use of them. In Sweden, social services are provided as much for middle as the working classes – all classes use the social services they need, and pay for those which are not free on a graduated scale according to their ability.'

Once universalism was accepted as the bedrock of the social democratic welfare state, this allowed means testing to be abolished for those who qualified for benefits. Now, instead of implying a lesser form of citizenship, 'social benefits should be provided as a general *right of citizenship*' (Möller, 1952: 392, our italics); hence the expansion of services for the whole population from this juncture, not just the poor. As regards benefit levels, for example, Michanek (1964: 10) explained that 'it was vital . . . to do away once and for all with the idea that . . . social assistance was something shameful, something of personal disgrace to the recipient. So we tried to tie the special benefits to certain objective criteria in the same way as under the social insurance system: a certain age, certain dwelling standards, number of children or a certain income gave the right to a certain benefit. We tried to restrict to a minimum any discretion in the assessment of the individual's need for help . . . We tried to do away with stinginess in the aid measures, to provide what might be termed as "help towards self-help", and to restrict to a minimum the necessary control.' The codification of entitlements then greatly reduced the discretionary powers of social security officials, meaning that benefits could be advertized as rights, rather than hidden away and jealously guarded behind layers of impenetrable bureaucracy, as in the operation of the liberal welfare state. Castles (1978: 96–7, our italics) thus observed that, 'in [Britain], large numbers do not claim the benefits they are entitled to – which is attributed to a mixture of lack of information *and an unwillingness to apply for charity* . . . But in Sweden, part of the curriculum in all comprehensive schools involves social studies courses which teach teenagers about the range of benefits *to which each citizen is entitled.*' And Huntford (1971: 201) noted that, 'if a Swedish mother is away from Sweden while her child allowance is due, she receives a notice from the Department of Social Security which says "don't forget that, even if you are abroad, you can still enjoy your social benefits. Fill in the enclosed form, and we will send your children's allowance to you wherever you may be."' In such ways, the social democratic welfare state buttressed and formalized the inclusionary characteristics of these societies. Instead of the preoccupation with 'welfare cheats' that came to be one of the characteristics of the Anglophone press during the development of the liberal welfare state,[9] Jenkins (1968: 196) observed that 'newspapers frequently carry lengthy articles about individuals who are not completely covered by the social security system': scandals emerged not in relation to welfare profligacy but in relation to those not receiving their due entitlements. Such differences point to the way in which the social democratic welfare state was not merely intended to prevent destitution, the function of the liberal model, but was also intended to reduce social distances – to bring about a greater egalitarianism in these already egalitarian societies. It should thus not 'ostracize the weakest', but seek an 'active redistribution of prosperity to create a society without pockets of poverty' (Myrdal, 1971: 89).

Nonetheless, from the 1980s, the parameters of the social democratic welfare state have become narrower. Claimants, as in the liberal welfare state, may now have to work longer to become eligible for earnings related benefits, and be more willing to take up work for means tested benefits; some benefits have been de-indexed from inflation and wage rates; levels of direct taxation have eased; government debts have been paid off, rather than further investments made in welfare provisions; and forms of 'workfare' have been introduced for unemployed 18–24-year-olds (Kuhnle, 2000; Timonen, 2003; Jutila, 2011). Furthermore, there has been strong resentment of those with no records of employment who have to claim the discretionary social assistance – particularly new immigrants. The right wing populist parties of this region[10] have enjoyed mercurial electoral successes by being able to exploit this matter. However, *none of them* espouse economic liberalism: rather than reduce welfare benefits, they argue that these should be reserved for 'real' Finns, Swedes and so on. As such, while there may have been some tightening around its edges, this model of welfare largely retains much of its universalism and relative generosity,[11] while avoiding the divisions and inequalities that the liberal welfare state, with its restricted scope, has been unable to address. As Rothstein and Uslaner (2005: 59) argue, 'if a state is going to tax the rich and give to the poor, the rich (especially the middle classes) will not agree to pay high taxes because they perceive that they do not get enough in return. They will perceive such [welfare] programmes as policies "only for the poor", and the middle classes in particular will turn away from political parties that argue for increasing taxes and social policies.'

In these more egalitarian and homogeneous societies, 'being poor' carried much less stigma than in the Anglophone, and pre welfare state mechanisms had been able to ensure their inclusion rather than exclusion. As the structure of the social democratic welfare state then began to be put together, its more formal mechanisms continued to perform this function, largely without the differentiating less eligibility emphasis of the liberal welfare state.

Different attitudes to state-provided security

The need for state welfare to provide security for the population – from mass unemployment in the 1930s followed by wartime destruction and terror in the 1940s – had been recognized in both clusters, and gave momentum to post-1945 welfare reforms. Thereafter, however, the association between state-provided welfare and security has remained strong in the Nordic countries, but has become much weaker in the Anglophone. One reason for this difference is related to the central importance of *trygghet* in the former. This Norwegian and Swedish word means both stability *and* safety, making it more multi-layered and deeply felt than the nearest equivalent English term, 'security'. As the then Swedish Minister of Social Affairs (quoted by Fleisher, 1967: 197) warned, 'nothing good has ever come out of insecurity. Security is the most basic foundation of the individual.' The obvious dangers posed by the natural elements; endemic poverty; and the proximity of large, bellicose, neighbours, such as Germany and Russia, meant that *trygghet* always had a high value in the Nordic region. When this began to be further undermined by the onset of industrialization and accelerating land enclosures, civil servants and intellectuals argued that these dangers should be countered by further extensions of protective state power: in this region, there was nothing unusual or undesirable about state assistance and administration per se. There was already an accepted place for this in the governance of these societies, as we have seen. Now, however, with *trygghet* under threat, there was *a necessity* for this. Policy makers thus disavowed British economic liberalism and looked to the way in which state intervention had been given legitimacy in Germany, in the form of the *kulturstaat* (the 'social service state'): 'the state machinery must, it was asserted, be used to regulate the economy in certain spheres, and the workers must be given protection and security, and a more just share in the distribution of wealth' (Seip, 1984: 334).

Initially, insurance became the mechanism to safeguard *trygghet* from the social changes threatening it. The 1871 Swedish Poor Law thus encouraged the development of Societies for Assistance (*skyddsförening*): 'every poor union shall endeavour, by the establishment of savings banks and mutual relief associations or by other suitable measures to obviate as far as possible the necessity for future poor relief.' From such beginnings, *preventing social problems* to safeguard community well-being, rather than reacting to them with punishment and penalties, became an important feature of the social democratic welfare model. Nelson (1953:

379, 383) later wrote that 'prevention is better than cure. This axiom lies at the root of the [Nordic] welfare policies today . . . the past 60 years have been dominated by the gradual development of social insurance. In some cases, for example health insurance and unemployment insurance, the schemes have built upon the mutual benefit societies voluntarily developed to provide a measure of protection against short term risks . . . in other cases, for example employment injuries insurance, disablement and old age insurance, where the issue was predominantly one of securing protection against certain long-term risks, the schemes were the direct result of legislative initiative.' However, during the course of the twentieth century, increasing affluence, in Sweden, especially,[12] also made it possible for the state to extend and enlarge its guarantees of security. *First*, from the 1950s, in the provision of earnings related benefits, reaching 90 per cent replacement value in the 1970s to ensure that recipients would be able to maintain their standard of living. This would then strengthen their support for welfare policies, while preventing the development of a beneficiary 'underclass', as in the Anglophone countries, kept from destitution but at the same time immured in poverty. *Second*, in the provision of enhanced training (symptomatic of the importance given to education in these societies), both to renew the skills base of society at large, and to ensure that those who were unemployed or suffered a disability would not be left as outsiders: 'social welfare policy is being transformed into a policy of social planning, having for its pivotal points the programmes of full and productive employment, family welfare and housing, prophylactic health and the rehabilitation of the handicapped' (Nelson, 1953: 488). As *The Economist* (1 January 1977) later explained, 'redundancy in Sweden does not mean unemployment. It means retraining and redeployment.' *Third*, as investment in public services increased (by 1980, the state sector accounted for 60 per cent of GDP in Sweden), so the use of the private sector was discouraged (Lindbeck, 1997). It was thought that the public sector provided better trained welfare professionals and standardized services, and was a more certain means of ensuring that the state's duty to provide universal services would be fulfilled (Trydegård, 2000). For Nelson (1953: 502), these extensions of state powers and responsibilities had brought about 'the reduction of social tensions and the promotion of social solidarity'. Similarly, Einar Gerhardsen (1971:167), Norway's Prime Minister for 17 years between 1945 and 1965: 'social policy, and in particular social security, is solidarity in practice. Those who are healthy help the sick and disabled, those who are in employment help the unemployed, those of working age help the elderly.' It is as if there was a taken-for-granted assumption in these societies, in which *likhet* and *lagom* were such strong characteristics, that the fortunate would readily assist – or, at least, finance state assistance of – the unfortunate.

There were grumblings, certainly, about the 'red tape' (*krångelsverige*[13]) that came with these levels of administration and bureaucratic regulation. There were also economic costs that came with them. By 1970, Sweden spent the most on welfare per head of population in the OECD, but it was also the most highly taxed member.[14] However, this was much more bearable in a society in which moderation was so deeply ingrained than in one which put much more emphasis on self-advancement ('in a civilized society, it is not only the striving for economic growth, but also the striving for security that illuminates the supreme goal of public policy, anchored in respect for human dignity': Kuusi, 1964: 57). There was also a high moral cost to the expectation that the state not only could, *but also that it should*, regulate and control all those unpredictable social forces that put *trygghet* at risk (Tham, 1998). With all the self-belief and confidence that came with being a state-employed intellectual in these societies, Alva and Gunnar Myrdal (1934: 244), also prominent Swedish Social Democrats, explained that 'we can prevent – technically it is possible to quite a high degree – illness, crime and asocial tendencies of different sorts'. The nature of these regulations and controls in civil society led, at one level, to the comedy of 'alcohol spies', employed by the Temperance Board to ensure that the small amount of alcohol that was allowed to be consumed by restaurant diners was not exceeded: 'a Swede who dined out never knew whether his innocent-appearing neighbour at the next door table might be checking his drinking . . . if the spy's suspicions were aroused, he would send of a report to the Board signed with his code number' (*Time*, 9 November 1953: 12). At another, it led to the tragedy of the compulsory sterilization laws. However, all these costs had seemed worth paying. As Swedish Prime Minister Tage Erlander [quoted by Fleisher, 1967: 4] put the matter, 'the state is not a threat to or an enemy of the individual. On the contrary, many of his problems can only be solved through cooperation and solidarity, through the state and municipality.' In these societies, the state's preventive policies were to be welcomed: community stability and cohesion superseded individual rights to be 'different' or to challenge these values.

Since the 1980s, however, economic changes have meant that the state is no longer the exclusive provider of *trygghet*. Unemployment in Sweden and Finland in the 1990s reached its highest levels since the 1930s, greatly undermining the revenue base for extensive welfare services.[15] As a consequence, some measure of privatization has been introduced in areas such as aged care and child care (Stolt, Blomqvist and Winblad, 2010). Nor are expensive welfare services so readily available: mental health services have been largely deinstitutionalized, for example (Zetterberg, 1995). At the same time, to bring about more efficiency, value for money and competitiveness, government ministers have set KPIs for the public sector organizations to achieve (see, for example, Temmes, 1998). Nonetheless, public support for state provided welfare remains strong (see Kvist, 1999; Nordlund, 2000; Jutila, 2011). In addition, 'private pensions are still less important than in other countries . . . health care to a larger degree than in other countries is publicly financed . . . child and elder care are relatively more developed in comparison with most other countries. In modern times, these services have not been stig-matizing, rather the opposite. For example, the middle class was for a long time *over-represented* among the users of public childcare . . . the [social democratic] welfare state has been changed in a liberal direction, but the changes are not significant enough to transpose the original model' (Lindbom and Rothstein, 2004: 5–7). The economic framework that made the social democratic welfare state possible may have contracted somewhat, but is still largely in place, and the levels of state power that come with this are still largely accepted.

In contrast, support for extensions of state power to provide security has always been much weaker in the Anglophone countries, because of the historical importance given to the rights of the individual over more general community norms (although there have been few qualms about extending the repressive power of the state to keep those at the bottom of these societies in their place, as with the development of the remarkable infrastructure necessary to run the nineteenth century Poor Law in England). Post-1945, there were certainly those who had high hopes that the British welfare state, modelled on the intentions of the Beveridge Report (1942),[16] would do more than make the lives of the poor more tolerable. T. H. Marshall (1950: 56), the most prominent British sociologist of the period, wrote that 'the extension of the social services is not primarily a means of equalising incomes . . . What matters is that there is a general enrichment of the concrete substance of civilised life, a general reduction of risk and insecurity, an equalisation between the more or less fortunate at all levels.' Similarly, for Richard Titmuss (1950: 70), the welfare reforms were a sign of 'national consensus'. However, among many others, there was alarm at the prospects of the growth in state power that this conjured. Friedrich von Hayek (1944: 200), later a great influence on Margaret Thatcher, warned that 'the increasing veneration for the state, the admiration of power, and of bigness for bigness' sake, the enthusiasm for "organization" of everything (we now call it "planning") and that the inability to leave anything to the simple power of organic growth . . . are all scarcely less marked in England now than they were in Germany'.[17] Thereafter, Geoffrey Gorer (1955: 286, our italics), in *Exploring English Character*, found a preference for privacy and independence from the state in post-1945 values, and that 'what seems to have remained constant *is a great resentment at being overlooked or controlled*, a love of freedom, fortitude'. Furthermore, civil servants in these countries, armed with new powers by the welfare state, commanded little of the status and respect they enjoyed in the Nordic. As J. L. Hodson (1948: 106) complained in *The Way Things Are*, 'what happens to civil servants? Does their common sense become atrophied? Or does too much security breed arrogance?'

In these societies, the state was, at best, an undesirable entity, rather than a saviour. It should be kept at a distance, rather than given sweeping powers of social engineering. Hence Barker's (1947) preference for 'muddling through', as if the market, or serendipity, or a few determined and brilliant individuals, would better shape the course of these societies than the state and its employees. Indeed, the British Conservative Party won the 1951 General Election with a manifesto that repudiated England's brief embrace of a powerful, interventionist central state during the war and its immediate aftermath: 'a worthwhile society cannot be established by Acts of Parliament and Government planning. Adequate rewards for skill and enterprise and for the creation of wealth, belief that saving and investment are worthwhile, diffusion of property, home ownership, the rule of law . . . personal responsibility and the rights of the individual – these are the true foundations of a free society' (quoted by Kynaston, 2010: 33). Thus, at the point when the social democratic welfare state was becoming more deeply embedded in Nordic society, so we find increasing limitations on the further development of the liberal welfare state. In 1961, welfare expenditure in both Sweden and New Zealand was 12.9 per cent of GDP. A decade later, while this had nearly doubled in Sweden, New Zealand had become one of the few OECD countries in which welfare expenditure had been reduced (Sutch, 1971). Furthermore, the inroads that the liberal welfare state had been able to make in adjusting the inequalities of the Anglophone countries had been very limited. In his *Anatomy of Britain*, Anthony Sampson (1962: 17) suggested that what redistribution had taken place had been amongst the top tiers of British society, rather than from top to bottom: 'interacting with the traditional Society of old families is the new Society of the self-made rich, the entertainers, the communicators, and the urban hurly-burly sometimes called café society . . . one recent survey estimated that the top one per cent of British adults owned 43 per cent of total net capital. The authors estimated that 20,000 people owned more than £100,000, and that their average holding was £250,000. (While at the bottom there are 16,000,000 people with less than £100 each, and an average of £50) . . . A hint of private wealth is provided by servants: the Ministry of Labour in 1960 recorded 30,000 men and 275,000 women in "private domestic service".' And the antipathy towards 'experts' was still in place. As the Oxford academic, and subsequent Labour cabinet minister, Anthony Crosland (1962: 62) lamented, 'we still have a cult of the amateur . . . and a strong basic hostility to professionalism and expertise and technology . . . top managers, civil servants and the rest, have the attitude of amateurism, and the belief that we can muddle through as we used to in the past'.

In effect, the liberal welfare state's penetration of the Anglophone social fabric was relatively shallow, and its inroads much more easily reversed than the social democratic model in the Nordic countries. Hence, from the 1970s, the commitment to 'getting the state out of people's lives' had a much greater political and cultural resonance in the Anglophone societies. Here, anything more than a very narrowly defined, residual role for the liberal welfare state came to be seen as a threat to the well-being of both individual freedom and the well-being of the nation. Hence the concerted efforts to terminate what is known as 'dependency culture', whereby 'the payment of certain types of social security encourages people to become dependent on benefits and lowers their desire to work or behave in a responsible manner' (McGlone, 1990: 171). As the USA policy analyst Charles Murray (1990: 4), highly influential on post-1970s Conservative governments, explained, 'Britain has a growing population of working aged, healthy people who live in a different world from other Britons, who are raising their children to live in it, and whose values are now contaminating the life of entire neighbourhoods.' Indeed, it was as if the welfare state had not only failed to address material problems, it had also led to the moral collapse of those segments of society that had become dependent on it. 'The national crisis'[18] of dependency culture then justified increasing penalties for welfare fraud and more checks, surveillance and scrutiny of beneficiaries.

Hence, as well, the attempts to reduce the size of the state and the services it provides. The Conservative Party (1979: 20) won the 1979 British general election with a manifesto that read: 'no-one can fail to be aware of how the balance of our society has been increasingly tilted in favour of the state, while diminishing the role of the individual . . . [Conservatives want to reverse that] and thereby restore the balance of power in favour of the people.' By the 1990s, New Labour also wanted to distance itself from the association between state provided welfare and security. As Tony Blair (2002) explained, 'we need to put behind us . . . the 1945 "big state" that wrongly believed it could solve every social problem [and instead build] an enabling state founded on the liberation of individual potential'. As has happened in the Nordic countries, welfare services have been privatized, downsized and contracted out. Here, though, this is not just designed to bring about more efficiency; *it is also designed to bring about a much more extensive restructuring of society at large* – as if individuals will finally be liberated from the tyrannies of state power and the post-1945 welfare aberrations thought to be responsible for this. As the New Zealand Prime Minister explained in 1993, 'for a while, New Zealand lost its way. We forgot the pioneer spirit, the sense of independence, and the community's responsibility for those who fell by the wayside. We said the state can look after this – and that – and eventually we expected the state to look after everything. What we are dealing with here is nothing more nor less than the renaissance of the Kiwi spirit. The pulse of New Zealand is beating again. And with it we are seeing the true spirit of New Zealand: proud, independent, hard-working and caring for your neighbour' (quoted by Kelsey, 1995: 337). And in David Cameron's (2009: 2) invocation of 'the Big Society', the state is to be vanquished altogether: 'the size, and scope of the government in Britain has reached a point where it is now inhibiting, not advancing the progressive aims of reducing poverty, fighting inequality and increasing general well-being . . . the recent growth of the state has promoted not social solidarity but selfishness and individualism. There must be a new focus on empowering and enabling individuals, families and communities to take control of their lives, so we create the avenues through which responsibility and opportunity can develop.' To prevent any obstruction in carrying out these missions, the state's apparatuses of government have also been weakened (it is as if the very term 'bureaucrat' has abusive connotations in these societies[19]). The civil service in Britain was thus reduced in size, from 746,000 employees in 1978 to 480,000 in 2003 (Wilson, 2003). And it was also emasculated, with recruitment to senior positions, particularly under Blair's 'New Labour' governments, from outside the civil service. These 'tsars' are usually funded on short-term contracts with responsibility for the development of specific aspects of government policy, as with the Rough Sleepers Unit noted earlier, in the belief that this will then allow them to cut through bureaucratic obstacles that might otherwise impede policy development.

In these respects, while the universal framework of the social democratic welfare state remains largely in place, that of the liberal welfare state has become still more residual, indicative of the historical differences to the presence of state power in these societies and the way in which it should be used: preventive and protective in the Nordic countries, reactive and punitive in the Anglophone.

Social democratic v Conservative images of society

Francis Castles (1978) used the phrase 'the social democratic image of society' to capture the way in which the Nordic Social Democratic and Labour parties not only regularly won elections (the Swedish Social Democrats were in government, sometimes alone, sometimes as coalition members, from 1932 to 1976), but also the way they had been able to indelibly imprint what they represented themselves as – humane, egalitarian, and inclusive – on the fabric of these societies. Indeed, by 1969, because the very name of Sweden's Conservative Party had become associated with ideological extremism (which meant, in this country, the privatization of welfare services and cuts to direct taxation), it was changed to *Moderaterna* (the Moderate Party). While there might be movements and adjustments within the social democratic welfare polity, it would be very difficult for any political party with aspirations of governing to stand outside of it. Castles has since been overtaken by events, though. Social Democratic and Labour parties no longer automatically win elections in this region. From 1979 in Sweden, Conservative and Centre parties have won four of 10; in Norway, five of 11 since 1981; and in Finland two of seven. Even so, governments of Right and Left have largely continued to develop policy within the social democratic framework. Radical departures from it can lead to electoral disaster: after promising tax cuts at the expense of welfare funding in the 1998 election, the *Moderaterna* vote then declined from 22.9 per cent at that time to 15.2 in 2002. Thereafter, the Swedish Conservative body politic, to distance itself once again from extremist taints, became the 'New Moderates'. In contrast, Anglophone Conservative parties and their equivalents have had most electoral successes, particularly during the 1950s and 1960s, crucial years for determining the overall size and structure of the welfare state.[20] Here, the core beliefs of these parties – free market economics, anti-trade unionism, freedom of the individual and hostility to the idea of the 'big state' – have become the dominant image of these societies. Departures from *this imagery* are then characterized as extremist and irrational. Indeed, since the 1980s, Labour's considerable electoral successes in these countries[21] have usually been accompanied by avid demonstrations of its own commitment to these Conservative principles and disavowals of any socialist heritage it might once have had.

There are four underlying reasons for the presence of these differing images of political dominance. *First*, the route to electoral success of Nordic Labour and Social Democrat parties was facilitated by the relatively small scale nature of industrialization – sufficient to create an industrial working class, but never an urban proletariat whose numbers would sweep it into government. The size of the natural constituency of these parties (that also included religious revivalists and prohibitionists) thus necessitated alliances, compromises and moderation, if political power was to be won. Accordingly, aspirations to achieve 'ownership of the means of production' and to ensure 'dictatorship of the proletariat' became polarizing symbols of class warfare and were dropped in the early twentieth century, leading to an exodus of leftist radicals who then formed their own socialist/ communist parties. As a consequence, the Social Democratic and Labour parties were not seen to pose a threat to the capitalist structure of these societies: they were not going to take over private firms (many industries, such as the railways, were, anyway, state owned), nor were they going to threaten the ownership of private property. On this basis, they were well placed to widen their support base amongst the middle classes (Ericsson, 2004). At the same time, the trade union core of these parties was not the electoral liability it became in the Anglophone countries, where the unions, because of their associations with closed shops, collective bargaining, strikes and conflict, were seen as inimical to national well-being, rather than central to it. Although the unions became particularly strong in Australia and New Zealand, where labour shortages had given these countries reputations of being 'workers' paradises' by the end of the nineteenth century, they remained in fundamental opposition to employers.[22] However, in the Nordic countries, the unions were seen more as another branch of the extensive social movement tradition – indeed, employers' federations were also strong by the end of the nineteenth century – and they had an accepted and central place in industrial relations (Therborn, *et al.*, 1978). In Finland, Norway and Sweden agreements were made in the 1930s between unions, management and government that consensually set economic and social goals.[23]

Second, there was no patrician class able to dominate political life and thought in the Nordic countries. Nor was there a rural proletariat, subservient, deferential and loyal to the great landowners, as in England. Instead, with the family farm as the basic unit of agricultural organization, the *bönder* were able to use their political power against urban elites, to demand the eradication of inequalities and upper class privileges. As such, the drive towards the democratization of Nordic society, coming primarily from rural smallholders rather than a radicalized working class, made possible the emergence of strong Agrarian/Farmers' – eventually Centre – parties. These then provided Social Democratic and Labour parties with opportunities for coalition government. At the same time, their proportional representation electoral systems led to coalition compromises that better fitted the emphasis on agreement and cooperation in these societies than the 'first past the post, winner takes all' majoritarian electoral systems that, for the most part, have been favoured in the Anglophone countries. As Lacey (2008) has shown, the former system also tends to favour left-leaning parties, thereby cementing in the left/centre dominance in this region.

Third, in the 1930s, Social Democrat policies were hailed as outstanding successes. Nationally, the response of the Swedish Social Democrat/Agrarian coalition government to the economic crisis and industrial disorder of the early 1930s had been to reverse economic orthodoxy: rather than cutting public expenditure and imposing further restrictions on welfare benefits, they embarked on a 'massive reflationary policy of government sponsored public works and deficit financing' (Castles, 1978: 25), while simultaneously raising income tax by 20 per cent. Unemployment then fell from 136,000 in 1932 to 21,000 in 1936, while strikes and industrial unrest sharply declined under the new arrangements for corporate government and the planning and development of economic and social policy. In a country where there were few inhibitions about the state's involvement in the economy, and where guarantees of *trygghet*, rather than the pursuit of individual riches, were more compelling, these achievements procured subsequent Social Democrat electoral successes. Their share of the vote increased from 43 to 48 per cent in the 1936 election, which it won with slogans such as 'welfare policy' and 'remember our poor and old people'. They had discovered the key to political power, as Gruchy (1966: 437) later noted: 'to maintain its support . . . the Social Democratic Party has to keep the matter of what is of primary importance . . . in the forefront of economic policy considerations – *and of primary importance is the high level of employment*. Any [Nordic] political party that would not assign very high priority to full employment policy would have a dim political future.' This was vital for the economic well-being of individuals, whose taxes would then help to fund extensions of welfare services. It also fulfilled the deeply embedded Lutheran values given to work. Credentials such as these further ensured that the Swedish right-of-centre parties were drawn into the social democratic framework. As this happened, political debate and strategy became all the more marked by high levels of consensus rather than division. Adler-Karlsson (1969: 18) wrote that 'all the parties of the economic process have realized that the most important task is to make the national cake grow bigger and bigger, because then everyone can satisfy his demanding stomach with a greater piece of that common cake. When instead, there is strong fighting between the classes in that society, we believe that the cake will often crumble or be destroyed in the fight, and everyone will be losers.'

Internationally, the Swedish Social Democrats also received considerable acclaim. For example, the USA journalist Marquis Childs (1936: 3) famously characterized their programme of governance as 'the middle way', bridging the gap between the 'concentration of economic power in the hands of a few men' in the USA and 'the trials and hardships in Russia'. The USA business journal, *Fortune* (May–September 1938: 65), similarly reported that 'Sweden has gone in for a far reaching New Dealism without scaring, overtaxing, or otherwise discouraging private enterprise and investments . . . Sweden has created the greatest boom in her history, the greatest in any peaceful country today – industrial production is up 50 per cent on the 1929 peak . . . unemployment is reduced to a minimum . . . the government has emerged from five years of extensive agricultural subsidies and public works with a healthy budget and a startling method of handling depressions.' In such ways, the Social Democrats were able to present themselves as the natural party of government in this region, locking in a policy framework and structure that would be politically, culturally and bureaucratically difficult to unravel (Lindbom and Rothstein, 2004). Their policies of high taxes and extensive state direction and services had brought prosperity and security to all while maintaining narrow wage differentials. These were not then seen as some sort of aberration, to be jettisoned in favour of the realities of market forces; instead, they became guarantees of *likhet* and *lagom*.

Since the 1980s, although Social Democrat electoral successes have been fewer, radical departures from the social democrat programme have been short lived. For example, after the 1991–1994 centre/right coalition government in Sweden cut taxes and public expenditure and privatized some welfare services, the Social

Democrats were then returned to power in 1994, with an increased share of the vote (from 37.6 to 45.3 per cent). Learning from this, centre/right governments have since concentrated more on the mode of delivery of welfare services, rather than questioning the validity of these services themselves. Both the Social Democrats and the Moderates thus fought the 2010 election on the theme of 'Jobs First'. And, while the right wing populist parties have made political capital out of immigrants receiving the generous welfare benefits of this region, they have been shunned and isolated, rather than given limelight in coalition arrangements, in Finland, Norway and Sweden.[24] Furthermore, the Social Democrats feel no need for name changes or rebranding. Even if it now shines rather less brightly, the same image is still projected: 'our aim is clear: everyone shall be included' (*alla ska med*) . . . when we support each other, everybody wins' ([Swedish] *Social Democrat Manifest*, 2006: 10).

Meanwhile, in the Anglophone countries, the Conservative image of society became dominant. In England, its roots lay in the liberal political culture that was upheld and reinforced by a network of patrician families whose urban and rural interests merged during the course of the nineteenth century. In Australia and New Zealand, these roots lay in the very strength of the labour movement itself. In contrast to the shared Nordic cake that was to be the product of social democratic engineering, in these two colonies, as Siegfried (1914: 211) observed, 'there is a cake to be divided, think the workmen, "let us be as few as possible when the division comes".' Rather than equal shares, each individual had hopes of gaining the largest slice: self-advancement had a higher priority in these societies than in the Nordic. Moreover, the very success of trade union bargaining power in Australia offset demands for any stronger development of the welfare state (Castles, 1978). There was, thus, little political pressure on Conservative-minded governments to introduce more extensive welfare measures. Instead, a particularly restricted version of the liberal welfare state was constructed in this country, leading to the dominance of Conservative values of low taxation and individual freedom, alongside a dislike of 'welfare bludgers' and state officials, following the mateship traditions from the early nineteenth century.

Furthermore, in contrast to the way in which the social democratic welfare state was heralded as a great success, the liberal welfare state neither satisfied those who paid the most in taxation for it, with seemingly little by way of return: Hodson (1948: 74) noted that 'men grow restive under the burden of taxation for how is the middle class man to send his children to university or save up for his old age . . . [T]he government gives singularly little help to the father of a middle class family for rearing his children.' Nor, with its flat rate discretionary benefits, was it able to secure the loyalty or win the trust of claimants and beneficiaries: in *The Family Life of Old People*, Peter Townsend (1957: 159, our italics) reported that 'in old age there were personal needs of a special kind: medicines and appliances to buy which could not necessarily be provided through the National Health Service . . . as well as compensatory things such as radios, house pets, newspapers and periodicals for the housebound and infirm . . . there is virtually no provision for them in "subsistence" payments to the old. *The object of National Assistance is largely to make up income, on test of means, to a subsistence level* . . . a general definition of need is incorporated in its scale rates, and these are applied to individual circumstances, with certain discretionary disregards and allowances . . . this definition of "subsistence" appears completely unrealistic.'

Fourth, the structure of the Nordic media also projected the dominance of the social democratic image. Its prevalent themes were moderation and agreement, and the avoidance of unnecessary emotion, excess or glamour: key values of Nordic society, and values that the social democratic welfare state seemed to safeguard and protect. Scobie (1972: 199) thus observed that, in Sweden, 'the authorities have assiduously avoided any form of advertising on either radio or television, being anxious to escape what they consider to be the awful excesses of American commercial television'. Similarly, Jenkins (1968: 259), on the conduct of current affairs programmes: 'so harmonious and so unwilling to engage in controversy are the Swedes that these programmes are invariably punctuated by long silences and often seem to be on the point of running down altogether.' As regards the widely read Nordic press,[25] 'there are certain boundaries of tolerance that the Norwegian press never crosses . . . a sensation press is unknown in Norway' (Grimley, 1937: 158); 'the Norwegian press reflects a culture with which the vast majority are identified. Yet this "common man's'' culture is not based upon emotional sensationalism or a tendency to simplify human problems in terms understandable to the least common denominator of the Norwegian population' (Rodnick, 1955: 65); 'even if the presentation [of the Norwegian press] was often pedestrian, it was inevitably free from sensationalism and mob appeal' (Derry, 1979: 436).

In contrast, the structure of the media in the Anglophone countries ensured the projection of a dominant Conservative image – one of worthy, aspiring, individuals, held back by state officials or put at risk by dangerous outsiders, such as criminals, immigrants, scroungers, beggars and so on, amidst strident calls for their punishment and exclusion. This has then been exaggerated by the much greater tabloidization of news and features in these countries. Chibnall (1977: 74) has claimed that 'it was not until 1969 and the arrival of Rupert Murdoch's revitalized *Sun* [newspaper] that crime reporting began to sail out of the doldrums'. Its sensationalism not only guaranteed its own success, but also influenced other proprietors and editors to follow in the same direction. Thereafter, Reiner (2007: 142) noted that 'in the last four decades there has been a hugely increasing media focus on crime . . . the proportion of crime stories in two major British newspapers, *The Times* and the *Daily Mirror*, doubled after the late 1960s, from 10 per cent to 20 per cent [of content]'. Of course, since the 1970s, the Nordic countries have not been immune from the deregulation of broadcasting and the introduction of new media technologies that have facilitated the trends towards sensationalism and trivialization in the Anglophone media. State broadcasters in these countries now have to shrug off some of their staid, educational, role and compete with private sector rivals. In all three of these Nordic countries there are now indicators of tabloid-style reporting that then has an ability to undermine the social democratic frame of reference for understanding the world: instead of seeing it in terms of cohesion, solidarity, and the need to redress the injustices experienced by society's victims, those same 'victims' – criminals, refugees, asylum seekers and so on – are now more likely to be seen, in a revamped media, as the enemies of such values.[26]

Nonetheless, the tabloidization of the Nordic news media remains comparatively modest, especially by comparison with England, and its impact continues to be mediated by influential broadsheet journalism that seeks to educate, rather than sensationalize (Lappi-Seppälä, 2007; Green, 2008). Indeed, it would be inconceivable that the levels of intrusion and corruption of the tabloid press in Britain that have been revealed in the Leveson Inquiry[27] could take place in this region. The ethical codes covering journalistic practices are much stronger in these countries and are more rigorously enforced (Green, 2008): a way of protecting relatively powerless citizens from the obtrusions of the powerful, in keeping with social democratic values. Meanwhile, state owned television channels, where programmes with violent themes are little in evidence, still perform public education functions and attract much higher audiences than in other Western countries (Wilensky, 2002). In contrast, in New Zealand, after deregulation and privatization, there is, to all intents and purposes, no longer a state broadcasting company that performs this function (the only country in the OECD where this is so). Overall, while social democratic values are still central to the Nordic media, the Conservative view of the world continues to dominate the Anglophone.

The relationship between welfare provision and population politics

The purpose of the social democratic welfare state was to both improve the material conditions of life of its subjects and also ensure the reproduction of the nation itself. By 1930, Sweden's birth rate was the lowest in Europe, raising concerns about the viability of the Swedish race. Alva and Gunnar Myrdal (1934) were asked to address the problem for the Social Democrat-led coalition government. The central theme of their report, *The Population Crisis* [*Kris i befolkningsfrågan*], was that low fertility was caused, first, by unemployment, which disproportionately affected child-rearing families, immiserating them in poverty and driving married women to have abortions; and second, by poor, overcrowded housing that, again, impacted most on those who wanted children. If the state were to remove these 'living standard penalties', fertility would increase. In effect, reproduction was an issue for the state as well as the individuals involved. By providing the social conditions whereby 'every child would be a wanted child', it would then be able to guarantee its own reproduction: 'the population question powerfully raises the political demand that social relations be altered in such a way that citizens will voluntarily bring a sufficient number of children in the world so that our nation shall not become extinct' (ibid.: 117). However, as Alva Myrdal (1947: 175) later wrote, 'a population policy could not aim at obtaining just more children, regardless of whether they had parental care, regardless of whether they were wanted or not, regardless of whether they were being born at the right time in the right families'. In addition, population policy had to respect the rights of women to seek paid employment –

in accordance with the egalitarian ethos of social democracy and broader Nordic values – rather than confine them to domestic labour. In this way, the 'living standard penalties' that had worked against child-bearing would be minimized. What was then needed, to make up for the deficit of home care, were wide ranging measures of assistance that would allow women to both pursue careers *and* bear children. As such, and indicative of the levels of trust and interdependencies that the homogeneity of these societies engendered, child care provision should be a community – not simply a family – responsibility: 'as the family deteriorates as an environment for raising children, the school or society through some other organ must conceive its task as assuming the functions that have come uncoupled from the family. It must organize collective care for children, so that it harmlessly and efficiently replaces and expands on care at home – in just the measure that home care becomes insufficient' (Myrdal and Myrdal, 1934: 368).

By putting the Myrdals' recommendations into policy (illustrating the links between the intelligentsia and policy making in this region[28]), the Social Democrats were not only able to engineer the reproduction of the nation, they were also able to engineer the reproduction of social democratic polity itself – a large part of the population had a vested interest in maintaining its dominance because of the welfare advantages it gave them: maternity benefits that covered 90 per cent of the population, marriage loans, additional grants for needy mothers and free school meals for all children were introduced in 1937. To ensure that child-bearing was a matter of choice, abortion was legalized in 1938 while, through its sterilization laws, the state would make this choice on behalf of those judged 'legally incompetent' to do so – another demonstration of what was to become a familiar dualism of social democracy: humane and progressive policies on the one hand, authoritarian and coercive policies on the other. In addition, and in contrast to the Anglophone emphasis on home ownership as a means of establishing privacy, boundaries and status, new homes, *designed around the idea of collective living*, were provided by the municipalities and housing associations. Once again, the already existing values of trust and cooperation, emerging from the homogeneity of these societies, informed and were incorporated into the arrangements of the social democratic welfare state. Childs (1936: 51) observed that '*it is the cooperative method,* together with assistance from the state in a variety of ways, that has made low cost housing possible in Sweden. In Stockholm 15 per cent of all families live in cooperative apartment houses . . . there are many cooperative advantages of all member tenants . . . cooperative laundries are equipped with most modern washing machines and mangles. Each woman who desires it is assigned a laundry period by a committee in charge of the laundry. The cost of power for the machines and gas for the mangles and special drying racks is a part of the general cost of maintenance of the apartment building and is shared among all member tenants.' Strode (1949: 205) then noted that 'the Swedish improvements in designs for city living, in which there are no ugly alleys and no unsightly backyards, but green areas for children's play and landscaped gardens, are due in considerable measure to the cooperative housing movement . . . many blocks are equipped with public dining rooms . . . in the kitchens equipped with stainless steel sinks, smooth faced cupboard doors, and glass brick walls, everything is made as convenient as possible. A garbage disposal chute is conveniently located, and beside it a laundry chute. In the basements are washing machines and drying rooms where the housewife may do the family laundry . . . Apartment house nurseries are located on the top or ground floor.'

The state also provided free or heavily subsidized holidays for children and housewives: 'due to the length and severity of the Nordic winter it is of special importance that the brief summer be utilized to build up the health of children . . . since 1945, all Swedish children in families below certain income levels are entitled to travel once a year for a nominal fee' (Nelson, 1953: 265). From the 1950s, it provided daycare centres – the intention was to build up an encompassing system of public child care that would allow both parents to pursue their careers (Lundberg and Åmark, 2001). Thereafter, all the Nordic countries provided financial support during pregnancy and maternity. In Sweden, housewives were given the right to claim sickness benefit. In 1991, *a right* to state-provided daycare for children was introduced and extended in 2000 to unemployed parents. These arrangements may be free, or a nominal fee may be charged – in Sweden, this is one to three per cent of one's salary, compared to around 20 per cent, or around £7,000 *per annum*, in the Anglophone countries. Parental leave entitlements have been gradually extended to their existing levels and provide some of the most obvious distinguishing features between the levels of assistance provided by the two models of welfare state, as Table 3.1 indicates.

Women have been the most obvious beneficiaries of these policies. They have not only been more able to pursue careers but, at the same time, by the nature of 'care work' in the welfare state, are more likely to find employment within it. As it is, public sector employment in the Nordic countries – around 30 per cent – is nearly twice the level of that of the Anglophone. At the same time, it is accredited with considerable status, contributing to the well-being and solidarity of the community, rather than the impediment to economic growth that it is seen as in the latter.

Depopulation had also been a significant concern in England, Australia and New Zealand in the 1930s (see, for example, Hogben, 1938). Beveridge himself had warned that 'the possibility of preventing the ultimate disappearance of the

Table 3.1 Paid maternity leave entitlements, 2010

Country	Entitlement
Finland	18 weeks at 70% salary, followed by 26 weeks shared parental leave at 70% salary
Norway	56 weeks at 80% salary, or 46 weeks at 100% salary
Sweden	69 weeks: 56 weeks at 78% salary, then flat rate of SEK 180 per day
New South Wales	18 weeks at federal minimum wage of A$590 per week
New Zealand	14 weeks at 100% salary or NZ$459 per week, whichever is the lowest
United Kingdom	39 weeks: 6 weeks at 90% salary, then 33 weeks at 90% salary or £129 per week, whichever is the lowest

population' was dependent on 'the kind of world we make for people to live in' (*The Listener*, 6 February 1935: 226). However, although married women had been employed in large numbers during the war, the Beveridge Report had been based, and costed, on the assumption that they would return to the pre war norm of not being in paid employment (as had been the case for seven out of eight married women in the 1931 census): 'in the next 30 years, housewives as mothers have vital work to do in ensuring the adequate continuance of the British race . . . with its present rate of reproduction, [it] cannot continue; the means of reversing the course of the birth rate must be found in incentives for marriage and child bearing' (Beveridge, 1943: 145). Thereafter, if women did depart from their destinies of motherhood and domesticity and seek paid employment, a range of benefit restrictions and disqualifications from entitlements further disadvantaged them (Riley, 1983). Women's exclusive role as mothers received strong ideological support from the medical and psychiatric professions, one area in which experts *were* influential on public and political discourse in these countries. In *Forty-Four Juvenile Thieves*, John Bowlby (1947) argued that the growth of delinquency was due to the wartime separation of children from their mothers. To avoid these consequences of 'maternal deprivation', 'the infant and young child should experience a warm, intimate *and continuous* relationship with his mother . . . in which both find satisfaction and enjoyment' (Bowlby, 1951: 11). In effect, then, child care was the specific and necessary duty of the mother. Similarly, D. W. Winnicott (1957: 126), a leading British psychiatrist, clearly articulated the appropriate post-war role for women in a BBC broadcast: 'talk about women coming back from the Forces not wanting to be housewives seems to me just nonsense, because nowhere else but in her own home is a woman in such command.' And, in conjunction with the same emphasis in popular culture (Kynaston, 2010), the *Royal Commission on Population Report* (1949: 36) reinforced 'the wife's role as companion to her husband, as well as a producer of children'.

These ideological and material pressures to put women back in the home and keep them there after the war had been even stronger in Australia and New Zealand. In the contemporary social policy and welfare literature of these countries there is no discussion of any other possibility. Indeed, in these two countries, only 10 per cent of married women were in employment in 1951, compared to 21.4 in Britain and 70 per cent in Sweden. As Nolan (2002: 63) explains, in relation to New Zealand, the main political parties were 'locked into a political race over domesticity, each trying to outdo the other in their defence of home and family'. Similarly in Australia: the expectation was that, whatever their employment, on marriage women would give this up and become 'homemakers' (Murphy, 2002). Thus, in contrast to the extensive provisions of the social democratic welfare state, the liberal welfare state provisions on population policy were again at a residual level. Family allowances were paid, and visiting nurses were provided for new mothers. Other than this, child care and child-rearing were left to individual families to work out for themselves, rather than the community responsibility such matters became in the Nordic countries. Although Beveridge himself had recommended subsidized holidays for mothers and children, these features of his report were never pursued.

Instead, in the immediate post-war period, the state *withdrew* financial support from the approximately 2,200 child daycare centres in existence in Britain in 1944 (a tenfold increase from 1938), when working mothers were the norm. The vast majority were gradually closed during the late 1940s on the basis that there was no further need for them (Riley, 1983). It was not until the 1980s, when child care and parental leave began to be addressed through the prism of gender equality, that these services materialized again. Now, though, these would be provided mainly by the private sector, some 40 years after these services, provided by and heavily subsidized by the state, had become routine in the Nordic countries. Parents wanting them would usually have to make their own arrangements and pay substantial fees (paid parental leave entitlements were not introduced until the late 1990s in these countries). Unlike their Nordic counterparts, they thus owed no debt of gratitude to the welfare state for relieving them of these burdens: for most, the state's welfare services largely passed them by.

In these ways, then, the two welfare state models – and the ways of thinking about the world on which they were based – built on and reaffirmed the value systems of these societies. The Nordic countries were able to become more cohesive and inclusionary through the universal network of assistance of the social democratic welfare state; at the same time, its universalism attracted high levels of public support. In contrast, because of the limitations of the liberal welfare state, old divisions remained in the Anglophone societies, while new ones opened up, as 'worthy' claimants were pitted against the unworthy, and the deserving against the undeserving: pensioners against the unemployed, those incapacitated by injuries at work against those never able to work because of disability, and so on. At the same time, the discretionary, subsistence level benefits of this model of welfare meant that it both alienated those excluded from receipt while never being able to build up a debt of gratitude from those who did receive them.

Exclusion and inclusion in the age of anxiety

As we have seen though, both welfare models have undergone varying levels of restructuring from the 1970s. This has coincided with, or has contributed to, the disappearance of many of the previous landmarks of security, certainty and stability across modern society as a whole (Bauman, 2001): employment has lost its permanence; religiosity has continued to decline (the Nordic countries have become the most secular in the world, Sundin, *et al.*, 2005); trade union membership and that of other community organizations has reduced; immigration has increased; local neighbourhoods have become unrecognizable through gentrification and migration patterns; the vast riches that the mobility of labour can now bring for a favoured few has been accompanied by the dead weight of poverty for those who have remained immobile; family life and personal relationships have become sites of instability and transience, rather than reassurance and security. These changes in the social landscape of modern society have brought new areas of danger, uncertainty and vulnerability into existence. At the same time, many of the roadmaps of everyday life that had previously been available to bring attention to hazards along the way – often drawn up by the state on behalf of its subjects – have been removed; the new ones that replace them provide only vague sketches of how they should negotiate their way around these new menaces. In this 'age of anxiety' (Holloway and Jefferson, 1997), risks have thus become more incalculable and unpredictable.

What, though, have been the effects of these general transformations, in conjunction with the reconfigurations of their own welfare arrangements, on the particular value systems of the Anglophone and Nordic clusters? In the former, the extent of these transformations has been deepened by a series of political choices to reduce the presence of state governance. There was always something highly suspicious and undesirable about the equality and uniformity that state services demanded, about the regulations to enforce them and the officials presiding over them. During the course of this restructuring, the message from both right and left of the political spectrum has been that the freedom of the individual is to supersede guarantees of state protection, as citizens are exhorted to stride out and make their own way in the world again. Their riches can be celebrated and enjoyed once more, rather than hidden away or removed by confiscatory levels of taxation. But the ties between the individual and the state, which have always been loose in these societies, have become much more flimsy and unreliable in this process. For some, the impediments that the state represented have been taken off them; for others, who have nowhere else to look for help, its promises of assistance have been withdrawn. This means that the distances each individual can travel in their new-found freedoms of choice are even more likely to be determined by their wealth and status. Not only this: they are also likely to have to negotiate all the anxieties and uncertainties they meet on these journeys on their own – the liberal welfare state has neither the power, nor the inclination, nor the resources to alleviate them. It was never intended to act as a 'people's home', of course, but it has since turned into a house to be avoided, if possible, and should be visited only by those on the margins of society. At the same time, secure and wide-ranging interdependencies, that might have provided support, are more likely to have themselves been dissolved.

A growing intolerance has emerged from the loss of familiarity and certainty and the attendant increase in anxiety and insecurity: of those, for example, who are still able to find some relief from the state, even when this has been cut off to many others: *British Social Attitudes* (Park, *et al.*, 2012) thus reported that 54 cent of the British public thought that benefits were too high and 63 per cent thought that child poverty was caused by parents who did not want to work – exact reversals of its findings in 1991. And of those whose race makes them seem 'different': opinion polling in 2010 showed that 68 per cent of the population thought that 'there were too many immigrants in Britain' and 75 per cent favoured a reduction in immigration (Blinder, 2011). Furthermore, Britain's membership of the EU invokes fears of the erosion of national identity and the imposition of threatening or 'different' values by the European Parliament and Court. In Australia, in the late 1990s, there was a sudden surge in support (peaking at 10 per cent nationally, although over 20 per cent in some states) for the One Nation Party, which campaigned against 'race based welfare' and 'the Asianization of Australia'. Notwithstanding the subsequent demise of One Nation as a political force, Australian public opinion polling indicates a significant majority who think that the level of immigration is 'too high' (Markus, 2011). In New Zealand, where 'strangers' have been always been met with a mixture of avid curiosity and suspicion (Pratt, 2006), there were protest marches against Asian immigration in the 1980s and 1990s, as well as high levels of support for the anti-immigration New Zealand First Party. In contrast to the approach taken to its counterparts in the Nordic countries, it became a member of the National-led coalition government of 1996 to 1999, and then the Labour-led coalition from 2002 to 2008. At the same time, with state guarantees of security now much more limited and restricted in these societies, there has also been a decline in trust between the public and governments that tell them their well-being and destiny is now in their own hands. *Eurobarometer 71* (2009) reported a level of only 21 per cent who 'trusted the government' in Britain. In Australia, 30 per cent of the public trusted government (Markus, 2011). In New Zealand, levels of trust in government fell so low in the 1990s[28] that proportional representation replaced the previous majoritarian electoral system, in the hope that this would bring a broader section of public views to parliament and help to rebuild trust in it (in fact, it made it possible for New Zealand First to enter parliament in larger numbers).

In Finland, Norway and Sweden, as well, it is evident that the characteristics of egalitarianism and 'sameness' are no longer so strong. While these three Nordic countries are now among the wealthiest of the Western nations, rather than the poorest, income inequality in Finland and Sweden has increased faster than in most other OECD members, from the mid-1980s to the early 2000s (OECD, 2011: 6). At the same time, Norway's oil wealth has created significant economic disparities (Wessel, 2001). Growing prosperity and consumerism have challenged the hegemony of *lagom*. While country cottages, for example, are as popular as ever in the Nordic countries – ownership of these properties had increased to around one in four Norwegian families by 2005 – 'the main difference from earlier times is that most cabins today have electricity and running water. Many are located next to a skiing resort . . . a new trend is to build luxury apartments in the mountains with outdoor jacuzzi and a panoramic view of the mountains' (Aase, 2005: 23). Or, many Nordic citizens prefer, instead, to purchase holiday apartments in exotic Thailand and similar locations.[30] In Sweden, while the tradition of mass produced but good quality furnishings has been maintained, these products are no longer solely designed with the aim of 'practicalness, durability and cheapness'. Purchases of luxury Swedish glassware, for example, are recommended on the basis that 'it is beautiful . . . it can be a great piece of décor for your home . . . Owning art glass will give you a hobby. You can go out and find new pieces and collect them as you see fit, allowing yourself to have something that is enjoyable to do. It doesn't matter if you collect a few pieces or if you have a whole room full, because everyone can do as they please . . . Collecting art glass is a great investment . . . at a later time in life you can sell off all your glassware and earn substantially more than you paid for it.' [31]

Likhet, too, has been undermined by changes in the racial composition of these societies. Austin (1970: 16) had written that, 'like other [Nordic] peoples, the Swedes are one of the least mixed races in Europe. Their striking appearance, somewhat less varied than that of many peoples, witnesses to their common descent.' However, the subsequent level of immigration, mainly from Eastern Europe and the Middle East, has meant that one in eight Swedes were born outside this country in 2009. Immigration reached record levels (102,000) in 2010, in Norway in 2008 (100,000) and in Finland in 2009 (29,100). The consequences of this swift transition from extreme homogeneity to multiculturalism has meant that Sweden is now characterized, by some, as a place of profound alienation and dislocation, rather than a 'model for a world' (Strode, 1949). In *What happened to Sweden?*, the journalist Ulf Nilson (2007: 154–5) complains that, 'during the early 1990s, immigration rose to record levels with the country's population growing fast, exclusively because of foreigners . . . the newcomers were mainly Bosnians, Albanians from the Serbian province of Kosovo, some Croats and yet more Kurds, Somalis and Iranians. Almost all were Muslims and several mosques were built but no churches . . . in 1994 no less than 83,598 were admitted, which meant that the population grew by almost a full percentage point in that year alone. Another revealing statistic tells us that the number of gainfully employed Swedes, aged 16 to 64, declined from 83 per cent in 1990 to 72 per cent in 1999, a net loss of 420,000 jobs. During the same years the country took in 350,000 asylum seekers. More than 90 per cent could not prove that they risked torture or death if they were sent back. Legally they had no right to asylum, but were given permanent residence permits for humanitarian reasons.' In *Fishing in Utopia*, Andrew Brown (2008: 204), himself an English immigrant to Sweden in the 1970s, writes of returning three decades later to a housing estate, where he had lived, in the provincial town of Uddevalla: 'in the little pizzeria beside the entrance to an underground car park . . . a father and daughter were speaking in Arabic to each other while I sipped my Coca-Cola. Anywhere else they would be classified as white – she in particular was very fair-skinned but I could see that [here] they would count as "black". Their knowledge of immigration seemed infinitely distant from mine, and the Sweden that they had moved to seemed a place about which I knew nothing. The bus I caught back to town in the middle of the day had 10 other passengers. Only the driver spoke Swedish to anyone, which he did with a thick foreign accent.'

It is as if these changes to the texture of the social fabric of these societies has brought risks and dangers that are now beyond the ability of the state to remedy, or has led to high levels of corruption within it. Hence, the themes in the new genre of Nordic crime fiction. James Thompson's (2009) *Snow Angels*, set in Finland, has Inspector Vaara investigating racially motivated killings; Jo Nesbø's (2009) *The Leopard* has the chain-smoking, regularly reforming but just as regularly lapsing, alcoholic detective Harry Hole investigating, not for the first time, serial killings in Oslo. Henning Mankell's (2011) *The Troubled Man* has the disillusioned, troubled and unhealthy Inspector Wallander uncovering political intrigue and corruption as he investigates a murder. And in Stieg Larsson's (2005–7) *Millennium*

Trilogy, a series of gruesome serial murders investigated by the journalist Mikael Blomkvist and Lisbeth Salander, a female computer hacker working for a *private* security firm, unlock the door to intrigue involving corrupt state officials and right wing political conspiracies. Of course, the disenchanted, dissolute detective, working in a quasi-independent capacity from his own police authority, which is, at best, ineffective and, at worst, sinisterly corrupt, is nothing new in Anglophone detective fiction. State power has always been viewed with suspicion in these societies: gifted amateur 'sleuths'[32] working outside of state organizations showed up their incompetence. Now, however, the need to work outside of the state itself, whether this is because there is much less chance of working successfully within it, or because the state and its bureaucracies have become organizations to be feared, has come to the Nordic countries. That crime in this genre is now solved by outsiders, or by individual detectives who have personal lives that in the past would have been thought to be highly reprehensible and dysfunctional, rather than, *or in spite of*, the organizations of government, is emblematic of the weakening of the ideal of the Nordic 'strong state' and all that it could accomplish. This has become a prevalent theme in the business and current affairs periodicals that had once been so full of wonder at Swedish welfare developments. *The Economist* (16 November 1991: 12), for example, carried a report headlined 'Government Shakes Off the State', going on to quote 'an imaginative representative of the building industry' who told its reporter that '"This is like the fall of the Berlin wall. Socialism has gone."' Similarly, eminent voices from the academy proclaim 'the fall' of Sweden's 'strong state', and that 'centralism, rule by experts and large-scale solutions are criticized. Policy steering has been reshaped, as central planning and common national norms have had to bow to demands for local influence, decentralization and individual freedom of choice' (Lindvall and Rothstein, 2006: 50).

Nonetheless, these changes, this disenchantment, along with the political decline of the Social Democrats and the dimming of the social democratic image of society, *have still not been sufficient to drain away the longstanding characteristics of moderation, restraint and forbearance in the Nordic countries*. Racial tolerance, in fact, seems strikingly high in comparison to the Anglophone countries. The *Stockholm News* (27 December 2009) reported opinion poll findings of 56 per cent of Swedes responding in the affirmative to the question 'whether or not immigration has been for the most part positive for [this country].' In another poll undertaken by *The Christian Science Monitor* (29 July 2011), '60 per cent of Norwegians had a positive attitude towards immigrants'. As do levels of trust in government: 57 per cent in Sweden and 54 in Finland (*Eurobarometer 71*, 2009). If the state's capability to provide security is no longer as extensive as it was, there has been no significant departure from the expectations that this *should* be its role. Ultimately, when social problems do occur in the Nordic countries, *these are not represented as the failure of the welfare state but as demonstrations of the need for more welfare resources*. Thus, after a shooting massacre at a school in Jokela, Finland, in 2007, the Finnish President, in her New Year address, stated that 'we have grown accustomed to seeing the functioning of our society to be self-evident, and it is good that we can have confidence in the security of everyday life. But it must not mean indifference, and should not lull us into a false sense of security. *Basic services need to be taken care of.*' (*Helsingin Sanomat*, 2 January 2008: 1, our italics).

At the same time, despite the changes to the structure and parameters of the social democratic welfare state, there is no intention to dismantle it, as has been the boast and intention of mainstream politicians in the Anglophone countries. Instead, Ugelvik (2013: 2) writes, of Norway, that 'the welfare state is everywhere and everywhere it is trusted and regarded as mostly benevolent . . . It is a source of Norwegian pride and identity and, as a national symbol and rhetorical trope, all-important for the legitimacy of many state initiatives.' It remains the case that the Nordic countries have the highest expenditures on social welfare, the highest direct taxes and the lowest income differences in the OECD (Lappi-Seppälä, 2011). They also have some of the highest *per capita* expenditure on education.[33] In Finland, in 2010, free education, up to and including MA level, was available to all. In Sweden, 'immigrants are entitled to free Swedish language instruction, and children of immigrants can receive both extra Swedish language for schoolwork as well as extra lessons in their native language' (Svensson, 2009: 106). The respect for distinguished scholars remains. The internationally renowned law professor Johannes Andenaes, at the University of Oslo, was given a state funeral on his death in 2003. Rather than eroding social capital – shared norms or values that promote social cooperation, instantiated in actual social relationships' (Fukuyama, 1995: 27) – the framework of the social democratic welfare state has been able to strengthen and sustain it, in contrast to the vague evocations of 'community spirit' and 'Big Society' that are somehow meant to spring into life in the Anglophone countries once state organizations have been weeded out of the social fabric. Rothstein (2001: 234, our italics) argues, in relation to Sweden, that 'the amount of social capital seems to have *increased* since the 1950s'. Not only are there high levels of confidence in political institutions, but there are also still high levels of involvement in civil society and social movements. Thus 'around 48 per cent of the adult population is regularly engaged in volunteering . . . [for] around 16 hours of work a month . . . Sweden has a long history of volunteering, dating back to the early twentieth century, which rose out of popular movements fighting for temperance, free churches or labour rights' (Fouche, 2010: 1).

In these ways, the strong interdependencies, reciprocities and civic respon-sibilities that became a feature of Nordic life during the course of the nineteenth and early twentieth centuries can still direct and inform everyday relations and interaction. A sign at the entrance to woods on the outskirts of Oslo, in 2006, thus read, 'Welcome to the City's Forests . . . These are our common property. Wherever you move around in these forests, you have rights and responsibilities. Take care of the forests and the animals and plants there. Help us keep the area clean . . . You can ride on all roads covered with gravel during the summer and on roads cleared of snow during the winter. But riding is forbidden between 11.00 am and 15.00 pm on Saturdays, Sundays and holy days. For other travel by horse, you need permission from the authorities. When on horseback, you must pay attention to other users of the forests . . . You can bathe in all rivers and lakes where there are no restrictions to protect drinking water. The same rules are valid for rowing and paddling in a boat you might have brought with you . . . Fishing is permitted from land in all rivers and lakes that are without restrictions to protect drinking water . . . You can camp (with tents) wherever you want, except at spots with restrictions to protect drinking water and at special shores reserved for bathing.'[34] In contrast, in Wellington, New Zealand, there were three signs to the entrance to woods on its outskirts in 2006. One indicated, with drawings in circles with red lines through them, that no guns, fires, bicycles, camping or taking of plants were allowed. A second warned car owners to 'lock it or lose it' – the responsibility for its safety was all theirs. A third warned dog owners, 'Don't risk a fine. Keep your dog on its lead and clean up its mess.' The Norwegian sign, which speaks of shared rights and responsibilities, that needs no threats or warnings to enforce its rules, that emphasizes all the activities that are permitted in the forests, rather than everything that is disallowed, is characteristic of an inclusionary society. Here is another illustration of the way in which social control can be internalized by informal mechanisms in these societies – through self regulation, family, friends, keeping face by maintaining or not deviating from expected standards – without the need for more punitive state sanctions. However, the New Zealand signs, which proliferate as each new problem behaviour comes to light, and where each individual is informed that they are responsible for their own conduct, where they are warned of what is not allowed rather than what they can do, and of the criminal penalties that follow rule breaking, are indicative of a more exclusionary society: a society where individuals are taught, formally and informally, to look after themselves rather than the general community, and where, because of weak interdependencies and declining levels of trust, the threat of punitive action by the state is necessary to maintain order and stability. These signs did not come about by accident or happenstance. Instead, they incorporated ways of seeing, understanding and thinking about the world that have been developed over the last two centuries in the value systems of these societies.

What now follows is an account of the way in which these different ways of seeing, understanding and thinking about the world have informed the respective routes of modern penal development in these societies.

4 The introduction of modern penal arrangements

During his tour of the Nordic countries, Edward Clarke (1823: 223) came across 'testimonies of capital crime and punishment [in a Swedish forest] . . . These consisted of three trunks of fir trees, stripped of the branches and leaves. Upon the tops of which as gibbets were fastened three wheels, for exposing the mangled carcass of a malefactor in three separate parts . . . this man, it seems, had committed murder.' He had come across the Nordic equivalent of England's 'Bloody Code'. At the end of the eighteenth century, there were 68 capital offences in Sweden and around 300 in England. Executions took place in public across these societies. Tyburn Gallows had been the most well known location for public hangings in England, until this came to an end in 1783 because of the prolonged disturbances associated with these events. Thereafter, executions were usually held outside the local prison – Newgate prison in London, for example – before crowds of up to 50,000. In the Nordic countries, the location of the execution varied: it might be at the scene of the crime, or at a prominent place in the offender's home community (where, in Sweden, attendance was compulsory for local citizens), or at a crossroads, for obvious symbolic reasons. And, in both clusters, if death itself were not sufficient expiation of the crime, a series of aggravated penalties were still available, variously involving the mutilation and exposure of the corpse. Dickens' (1860/1996) *Great Expectations* opens with an English country landscape that had gibbeted corpses swinging in the wind in the background. In the Nordic countries, execution usually involved decapitation by axe, followed by dismemberment and the public display of body parts; this is what Clarke had seen.

All the drama and theatre of punishment, and the messages it was meant to convey, were associated with these spectacular public executions. The prison at this juncture played only a minor administrative and significatory role. Used mainly as a holding place until the accused's fate was determined, its conditions were squalid, disorganized and chaotic, as John Howard discovered in his tours of British and Nordic prisons. In the former, he saw 'half-starved prisoners, some come out almost famished, scarce able to move, and for weeks incapable of any labour' (Howard, 1777/1929: 30). As he later reported, things were much the same in the Nordic countries. In Stockholm, for example, 'one prison had six rooms, four of which, having their windows nailed up, were very dark, dirty and offensive. Here were Swedish prisoners almost stifled, in consequence of receiving no air except through a small aperture in the door of each room. The gaoler here, as in other prisons, sells liquors . . . His room, like those I have seen too often in my own country, was full of idle people who were drinking' (Howard, 1792: 83).

Around 1870, however, the death penalty had been almost wholly restricted to offences of murder[1] across these societies, and public executions had been abolished.[2] Furthermore, all the aggravated death penalties had been removed: in England, the beheading of the corpse, in 1820; gibbeting, in 1832; hanging in chains, in 1834; in Norway, all aggravations came to an end in 1815; from 1832 the body parts and head were to be removed from their poles three days after execution (rather than left indefinitely) and buried; from 1833, the head was still to be placed on a pole after execution, but the body was to be buried immediately after the event; and all displays on the pole were abolished in 1842 (Sørnes, 2009: 55–6). Meanwhile, as punishment to the human body declined in use and became more restricted in scope, so the prison became more central to the development of modern penal systems. The early nineteenth century penitentiary experiments in the United States, involving the Philadelphia separate system (cellular confinement for the duration of sentence with visits only from the prison authorities) and the Auburn silent system (work in association during the day in silence, separate confinement at night), were highly influential in both clusters.[3] Ultimately, however, the separate system (with its echoes of Jeremy Bentham's panopticon[4]) became the prototype for the design and operation of Pentonville Model Prison, opened in London in

Figure 4.1 Botsfengslet, Oslo, Norway, seen from across the cabbage field maintained by the prison. Photograph: Wilse/Oslo Museum.

1842, and Oslo *Botsfengslet* [penitentiary], opened in 1851 (see Figure 4.1). In England, another 55 prisons were built in this style between 1842 and 1850 (see, for example, Figure 4.2). Sweden had built 45 'separate system' prisons by the 1880s and, with 2,500 cells, it could house virtually all its prisoners in this way. Although there was more piecemeal development elsewhere in these clusters, separate cell confinement remained the aspiration of both Anglophone and Nordic prison administrators during the second half of the nineteenth century.

Unremarkable similarities, then, in the respective transitions from pre modern to modern penal arrangements in these societies, and the introduction of a new 'economy of punishment', whereby one would now pay for one's crime through

Figure 4.2 Armley prison, Leeds, exterior, south elevation. An example of the new style prison architecture in the mid-nineteenth century. Photograph: Courtesy of English Heritage.

deprivation of time and enforced isolation, rather than intense physical pain (Foucault, 1977). *However*, there were also important differences in the respective Anglophone and Nordic adaptations of the modern penal arrangements that were then put in place. *First*, in relation to the death penalty: although it steadily declined in use from the mid-nineteenth century in the Anglophone countries, it remained available as a sanction for murder until the mid-twentieth.[5] In the Nordic countries, however, it had virtually come to a *de facto* end in the 1870s. In Finland, the last execution was in 1826, although formal abolition was not until 1949; in Norway, the last was in 1876 with abolition in 1902; in Sweden, there were only five between 1877 and 1910, with abolition in 1921. *Second*, in relation to the prison. This became a place of *deliberate* suffering, hardship and privation in the Anglophone countries during the second half of the nineteenth century. In England, the Report of the Commissioners Appointed to Inquire into the Working of the Penal Servitude Acts (1879: 1, our italics) stated that '*penal servitude is a terrible punishment. It is intended to be so; and so it is*'. In New South Wales, the Report of the Comptroller-General of Prisons (1892: 2, our italics) explained that 'those who complain that prisoners are not reformed in gaols should remember that gaol is not a reformatory, nor is it an asylum. *It is a place to which offenders against the law are to serve certain periods under stern and strict discipline as a punishment for crimes and as a warning to others.* It cannot reasonably be expected that a prisoner who reaches the hands of the gaol authorities as a dishonest man, with criminal tendencies, can be turned into an upright and respectable citizen by prison treatment.' And, in New Zealand, the Report of the Inspector of Prisons (1899: 3, our italics) noted that '*the main object of imprisonment is to punish* . . . [and] it behoves others to undertake the work of reformation'.

In the Nordic countries, however, imprisonment was intended to have more productive possibilities, leading to reformation. This had been signalled in the Norwegian Report of the Penal Institutions Committee (1841: 707): 'there can be no talk of throwing away the fruits of the Enlightenment, civilization and industrialization; hence, the classes who have so far not been able to utilize these must be included in them.' In these respects, the purpose of imprisonment was designed to bring about the moral improvement of the inmate by 'making him used to order, discipline and industriousness', so that he would then become an 'impeccable, productive and useful citizen' (ibid.: 462). In Finland, the 1864 Report of the Penal Law Commission stated that 'the penal law should not be used solely to support general legal security and the maintenance of the authority of the law and to provide for the possibility of meting out punishment in a just proportion to the seriousness of the offence; *instead, in a truly Christian spirit it should also attempt to further the reform of the fallen offender and his achieving a new start* through the use of measures which can be connected with the force of punishment without the punishment losing its severity and repressiveness' (quoted by Lahti, 1977: 122, our italics). Even if, as here, severity was to be built into the penal system, this was not to be its only focus: it was to be exercised in combination with other influences intended to make the inmates better people. Indeed, in Sweden in the second half of the nineteenth century, the penitentiaries were referred to as 'betterment prisons' (Nilsson, 2003: 9). The Director of the Royal Prisons Board, Sigfrid Wieselgren (1895: 3), thus affirmed that 'the [separate cell] prisons . . . replaced the old means of punishment that was obliged to the retribution and deterrence theories; one is looking [instead] to accomplish the perceptible discipline through separate confinement, by which the punishment always should be united with the elimination of bad influences, without which the rehabilitation of the fallen, as far as one can judge, will be made impossible and his human rights violated'.

In such ways, the inclusionary and exclusionary value systems of these societies had already begun to influence their respective courses of penal development: in the Nordic countries, we see moderation and restraint – these societies no longer needed the dramatic excesses of pre modern corporeal sanctions to maintain order and cohesion, and lawbreakers were thought to be redeemable; the prison was not to act as an impenetrable barrier between them and the rest of society. In the Anglophone countries, however, punishment, for most, had come to be remorseless and unforgiving in their modern prisons, rather than confined to a few moments of agony during execution. In these respects, the prison now assumed most of the death penalty's significatory role, sending out warning messages of its capability to break offenders down and crush them. It was at this point only that reformers could get to work on whatever remained. How, though, did these different adaptations of modern penal arrangements come into place?

The death penalty in modern society

One reason for the more rapid termination of the death penalty in the Nordic countries is to be found in their constitutional arrangements. In the first half of the nineteenth century, the monarch was more directly involved in governing the Nordic countries than in England (and its colonies[6]). In the latter, particularly in the aftermath of the Great Reform Act 1832, parliamentary democracy was well established, and the monarch had already become a largely symbolic non-political head of state. Sweden, in contrast, was still governed by its Diet, and Finland was ultimately ruled by the Russian Tsar. Accordingly, the commutation of Finnish death sentences to transportation to Siberia in 1826 is attributable to the anti capital punishment sentiments of Nikolai I, who became Tsar of Russia and its dominions in 1825. In both Sweden and Norway (where the monarch still held executive powers and responsibilities), the power to commute death sentences was vested in the King in person, rather than a crown minister. In his book *On Punishment and Punishment Institutions [Om Straff och Straffanstalter]*, which was particularly influential because of the high standing of the Swedish monarchy at that time,[7] Crown Prince Oscar of Sweden (1840: 11–2) emphasized what, for him, was the repellent nature of this task: 'before the decision is made, the mind is painfully engaged in a search for what is the most just, and afterwards the memory of the sorrowful topic lies heavily on it . . . In order to fully comprehend the importance of this remark, it would be necessary to imagine oneself in the place of the Monarch; and to consider, when an average of 61 cases of death penalty sentences yearly are brought forward in Sweden [around three quarters of which were pardoned] how great a portion of his time is taken up, for the nature of these cases cannot be compared with ordinary administrative questions.' In England and the colonies, however, although decisions regarding commutations and pardons were made by the King in Council, in practice it was the King's ministers, as members of the Council, who took these decisions (see Gatrell, 1994: 543–4).

But there is more to understanding the different place of the death penalty in the modern penal arrangements of these societies than the whims and consciences of monarchs, on the one hand, and the constitutions of governments, on the other. There is also the way in which their respective cultural values were instrumental in providing different ways of seeing, understanding and thinking about this sanction. This is reflected, first, in *the differing modes of knowledge* that were brought to bear on this matter, and, second, in *the differing behaviour of the crowds* at public executions in the two clusters of societies during the first half of the nineteenth century, and the subsequent reactions of the authorities to them.

Modes of knowledge

In the Nordic countries, the most important part of the legislative work of government in the nineteenth century was (and still is) carried out by specialized committees (nominally, at least, independent of government) which considered Bills before they were submitted to parliament. The purpose of these committees has been to interpret legislation in advance in the form of *travaux préparatoires* (Schmidt and Strömholm, 1964). Furthermore, 'when a committee is appointed . . . it is often constructed so that the results of its work cannot be affected by petty things like parliamentary process or public opinion' (Elwin, 1977: 290): in other words, the experts sitting on the committees drove policy – parliamentary processes and debate became secondary to it. In contrast, law reform bodies in the Anglophone countries – Parliamentary Select Committees or Royal Commissions – had their memberships selected by the government of the day, meaning that these bodies were likely to be dominated by its own members and sympathizers. In the first half of the nineteenth century, the various appointed Nordic Criminal and Penal Law Commissioners were jurists, law professors and civil servants, as well as practicing lawyers and judges. However, it was the law professors and civil servants who seem to have had the most influence on the contents of the various reports – as was to be expected in these societies in which a high value was placed on education, and where employment in the state bureaucracies carried high status.[8]

By the same token, judges in these societies have never enjoyed the elite status they have had in the Anglophone. Instead, from the Middle Ages, Nordic judges have sat with lay assessors (who have had the power to override them) in making findings of guilt and deciding sentence. In effect, the Nordic judges were neither above the rest of the community nor detached from it, nor did they wear any of the wigs and gowns that, for the English judges, were meant to signify such superiority and detachment: 'a Swedish law court studiously avoids all the bewigged pomp and circumstance of a British court' (Austin, 1970: 45). Rather than being selected for a life 'on the Bench' on the basis of charismatic and dazzling courtwork, as in

England, the Nordic judges have trained for this profession as a career ('high flown eloquence and appeals to sentiment [by counsel] are almost completely unknown in Sweden': Schmidt and Strömholm, 1964: 11). Beforehand, they are likely to have been career civil servants, with experience in drafting Bills, or other forms of judicial administration. They thus have different experiences of life than the Anglophone judges, with their privileged backgrounds – most certainly in the nineteenth century – revolving around private education or attendance at leading public schools and universities, followed by induction in courtroom gossip and anecdote.[9] Such elitism in England had been further strengthened by the judges' constitutional standing as a counterweight to any overreaching parliaments. However, in the Nordic countries, any such displays of pomp and grandeur were wholly out of place. In addition, the judges were not exempt from the insistence on uniformity and consensus: 'among the general public . . . *there is much suspicion against an independent judiciary* . . . All in all contemporary political life reflects a general view that the judiciary may not carry out a policy of its own but must identify itself with the policy of the ruling majority' (Schmidt and Strömholm, 1964: 36, our italics). At the same time, the Lutheran heritage provided an innate caution against making outspoken, condemnatory judgments of others. Thus, while the Nordic judiciary are likely to consider themselves as members of a select corps within the public service, they have never looked upon themselves as having greater influence or 'say' in public affairs than other officials. Their task has been to state what the law is, without the pontificating and moralizing that came to be one of the characteristics of the Anglophone judges[10] whose status, upbringing and constitutional position encouraged them to do exactly this. At the same time, the scope for Nordic judges to act in such ways was, anyway, greatly restricted: the intent of the law had already been set out for them in the accompanying legislative prescriptions. In contrast, in the common law Anglophone societies, it was the judges who interpreted intent and fitted this to existing case law (which, in itself, was framed through their own elitist understandings of the social order).

Accordingly, the respective law commissions and advisory bodies set up to bring about the modernization of penal law in the early nineteenth century brought very different modes of knowledge to this task. In the Nordic countries, Enlightenment thought was very influential, particularly Beccaria's (1764) *On Crimes and Punishments* (it had been translated into Swedish in 1770). He was opposed not only to the aggravated death penalties of the pre modern world, but the death penalty itself: 'the punishment of death is pernicious to society, from the example of barbarity it affords. If the passions, or the necessity of war, have taught men to shed the blood of their fellow creatures, the laws which we intended to moderate the ferocity of mankind should not increase it by examples of barbarity.' In addition, he envisaged a democratization of the criminal justice process. Rather than the criminal law being used to uphold the privileges of the powerful, legal power and authority should be invested, instead, in the civic body as a whole: 'laws which surely are, or ought to be, compacts of free men, have been, for the most part, a mere tool of the passions of some, or have arisen from an accidental and temporary need. Never have they been dictated by a dispassionate student of human nature who might, by bringing the actions of a multitude of men into focus consider them from this single point of view: the greatest happiness for the greatest number' (ibid.: 12). At the same time, the quantity of punishment to be imposed should be proportionate to the crime committed (to prevent unnecessary excesses) and determined in advance in penal codes written by these '*dispassionate students of human nature*', rather than left to the discretion and whims of judges: 'when a fixed code of laws, which must be observed to the letter, leaves no further care to the judge than to examine the acts of citizens and to decide whether or not they conform to the law as written: when the standard of the just or the unjust, which is to be the norm of conduct for all; then only are citizens not subject to the petty tyrannies of the many which are the more cruel as the distance between the oppressed and the oppressor is less, and which are far more fatal than that of a single man, for the despotism of many can only be corrected by the despotism of one; the cruelty of a single despot is proportional, not to his might, but to the obstacles he encounters' (ibid.: 24).

Such ideas – reductions in the intensity of punishment, with a view to bringing about greater social cohesion, and codification as a means to preventing tyranny – variously informed the Nordic penal reform commissions of this period. The Swedish Law Commission (1815) took the view that the death penalty was 'barbaric and could only make people hardened and alienated towards the law . . . It could neither improve nor deter and goes against the civilisation of the times.' It was the opinion of the Commission that the sanction would disappear altogether as society itself continued to evolve, driven on by the emphasis now given to rationality and science, rather than the superstitions and emotions of the pre-modern era, even if the Commission was not convinced that this level of cultivation had yet been achieved in Sweden (which led to its decision to recommend the retention of the death penalty for murder cases and those that endangered 'the safety of the state'). In addition, the Commissioners situated penal reform in the context of broader international developments, as if, in so doing, this gave further legitimacy to their proposals: these would ensure that Sweden would be part of the progressive, post Enlightenment world of reason and civility that was sweeping through the rest of Europe. Thus, the Swedish Law Commission's (1826) Proposition refers to German and French jurisprudence, as well as abolitionist reforms in other jurisdictions – Hanover, Saxony, Wurtemberg and Weimar in Germany, Swiss cantons, and Louisiana in the USA. As a subsequent Proposition (Swedish Law Commission, 1832) concluded, the continued presence of the death penalty went against 'the civilization of the times'. Furthermore, any arguments based on the supposed deterrent effect of the death penalty had little purchase in these homogeneous, egalitarian and poor societies. There were no great accumulations of wealth and property that needed to be protected from the predations of the lower classes by this sanction; and its use appeared unseemly and unnecessary because of the sense of solidarity that the high level of uniformity in the population had created: those who were executed were likely to be seen as being just the same as any other citizen, rather than wild outsiders.

In addition, in societies where moderation and restraint were paramount, revenge and the emotions underpinning it should have no place in the administration of punishment. Crown Prince Oscar (1840: 6) thus wrote of the quandary of retaining the death penalty: 'society has undeniably the right, as well as the duty, to punish every action which can interrupt the public order of justice . . . But should this right go further than the loss of freedom? Every punishment that reaches outside of this boundary enters the territory of revenge.' The Norwegian Report of the Penal Institutions Commission (1841) thus argued that the death penalty should be abolished: those who supported it 'did not understand human nature – utterly harsh punishment hardens instead of deterring.' Instead, it was the duty of the Norwegian state to move the human race towards its 'great goal' of allowing 'justice and truth to rule in a reasonable world', without the need for its authority to be upheld by such a dramatic sanction; this was how the world should be (even if at that time, it was still thought necessary to retain the death penalty in 'extreme cases', specifically premeditated murder, aggravated robbery with loss of life, and treason). In Finland, the decision on whether the *de facto* abolition of the death penalty that had been in place since the 1820s should become *de iure* periodically resurfaced, as successive law reform commissions resumed their work on drafting the penal code. That of 1862 had proposed to retain the death penalty for treason and murder, safe in the knowledge that any such sentence would be automatically commuted to transportation, following Nikolai I's dictat. Here, too, prominent jurists played a leading role in popularizing the abolitionist cause, particularly Karl Gustav Ehrström, Professor of Law at the University of Helsinki. For him, the death penalty represented 'the disgrace of our time'. In a series of newspaper articles in 1859, he explained that reducing crime was not attainable by fear, but through the strength that came from religious and moral education: 'punishment has to be a just atonement that should generate the reform of the offender' (quoted by Blomstedt, 1964: 439–40).

However, Enlightenment influences were much less prominent in corresponding attempts to modify penal law in England. When introducing legislation to restrict the availability of the death penalty in 1808, Sir Samuel Romilly, then the country's leading jurist and an enthusiast, himself, of Beccaria, complained that 'in the criminal law of the country, I had always considered it a very great defect that capital punishments were so frequent . . . No principle could be more clear than that it is the certainty, much more than the severity of punishments which renders them efficacious. This had been acknowledged ever since the publication of the works of the Marquis Beccaria; and I have heard . . . that upon the first appearance of that Work it produced a very great effect in this country. *The impression, however, had hitherto proved unavailing; for it has not, in a single instance, produced any alteration of the criminal law; although in some other states of Europe such iterations have been made*' (Hansard [UK], HC Deb, 18 May 1808, col. 395, our italics). Indeed, any limitations on the Bloody Code were unwelcome amongst powerful sections of British society. Lord Ellenborough, for example, a judge himself, was of the view that '*terror alone could prevent the commission . . . of crime* . . . although the law as it stood was but seldom carried into execution, yet the terror was precisely the same . . . the apprehension of no milder punishment would produce anything like safety to the public interest' (Hansard [UK], HL Deb,

30 May 1810, col. 197, our italics). In societies with such lengthy social distances and wide social divisions as England, there was still a place for terror in its penal practices: these made it too insecure a society to do away with this sanction, while the lack of interdependencies that was the result of these divisions gave no encouragement to the development of abolitionist sentiments. Indeed, it was claimed that Romilly's intentions to reduce the ferocity of punishment were based on mere 'speculation' and 'theories' – which was enough to damn them in a society that preferred hard facts to ideas, and was highly suspicious of its intellectuals. Sir James Mackintosh MP, for example, thus preferred 'the testimony of bankers and merchants to the mere declarations of the learned gentlemen' (Hansard [UK], HC Deb, 23 May 1821, col. 967).

Thus, while the infliction of the death penalty was indeed restricted during the first half of the nineteenth century in England, there was little reference to this being part of a more general move towards a 'better society' that was characteristic of similar developments in the Nordic countries. Instead, reducing its availability was justified on the basis that this would make the criminal justice system more efficient and *more of a deterrent* than it currently was. The multiplicity of death sentences only created sympathy for offenders: juries refused to convict and, even if they did, judges might then use their discretionary powers to avoid execution. As a consequence, justice, Romilly (1820: 126) explained, had become a 'lottery.' Fewer and less severe penalties – but greater regularity in their imposition – would bolster the element of fear in the criminal justice system while eliminating the 'dangerous sympathies' for the offender caused by the capricious brutality of the Bloody Code. In this way, punishment would be used more sparingly but with greater certainty: it would *inevitably* expel and destroy under these circumstances, thereby more effectively bolstering and protecting the existing social structure and its divisions and hierarchies (McGowen, 1983). In contrast, in the more egalitarian Nordic countries, the death penalty was not needed for these purposes: this sanction, it was anticipated, would eventually have no place in the 'reasonable world' that these societies were moving towards, one where 'justice and truth' would prevail.

These Enlightenment principles were then built into the penal codes that the respective Nordic law commissions drew up during the nineteenth and early twentieth century: codification was essential to ensure that the quantity of punishment was determined by experts at this stage, rather than judges presiding in a particular case: the Nordic judges had no right (nor did they claim any such right anyway, given the different juridical cultures of these societies) to stand between government intentions and policy development. However, attempts to limit judicial discretion in England for these same purposes were met with fierce resistance (resulting in *consolidation*, but not codification, of the criminal law in the 1860s): the different standing of judges gave them the right to occupy exactly that position. Replying to a further attempt by Romilly to reduce the number of capital statutes in 1813, the Solicitor-General stated that 'if discretion must be vested somewhere, where it could be so safely reposed than as with the judges of the land? Always reserving too, an appeal to the fountains of mercy – an appeal which, whenever good cause could be shown in support of it, had never been made in vain' (Hansard [UK], HC Deb, 17 Feb 1813, col. 562). Indeed, it was as if the intended modernization of penal law was merely some sort of undesirable continental practice that led to greater tyranny rather than less, endangered individual freedom rather than protected it: William Windham MP stated that 'he could not help looking with an eye of jealousy on all such visionary schemes, which had humanity and justice for their ostensible causes. What had we witnessed within the last 20 years? Had not the French revolution begun with the abolition of capital punishments in every case? But not till they had sacrificed their sovereign, whom they had thus made the grand finale to this species of punishment' (Hansard [UK], 1 May 1810, col. 768). In this society, punishment, in the form of the death penalty and the signs and symbols it gave out, was seen as a *guarantee* of freedom (it would frighten the lower classes, in particular, away from crime), whereas in the Nordic it was thought to *endanger* freedom.

By the same token, the standing of the English judges and the deference to their opinion also ensured that they, rather than any criminal law intelligentsia, were particularly influential on the law reform bodies. This can be seen in the conclusions of the Royal Commission on Capital Punishment (RCCP), which sat from 1864 to 1866. Its membership consisted of one lord, eight MPs (five of whom were lawyers), two judges and one civil servant. It had been convened to consider 'the provision and operation' of capital crimes and whether 'any alteration is desirable . . . in the manner in which such sentences are carried into execution'. To these ends, it heard evidence from 36 witnesses and, in addition, '*the opinions of all Her Majesty's judges as well as of other prominent criminal lawyers have been researched*' (RCCP, 1866: 1, our italics). The Commission was not prepared to consider the case for abolition but, instead, took the view that, in addition to treason cases, the death penalty should remain for those murders committed with 'malice aforethought'. What seems to have influenced it, and have given it the authority for its conclusions, was the evidence of the judges and 'prominent lawyers' in the extensive discussions on the deterrent effects of this sanction. Although 30 witnesses were heard on this particular matter, with only the narrowest of majorities (16–14) in the affirmative in the evidence, the judges and barristers unanimously maintained it did act in this way. Only one jurist gave evidence – the little known Dr Leone Levi, Professor of Commercial Law at the recently established, but still low status, King's College, University of London (it then offered only evening classes to 'working people'). Levi was an abolitionist, and quoted Beccaria in support of his arguments. However, his evidence was then followed by that of James Fitzjames Stephen, barrister-at-law and judge, educated at Eton, Britain's most exclusive public school, and Trinity College, Cambridge, and subsequently renowned for his views that 'criminals should be hated' (Stephen, 1883: 82). In his opinion, based entirely on the death penalty cases in which he himself had prosecuted or adjudicated, 'the sentence of capital punishment deters people from crime more than any other . . . people are aware that murder is punishable by an ignominious expulsion from the world. They therefore get to consider murder as a very dreadful thing. They associate it with an ignominious death long before they have ever had any notion of committing the crime' (Minutes of Evidence,

RCCP, 1866: 254). He peremptorily dismissed international evidence that contradicted his assumptions. When questioned about Tuscany, for example, where the death penalty had been abolished for 80 years, his reply was that, 'I do not know anything about the state of society, or the national character or the circumstances of Tuscany and I therefore cannot give an opinion on that point . . . what I have written upon the subject I have based principally upon my own experience' (ibid.: 255).

The evidence of three of England's leading judges, all members of the Court of Exchequer,[11] was similar in tone. Lord Cranworth (also educated at Eton and Trinity College, Cambridge) maintained that 'murder is a crime so much beyond all other ordinary crimes, that I think society is justified in restricting, as far as possible, its commission by the most deterring punishment, and I have no doubt whatever that the fear of death is infinitely more deterring than the fear of any other punishment' (ibid.: 1). For the privately educated Baron Bramwell, 'you punish because the law threatens punishment; if punishment were not inflicted, the law which threatened it would be idle.' As for the international abolitionist trends, his view was that 'we cannot rely upon the effects of a change from capital punishment to some other punishments in foreign countries because we do not know enough of the particulars to place any dependence on the reported results' (ibid.: 29–31). As with Stephen, evidence from societies that showed how it was possible to live without the death penalty was not thought worth considering. Baron Martin, educated at Winchester (a close rival to Eton) and Trinity College, Dublin, acknowledged that he appeared 'very seldom in a criminal court' but was nonetheless confident that 'for the purpose of forming a real judgement upon the efficacy of capital punishments you must have recourse to persons who are well acquainted with the lower classes . . . *my idea is that punishment must be a terror to them*, and that in the event of the committing of murder they will be punishable by death' (ibid.: 56, our italics). The main body of the Nordic penal law intelligentsia had taken the view that the death penalty was associated with pre modern excesses that should have no place in the modern world, a world to which they wished to belong, and a world that was now offended by the presence of the death penalty, as they saw beyond their own Nordic boundaries. Here, though, such lofty ideals were irrelevant to the senior judges and lawyers who provided pivotal opinion on its future in the Anglophone societies. For these elite members of British society, it remained a necessary sanction if the awe and power of the state, that was embodied in it, was to be maintained: punishment still needed to be a 'terror' to those on whom it would be inflicted – 'the lower classes' – far removed from the high status coterie who decided this on their behalf. Furthermore, failure to use this sanction when it was available would only bring the law and, by inference, the judges, into disrepute.

Crowd behaviour

By the mid-nineteenth century, crowd behaviour and the general conduct of public executions also demonstrated great differences in the way in which the death penalty was seen and understood in the two clusters of societies. The 1840s witness accounts of William Thackeray, in England, and Bjørnstjerne Bjørnson, in Norway, provide clear illustrations of these differences. Thackeray (1840: 154–6) described the execution of François Courvoisier outside Newgate prison: 'the character of the crowd [at 6.00 am] was as yet, however, quite festive. Jokes bandying about here and there, and jolly laughs breaking out. All sorts of voices issued from the crowd, and uttered choice expression of slang . . . the front line, as far as I could see, was chiefly occupied by blackguards and boys – professional persons, no doubt, who saluted the policemen on their appearance with a volley of jokes and ribaldry . . . the audience included several peers, members of the House of Commons, a number of ladies armed with opera glasses, some foreign princes and Counts . . . from under the black prison door a pale quiet head peered out. It was shockingly bright and distinct; it rose up directly, and a man in black appeared on the scaffold, and was silently followed by about four more dark figures. The first was a tall, grave man: we all knew who the second man was. "That's he, that's he", you heard the people say . . . His mouth was constricted into a sort of pitiful smile. He went and placed himself at once under the beam . . . the tall grave man in black twisted him round swiftly in the [right] direction, and drawing from his pocket a night cap, pulled it tight over the patient's head and face. I am not ashamed to say that I could look no more, but shut my eyes as the last dreadful act was going on which sent this wretched guilty soul into the presence of God . . . 40,000 persons of all ranks and degrees – mechanics, gentlemen, pickpockets, members of both Houses of Parliament, street walkers, newspaper writers, gather together at Newgate at a very early hour; the most of them give up their natural quiet night's rest, in order to partake of this hideous debauchery, which is more exciting than sleep, or wine, or the last new ballet, or any other amusement they can have. Pickpocket and peer, each is tickled by the sight alike.'

Bjørnson (1898: 113, our italics) remembered how, as a child, he had watched the execution of Peer Hagbo in Norway in 1842. This had taken place at a crossroads seven miles from Hagbo's village. As the procession, made up of the condemned man, the clergy and a military escort, moved towards it, 'by the wayside stood people curious to see [Hagbo], and they joined the procession as it passed along. Among them were some of his comrades, to whom he sorrowfully nodded. Once or twice he lifted his cap . . . it was evident that his comrades had a regard for him; and I saw, too, some young women who were crying, and made no attempt to conceal it. He walked along with his hands clasped at his breast, probably praying . . . *A great silent crowd stood round*, and over their heads one saw the mounted figure of the sheriff in his cocked hat. The Dean's speech [in Danish] was neither heard nor understood, but it was short. His emotion forced him to break off suddenly. One thing alone we all understood: that he loved the pale young man whom he had prepared for death, and he wished that all of us might go to God as happy and confident as he who was to die today. When he stepped down they embraced each other for the last time . . . [Bjørnson's father, the local pastor, then spoke], following up the thunderous admonition of the execution itself, he warned the young against the vices which prevailed in the parish – against drunkenness, fighting, unchastity and other misconduct . . . as for me, I left the place sick at heart, as overwhelmed with horror, as if it were my turn to be executed next. Afterwards I compared notes with many others, who owned to exactly the same feeling.'

Both authors were profoundly affected by what they had witnessed – but they had witnessed very differently conducted events. For Thackeray, the crowd's total lack of empathy for Courvoisier seemed even more disturbing than the execution itself. Crowd behaviour had not always been like this on these occasions, though. In the eighteenth century, it could be sympathetic to the condemned, to the point of trying to rescue them, or bawdy and insensitive; similarly, the condemned might make a bold speech against injustice, might be joyfully anticipating an imminent heavenly welcome, or might be desperate with fear (see Radzinowitz, 1948; Gatrell, 1994). Now, however, with the weakened social bonds and interdependencies brought about by industrialization and urbanization, the loss of another person's life, in this particularly demeaning and humiliating way, led only to carnival and ribaldry (probably exacerbated by the increasing rarity of these occasions[12]) – nothing more than this. Meanwhile, Courvoisier's exchanges with the crowd had been reduced to 'the pitiful smile' he gave before the hood was placed on his head. In the pre modern era, the fate of the condemned had often been vicariously shared by the crowd, as if they experienced the pain of one of their fellow citizens being torn away from them. By the mid-nineteenth century, however, the unity between the onlookers was brought about by avid curiosity and unrestrained celebration that the imminent despatch of the person on the scaffold – now known only on the basis of his difference to the surrounding crowd – provoked.

At the Norwegian execution, though, it was as if those in attendance had no wish to lose a citizen who still seemed very similar to themselves in all other respects. The loss was met with sorrow, rather than celebration. In addition, the pastor played a much more central role in the event than the chaplain in England, where their public ministrations had become minimal. Indeed, whereas Thackeray is preoccupied with the crowd scene, Bjørnson gives predominance to the work of the pastors. On such occasions, the pastor's presence marked the culmination of lengthy preparations with the condemned (that sometimes could take months). It was the pastor's duty to instruct the prisoner that it was possible for the latter to influence his own salvation, and that it was never too late to ask for God's forgiveness, no matter what the crime had been: for Lutherans, forgiveness did not come from deeds, but from faith. Sofie Johannesdatter, who was, in 1876, the last woman to be executed in Norway, is reported to have said before her beheading, '"Now I am going home to Jesus." She then read a hymn to the 3,000 people who had gathered to watch the execution' (*Aftenposten*, 18 February 1876: 1). At the same time, such occasions obviously provided the pastors with the opportunity to affirm their own civic authority in these communities – for which there was, then, no equivalent in the more fractious Anglophone societies.[13]

Not every Nordic execution followed the pattern described by Bjørnsen;[14] nonetheless, the solemnity of the occasion and the sorrow of the crowd were the predominant themes of nineteenth-century witness accounts in Norway and Sweden. Clarke (1823: 261, our italics), describing an execution in Stockholm, noted that 'at nine in the morning the throng in the road was so great that carriages could not approach. *Many spectators were in tears.*' Not only this: it also seemed that the executions were likely to threaten social cohesion and solidarity, rather than bring fragile unity, as in England. After another execution in Stockholm, 'An Old Bushman' (1865: 84) observed that 'if the public papers speak the feelings of the people, in all probability this will be about the last capital punishment in Sweden.' Indeed, the influential Swedish law professor, Knut Olivecrona (1866/1891: 237, our italics), in *On the Death Penalty* [*Om dödsstraffet*], maintained that '*the execution of the death penalty has a demoralizing effect on the people*'. After it took several blows of the axe to deliver the *coup de grâce* to Olaves Andersson, near Oslo, *Aftenposten* (17 July 1868: 1) complained that 'outstanding people from all kinds of professions now want to abolish the death penalty. Why do the authorities need to force a man to perform the barbaric act of chopping the head off another man with an axe?'

While there were a handful of private executions still to come in Norway and Sweden from 1870 to 1910,[15] this sanction was allowed to fall into disuse in this region with little further controversy. In Norway, it ceased to be mandatory for murder in 1867, although, by then, commutation to life imprisonment had become the norm, rather than the exception, in these cases. Rather than routine commutation bringing the law into disrepute – the fears of some of the English judges – it was claimed in the Norwegian parliament that 'it is almost 20 years since the last execution was held in this country, and the consistent use of the right to pardon seemed not to have offended the common sense of justice or reduced the rule of law' (Stortinget, 1896: 27). Indeed, it was more likely that these sentiments were strengthened by commutation rather than weakened by it: again, judges were expected to support public policy, not demonstrate their detachment from it. Thereafter, the abolition recommendations of the 1896 Penal Code Commission, with Professor of Law Bernard Getz as its chairperson, were incorporated in the 1902 Penal Code. In Finland, the recommendation of the 1880 Law Commission that the death penalty should be *optional* in murder cases was finally incorporated in the 1889 Penal Code. Although six death sentences were passed between 1895 and 1917, these were all commuted. There were no more, in peacetime conditions, before eventual *de iure* abolition. In Sweden, Olivecrona (1866/1891: 199) proclaimed that, 'while the process of civilization has ensured that many of the previous barbaric practices and punishments, such as slavery and torture, have disappeared . . . it now only remains to obliterate the death penalty – this last remnant of barbarity'. As a member of the nobility estate, he had been able to put forward these views in the 1863 Penal Code debates in the *riksdag*, resulting in it becoming an *optional penalty* in murder cases in 1864. After being made a judge of the Supreme Court in 1868, he was then able to ensure that virtually all applications for pardons and commutations were granted. In the foreword to the second edition of *On the Death Penalty*, he (ibid.: i) maintained that 'with the level of civilization now reached amongst the Swedish people, *the death penalty is no longer absolutely necessary to fully secure the legal security in the country, and as all punishment that oversteps the limit of necessity, it is unfair and should no longer be used'*. That is, the stability and cohesion of this society did not need the threat of this sanction to reinforce it. Eventual abolition in Sweden, in 1921, was mentioned by only one newspaper, which simply stated the decision had been 'long overdue'.[16] This was what the awe and theatre once associated with the death penalty had been reduced to: an irrelevance to the social arrangements of these societies, which were conducted according to the principles of moderation and restraint.

However, while the Nordic authorities had wanted to protect the crowd from the sights of public executions, in England it was the behaviour of the crowd itself, rather than the executions, that had become repellent to observers such as Thackeray. At the execution of Franz Muller, *The Times* (15 November 1864: 5, our italics) complained that 'he was hung in front of Newgate. He died before such a concourse as we hope may never be again assembled either for the spectacle which they had in view or for the gratification of such lawless ruffianism as yesterday found its cope around the gallows . . . *Muller died with dignity, the only one showing this.*' But, both the Report from the Select Committee of the House of Lords (1856) and the RCCP (1866) recommended the abolition of *public* executions, while maintaining support for the death penalty per se. Sensibilities relating to the death penalty extended to the manner of its application but not its very existence. Here, the death penalty seemed to maintain and secure the social fabric rather than endanger it. When conducted with due solemnity, its presence, even if now set 'behind the scenes', would continue to provide an important symbolic message in these more divided and less solidaristic, less forgiving, societies. On this more restricted basis, capital punishment maintained the support of prominent public figures such as Dickens, Thomas Carlyle and John Stuart Mill.[17] The shift from public to private executions, rather than abolition, also occurred in New Zealand and New South Wales, notwithstanding some settlers who argued that public executions gave important messages to Maori and Aborigines about the might and strength of Imperial power (although there were also worries amongst them that this mode of execution put disconcerting ideas into the heads of these indigenous races).[18]

Ultimately, while the abolition of the death penalty was taken for granted in the Nordic countries at this juncture, it was its retention – as a punishment to be carried out in private – that was taken for granted in the Anglophone. In England, *The Times* (14 March 1878: 9, our italics) reported that 'the storm which once seemed to be gathering has subsided and has been followed by a great calm. *Abolition no longer has a place among the real questions of the day.*'

Executions, symbolism and solidarity

During the first half of the twentieth century, there were further restrictions on the use of the death penalty in the Anglophone countries (it had already fallen into abeyance in New South Wales before final abolition[19]). Any ostentatious remnants of its presence, such as tolling chapel bells and the hoisting of a black flag at the prison where the execution was taking place, were removed, and press attendance was prohibited from 1934 in England, so that its only public manifestation would be in the form of a small death notice posted outside the executing prison. Nonetheless, important sectors of these societies clung on to this sanction, still fearing that social order would collapse without its support.[20] These included senior judges and leading members of the Church of England, most members of the respective Conservative parties, most of the British House of Lords, and, post-1945, a sizeable majority of public opinion.[21] In these societies, replete with barriers and divisions, with strong senses of individuality but weak interdependencies, where extensive social distances led to fears and fantasies rather than restraint and moderation, the presence of the death penalty, even if now more symbolic than real,[22] was still needed. It protected the rest of society against the monstrous out-siders that seemed so much more plentiful here than in the more homogeneous Nordic countries. 'Why should depraved creatures . . . be kept alive, imprisoned at vast expense to the public purse, spreading corruption with their baleful influence . . . with the opportunity of hatching further diabolical plots against their fellow men?' (Hansard [UK], HL Deb, 19 July 1965, col. 456). In New South Wales and New Zealand, especially, those who argued against this were regularly accused of 'sentimentality': those who had failed to prosper in these lands of opportunity should be held responsible for their own fate. Indeed, in these colonies it was thought that there was something effete and unmanly about arguing for abolition and about the fanciful metaphysics on which the abolitionist cause was based: 'whether we deal with this from an emotional or sentimentalist point of view, or what is called a humanitarian point of view, we have eventually got to deal with the world as it is, and the world is not made up too much of sentimentality or emotion but of the stern facts of reality' (Hansard [NSW], 3 Sept 1925: 578); 'all this pseudo-humanitarianism is undermining our social stability', (Hansard [NSW], 23 March 1955: 3257); 'in my opinion, the evidence of those men of practical experience deserves far greater weight than the evidence of what I should like to call . . . misguided sentimentalists' (Hansard [NZ], 16 Nov 1950: 4285).[23] By the same token, during the first half of the twentieth century, research that contradicted the death penalty's assumed deterrent powers could be simply ignored. As usual in these societies, the work of experts and intellectuals was held in low regard: one British MP thus claimed that 'statistics do not conclude the matter. Not all human reactions can be measured by statistics, and statistics of crime have little to say about the deep-seated beliefs that govern the conduct of those who refrain from crime . . . It is important that murder should be regarded with peculiar horror – that horror is in itself a powerful psychological barrier against killing. Since statistics give us no help, let us try common sense. Death, I should have thought, is more feared than any other punishment' (Hansard [UK], HC Deb, 16 Feb 1956, col. 2560). In contrast, the support of *public opinion* for this sanction was thought to be a further justification for retention. The thinking of 'ordinary people' – always a potent argument in these countries – should lead policy development, rather than have this entrusted to the state and its officials. As the Conservative peer Lord Salisbury[24] explained in 1956, 'abolitionist members [of parliament] are not only ignoring their electors, but defying them. The public must be trusted all the time, and we must be guided by their views when they are ascertainable, whether we personally consider them right or wrong. Anything else makes nonsense of our democracy' (quoted by Christoph, 1962: 149–50).

Nonetheless, it was in the post-war period that social cohesion finally seemed strong enough to hold together without the prop of the death penalty. Only now did it become possible, in these Anglophone societies as well as the Nordic, to argue that 'we do not punish for the sake of punishment. Retribution has long since ceased to have any relevance' (Hansard [NSW], 24 March 1955: 3226). In an editorial in support of abolition, *The Times* (18 December 1964: 11) made the point that 'execution has degenerated into a totem, and totems have no place in adult societies': the drama and emotion that this penalty had previously invoked, to help hold this society together, had become superfluous. Indeed, at this junction, there was also more willingness to allow rationality and knowledge to supersede common sense and anecdote in the determination of policy. In a debate on capital punishment in the New South Wales Assembly, it was thus claimed that 'psychology and psychiatry have a greater place in deciding what punishment shall be inflicted on offenders. The modern school favours corrective punishment – over the old revenge or deterrence' (Hansard [NSW], 28 May 1949: 574). In England, a new RCCP was established in 1949, with its 12 members now including the famed Professor Leon Radzinowitz, a psychologist, 'a writer', a trade unionist, a professor of law, and two lawyers – but no judges. Its subsequent conclusion (RCCP 1953, para 65) that 'there is no clear evidence that the abolition of capital punishment has led to an increase in homicide' removed its deterrent credibility, and was influential in Australia and New Zealand, as well as England.[25] At the same time, a new belief in the power of the state, after its wartime accomplishments, would allow public opinion to be overridden: as one British abolitionist MP put the matter, 'I doubt very much whether at the moment public opinion is in favour of the change, but . . . there are occasions when this House is right even if the public may not at that moment be of that opinion' (Hansard [UK], HC Deb, 10 February 1955, col. 2083).

While it remained, for some, a legitimate symbol of the state's power to punish, the death penalty had now also become a symbol of tyranny and barbarity that had no place in the Western democracies: 'repressive punishments belong to the systems of totalitarian states and not democracies. It was no accident that the chief exponents of violence and severity in the treatment of criminals in other times were Nazi and Fascist states' (Hansard [UK], HC Deb, 14 April 1948, col. 1014–5). Even so, although abolished in New South Wales in 1955 and New Zealand in 1961, it endured a lingering death in more divided England: it was merely 'suspended' in 1965 (the House of Commons voted 200 to 98 in favour, the House of Lords 204 to 104), before final abolition in 1969.

Imprisonment

These clusters of societies had had a shared involvement in the birth of the modern prison. Why, then, did their respective prison systems begin to diverge so sharply in the second half of the nineteenth century?

Prison as deterrent

What the purpose of prison should be had been highly contested in England from the 1840s to the 1860s. The champions of the separate system as put into practice in this country (18 months of isolation from 1842, rather than the entire sentence as at Philadelphia; and then reduced again, to nine months in 1850, following concerns about its deleterious mental and physical effects[26]), particularly the prison chaplains, believed that it could bring about the prisoners' penitence and reformation (Anderson, 2005: 147).[27] Indeed, in the mid-nineteenth century, the chaplains were pivotal figures in the administration of English prisons, reporting only to the governor and even, in some instances, sharing prison management with them (see, for example, Nihill, 1839). However, the design and administration of the new model prisons that were conducive to the separate system also provoked great criticism: while less eligibility had been injected into the administration of the Poor Law, it had not yet found its way into the penal system – quite the contrary, in fact. The journalist Hepworth Dixon (1850: 153) found that, at Pentonville, 'the diet is better, richer than in other prisons'. And Mayhew and Binney (1862: 120), also visiting Pentonville, reported on the 'wondrous and perfectly Dutch-like cleanliness pervading the place . . . [It was] extremely bright and cheerful . . . with its long, light corridors, it strikes the mind, on entering it, as a bit of the Crystal Palace, stripped of all its contents.' Furthermore, Home Office civil servants were, at the time, of the opinion that it would be unconscionable for the prison diet to be used as 'an instrument of punishment' – hence Dixon's comments, and those of Mayhew and Binney (1862: 130) that 'the most genuine cocoa we ever supped was at a Model prison'. However, these conditions of confinement seemed utterly luxurious when compared to those of most of the populace, as Dickens (1849–1850/ 1992: 714) satirized in *David Copperfield*: making a tour of what was meant to be Pentonville, Copperfield observed that 'it being, then, just dinner time, we went first into the great kitchen, where prisoners' dinner was in the course of being set out separately, with the regularity and precision of clockwork . . . I wondered whether it occurred to anybody that there was a striking contrast between these plentiful repasts of choice quality and the dinners, not to say of paupers, but of soldiers, sailors, labourers, the great bulk of the honest, working community; of whom not one man in 500 ever dined half so well.' Similarly, the essayist Thomas Carlyle (1850: 44) wrote of one 'palace prison' he visited: 'gateway as to a fortified place; then a spacious court, like the square of a city; broad staircases, passage to interior courts; fronts of stately architecture all round . . . surely one of the most perfect buildings within the compass of London'. Such was the disquiet at the revelations of conditions within these 'palaces' that the architect Henry Roberts (1850: 4) warned that 'the nation surely cannot long allow such a contrast to exist between the comparative domiciliary comforts enjoyed by those who have forfeited their freedom as the penalty of crime, and the wretched home from which at present too many of our labouring population are tempted to escape to the gin palaces or the beer shops'.

In these new prisons, those whose criminality had made them the least deserving members of these societies experienced little of the miseries of institutionalization now forced on those whom not even the most hard-nosed economic liberal could hold responsible for their own travails: workhouse orphans such as Oliver Twist (Dickens, 1838/1992), for example. The Prisons Acts of 1865 and 1877 were intended to rectify these distortions and injustices, and the way chosen to do this was by *lowering* the living conditions in the prisons, rather than *raising* those in the workhouses. Driven by the ferocity of the criticisms of the 'palace prisons', the Report from the Select Committee of the House of Lords on Prison Discipline (1863) had recommended that imprisonment should be used for deterrent, rather than reformative, purposes. Accordingly, the first part of the progressive stage system (initial separation followed by increasing levels of association with other prisoners) would be transformed from being a period of reflection and penitence to one that was intended to break the spirit of the prisoner: 'the especially penal character of the first month of sentence – a period of strict and so far as is possible, unbroken isolation – is maintained for all prisoners' (Report of the Commissioners of Prisons, 1884: 11). But this, rather than being the centrepiece of the prison experience, as originally envisaged, was merely the preliminary to a much more systemic routine designed to break and overwhelm.[28]

This was to be achieved by unifying and modelling the prison regime on 'hard bed', 'hard fare' and 'hard labour' principles, as provided for in the legislation of 1865 and 1877. It was Du Cane who then put these principles into effect (and those who served under him subsequently brought his ideas to the colonies of Australia and New Zealand[29]). Now, less eligibility was able to make a grand entrance to the prison systems of these societies. *'Hard work'*: prison labour was to be afflictive rather than productive, with much of it performed on treadwheels and cranks (see Figure 4.3).[30] These 'hard labour machines' were installed in each English prison after the 1865 legislation, with the effect that '[prisoners are] placed on the treadwheel during the first month for six hours each day . . . the speed of the wheel being 32 feet per minute and five minutes rest is allowed for each 15 minutes of work . . . In places where for any reason a treadwheel is not available, cranks are made use of' (Report of the Commissioners of Prisons, 1888: 10). *'Hard beds'*: the prisoners would sleep on wooden planks. *'Hard fare'*: the prison diet was to be severely restricted. The Report from the Select Committee of the House of Lords on Prison Discipline (1863: 498, our italics) explained that 'cocoa and meat were unnecessary luxuries and that the functions these provisions performed could be provided by other less extravagant means: cocoa as a stimulant could be replaced by fresh air; meat as a nutrient should be replaced by other farinaceous substances and vegetable foods, *so that the main elements of prison diet would consist of bread, rice, oatmeal, potatoes, milk and liquor.*' Thereafter, the Report of the Commissioners of Prisons (1878: 10) noted that the prison diet 'has the great merit of simplicity and economy, and we have every reason to believe that it furnishes sufficient and not more than sufficient amount of food to all persons subjected to it'. Food servings then came to consist mainly of 'stirabout' (low quality porridge), the quantity of which was measured to the last 1/16 of a gramme,[31] such was the exactitude in the degree of deprivation that was to be inflicted. In New South Wales, the diet was designed to be 'as low as is consistent with health with

Figure 4.3 Treadwheel at HMP Kingston, Portsmouth, Hampshire. Photo: English Heritage.

due provision for exercise' (Report of the Comptroller-General of Prisons, 1885: 2). In New Zealand, Captain Arthur Hume, the first Inspector of Prisons, introduced a new diet 'to make imprisonment more rigorous' (Report of the Inspector of Prisons, 1895: 3).

Furthermore, rules regarding hygiene, dress and diet were also designed to humiliate the prisoners, to make them aware of the shamefulness and degradation to which they had been reduced, and the gulf that now existed between them and the rest of society. Their heads were thus regularly shaved and they had to wear highly stigmatic, often multi-coloured uniforms. Balfour (1901: 36) remembered how, on being received into prison, 'there appeared a person dressed in the most extravagant garb I had ever seen outside a pantomime. It was my first view of a convict . . . the clothes were of a peculiar kind of brown (which I have never seen outside of a prison), profusely embellished with broad arrows. His hair was cropped so short that he was almost as closely shawn as a Chinaman. A short jacket, ill-fitting knickerbockers, black stockings striped with red leather shoes completed his appearance.' Notwithstanding periodic reservations from some officials about these practices, the Report of the Committee of Inquiry on Prison Rules and Prison Dress (1889: 44, our italics) was of the opinion that any relaxation of the rules on uniform *'would produce in the mind of the prisoner and of the public the impression that certain classes of offenders are exceptionally favoured'*.

As these exclusionary, deterrent policies began to thread their way through the prison systems of the Anglophone societies, so the values and standards of the world outside the prison began to shrivel away within it. The prisons would increasingly be run according to their own, specifically penal values. Furthermore, those who might have had the power to challenge these intentions now found that their authority had been largely removed. *First,* under the provisions of the 1865 legislation, the chaplains were made subservient to uniformed chief officers, to whom they had to report, thereby signalling an end to their status in prison administration and the redemptive possibilities of the prison that they envisaged (a downgrading that matched what was happening outside the prison, as the values of industrialists and entrepreneurs became more significant than those of clerics: Perkin, 1969). They now wrote little of note in their annual reports, which were appended to the main report of the governor. In some cases, they wrote no report at all, and were given only a passing reference in the governor's document – as at Birmingham prison, for example: 'the services in the chapel have been thoroughly performed by the chaplain, who reports favourably on the behaviour of the prisoners' (Report of the Commissioners of Prisons, 1879: 18). Sir Edmund Du Cane (1885: 158), Assistant Director of Prisons from 1865 and then, from 1877 to 1895, Director of the English Prison Commission, the centralized bureaucracy that had been established to ensure uniformity in prison administration, was contemptuous of them. He spoke, for example, of the 'burlesque absurdity' of making inmates learn sections of the Bible by heart, as had occurred at Reading prison under the Reverend John Field's chaplaincy. Indeed, with their post-1865 change in status, they became peripheral figures around the prison, decorative but largely powerless. The embezzler Jacob Balfour (1901: 68, our italics) was greeted with the following advice from the chaplain as he began his prison sentence: 'it's lucky for you . . . that you have come just at this time. The governor who has recently left was a very severe man indeed. Things are bad enough at present, and even now I would warn you to be very careful of the warders. *You are wholly in their power.*' So too, most likely, was the chaplain himself. When he and Balfour witnessed the beating of a prisoner by officers, he dolefully remarked: 'it's no good . . . there's nothing we can do' (Balfour, 1901: 224). In the Australian and New Zealand reports, the chaplains hardly receive any mention at all. For example, in New South Wales, the Report of the Comptroller-General of Prisons (1901: 4, our italics) states that 'moral and religious instruction is carefully conducted by the various chaplains . . . *it is to be regretted that unavoidable circumstances render it impracticable to increase their visits to various prisons*'.

Second, the doctors now had to perform their work in accordance with the values of the prison system, rather than their Hippocratic Oaths. Their previous discretionary power to award extra rations or to supplement the prison diet had been removed by the 1865 legislation. They now had to justify, in writing, any additions to the 'hard fare'. The Report of the Commissioners of Prisons (1878: 10) noted with approval that 'a check may be put upon the very undesirable practice which prevailed in some prisons of supplanting the authorized diet by extra issues, which has been carried to such an extent in certain instances as virtually to set aside the authorised diet'. In addition, educational provision – of a minimal nature for most outside the prison, anyway – was even more so within it. In some English prisons – Bristol, for example – no education at all was provided (Report of the Commissioner of Prisons, 1879: 18). At Strangeways, Manchester, 'there is one schoolmaster for 741 prisoners, and he is not a schoolmaster really, he is a warden schoolmaster' (Report of the Departmental Committee on Prisons, 1895: 261). It was similar in the colonies. In New South Wales, it was noted that 'at present the female prisoners receive no educational attention. Male prisoners in six gaols have fair opportunities for schooling. [But] not much is practicable in this direction, nor is much done. *The teachers combine scholastic duties with those of storekeeper, clerk or some other office, and possibly attach more importance to the latter work. They are not trained men and consequently labour under serious disadvantages*' (Report of the Comptroller-General of Prisons, 1896: 75, our italics). In New Zealand, Hume was of the view that 'endeavouring to educate prisoners is a mistake . . . The assembling of prisoners together for the purposes of school tends to great irregularity . . . it stands to reason that a man who has performed his day's allotted task of hard labour cannot possibly benefit by attending school in the evening' (Report of the Inspector of Prisons, 1881: 20). Du Cane (1885: 79) himself was anyway of the opinion that 'many prisoners form a class of fools whom even experience fails to teach'. The result was that, where it was provided at all, education became a privilege that had to be earned, rather than an essential component of improvement and reintegration. As the Report of the Prisoners' Education Committee (1896: 6) noted, '[in England] secular education has hitherto been subservient to labour and no evidence has been adduced in favour of any alteration to this principle amongst the chaplains and schoolmasters'.

England led the way in the construction of these meticulously tailored regimes of suffering, but Australia and New Zealand pursued the same intentions, if sometimes with other means. In the former of the two colonies, a reintegrative approach to most lawbreakers had marked the earlier years of transportation (Braithwaite, 2001).[32] However, as free settlement increased from the 1830s, the convict origins of the country were thought to be a shameful stain that put off investment and endangered further immigration. As Harris (1847: 223) put the matter, 'general society cannot be said to exist in [New South Wales], particularly in the shape of public balls, reunions and concerts when you may expect to find the person on your right a murderer; him on the left a burglar'. Thereafter, a concerted effort was made to write Australia's convict origins out of its own history (Hughes, 1987; Tsokhas, 2001; Smith, 2008). Hence, the development of a much more exclusionary penal policy based around imprisonment, rather than assigned works, as had initially been the case. Furthermore, whatever the power of 'mateship' to provide social cohesion outside of the prisons, there was little semblance of this within them. Prisoners embodied the convict past that all respectable Australians now wanted to forget. This not only further distanced them from the rest of society but seemed to give justification to the prison authorities to assemble their own instruments of discipline in order to ensure complete subjugation: irons, variations of wooden and leather gags, 'spreadeaglings' and whips.[33] Meanwhile, in New

Zealand, Captain Hume maintained that 'prisoners should have their meals in their cells, and be kept quite separate, except when on the works, at exercise or at Divine service. The existing system of prisoners having their meals and spending spare time in association is most detrimental to prison discipline' (Report of the Inspector of Prisons, 1881: 1). He then continued: 'I would also recommend that the birch rod [that is, whip] be introduced in prisons, as it has been found in English prisons that birching, whilst being a safer punishment than flogging, at the same time, by placing the recipients on the footing of boys, has a humiliating effect and is therefore a deterrent and a valuable addition to the cat[34] as a means of punishment' (idem). In this country, the very existence of prisoners threatened its claim to be a 'Better Britain': their presence reduced this otherwise pristine and pure society to the level of Australia, and thereby justified and provoked the additional brutalities that were inflicted on them – as if strokes of the birch would have the effect of some sort of social cleansing and purging of the impurities they represented.

Such strategies were reflections of, rather than aberrations from, the social arrangements of these societies, in which prisoners were seen as being at the bottom of their lengthy hierarchies of moral worthiness. Du Cane (1875: 302–3) was of the opinion that they had characteristics that were 'entirely those of the inferior races of mankind – wandering habits, utter laziness, absence of thought or provision, want of moral sense. The cunning and dirt that may be found in their physical characteristics approach those of the lower animals so that they seem to be going back to the type of what Professor Darwin calls our "arboreal ancestors".' Even prison reformers were repelled by them. William Tallack (1889: 216), the founding Secretary of the Howard Association, thought that prisoners were 'not very drunken as a class, but incorrigibly lazy. Work is the one thing they most abhor; they are often too indolent to wash themselves; they prefer to be filthy; their skin in many instances almost ceases to perform its functions. Nearly all the discharge from some of their bodies is by the bowels; and when completely washed such people become sick.' By the end of the nineteenth century, prisoners in these Anglophone societies had thus come to be thought of as a different species of humanity altogether, as if they had been excommunicated from membership of them: a way of thinking that, in turn, reinforced the need for their exclusion and justified the humiliation and deprivation that being sent to prison in these unforgiving societies had come to involve.

Prison as sanctuary

In the Nordic countries, the terms of separate confinement could be significantly longer than in the Anglophone: a maximum of four years in Norway, from 1848 (although reduced to two in 1900); the 1864 Swedish Penal Code prescribed a maximum of 12 months, extended three years in 1892; in Finland, the 1889 Penal Code prescribed a *minimum* of four months' separation. It was rigorously enforced: inmates could be punished for climbing on their cell window to look outside. Windowsills were inspected to see if the layers of dust had been disturbed by any such activity. While prisoners in England, under separate conditions, were allowed to dispense, in 1878, with wearing masks (to prevent recognition) on leaving their cells, this practice continued in some Swedish prisons until the 1940s.[35] In these respects, separation was more central to the organization of the Nordic prisons. However, it was not intended to act as some sort of interim phase designed to break the spirit of the convict and which, once completed, would be followed by the grotesque displays of human dressage that Du Cane and his acolytes had prescribed for them in England.[36] It might well do this, of course; but nevertheless in these societies, separation was understood, justified and thought of as a 'charitable deed . . . the prison officials saw much to be gained from this since, as a consequence, the destructive influence of the association prisons was, as far as possible, removed' (Almquist, 1924: 47). As such, these prisons remained true to their original purpose of ensuring that inmates were kept away from the corrupting influences of their peers and providing them with the opportunity to find redemption through self-reflection and knowledge of God (Nilsson, 1999: 312). As Crown Prince Oscar had explained (1840: 56), 'the Philadelphian solitude has a more immediate impact on the mind, or on the intent of good or evil, and the liberated prisoner takes with him the fruit of a wholesome self-examination, and of the internal warning voice, to whose punishing severity he has been left'. In contrast to Du Cane, his Swedish counterpart Wieselgren (1895: 386) took the view that 'solitude, interrupted only by the officials' visits, has proved effective to induce the prisoner to introspection, open the mind to repentance, and create a need for industriousness'.

This is not to say that there were no critics of these Nordic variations of the separate system – deterrence had its supporters here, as well. In Sweden, Olivecrona (1872: 65), notwithstanding his fierce opposition to the death penalty, argued that 'by harshening the sentence, intractable minds will always during its first part of the sentence [be] mortified and the prisoner driven towards remorse and made more receptive to instructions promoting an improved living'.[37] But the separate system, *and the way in which it was thought that this would facilitate reintegration, rather than frighten prisoners into obedience*, as in England especially, also had powerful supporters: Wieselgren (1895: 258) was of the view that separation needed to be longer – a short period would only be a 'recreation'. In addition, it was strongly endorsed by most of the prison pastors. One, in Sweden, had claimed that 'the great advantages [of separation] have now been sufficiently proven . . . seldom has any-one condemned for crime returned' (Report of the National Prison Board 1849, quoted by Nilsson 2003: 9). Their support is unsurprising, given that separation would ensure that they then had a much larger role to play in the life of the prison than their Anglophone counterparts after 1865. Thus, while the Report of the [Norwegian] Penal Institutions Commission (1841: 458, our italics) recognized that 'undoubtedly, [the prisoner] will feel unhappy; unless someone came to his aid in this state, he would succumb to despair, insanity or suicide. But the prison's administrative officers, *and above all the priest*, stand by his side . . . the gentle light of religion can illuminate the sinner's dark soul, and arouse his faith in the eternal truth . . . and lead him from despair to the well of hope and comfort.' To this end, the 1886 Rule Book for Långholmen prison, Stockholm, (quoted by Rudstedt, 1994: 34) stated that, 'during the first eight days of the cell time, the prisoner should not be given any work. During this time he is visited by the pastor who during conversations should try to establish the state of the prisoner's soul, his moral development and living conditions, and the reasons for his crime and the circumstances under which it was committed.'

If the power and influence of the pastors was now receding in society at large, with the rise of anti-clerical religious revivalism and new professional groups – schoolteachers, civil servants and doctors, who took on many of the duties that the pastors had previously performed[38] – it was as if the prison had become their last bastion of power. Here, at least, they would continue the broader responsibilities and enjoy the authority they had once held beyond the prison: holding services, usually in the wing corridor so that prisoners could participate from inside their cells, and preparing novitiates for confirmation, while teaching them to read and write so that they would be better able to know God themselves (the pastors also ensured that each prisoner's educational standard and religious knowledge was checked on arrival and throughout their sentence). Faith in God would still bring their salvation, irrespective of the crimes they had committed: 'no sin can separate us from Him, even if we were to kill or commit adultery thousands of times each day' (Luther, 1521/1880, Letter no. 99). The Report of the [Finnish] Prison Service for 1886 (1888: 43) thus makes references to confirmation classes: those who had yet to be confirmed in the Lutheran church were expected to attend, while 'every Sunday there is a [religious] service. This involves explaining the Bible and teaching the catechism. There is religious instruction on the other days.' In addition, the section on 'Soul Care and Education' in the Report of the Prison Service for 1885 (1887: 43–5) notes that '300 prisoners visited the prison school . . . during the year'. The report then goes on to grade them all in terms of 'reading, writing, and counting'. At the end of the year, it claimed that there had been large advances in each category. Here, then, education was an integral feature of the prison timetable: it was to be encouraged, rather than disavowed as in the Anglophone prisons. As well as the pastors, qualified teachers worked in these prisons. Although Finland was then one of the poorest countries in Western Europe, money was set aside to provide them (Report of the Prison Service for 1890, 1892). This then remained so, despite the repression and poverty of the post-civil-war period: 'education is provided to those under 40 serving three months and more and those who previously had not been to school' (Report of the Prison Service for 1922, 1925: 30). Then again, the importance of literacy was much stronger and more deeply embedded in these countries. While, in England, 21 per cent of prisoners were thought to be illiterate and 75 per cent 'could only read or write imperfectly' (Report of the Departmental Committee on Prisons, 1895: 337), the 1911 Report of the Swedish Royal Prison Board (1912: 42), noted that only one 'protectee' [that is, prisoner] was illiterate, out of a daily average prison population of 1,980.

Furthermore, the commentaries of the pastors provide the main descriptions and documentation of prison life in the Nordic annual reports, in contrast to the format of the Anglophone, which, after 1877, were principally written in a few *pro forma* lines by individual governors, following a lengthy introduction from the Director of the Prison Commission. We thus find that, in the former, it was not the prison that was to be feared but what lay beyond it, as if the prison was able to act as a sanctuary from the world and its sins. One pastor working in Oslo *Botsfengslet* thus reported that 'the ability to receive religious instruction is higher among the prisoners than would be expected. The fact is that these people are often deeply unhappy and have several times tried to get away from their earlier bad ways' (Report of the Director of the [Norwegian] Prison Board 1903–1905 (1907: 7). 'The moral state of the prisoners is characterised by a sense of hopeless loneliness . . . *[but] the effect of punishment seems to be beneficial in most cases*', said another. 'A large majority admit that they deserved punishment and find the courage to start a new life through their shame and remorse' (ibid.: 6. our italics). A third pastor wrote (ibid.: 8) that, 'under the influence of life's seductions outside prison, the budding religiosity acquired in prison is often compromised . . . however, it is only the very thick skinned anti-social types who are hopeless. Religion in prison almost always has a disciplinary effect.' Here, then, prisoners were thought redeemable; they simply needed pastoral guidance and leadership to bring them to this: they were not to be beaten into submission, flogged (corporal punishment had been abolished in Norwegian prisons in 1841), have wooden gags stuffed in their mouths or to be broken on treadwheels.

Instead, the values of *likhet* and *lagom*, in conjunction with the Lutheran insistence that God alone could make judgments on an individual's redemptive possibilities, had produced a very different way of thinking about prison life. The 1911 Report of the Royal [Swedish] Prison Board (1912: 45) thus noted that 'solitary confinement is good for those not sentenced to labour [in Sweden]. They work in their cells without moral contagion . . . [this] separates them from normal friends or gangs. They feel shame when thinking about their crime . . . All this contributes to the more important question of the soul.' Nonetheless, worldly temptations were never far away: 'freedom can be very dangerous for some people. Freedom can release the most basic instincts. *The road from prison to freedom for many leads to them taking the wrong paths*' (ibid.: 46, our italics). In other words, once released from the sanctuary that prison had provided for them, former inmates could not be relied on to resist, on their own, the temptations that reappeared. In Norway, it was the practice that 'if the prisoner's own clothes are of too low a standard, he will be provided with clothes so he can be released in a decent, not too eye-catching outfit. He should be assisted with travel to his home place, or elsewhere in the country if he can demonstrate to the [Prison] Director that he can make an honest living there' (Report of the Director of the [Norwegian] Prison Board 1901–2 (1904: 123). But what was also needed was a supervening authority that would protect and guard them from subsequent transgressions. Thus, prisoners on conditional release were given stringent reporting conditions and their employers were to report back to the pastors with details of their progress. The Anglophone prisoners, however, were likely to find that they had been simply cut adrift from the rest of society on release. In England, the Report of the Commissioners of Prisons, 1878: 7, our italics) thus stated that 'we have endeavoured in framing this system to provide that the rigour of the discipline to which each prisoner will be subjected *shall be in some degree in his own hands'*. In the Anglophone societies, individuals were responsible for their own journey through life, in prison as well as out of it, great or small, those best equipped to make this journey, and those least well equipped.

At the same time, prison labour in the Nordic countries was intended to be productive rather than afflictive – more Martin Luther than less eligibility. Although in Norway the prison doctor, and subsequent Law Commissioner, Fredrik Holst (1828: 34) had written favourably of the treadwheel he had seen in use in England, the Report of the [Norwegian] Penal Institutions Commission (1841: 491) took the view that work should be meaningful, should teach the prisoners a trade and, in general, should have a 'positive and healing effect on the mind'. Afflictive labour, in contrast, did not 'bring the desire for and the habit of work'. It was also important to avoid work being seen as 'repugnant' – Lutheranism insisted on the *redemptive* possibilities of work through the contribution it allowed each individual to make to community well-being ('a man does not live for himself alone, he lives only for others': Luther, 1521/1880: 364–5). The different approach to prison labour in the Nordic countries is seen in Enoch Wines' (1878: 14) opening address to the International Prison Congress of Stockholm: 'effort has been made [in Norwegian prisons] . . . to develop and improve scholastic instruction in the prisons; to enlarge the prison libraries; and to organize the labour in such a manner that prisoners will be occupied in such kinds of work as will best enable them, on their liberation, to honestly and honourably provide for the wants of life'. And, in Sweden, while the work undertaken in the cell prisons was of a simple kind, from 1895 entrepreneurs were allowed to hire prisoners working on contract in weaving and knitting, basket-making, pram-part making, leather work and shoemaking (Rudstedt, 1972: 185). The prisoners were then able to have some share in the profits of their labour. As in Norway earlier, Swedish prison legislation of 1916 stipulated that '*the work undertaken in prison should be such that it provides vocational training or the education that can aid their chances to make a living after release'*. To emphasize its positive value, punishments for indiscipline in these countries included *being deprived of work*. In England, though, indiscipline might lead to the imposition of *more* penal/afflictive labour tasks (Radzinowicz and Hood, 1986: 556). Furthermore, the expectations of what prisoners were capable of achieving in their work were very different. Thus, in New South Wales, 'as regards the employment of prisoners on useful or productive work, it must be repeated that . . . *the prison population is chiefly recruited from the idle and vicious classes, not from the hard working and industrious'* (Report of the Comptroller-General of Prisons, 1893: 1, our italics): in effect, the labour of prisoners was as worthless as every other feature of their lives. In contrast, Wines (1878: 15) referred to 'an exhibition [that] will be made of the products of labour in the prisons of the [Nordic] countries. Such an exhibition cannot fail to be at once interesting, instructive and inspiring.' Here, then, prisoners' work could be displayed with honour: there was nothing similar to the disqualificatory distance that now separated them from the rest of society in the Anglophone countries. Without this barrier, they could be given the opportunity to demonstrate their *worthwhile* capabilities.

For the same reason, there was far less importance given to ensuring that prisoners experienced a level of deprivation that set them apart, in a special category of unworthiness, from the rest of society: less eligibility had a much more reduced presence in the Nordic prisons, just as it did in Nordic social policy. In Sweden, prisoners ate much the same as everyone else at that time: boiled potatoes, a little meat, herrings and porridge (Rudstedt, 1972: 123). In addition, each prisoner had the right to purchase bonus items, such as bread, milk, margarine, pork, cheese and sausage from the money they earned. Although in the early twentieth century this was restricted to coffee, tea, cocoa, sweets, tobacco and snuff, because of the friction the purchases generated (ibid.: 209), prisoners at least had some capacity for autonomy and choice that was entirely absent from the Anglophone prison systems at that time. In Norway, the diet had been determined with a view to satisfying 'all of the prisoner's real physical needs and as far as possible avoiding all physical suffering and deficiencies that could damage his health, but to deprive him of all sensory pleasures, which lies beyond the satisfaction of basic necessities' (Report of the [Norwegian] Penal Institutions Commission, 1841: 532). Therefore, 'preparation methods or additives whose only purpose it is to improve the flavour of food, should be abolished, and it should be ensured that naturally good tasting foods are not too prominent. It should be . . . healthy, monotonous, and everything that can be classified as fine nourishment should be forbidden, as should tobacco, liquor, wine, beer and other alcoholic beverages' (ibid.: 534). But, if food lost its quality in these ways, at least it retained its quantity. There seem to be no accounts from the Nordic countries, as there certainly were in England, of prisoners punished for eating – driven by hunger to eating – 'candles, boot oil, and other repulsive articles' (Davitt, 1886: 18).[39] Indeed, subsequent improvements to the Norwegian prison diet were celebrated, rather than hedged around with assurances, as in England, that there were still no luxuries in the prisons, and that prisoners would gain no advantage from being there.[40] Thus: 'May 5th was a day of joy in the prison, since it was the first time the prisoners were served beef and beef soup for dinner. It was a festive meal, and many were exclamations of happiness and contentment' (Report of the Director of the [Norwegian] Prison Board 1903–4, 1909: 9).

Furthermore, community values were still able to penetrate the Nordic prisons: they had not been turned into a micro-world that was set apart from the rest of society. Wieselgren (1895: 442–3, our italics) refers to the way in which one of the Swedish prison doctors, in 1849, complained that 'every cell had a New Testament, a catechism, and a devotional manual for prisoners . . . but this was not enough. He was therefore of the opinion that every cell prison should own "a small collection of educational, useful and moral books", of which the pastor could entrust suitable reading for deserving prisoners . . . *But to the extent that a rising standard of the general education outside the prison had a positive effect on that of the prison*, . . . it gradually became a necessity to accommodate both prisoners and the prison service's own veritable interests, by obtaining libraries for the prison.' In Finland, the Report of the Prison Service for 1885 (1887: 48–9, our italics) referred to a prison doctor discussing links between prison conditions, diet and prisoner health in a way that had, by then, become impossible in the Anglophone countries: 'it is not clear if ill health amongst prisoners is due to prison conditions, or if they were in bad shape when they arrived. However, *he thinks that the large number of prisoners with disturbed digestive systems is due to the prison diet.* It consists of too much vegetables and too few meat products; he also thinks that the bread ration could be reduced in favour of cheese, as a surrogate for milk . . . The drinking water is also of a low quality.' Here, then, deficiencies in the prison diet – deficiencies that were linked to ill health, rather than how many grammes of food prisoners were allowed to eat – could be publicly recognized and discussed: prisons belonged within these Nordic societies, rather than existing beyond their boundaries.

Similarly, prison clothing in Sweden and Norway was the same as that of manual labourers.[41] In Sweden, this was grey for those working inside the prisons and brown for those working outside. It was distributed as follows: 'after having been searched, the prisoner is ordered to bathe, after which he is dressed in the prison uniform. This consists of undergarments made out of *buldan* [thick linen], an overcoat, pants, vest and hat made out of grey *vadmal* [thick wool] with socks and *buldan* slippers, which when outside would be swapped for leather shoes with a wooden sole' (Långholmen Prison Rules, 1890, quoted by Rudstedt, 1972: 36). In Norway and Sweden, there were none of the elaborate stripes, arrows or colouring that were characteristic of English prison uniforms until the 1920s. More care seems also to have been taken to ensure that the prisoners were given clothing that actually fitted them. As the 1911 Report of the Royal [Swedish] Prison Board (1912: 54, our italics), observed, 'many of our *protectees* look like rubbish. It is impossible to send them to work until we have given them new clothes from hat to shoes. *Within the [prison offices] there is a big wardrobe with a changing room where they can try on new clothes.*' In the Anglophone prisons, inmates were simply issued with a standard kit on reception, based on an estimate of their size or, failing this, whatever was available. As the former prison chaplain Rickards (1920: 130) noted, 'nothing more disfiguring and disgusting than the dress and tenure of the man in prison is it possible to imagine, and some of them feel it acutely, especially when a friend or relative is allowed to visit them, and they see how shocked their visitor is when [they] realise that it is the man he has known outside in decent garments.' Although in the late nineteenth century Swedish prisoners were either shaved or 'given a very short haircut', the 1912 Report of the Royal [Swedish] Prison Board (1913), notes that they were now allowed to grow their hair and wear a beard. In England, however, Rule 95 (1948) still stipulated that 'arrangements shall be made for every prisoner to wash at all proper times, to have a hot bath at least once a week and for men . . . to shave daily and to have their haircut as required'.

It is also evident that the social distances between inmates and officers were significantly shorter in the Nordic countries. The 1874 Prison Rules in New South Wales stated that 'prisoners will be very respectful to all officials of the government and will never pass a superior officer of the prison without touching his hat. When visited in his exercise yard by any officer he will stand at attention, facing off' (that is, he was not allowed to look the officer in the face, Report of the Comptroller-General of Prisons, 1874: 11). However, the 1885 Swedish Prison Rules merely stated that 'the prisoner should politely and decently greet the prison's Director, preacher, doctor and staff and follow the directions given by these persons . . . When he is visited by the Director, preacher or other person he should not talk louder than is necessary' (Rudstedt, 1994: 24). While the Swedish prisoners clearly have to show deference in their conversations with officials, they are not called upon to physically demonstrate their subjection to them. However, the 1899 New South Wales Rules (our italics) maintained that 'the prisoner will be very respectful to all prison officers, and should any visit him in his exercise yard, *he will immediately come to attention*'. Similarly, 'prisoners will invariably touch their hats when passing or addressing an Officer, excepting when marching in company, when the Officer in Charge will give the direction "eyes right" or "left" as the case may be' (Report of the Comptroller-General of Prisons, 1916: 9). In the more egalitarian and homogeneous Nordic countries, there was no need for such elaborate rituals of deference and supplication in the interaction between prisoners and officers. There was less difference between prisoners and the rest of the population, and less need to advertize any that there might be – the provisions for clothing, diet, labour and education were much in keeping with the standards of life outside the prison. Ultimately, the prison sentence was intended to reclaim inmates, rather than aggravate their exclusion. As Wieselgren (1895: 393, our italics) put the matter, 'one finds that crime and moral degradation usually grow up in coarse and ignorant families and in the tracks of poverty. *Public safety should first be sought in a more extended religious and educational instruction, and in enlightened care for the able-bodied to pave the way for work and favourable employment.*'

The foundations of difference

At the end of the nineteenth century, punishment had a much larger role to play – both real and symbolic – in securing social order in the divided Anglophone societies than in the Nordic. This was reflected in the unwillingness to let go of the death penalty in the former whereas, in the latter, this sanction had long since ceased to be needed for these purposes; in addition, it was reflected in the emphasis on imprisonment as a deterrent penalty (and a greater willingness to use it) rather than the reintegrative mechanism it was thought to be in the latter. Furthermore, some of the different characteristics that are found in the prison systems of these societies in the early twenty-first century had already been put in place.[42]

First, prison size. Notwithstanding the initial attractions of the Benthamesque grand penitentiary, there was, by that time, an emphasis on small prisons in the Nordic countries: Almquist (1931: 200) noted that Norway had '12 district prisons and 106 auxiliary prisons of various sizes'. In contrast, there had been a drive towards the rationalization of the prison estate in the Anglophone countries. In England, from 1862 to 1877, 'no fewer than 80 out of the 193 prisons of that date, all of course the small ones . . . were entirely discontinued' (Webb and Webb, 1922: 202–3). Indeed, this fixation on large institutions reinforced the physical and administrative divisions between prisons and the rest of society.

Second, the sense of 'difference' between prisoners and the rest of society in the Anglophone countries, in contrast to the much more untroubled equanimity of the approach to them in the Nordic countries – there, they were just another group of sinners, and, like all others, redeemable through faith. The threatening, remote, appearance of the Anglophone prisons not only made them unwanted neighbours but further exaggerated the difference between their inmates and the rest of society. Indeed, the very sight of prisoners in the public domain had become intolerable. If, during the course of the nineteenth century, they had become objects of curiosity by virtue of their removal to prison, they had also been turned into objects of menace. In New Zealand, labour shortages had meant that prisoners had been employed on public works, but growing public antipathies drove them back inside: 'the influence of prisoners in cities is not good and when we see children in front of [Wellington gaol] playing prisoners, it showed a familiarity with the system which could not be for good' (Hansard [NZ], 13 August 1907: 191).

Third, the presence of much stronger militaristic features and traditions in the Anglophone prisons. In New South Wales, this justified prison watchtowers, still familiar features of the maximum security institutions of this state: 'either a central tower originally designed or an elevated platform should be erected in [Sydney] gaols, to enable officers in charge to command a fuller view of the prisoners' (Report from the Select Committee on the Public Prisons in Sydney and Cumberland, 1861: 10). Furthermore, there was drill for prisoners *and* prison officers: '[this] is enforced amongst warders, who are all supposed to be used to arms, and a handbook of drill has been compiled so as to bring about uniformity of practice; and in other directions a general straightening up has taken place' (Report of the Comptroller-General of Prisons, 1896: 5). In the Nordic countries, however, the emphasis was on developing the prisoners' educational achievements and engaging them in productive work. And, rather than drill for the officers, a 'school for the professional education of prison keepers' had been proposed in Finland in the 1860s (Wines, 1878). In contrast, education in the Anglophone prisons was only to be of the most basic standard, when provided at all, and then only available after prisoners' work had been completed.

Fourth, the justifications for harsh treatment and privations in the Anglophone prisons against the Nordic intents to reclaim their prisoners. The importance given to less eligibility limited the possibilities for any reductions in the severity of the Anglophone prison systems: their inmates had to remain in their place at the bottom of these societies, and prison itself had to send out signals that this was indeed so. In the Nordic prisons, however, we find that the binary system of governance of these societies was already beginning to take effect in their prison systems. On the one hand, there were more intensive systems of control and surveillance in the prolonged periods of solitude and silence. On the other, there was a sense of egalitarianism and cohesion that allowed prisoners to be seen as much the same kind of human beings as everyone else – there was no need to further stigmatize and humiliate them to emphasise their difference.

5 Two welfare sanctions

From the late nineteenth century, however, both ways of thinking about punishment were subjected to new social forces. For Garland (1985), this period marked the emergence of 'the welfare sanction'. In keeping with the broader trajectory of welfare governance, its characteristics included a 'distinct positivistic approach to the reform of deviants . . . extensive use of interventionist strategies . . . deployment of social work and psychiatric expertise, [a] concern to regulate, manage and normalize rather than immediately to punish' (ibid.: 128). Certainly, these characteristics began to feature in subsequent penal development all the way through to the late 1960s – the high-water mark of the welfare sanction per se – in these societies. However, *the range and extent* of these characteristics took place within the parameters of their respective models of welfare state development and the values embedded in them. The end product was that, just as there were two models of welfare state development, so there were *two distinctive welfare sanctions*, each corresponding to the broader welfare state typologies in which they were situated, and with similar consequences in their respective penal realms. Thus, while the social democratic welfare sanction of the Nordic countries began to be put into effect through new mechanisms, and was derived from secular, rather than religious, modes of knowledge, it also represented a line of continuity with the past in so far as *punishment was still intended to be used for productive and inclusionary purposes*. Similarly, in the Anglophone countries, there was a line of continuity with the penal past in the form of *disqualificatory, exclusionary punishments that the liberal welfare sanction was ultimately unable to eradicate*: while its reformist intents succeeded in significantly reducing prison levels in these societies in the inter war period, its own limitations and those of the liberal welfare state meant that this was unable to be sustained post war; similarly, its attempts to ameliorate prison conditions were consistently offset and ultimately undermined by the stamp of less eligibility that it carried with it.

How, though, did the two welfare sanctions come into existence, and what kinds of penal arrangements did they oversee and sponsor?

The emergence and development of the social democratic welfare sanction

The intellectual origins of the social democratic welfare sanction are to be found in the ensemble of Italian, French and German scholars who, from the publication of Cesare Lombroso's (1876) *L'Uomo Delinquente* to that of Enrico Ferri's (1928) *Principles of Criminal Law*, dramatically revised the post Enlightenment legal and religious foundations on which thinking about crime and punishment had been based in the Nordic region. Some of the central themes in this scholarship[1] were (1) the classification of criminals by type (rather than seeing them all as sinners); (2) the denial of free will (rather than crime being understood as the product of moral culpability); (3) the role of punishment as a form of *social defence* (rather than providing the opportunity for offenders to seek redemption from God), thus its extent should thus be determined by the *crime risks and dangers* that should be assessed in each offender (rather than be commensurate to the particular crime they had committed); and (4) punishment should then take the form of incapacitation, or *neutralization*[2] and, until those risks had been brought under control, some form of indefinite detention would be the principal means of achieving this[3] (thereby overturning the Enlightenment principles that insisted on finite punishments). The regular international conferences that were held in Europe and North America between 1872 and 1935 provided some of the main outlets and discussion points for this scholarship, although periodic ruptures within it led to the formation of competing associations (Alper and Boren, 1972). The International Prison Congress (IPC) was probably the foremost of these, but others included the International Union of Penal Law (IUPL).

Prominent Nordic scholars, penal administrators and civil servants regularly attended the congresses and the second IPC meeting was held in Stockholm in 1878. However, the German law professor Franz von Liszt who, with others,[4] founded the IUPL in 1889 (which had its second meeting in Oslo in 1892), was the most influential of 'the new penologists' in this region, even though his work remains little known in the Anglophone world.[5] The founding statement of the IUPL indicates the focus of this organization and his own *oeuvre*: 'crime is viewed more and more as a social phenomenon; its causes and the means to be employed in suppressing it are, then, *plainly as much the concern of sociological investigators as of judges and lawyers*' (quoted by Alper and Boren, 1972: 33, our italics). As with his contemporaries, von Liszt was prepared to accept that criminals were not responsible for their actions because of their absence of free will. However, in contrast to the biological determinism of Lombroso and his followers, he was also of the opinion that crime was as much the product of the social environment as any individual deficiencies or defects that criminals might have (von Liszt, 1882). This premise had three important implications for policy development. *First*, 'the concept of punishment gives way to those of curative rehabilitation and preventive detention. The conceptual dividing line between crime and insanity [also] gives way' (von Liszt, 1897: 76).[6] In these respects, there were no 'natural limits' to *how much* punishment should be inflicted, nor should there be any legal restrictions to it: crime was essentially an illness and, like any other illness, should be treated as such until it abated. *Second*, criminological research ought to provide the foundations for penal policy and assess its effectiveness, rather than leave this to be determined by judges using abstract legal principles. *Third*, there was an onus on the state to develop social policies that would reduce the criminogenic features of the criminal's environment (housing, public health, education and so on). In these ways, it would become possible to prevent crime by the use of social measures, rather than relying exclusively on punishment to bring about the 'neutralization' of the criminal. However, this aspiration was qualified with the proviso that, until the modern state and its organizations of government were sufficiently developed to perform these tasks, punishment should still be the main instrument for protecting citizens from crime risks (von Litsz, 1882). Again distinguishing himself from the determinism of Lombroso and others, he went on to argue that its form should provide 'safety from the incorrigibles [and] *the rehabilitation of the improvables*' (ibid.: 174, our italics). The former, by whom he meant selective recidivists, should be imprisoned indefinitely, with their cases reviewed every five years to assess signs of good behaviour and improvement – indicators that their risks of future crime had diminished. For the latter, he advocated a one to five year prison sentence, the release date to be determined by the inmate's progress in prison, rather than being set in advance by judges. Work and education would then provide the means for them to show improvement while serving their sentence. For a third group – the 'incipient chronic' or 'occasional offender' – fines or 'conditional' (that is, suspended) prison sentences would act as 'a rebuke to their selfish impulses' (ibid.), and would be punishment enough. The meetings of local criminalist associations that were formed in each of these Nordic countries in the late nineteenth century then provided opportunities for further dissemination of his ideas, as did the journal *Nordisk Tidsskrift for Kriminalvidenskab* (Nordic Journal of Criminology), founded in 1893 (Andenaes, 1959).

There are some obvious reasons for the resonance of his work with Nordic audiences at that time: his dislike of unnecessarily repressive punishment and belief that some offenders, at least, were redeemable sat well in these societies in which prison regimes were intended to reclaim offenders; as did his downplaying of the importance of judicial thinking in the development and application of the principles of punishment where judges administered law, rather than made it, and where civil servants and the criminal justice intelligentsia were held in high regard; as did his advocacy of indeterminate prison sentences for recidivists in a society in which collective well-being had priority over individual rights; as did his insistence that the state, rather than responding to crime with punishment, should develop preventative social policies – a state in which extensive powers were already in existence and would be extended further as the social democratic welfare state began to be constructed. The introduction of suspended sentences of imprisonment in Norway in 1894 was an indication of his immediate influence in this region, as were the provisions for the indefinite imprisonment of habitual criminals in that country's 1902 penal code, drawn up largely by Getz, himself a member of the IUPL (Stang Dahl, 1985). Suspended sentences were then introduced in Sweden in 1905 and Finland in 1918. In the latter, Professor of Law Allan Serlachius, petitioning for revisions to the penal code to this effect in 1905, used von Liszt's framework of criminal classification in his justification. Its existing provisions, he claimed, 'only applied to, and were apparently designed for "real", in other words chronic, offenders. For chance – that is acute – offenders, imprisonment, especially, did more harm than good, and society should show its disapproval of their acts through the use of conditional sentences' (quoted by Lahti, 1977: 130). Thereafter, with a view to restricting unnecessary entry to imprisonment for the 'occasionals' or 'chance offenders', legislation for 'day fines'[7] was introduced in Finland in 1921.

The more wide ranging penal reforms that were put into place in these societies from the 1920s to the 1960s situated the possibilities of punishment that von Liszt, in particular, had offered within the framework of social democratic welfare governance.[8] In this way, the reforms gave further impetus to the binary system of penal control and regulation in the Nordic countries. *On the one hand*, the state should be given increased powers of control and coercion over those whose *unpredictable or unproductive behaviour* put the well-being and security of the rest of the population at risk. *On the other*, rather than allowing such measures to seal their exclusion from society, these same groups of deviants and lawbreakers should be treated with moderation and restraint in a bid to more effectively bring about their social inclusion.

Control and coercion

This was manifested, *first, in the growing importance given to medico-psycho-logical knowledge* as a way of understanding crime – necessary if crime was indeed to be understood as an illness (von Liszt's position) and in need of treatment. Thus, in Sweden, Victor Almquist (1927: 322), the Director of Prisons, claimed that 'the criminal act is a manifestation of a moral disease, but only a manifestation, not the disease itself. Through its manifestation, one can make a judgement as to the seriousness of the disease, but without being able to judge, before the fact, if treatment, or the length of treatment, could have an effect on the disease.' Swedish legislation in 1927 and 1937 thus provided 'custodial care' for 'mentally abnormal' offenders and 'internment' for habitual criminals. In principle, such confinement was 'to continue just as long as the person is considered a menace to society' (Göransson, 1938: 125). Minimum, not maximum, terms of detention were set. In making their decisions, the courts would be guided by a 'Detention Committee' of psychologists and prison officials. In Norway, legislation in 1929 allowed for the indefinite detention of those who posed a danger due to 'abnormal conditions of the soul', an amalgam of religious and medico-psychological knowledge that marked the crossover point in the respective dominance of these discourses in criminal justice policy. Although, in Finland, medico-psychological knowledge was to have minimal impact on policy and administration,[9] the use of the indefinite sentence as a form of social defence was reinforced by the Dangerous Recidivists Act 1932: those who endangered 'public or private security' by their repeated offending would be contained indefinitely. In the spirit of von Liszt, the purpose was to reinforce the prevention of 'chronic criminality'. The length and terms of confinement would also be determined by a Prison Tribunal (Lahti, 1977).

New spaces were then opened up, within the criminal justice and penal system, that provided the opportunity for diagnosis and assessment of the risks each offender posed. As the Norwegian Director of Prisons, Hartvig Nissen (1935: 139, our italics), wrote, 'When modern criminal justice policy demands that society's reaction toward those who violate its laws must take into account the individuality of the offender, *the authorities must have the means to gather extensive and in-depth knowledge about the man's character and his entire personality.*' To achieve these tasks, psychological experts, rather than Lutheran pastors, now became pivotal figures in the penal system. Conrad Falsen (1930: 61), the Director of Opstad Work Colony in Norway, thus recommended the recruitment of 'psychiatric doctors' to the prisons. Furthermore, prison directors 'should undertake a course in psychiatry before being allowed to undertake this important job.' As Torsten Eriksson, subsequent Director of the Swedish Prison Commission, later explained, in an address to the Finnish Criminalist Society (1951: 67), 'If we treat offenders, we must have the same liberties in criminal care as they do in medical health care and this means we have the power to free a person immediately if the treatment requires or keep him in an institution for any length of time if it seems appropriate.' For these purposes, the new position of Professor in Forensic Psychiatry at the Karolinska Institute (Stockholm) and Chief Medical Officer at Långholmen Prison had been established in 1946.

Indeed, in conjunction with the increasing powers of the social democratic welfare state and the way in which it was prepared to absorb the responsibilities of individual citizens, so diagnoses of mental abnormalities and other personality deficiencies in offenders – and the need for specialist provisions for them – grew exponentially. While, from 1930 to 1935, 25 per cent of male defendants examined by psychiatrists in Sweden were diagnosed as 'probable recidivists', this increased to 68 per cent in the period from 1946 to 1950. While preventive detention was used in only three cases in 1928, there were 121 such sentences in 1946, and 204 in 1954, by which time preventive detention inmates constituted around 15 per cent of Sweden's total prison population (Eriksson, 1954). In addition, the number of offenders found to be insane and not punishable also reached high levels. Eight hundred out of the 164,000 who were convicted in 1945 were then committed to mental hospitals. Indeed, it was seldom determined that those defendants who were examined were *not* suffering from some sort of mental disorder – only 13, for example, out of 555 referrals in 1970 (Moyer, 1974: 810). Furthermore, 'every murderer has to be examined by a psychiatrist – the examination takes at least six weeks – *and most are found to be insane, needing hospital care instead of prison treatment*. The result is that murderers in Sweden – especially the most dangerous of them – are seldom convicted and imprisoned nowadays. Out of 63 murderers in the four years 1944–47, 48 were found insane and committed to hospitals' (ibid.: 806, our italics).[10] As Hardy Göransson (1938: 130), Director of Swedish Prisons, had pointed out, 'the prerequisites for such a judgement by the court are not so rigid as in countries that follow the M'Naghten rule[11] or similar precepts. This means, among other things, that many psychopaths are sent to mental hospitals on a finding of insanity.' In these societies, without the same level of insistence on individual responsibility in criminal law as in the Anglophone, the rigidity and narrowness of the M'Naghten distinction between sanity and insanity could be dispensed with, allowing for much more fluid interpretations of mental health and much higher numbers of positive diagnoses of mental deficiencies. By the mid-1950s, 255 psychiatric beds were available in the Swedish prisons, accommodating eight per cent of its total prison population (Rylander, 1954–1955). Indeed, the Swedish Social Welfare Board (1952: 6) reported that 'many penal institutions are provided with mental [health] departments. In fact there has been a strong tendency in recent decades to bring medical sciences, particularly psychology, to bear on treatment. The Prison Board has a department staffed with forensic psychologists, and to an increasing extent the courts order a mental examination of the defendant.' In the 1960s, there were 14 different centres of forensic psychiatry in Sweden.

Second, in the development of eugenics based penal strategies. In keeping with the power of Nordic social movements to define social problems, eugenics movements in each of these societies pressed for more extensive state controls over the reproductive habits of 'the unfit' in the early twentieth century (Broberg and Roll-Hanssen, 1996). In Finland and Norway, the sense of national identity, so important in their struggles for independence, became linked to the need to maintain racial purity. After the triumph of the 'Whites' over the Russian influenced 'Reds' in the civil war, the Finns were particularly anxious to assert their Nordic ancestry, rather than the Mongol with which they had previously been associated. As 'proof' of the former, beauty contests were organized, with the winners becoming 'representatives of a racially pure Finnish womanhood in the eyes of the rest of the world . . . independent Finland needed its national symbols to increase its own feeling of solidarity' (Hietala, 1996: 200). By the same token, though, vigilant 'race hygiene' was also needed to stamp out any impurities that jeopardized this desired identity, including those thought to be caused by the hereditary effects of alcohol – crime, mental disorder and unwanted children (see Roll-Hansen, 1996). In Sweden, similar concerns had been raised by the apparent decline of 'Swedish national character' (Sundbärg, 1911b). Mass emigration had contributed to population loss (ensuring that this society was able to reproduce itself was to be an important theme in the formation of the social democratic welfare state, as we have seen), while Norway's unilateral declaration of independence in 1905 was thought to have harmed its national prestige. Furthermore, the consequences of late industrialization and land redistribution in Sweden were now beginning to take effect. While the middle classes were becoming more prosperous (Ericsson, Fink and Myhre, 2004), the cohesion of the Swedish *bönder* class had fragmented, bringing into existence some 1,400,000 landless peasants in the early twentieth century, many of whom were thought to have alcohol problems (Fleisher, 1967: 15). Again, then, it was thought that racial health was being put at risk by alcohol and its degenerative physical and mental consequences. Moreover, the mere confinement of those so affected was not sufficient to counter the hereditary dangers that they posed to national well-being.

Olof Kinberg (1930: 367, our italics), the Swedish psychiatrist and 'Alienist to the Central Prison, Stockholm', thus called for 'the temporary *élimination* of criminals' through 'a registration of all individuals who are endangered by an asocial environment or whose course of activity already shows them to be asocial *and for a stop to the increase of such persons whom experience shows are predisposed to crime*'. In Norway, Nissen (1935: 134, our italics) maintained that, 'as true as it is that a significant cause of crime is poor human material, it is also true that the reduction of this *through preventing its continuation to the next generation* has to be the main aim of criminal justice policy in the future'. Thereafter, Göransson (1938: 132, our italics) observed that 'it is becoming more and more clear that the treatment of asocial persons is a question which concerns everyone, since criminality and other asocial conduct means heavy economic burdens on the community and constantly threatening danger to life and property. *It is not only humane but prudent to prevent and to combat such phenomena.*' In this context, 'prevention' did not merely refer to enhanced social measures of assistance. It also obliquely referred to the need for medical procedures on the reproductive capabilities of those thought to be 'asocial'.

The legitimacy of such proposals was affirmed by the commitment of Social Democrat and Labour parties to produce 'better quality citizens', as well as a better quality of life for them (Sundell, 2000). While the state would give right of entry to 'the people's home' to all, it would also be given, in return, the power to ensure that each individual member neither diminished nor threatened the well-being of the population at large; hence the justifications for the sterilization laws in the 1930s. Indeed, in Sweden, Myrdal and Myrdal (1934: 83) argued that this procedure should not only be administered on the degenerate and the defective, but that it should also be considered for much wider categories – '"the psychologically inferior" though not formally legally incompetent, with asocial disposition'. The 1941 Penal Law Commission then justified sterilization of those who were insane or mentally deficient, and those who had 'a marked asocial way of living that as a rule could be said to be combined with psychic inferiority of one kind or another' (quoted by Sundell, 2000: 508). Sweden also introduced a castration law for sex offenders in 1944, and Finland in 1950 (Norway rested with voluntary castrations). In this region, the grubby, sordid brutalities of punishment that involved the infliction of pain on the body of lawbreakers had no role to play in the sanitized framework of the social democratic welfare sanction. However, surgical operations that were carried out by white-coated medical professionals on those who jeopardized community health and security were to be encouraged.

Third, in the development of social democratic influenced social engineering, designed to bring about more cohesion, solidarity and security. This was reflected in the increasing regulation of normative behaviour as well as breaches of the criminal law. The temperance movement had been instrumental in bringing about restrictions on alcohol production and consumption from the late nineteenth century and the internment of alcoholics in Sweden under the provisions of the 1913 Inebriety Act. The Social Democrats then revised this legislation in 1932, and made it applicable to 'those addicted to alcohol who on account of such abuse are a danger to themselves or others, who depend on private or public charity, fail to provide for themselves and their families, or are incapable of taking care of themselves' (Göransson, 1938). It allowed for internment for between two and four years on the recommendation of the local Temperance Boards (similarly, in Norway). Their committees would also determine the release date. There were 10 such alcoholics' institutions in Sweden, with a capacity to hold 700, by 1938. In addition to these and the sterilization measures, the state's right to correct departures from normative expectations was also reflected in internment provisions for vagrants – along with 'pimps, confidence men, professional gamblers and liquor smugglers' – in a workhouse or labour colony where they would be made to undertake compulsory labour for between one and three years: 'the county administration or board also fixes the length of the internment period' (ibid.: 132). These kinds of social problems had now become matters of public health and national vitality to be addressed by the state, rather than being left to God to decide on redemption or otherwise for the individuals concerned. In these respects, *the very consumption of alcohol*, not simply those who were alcoholics, constituted a danger to social well-being. In addition to the existing restrictions on consumption, Sweden (1936), Finland (1937) and Norway (1941) became the first countries to introduce specific legislation relating to driving under the influence of alcohol (generally, imprisonment was likely for consuming anything more than one small alcoholic drink).

In the post-war period in Sweden, penal policy also reflected the *egalitarian* thrust of social democratic social engineering. Rather than focussing on crime committed by poor people, the Report of the Penal Code Commission (no. 55, 1956: 36) was of the view that 'white collar crime completely dominates the most serious types of crime in this country'. Nonetheless, the prosecution of alcohol related crimes also increased from 3,460 in 1950 (49 per 100,000 of population) to – in the post *motbok* era – 17,036 in 1970 (212 per 100,000). Indeed, the scourge of alcohol was thought to run right through the criminal population. The Report of the Penal Code Commission (1956) claimed that, in addition to those prosecuted for driving under its influence, '33 per cent of all criminals were drunk at the time of their crime'; 'violent criminals 84 per cent drunk; thieves 35 per cent drunk'; and, of men over 25 committing crime, '50 per cent had misused alcohol'. In the same period, more than half of the Swedish prison population was made up of those convicted of alcohol-related driving offences (for example, 1,154 out of a daily average population of 1,871 in 1947 (Report of the Royal [Swedish] Prison Board *1946–1947* (1947)).

The end product of this intention to control minor illegalities and breaches of norms as well as major crimes was *a rise* in the Swedish prison population even though, when the Social Democrats had come to government in the 1930s, they had launched a concerted drive to bring about its reduction, favouring (in the manner of von Liszt) preventative rather than penal solutions to crime. As Minister of Justice Karl Schlyter (1934: 17, our italics) explained, in what became his famous

Depopulate the Prisons speech, 'more important than all reforms of imprisonment and more important than removing a number of offences from the criminal code or reducing the sentencing scale, *are those social reforms that can change the environment that creates the prison customers in the first place*'. He also referred to the 'shame' of the unnecessary incapacitation of vagrants, young people, fine defaulters and alcoholics (ibid.: 12). To this end, and following Finland's earlier lead, day fines had been introduced in Sweden in 1931 (and Norway in 1933). In further legislation in 1939, imprisonment only became an option for fine defaulters if there was a deliberate refusal to pay. This had the effect of reducing the number of imprisoned fine defaulters from 13,358 in 1932 to 286 in 1946. *Even so, the rate of imprisonment then increased from 45 per 100,000 of population in 1950 to 60 in 1965.* This seems likely to have been caused by the almost absolute belief that this apparently benign, protective state was justified in using its extensive powers to take care of those who could not take care of themselves, in whatever capacity. Indeed, there were no qualms about removing children from home if necessary: the Report of the Penal Code Commission no. 55 (1956: 40, our italics) stated that 'it is important to recognize the importance of early influences on criminality. Childhood is very important in relation to crime . . . a bad upbringing justifies removal from the home. Crime prevention is very important from an early age in relation to training in values and morals. *The state is prepared to provide the upbringing children need.*' Moreover, policy in the post-war period was largely under the direction of welfare experts and civil service technicians, rather than Social Democrat politicians, imbued with evangelical faith in the curative powers and resources that had been invested in them (Lexbro, 2000).

Moderation and restraint

However, while the state's power to regulate and control was increased in these ways, the pain of its penal sanctions was significantly reduced. The medicalization of crime and alcohol problems had begun a process that would lead to the removal of pastoral power from the prison and the practice of cellular confinement that was its bastion. Amidst growing recognition in Sweden that this contributed to mental illness (despite the virtues that the pastors had attributed to it), from 1916 'the three year term was kept, [but] after the first year freedom from isolation was allowed during walks, school time and when in church' (Almquist, 1927: 324). It was then reduced to a maximum of one year in 1921. In Norway, the term of confinement had been reduced to three months in 1933 but, by this time, the authorities were, anyway, relegating its significance: 'the cell should make up the basis of prison treatment, used during the night-time, rest and for some individual work tasks. *But work should be undertaken together with other prisoners*' (Falsén, 1933: 139, our italics). Indeed, church attendance in Norwegian prisons was made voluntary in 1939. With this increasing secularization of the prison, so interest in the mental health of prisoners began to supersede interest in their 'soul care'. In the 1927 Report of the Royal [Swedish] Prison Board (1928), there are the first references to 'the mentally weak'. By the time of the 1938–1940 Report of the

Royal [Swedish] Prison Board (1941), prison classifications based on religious status ('confirmed' or 'unconfirmed') have disappeared. Instead, a new section, 'Treatment and Care', refers not only to religious instruction but also to education, training and medical and social work intervention.

By this juncture, the Social Democrats had also become interested in reform *within* the prison. To a degree, this had been prompted by the publication of Else Kleen's (1944) edited book, *Prisoner, Person, Punishment* (her marriage to the Social Democrat Minister for Social Affairs gave additional importance to the text[12]). In Sweden, there seems to have been virtually no tradition of prisoner biographies, as there was in England, and which gave very different accounts of prison life to those set out in the annual reports.[13] Now, though, Kleen (ibid.: 46–7) brought the debilitating consequences of cellular confinement to a wider audience: the prisoner 'has become a number and even in the best circumstances, can only hope to be treated as such. Others regulate all his actions in minute detail; he does not even possess everyone's birthright to be alone. Through the cell's Judas eye, his actions are constantly monitored, the space which he can call his own is not much bigger than a grave, in the workshop he is crowded by other people; if he has a right to be in communal areas he still cannot choose his own company even here . . . he can in no way give expression to his own personality in a way that he can keep to himself.' She was arguing, in effect, that the separate cell system was not only harmful, in itself, for prisoners, but also contradicted the value given to personal space in these increasingly secular societies.[14] Serene, rural solitude was prized now (as reflected in the popularity of summer cottages in the country), rather than the privations of monastic isolation in the cell. As such, this mode of confinement represented an archaic contravention of these values, and the opportunities for *all* to enjoy them, that egalitarian Social Democrat governments should be providing.

Thereafter, the world beyond the cell was welcomed in, rather than fearfully shut out. The 1941 Report of the Royal [Swedish] Prison Board (1942: 41) refers to a psychiatric prison where 'football is arranged between prisoner teams and those from outside'. Swimming pools were built where the inmates had 'no natural facilities'. The 1942 Report of the Royal [Swedish] Prison Board (1943: 43) refers to 'bigger cell windows, more light, air and the possibility of a view for the bodily and spiritual health of the intern.' Cellular confinement was then finally abolished in Sweden in 1945, under the provisions of the Penal Reform Law (although it lingered on in Norway until 1959 and Finland until 1971, it had never been anything like as extensive as in Sweden). Now, those admitted to prison should be treated, as Eriksson (1977: 132) later explained, 'with regard to their human worth. This deviated from many contemporary laws and came into being after all the revelations that had been made about the barbaric treatment of the prisoners in concentration camps by the Nazis.' The knowledge of what human beings were capable of doing to each other under such a regime had given additional strength to the Nordic values of restraint and moderation, and a determination amongst those developing policy that the treatment of prisoners should not be an exception to them. Accordingly, the 1945 legislation also stipulated that 'the loss of liberty . . . need not be accentuated by repressive means to be a deterrent. The loss of liberty can never be outweighed by any benefits . . . [but] *one should strive to make conditions in the institutions resemble life in free society as much as possible and encourage the prisoner's efforts and capacity for independent work . . . imprisonment should not be harmful to the prisoner's economic life and social status'* (quoted by Sellin, 1948: 23, our italics).

These intentions were further developed in the Report of the Penal Code Commission (no. 55, 1956: 40). Now it attempted to omit all oppressive connotations from the context of this document. For example the term 'punishment' (*straff*) should be replaced with that of 'consequences' (*påföljder*). Prisons were to be 'prisoner care institutions'; cells were to be 'living rooms'; prisoners were to be known as 'interns' and were to be addressed by name or by '*Ni*', the polite form of 'you'. Mentally ill offenders were held in 'protective custody', which was 'not seen as punishment' (Report of the Royal [Swedish] Prison Board, 1956–7). The report also stressed the importance of community involvement in reintegration – prisoners were not a race apart to be administered in isolation by Corrections officials: 'if a prisoner feels excluded from socializing with respectable people, he is likely to seek out other criminals. The community has a duty to take care of its criminal members.' Equally, the language of punishment had to change in ways designed to more clearly convey its inclusionary intents and soften its blow, with the effect that previous distinctions between lawbreakers and the rest of society became blurred. Prison design was also intended to reduce the 'difference' between prisoners and the rest of society. The *small, urban prisons* that have become characteristic features of the Nordic prison systems of the twenty first century were one such innovation. These were institutions that, as Schlyter (1946: 66) indicated, 'differ little from normal houses . . . the majority of prisoners are relatively harmless and do not need to be cared for in the fortress like institutions'. The 'open prisons' that also date from this time were another. Soine's (1964: 213) description of these latter establishments in Finland[15] dramatically highlights the transformation in the possibilities of imprisonment that had now taken place in this region: 'a common feature . . . is that they are operated in the same way as free working places . . . in all these institutions there are big dining halls with self-service. In addition to this, every barrack has a small kitchen of its own where the men can make coffee or tea or some other snack for themselves. The colony also has a canteen, a radio and often a television set, as well as a reading room where newspapers can be read and visitors received. There is also, of course, a Finnish bath, or "sauna".' The importance of personal space was also recognized, now, in the organization of both closed and open institutions. Eriksson (quoted by Fleisher, 1967: 188) thus explained that 'inmates should have to walk some distance to get to work, to watch a movie, to eat their meals. There should be enough space for a football field. Space is very important for the mental health of prisoners.' In Norway, during the 1960s, prisoners were allowed short periods of leave (a few hours) outside the prison 'for taking a walk with a visitor . . . this has also been used for some staff to take inmates for a walk to the village, to the theatre or a football match or to do some needed shopping' (Report of the Director of the Prison Board, 1973: 74). Similarly, in relation to internal living arrangements: 'productive work and security demands are satisfied through the physical design and surveillance technology. There are also common rooms, study rooms, a library and a small kitchen on each wing' (Report of the [Swedish] Prison and Probation Board 1961 (1962: 115)).

As the purpose and construction of prison changed, so too did the roles and expectations of prison staff. The emphasis on therapeutic rehabilitation, rather than spiritual redemption, demanded new professional standards across the prison service. Under the provisions of the social democratic welfare sanction, prison inmates were now to be restored to well-being *just like any other group of welfare clients* (they were no longer seen as sinners who should seek redemption). As Moyer (1974: 41) put the matter, 'prisoners and criminal patients are thus viewed in many ways the same as unemployed persons – a group whose existence detracts from the complex functioning of society and who thus must be trained and guided to find useful positions again'. Indeed, it was as if prisoners had become 'orphans of the welfare state' (*styvbarn i folkhemmet*[16]), in relation to whom the prison staff, *at all levels*, would be expected to act in an *uppfostran* capacity. That is, they would steer the 'interns', the 'orphans', onto 'the right path', and correct unwanted behaviour through the provision of education, trade training and so on. This was an attribute of the highly paternalistic nature of the social democratic welfare state, as a whole, towards those thought to have lost their way in life. The literal translation of the term *uppfostran* is 'to raise', as in 'raising a child', and implies the establishment and enforcement of rules, boundaries, firmness, education and approval of 'the child', with simultaneous disapproval of rule breaking actions. To better carry out and facilitate this role, there was to be a renewed emphasis on training and qualifications for those working in the prisons. As Soine (1955: 31, our italics) put the matter, 'the modern perception demands psychologists, psychiatrists, sociologists and social workers to treat offenders and that the guard, who is the prisoners' daily instructor and long term companion, is the prisoners' most important pedagogue. *This kind of perception sets a whole new set of quality requirements to* [sic] *prison staff beginning from the youngest guard. In this sense he can hardly be called a mere guard anymore.*' From 1954, the Swedish 'prisoner care' men would also be expected to contribute to a '"Treatment Collegium" consisting of a variety of prison staff and psychiatric experts, where the cases of prisoners serving six months or more would be heard. A treatment plan would be developed, with the inmate having the right, but not the obligation to participate in this' (Report of the Royal [Swedish] Prison Board *1953*, 1954: 28).

Importantly, then, it was intended that there would no division of labour between white collar treatment staff and uniformed guards: contributing to prisoner rehabilitation was the goal of all those employed in the prison.

Meanwhile, security would not be allowed to compromise the intention to place the pattern of prisoner employment on a par with that of the outside world. As Eriksson (1967: 199) put the matter, 'first we build the factory, then we build the prison'. That is, factory conditions would determine the nature of confinement, rather than prison conditions determine the kind of work that would be available to inmates. Accordingly, 'prison workshops . . . were organized in the same way as work outside the walls, with work measured per unit produced, clocking on and clocking off and so on' (Rudstedt, 1994: 149). Prisoners, like all other citizens, were expected to work in these societies – full employment was now central to the economic foundations of the social democratic welfare state, as well as the value that the Lutheran heritage had placed on it: 'a full employment policy is followed in the modern treatment of criminals. Inmates are under the obligation to work and all able-bodied offenders shall be employed. Idleness cannot be tolerated' (Report of the [Swedish] Prison and Probation Board *1961*, 1962: 16). At the same time, the Swedish trade unions, rather than seeing the workshops and other employment initiatives as a threat to free labour, had become involved in their development, indicative, again, of the high levels of solidarity and cohesion in this society. Gunnar Marnell (1974: 19), then Director of Stockholm Prisons, wrote that, 'in 1964, the trade unions of building and construction collaborated with one of our open borstals in such a way that the boys were members of the union when they left the institution . . . The Prison Board now has appointed a special official (from the trade unions) to promote this form of collaboration. Other unions may follow this example shortly since the central management of the unions has appointed a special working party to develop collaboration with prisons.' A similar pattern was taking place in Norway. The 1956 Prison Reform Commission stated that 'maximum effort should be made to make the work regulations of institutions resemble work conditions on the outside, and work should take place under conditions and in surroundings which stimulate work habits and work interests' (quoted by Mathiesen, 1990: 26). Thereafter, a prison visitor described modern 'prisoner care' at the newly built Ullersmo Central prison: 'well equipped, inmates have the possibility to learn a trade, and eventually receiving a qualification. Such things give self-confidence.' Indeed, the visitor goes on to report that '*the whole institution will be as little like a prison as possible* . . . Regarding warm water and internal phones, it is beneficial to have warm water to wash one's hands in after a long day at work, and the phone is useful when the inmate needs to use the toilet. His intestines are hardly different from those not in prison. Sport and swimming are of course important tools in education and discipline' (*VG*, 28 March 1966: 3, our italics). In Finland, the equivalent of a market wage was paid to prisoners working in its open institutions. Some Swedish prisoners were allowed to continue in their previous employment: *The New York Times* (30 October 1970: 9) reported that 'inmates travel each morning to civilian jobs and return to their quarters at night'.

At the same time, it was also recognized that prisoners, like any other group of workers, should be entitled to holidays. One Swedish 'treatment experiment' thus involved a three-week vacation for 10 long-term prisoners, with no obligation to work, on a remote farm in the company of 'a close friend or relative' (Report of the [Swedish] Prison and Probation Board, *1968,* 1969: 6). During the 1960s, various other pilot programmes involved prisoners and students sharing a hostel and studying together in Uppsala (*The Times*, 13 October, 1967: 10). In this country, prison could be a means of facilitating inmates' access to education, in relation to which they should be treated like any other student, rather than reinforcing their disqualification from society. In another, a 'prison hotel' was opened at Ulrikfors offering board and lodging to visiting relatives and intimate friends at weekends – with the prisoners accompanying them. Meanwhile, the high level of escapes and failures to return from leave[17] were not allowed to jeopardize these initiatives. Instead, for the authorities, escaping 'was a natural reaction to unnatural circumstances' (Report of the [Swedish] Prison and Probation Board, *1964*, 1965). Escapes represented a failure of state policy, not in relation to security, but regarding the unnecessarily repressive nature of imprisonment that contradicted social democratic values. As Eriksson (quoted by Rudstedt, 1994: 126, our italics) explained, 'our task, to guide ['interns'] towards a responsible use of freedom while in such a forced environment becomes impossible if the treatment is aimed towards demanding complete obedience . . . *We shall not forget that we live in a society that wants to show respect for the individual human beings – this is part of the essence of democracy.*' Rather than allowing the escapes to become a pretext for more security, the response of the Nordic authorities was to further liberalize the prison system: parole was increased, more staff were hired and they were provided with better training (in psychology, psychiatry, criminology and 'social care', as well as self-defence).

The responses of the authorities were facilitated by the way in which the Nordic media generally replicated the values of moderation, restraint and inclusion when reporting prison issues. Indeed, to ensure that there were no departures from them, 'rules of communication' were agreed between the Swedish Criminalist Association and the Publishers' Association at a meeting in 1953. While this, again, is indicative of the way in which corporate agreements were used to ensure consensus across these societies, it was also indicative of the standing of criminologists at that time in Sweden. As it was, the rules recognized that 'readers' confidence is the basis of all sound journalism'. It was thus important that 'all efforts were made to publish correct information *and to distinguish between news and opinion*, as well as a prohibition on judging anyone who had not yet been convicted – hence names, addresses and photographs of suspects could only be published after conviction' (Holmberg, 1953: 62, our italics). In effect, the Nordic press was as factual and dispassionate in reporting prison matters as it was other news items. The details of escapes were given, for example, but without explicit or implicit criticism of the prison authorities for not preventing them. Thus, in Sweden: 'five escaped from prison during one day. One person in the morning, using a plank to scale the wall; another four that afternoon via a roof in Gothenburg Prison' (*Svenska Dagbladet*, 4 January 1956: 3, 6). Similarly in Norway: 'Dangerous Opstad Prisoners on the Run . . . A large group of prison staff and police are today searching for three prisoners who escaped while working outdoors . . . they were spotted at 5.30 pm yesterday at Undheim, but since then there has been no trace of them. Two of them are seen as dangerous men who can cause a lot of trouble while on the run. One of them drove a horse and carriage yesterday when they were working, and it was this they used for their escape. Officers, who saw them drive away, presumed that they were just off to collect more materials. The prisoners left the horse outside the prison grounds' (*VG*, 9 June 1956: 1, 9). Then again, as prisoners were seen as 'just another group of welfare clients', with no great differences between them and the rest of the population, they were of no special interest anyway, and their escapes from prison were unlikely to attract sensational headlines for these reasons.

Instead, it was when the plans or reactions of the authorities seemed to contravene the prevailing penal values that critical comments were raised – there was too much security, rather than not enough. Kumla high security prison in Sweden, opened in 1965, was thus described as being 'too security conscious and austere': 'a psychologist working in the prison system has directed sharp criticism against the prison constructions at Kumla, which offers a particularly depressive environment that makes the readjustment of the prisoners much more difficult. From the low buildings, one cannot see over the seven metre high wall. All transports take place underground, and the technical equipment replaces human contact. Kumla has the character of a concrete bunker. The police, who have experience of [this prison,] emphasize that the inmates are worn down, they emerge much worse than they came in, suffering from claustrophobia and . . . apath[y], after long stays in small concrete cubes' (*Svenska Dagbladet*, 26 February 1966: 4).

'Almost the best of everything'

For the international community in the late 1960s, Sweden had become the leader of Western penal reform (although by now the parameters of the social democratic welfare sanction had also been set in place in Finland,[18] as well as Norway). While the rise in its rate of imprisonment over this period received little attention, a succession of visiting journalists and travel writers marvelled at its prison conditions (in much the same way that its welfare reforms had captured the attention of the international community): 'in the open prisons, guards are not armed, windows not barred and nothing prevents a prisoner from quietly strolling away over the fields' (Strode, 1949: 225); 'I asked what was done about escaping prisoners, since none of the guards had guns and the [prison] walls were not exactly formidable. [The governor] replied, "it is better to let the man go than to put a hole in him. . . we can always catch him later"' (Connery, 1966: 409–10); 'if the sentence is imprisonment, the prisoner has the comfort of knowing that Swedish prisons are world famous, the explicit aim being to reform, not to punish or take vengeance' (Jenkins, 1968: 65); 'if one should be sentenced to a work camp for driving under the influence of alcohol, it will not be in the newspaper even if one is well known; and one has some choice as to when he will serve his time, such as during vacations, so that even his employer need not know' (Tomasson, 1970: 276); 'Sweden's prisons are models of decency and humanity', claimed *The New York Times*' journalist Tom Wicker (1975: 201), under the headline, 'Almost the Best of Everything', linking its prison conditions to the quality of life outside of them in this society.

In reality, both sets of practices – the growth of imprisonment and the remarkable conditions of imprisonment – were complementary, rather than contradictory, features of the Swedish adaptation of the social democratic welfare sanction: an insistence that the state needed to correct, to whatever degree was necessary, deviation from social norms, as well as lawbreaking; and an insistence that the pains of correcting these deficiencies would be minimized for those individuals concerned.

The emergence and development of the liberal welfare sanction

Even though, in the late nineteenth century, there had been far fewer direct contacts with the European theorists and the international criminology associations (English officials, reflecting the suspicion of intellectuals, theorizing and anything 'foreign' that were such strong characteristics of these Anglophone societies, had been reluctant to participate in these meetings[19]), there were broad parallels in the intellectual roots of both models of welfare sanction. As with the Nordic societies, so in the Anglophone: criminals began to be classified by type: Havelock Ellis (1890: 1–21), for example, distinguished between 'the political criminal; . . . the criminal by passion; . . . the instinctive criminal; the occasional criminal . . . and the habitual criminal or the professional criminal'. Similarly, the assumption that criminals *chose* to break the law began to be disputed. Charles Goring (1913: 368), on the basis of his research on English prisoners, claimed that '[criminality is] inherited at much the same rate as are the other physical and mental qualities and anthropological conditions in man'. The need to reconsider the question of responsibility in criminal law came with these doubts. As the Prison Medical Officer J. M. Sutherland (1908: 57, our italics) observed, '*there is much to be said for the relativity of the responsibility of the derelicts of society* with all the drawbacks and disadvantages of environment, bad heredity and degeneracy bequeathed or acquired'. There was also support for punishment as a more extensive form of social defence, rather than the preoccupation with its use as a feared deterrent. Sir Robert Anderson, a senior figure in the London police, thus argued (1907: 36) for the compilation of criminal 'dossiers': 'these should consider the criminal and his antecedents and circumstances; and that, moreover, with the object of safeguarding the interests of the community, as well as dealing fairly with the culprit . . . the essential inquiry should be "Who is the offender?", "What is his character?", "What are his antecedents and circumstances?"' Under these circumstances, punishment should principally involve some form of bland, indefinite 'neutralization' rather than a finite term of misery and deprivation in one of Du Cane's prisons, as Sutherland (1908: 70) again explained: 'It is for the public and administrative bodies and individuals directly concerned with social order and good government to evolve a penal organization [that will] gradually eliminate from communities those elements which are unfit for its evolution and dangerous to society.' These new ways of thinking about crime and punishment in England then came to Australia and New Zealand through contacts between the respective prison authorities, visits to Europe by senior officials from these colonies, and correspondence between local penal reformers and the new penology fraternity.[20]

Nonetheless, the subsequent parameters and scope of the liberal welfare sanction took on a different form from those of the social democratic model. While the latter was concerned to provide greater protection of society as a whole through extending state power over individuals, the former was concerned with *providing more protection for individuals from excesses of state power* than had previously been the case (Bailey, 1997): excesses in the sense that in these Anglophone societies it was thought that individuals should be able to live their lives, for good or bad, without any unnecessary interference. This, rather than any elaborate development of psychodynamic treatment programmes, was the liberal welfare sanction's distinguishing feature. *However, while the social democratic welfare sanction intended to correct and normalize in such a way as to bring about the social inclusion of its recipients, the liberal welfare sanction was ultimately limited in its ability to reduce penal severity.* As with the distinctions that the liberal welfare state itself made in the determination of who should receive its assistance and who should not, distinction was made between the 'deserving' and 'undeserving': although some special categories thought 'deserving' might have their sentences reduced, those deemed 'undeserving' – most adult offenders – were still held responsible for their crimes and would be met with exclusionary penalties.

Protecting individuals from excessive uses of the state's power to punish

During the 1920s, the same elements that had coalesced around the development of the social democratic welfare sanction were also present in the Anglophone societies. *First*, in the form of the growing presence of medico-psychological knowledge in penal discourse. In *The Roots of Crime*, Edward Glover (1922: 4) argued that 'crime is not simply an anti-social phenomenon to be dealt with by the judiciary in accordance with fixed penal codes, but also a psychological problem involving close study on the part of all who are concerned with the motivation of human conduct'. From this point, and similar to the transformations taking place in Nordic prison discourse in the early twentieth century, references began to be made in the Anglophone prison reports to the 'mental weakness' of inmates; to courts 'becoming more interested in the mental condition of prisoners' (Report of the Commissioners of Prisons, 1919: 15); to 'mental instability' (Report of the Comptroller-General of Prisons (1927–9); to 'disordered impulses'; and to offenders 'who cannot be certified as insane, but whose mentality is such that their power of inhibition is below normal' (Report on the Prisons Department, 1926: 9).

Second, in the promotion of eugenics-based penal policies. It was not only the case that the British race was in danger of physical deterioration, it seemed, in the early twentieth century. It was also apparent that the breeding habits of 'the unfit', greatly exceeding those of the upper and middle classes,[21] were likely to exacerbate this dangerous trend. At the same time, the undesirable qualities of those judged to be 'unfit' were thought to be the products of heredity. The statistical innovations[22] of the prominent mathematician and eugenicist Karl Pearson (1903: 608) seemed to prove that 'we inherit our parents' tempers, our parents' conscientiousness, shyness and abilities, even as we inherit their stature, forearm and span'. Goring's subsequent research, as we have seen, then extended the powers of heredity to disposition to commit crime. Accordingly, if the British race was to be saved, the mere segregation of those who threatened its vitality and quality was insufficient. As Pearson (1907: 406) then explained, 'education for the criminal, fresh air for the tuberculous, rest and food for the neurotic – these are excellent, they may bring control, sound lungs and sanity to the individual; but they cannot save the offspring from the need of like treatment nor from the danger of collapse when the time of strain comes. They cannot make a nation sound in mind and body, they merely screen degeneracy behind a throng of averted degenerates.' To prevent their propagation, there had to be what the New Zealander W. A. Chapple (1903: 118) described, in *The Fertility of the Unfit*, as 'external restraint' (that is, vasectomy or sterilization). In particular, women offenders 'should be offered the alternative of surgical sterility or incarceration during the child rearing period of their life.' The respective Anglophone eugenics movements that favoured such proposals enjoyed support from all sides of the social and political spectrum. In England, the Fabian prison reformer Sydney Webb (1909: 3) was of the view that 'race deterioration, if not race suicide, has to be avoided, hence the legitimacy of compulsory sterilization'. Similarly, the novelist H. G. Wells (1904: 11, our italics): 'I believe that now and always the conscious selection of the best for reproduction will be impossible; that to propose it is to display a fundamental misunderstanding of what individuality implies. The way of nature has always been to slay the hindmost, and there is still no other way, unless we can prevent those who would become the hindmost being born. *It is in the sterilization of failure, and not in the selection of successes for breeding, that the possibility of an improvement of the human stock lies.*' In New Zealand, the leading eugenics advocate was Chief Justice Sir Robert Stout (1911: 6), who argued that 'sterilization or de-sexualization . . . will prevent breeding and also destroy the sexual desire that leads to sexual crime'. In New South Wales in 1927, Millicent Stanley, the first woman elected to its General Assembly, spoke in favour of legislation that would 'segregate the unfit' from the rest of society (Carey, 2007).

Third, in the rise of political forces committed to reducing social inequalities and lessening the severity of the state's response to crime. Around the turn of the twentieth century, reformist Liberal governments, along with the rising Labour party,[23] were prepared to widen the assistancial orbit of the state. Some of these politicians also pursued penal reform, most famously Churchill who, in 1910, minuted that its first principle 'should be to prevent as many people as possible getting [to prison] at all. There is an injury to the individual, there is a loss to the state wherever a person is committed to prison for the first time' (quoted by Bailey, 1997: 320).[24] There were also important links between radical politicians and pressure groups such as the Humanitarian League and the Howard League in England, even if these consisted mainly of middle class intellectuals and others with derided 'egghead' associations: their constituency was thus quite different to – more elitist and isolated than – the more broad-based Nordic social movements. In addition, some politicians were willing to take up the causes of political prisoners, imprisoned conscientious objectors and suffragettes in the early twentieth century.[25] These interconnections brought about some notable successes in reducing the levels and intensity of punishment. For example, a member of the Humanitarian League himself, John Galsworthy's (1910) play *Justice* featured a law clerk who, sent to prison for his first offence (embezzlement), suffered a nervous breakdown as he experienced separate confinement at the start of his sentence. After the uproar caused by these scenes (see Nellis, 1996), the Home Office rushed through further reductions to the period of isolation.[26]

In addition, the authorities were now prepared to loosen the rigidity that their predecessors had brought to penal administration. In England, Du Cane's successor, Sir Evelyn Ruggles-Brise, had been a student of the Oxford Professor of Philosophy, T. H. Green, whose work challenged the hegemony of economic liberals in relation to the role of the state in modern society. In *Prologemena of Ethics* (Green, 1883), he had argued that an extended, enhanced, state authority would provide each citizen with the opportunity to bring to fruition 'their best self', thereby providing the opportunities for more 'just' and 'efficacious' social arrangements. His influence on Ruggles-Brise can then be seen in the latter's comments, as Chairman, in the Report of the Commissioners of Prisons (1918: 8): 'a social system which could facilitate the means of employment while at the same time maintaining its sobriety at the present level would incidentally find in such measures the solution of the penal problem.' On the face of it, this was a retreat from the insistence that individuals had to accept full responsibility for their (criminal) conduct. Instead, the suggestion now was that it was the responsibility of the state to take preventative social measures to reduce their criminogenic surrounds.

In much the same way, then, as the Nordic countries, the coalescence of these forces provided a nexus for penal reform. Indeterminate sentences thus became entry and exit points of the prison in the Anglophone societies. This sanction was introduced for recidivists in New South Wales (1905) and New Zealand (1906) in habitual criminals' legislation. In England, preventive detention was introduced in the Prevention of Crime Act [PCA] (1908), taking the form of a double track penalty for third conviction recidivists: a finite sentence for the offence was to be followed by indefinite confinement at special prisons[27] for up to ten years, or until 'there is a probability that [the prisoner] will abstain from crime and lead a useful and industrious life' (s. 14(2) PCA 1908). Furthermore, the release of those sentenced in this way would be determined by an advisory committee of experts (much the same mechanism was also introduced for the corresponding legislation in New South Wales and New Zealand), rather than the judge at the time of sentence. Even then, this would not mark the end of their punishment, since release would instead be hedged around with conditions relating to employment, association and so on. In this way, their normative behaviour would be checked and regulated in addition to any lawbreaking propensities they might have. The use of the penal law to regulate norms as well as punish crimes was also reflected in inebriety provisions in England (1898), New South Wales (1905) and New Zealand (1906) that were similar to those for the internment of alcoholics in the Nordic countries. There were also proposals for the establishment of labour colonies for the unemployed in England, similar to those for Nordic work colonies. Equally similar was the way in which criminals with mental abnormalities could be detained indefinitely. In England (similarly, New Zealand from 1911), the 1913 Mental

Deficiency Act[28] allowed for 'moral defectives – 'those who from an early age displayed some permanent mental defect coupled with strong vicious or criminal propensities on which punishment had little or no effect' – to be held in this way.

However, it is also at this point that the similarities and parallels between the two welfare sanctions come to an end. Rather than the further extensions of the state's power to regulate, control and correct, which came with the subsequent development of the social democratic welfare sanction, any more systematic advances in this direction were largely blocked or impeded in the Anglophone countries. There were two main reasons for this. *The first was the residual suspicion of any such enhancement of state power and authority* – exactly what would be necessary for punishment to be transformed from being a juridical calculation of culpability to the administrative mechanism of social defence that it was becoming in the Nordic. Accordingly, those measures that did extend the state's power to punish by eliding breaches of criminal law and normative deficiencies became *peripheral*, rather than central, to the operation of Anglophone penal systems. The English judges, in particular – in contrast to their Nordic counterparts, who were more used to sharing their knowledge and authority in court and who, anyway, were civil servants rather than a specially selected elite group from an already elite profession – were antithetical to indeterminate sentences and the regulatory framework attached to them. Their judgments thus set carefully prescribed limits on these new penal powers. The Court of Appeal in *R* v *Sullivan* (1913, our italics)[29] recognized that '*it was necessary in the interests of the prisoner* that very watchful care should be exercised by this court and also by those who preside over trials in which a prisoner is charged with being a habitual criminal, to see that the prisoner's interests are jealously safeguarded'. Rather than allow state power to be used to provide protection for society as a whole, the judgment was focussed on protecting individuals – even the most worthless, as here, a criminal threatened with preventive detention – from undue enlargement of state power: 'persistence [in crime] is not proved by evidence of a number of convictions beyond the three. Where the interval between the crime charged and the offender's last release from prison is substantial, evidence of criminality must be submitted . . . *the mere fact that a convict on license had not reported himself to the police is not sufficient to establish that he is leading a dishonest or criminal life*' (*R* v *Mitchell*, 1912).[30] Furthermore, these laws should only apply to crimes rather than mere breaches of normative conduct. Thus: 'although association with other criminals was proven this was insufficient to result in a habitual criminal conviction' (*R* v *Hammersly*, 1925)[31]; 'it is impossible to say that the jury would inevitably have found the appellant to be a habitual criminal if the importance of his period of honest work had been explained, and the sentence of preventive detention must therefore be quashed' (*R* v *Winn*, 1925).[32]

These restrictions on punishment were in keeping with the thrust of the more egalitarian polity of this period. As William Crick, speaking out against the habitual criminals measures in the New South Wales Assembly explained, 'the tendency of modern legislation is not to brand a man as being incapable of reform because he has fallen once, but to give him a chance' (Hansard [NSW], 1905: 24). In these societies, 'giving him a chance' meant setting him free from the state, rather than entrusting him to it. Whatever prisoners might have done to justify their exclusion from the rest of society, this should not reduce them to the level of playthings of the state, to be tossed out of prison by bureaucrats at the point when they decided that they had amused themselves enough at their expense. Indeed, the penal authorities themselves were suspicious of the new powers they had been given under these measures. Ruggles-Brise (1921: 58, our italics) was thus at pains to point out that indeterminate sentencing provisions 'do not touch that large army of habitual vagrants, drunkards, or offenders against bye-laws who figure so prominently in the prison population. *[These are] weapons to be used only where there is a danger to the community from a professed doer of anti-social acts being at large*, and reverting cynically on discharge from prison to a repetition of predatory action or violent conduct.' There was also widespread public suspicion of any such measures, reflecting the way in which state authority, certainly in England, continued to be seen as something alien, frightening and unwelcome by many. The Report of the Departmental Committee on Sexual Offences Against Young People (1925: 61, our italics) noted that 'we consider special action is called for in cases of repeated sexual offences . . . [but] *we are aware that the public mind is distrustful of any kind of indeterminate sentence*'.

The overall effect of these limits and restrictions on the new powers of punishment that had been given to the state was that the highpoint of the use of preventive detention in England was in 1910, with 162 such sentences; by 1948 only six sentences were imposed in that year (Morris, 1950). By the 1960s, such measures had largely fallen into disuse (Bottoms, 1977). The pattern was similar in New Zealand and Australia: 'notwithstanding that approximately 30 per cent of total receptions in [New Zealand] prisons are of the petty recidivist type who are not deterred, or in respect of whom society is not protected, by repeated short sentences, there has been no recourse by the court to [habitual criminal declarations] at least during the past 20 years and possibly longer' (Report on the [New Zealand] Prisons Department, 1948: 4). In New South Wales, only 20 habitual criminal orders were made in the first 20 years of that legislation (Grabosky, 1977). Similarly, there was little enthusiasm amongst the body politic for the various plans and proposals to give the state the power to correct the habits and conduct of inebriates, defectives and vagrants. Even amongst those, such as Green, who favoured the idea of a more interventionist state, the intention was that *it should facilitate opportunities for self-improvement*. It was not intended that the state would become involved in anything like the social engineering programmes of the Nordic countries, Sweden especially. The inebriates' legislation thus came to a swift end. In England, two such institutions that had been established in 1899 were closed in 1923 because of lack of use. The only specialist institution in New South Wales (none were ever opened in New Zealand) was closed in 1929. The laws against mental defectives were much more likely to be used – when they *were* used[33] – against women of supposedly dubious sexual morality, rather than against all those male criminals whose defectiveness was thought to be conjoined with drunkenness and recidivism, and who had originally prompted these measures (Walmsley, 2000; Fennell, 2001).

As for the vagrants, the labour colonies that had been considered in England never came into existence. Nor was such a measure even considered in New South Wales and New Zealand. In these colonial societies, it was thought that there were ample employment opportunities that individuals should seek out for themselves without the need for any such direction from the state. Similarly, rather than compulsory sterilization being seen as a legitimate way to safeguard racial and national well-being, the prevailing view was that vulnerable individuals had to be protected from such an insidious use of state power. Sutherland (1908: 92–3), although a strong supporter of the indeterminate sentence, was also of the opinion that 'there is not the remotest chance of a British legislature entertaining or sanctioning such a proposal [for the sterilization of criminals and defectives, and even if there was] it would be impossible to find a public mutilator . . . no doubt it is a simple and speedy remedy to put the habitual criminal and delinquent "on the list" as persons who "would not be missed", but listing them for lethal, or mutilating, chambers is not the way either justice or humanity points'. And the New Zealand prison reformer and chaplain, the Reverend James Kayll (1905: 112–3), denounced Chapple's sterilization proposals: 'regard yourselves for the moment as being brute beasts and discuss [compulsory sterilization] upon that level. Murder the social instinct; murder the compassionate spirit; disregard the Divine Law and stifle all faith in the providence of God.' The subsequent Report of the Departmental Committee on Sterilisation (1934) in England extinguished any further interest in eugenics-based penal policies, concluding unanimously against compulsory sterilization. In these countries, the surgical interference with the body's reproductive capabilities to eliminate risks to normative well-being remained off the agenda, even though *punishing the body for crime*, by whipping, flogging or hanging, remained possible in them until the 1960s.[34]

The second reason for the departure of the liberal welfare sanction from the route of the social democratic model was because of a reluctance to retract the principle of individual responsibility in criminal law: at least, a reluctance to retract this beyond those categories of offender who qualified as being worthy of assistance from the state and who were thought deserving of some mitigation of their punishment. Medico-psychological knowledge, the main vehicle for this secular absolution of criminal responsibility in the social democratic welfare sanction, was only allowed to make limited intrusions into Anglophone criminal justice systems (notwithstanding the references to 'mental weaknesses' and similar comments in the prison reports in the inter war years). The idea that crime was some sort of predestined activity that individuals could do nothing to resist was met with considerable scepticism, not least amongst English prison medical officers. Common sense and pragmatism based on experience was valued, in these societies, more than theory and remote intellectualizing. William Norwood East (1923: 229), then medical officer at Brixton Prison, thus counselled against 'the hyper-enthusiasts for inherited degeneracy'. Ruggles-Brise (1921: 162–3, our italics) himself conceded very little ground to those who claimed exemption from responsibility for their crimes on the basis of inherited deficiencies. As regards the inebriates, '[this] is a constitutional peculiarity, and depends in many cases upon qualities with which a person is born, in many is acquired by vicious indulgence . . . [but] *it is erroneous and disastrous to inculcate the doctrine that inebriety, once established, is to be accepted with fatalistic resignation*'. As regards the mental defectives: '*defectiveness . . . must not be pressed so far as to affect the liability to punishment of the offender for his act*' (ibid.: 170, our italics). Thereafter, as psychological abnormality began to replace biological determinism in medico-psychological discourse, the Report of the Departmental Committee on Persistent Offenders (1932: 46, our italics) was dismissive of such explanations of crime: 'we do not agree with the view that crime is a disease, or that it is generally the result of mental disorder . . . *and further, if we accept the psychological explanations in certain cases of crime, we do not regard it of necessity as an excuse for the offence*'. Under the operation of the liberal welfare sanction, any attempts to challenge the deeply embedded emphasis on individual responsibility by reference to this knowledge would be more likely to be seen as an 'excuse' for crime than under that of the social democratic welfare sanction, which demonstrated a much greater readiness to shield individuals from their culpability.

Thus, while psychological deficiency was eagerly diagnosed by prison medical staff in Sweden, Norwood East and Hubert (1939: 7), in their research on a prison cohort of men aged under 40 who had been convicted of sexual or arson offences,[35] maintained that 80 per cent of them were 'psychologically normal'. And only seven per cent of the remainder, they then claimed, were actually 'treatable': not only was there little evidence of the psychological abnormalities that the Swedish authorities had found so readily but, in addition, even when discovered, there seemed little that could be done to correct them. There was no corresponding enthusiasm, then, for the great investment in treatment facilities that came to be characteristic of the Swedish version of the social democratic welfare sanction. This remained so even in the post-1945 period, after medico-psychological knowledge had been able to demonstrate successes in alleviating Allied physical and mental wounds during the war, as well as in operations it had helped to conduct against the Nazis (Rose, 1985). This was the period when liberal elites situated at leading British universities, in conjunction with senior civil servants and members of the legal profession, were at their most influential on the development of penal policy (Loader, 2006), as already seen in relation to the death penalty debates of this period. The Advisory Council on the Treatment of Offenders (ACTO) was established in England in 1944 and was followed by the Home Office Research Unit in 1957.[36] Nonetheless, considerable scepticism about the claims made for medico-psychological treatment in the criminal justice system remained amongst these elites; in addition, there were concerns that this masked more intrusive forms of state power. As one of this circle's leading lights, Baroness Barbara Wootton (1959: 218) put the matter, 'fine phrases cannot, however, obscure the fact that "adjustment" means adjustment to a particular culture or to a particular set of institutions; and that to conceive adjustment and maladjustment in medical terms is in effect to identify health with the ability to come to terms with that culture or those institutions'. Similarly, the authorities continued to warn that 'it is a mistake to assume that every person who fails to adapt themselves to social conditions is a psychopath' (Report of the Commissioners of Prisons, 1946: 64); and 'the aim should be for more intensive individual investigation . . . in such a way that an individual offender will accept it and not use it as a reason for regarding themself as a medical case or psychiatrically abnormal person' (Report of the Commissioners of Prisons, 1951: 86). Clearly, as the latter comments indicate, inquiries into an individual's background, to elicit the cause of their criminality, *were* permitted within the liberal welfare sanction – the Home Office (1959: 13) White Paper, *Penal Practice in a Changing Society*, thus favoured the development of 'more humane and constructive methods' of responding to crime. This, though, was very different to allowing psychological knowledge to absolve criminals from any responsibility for their conduct and, in so doing, turn them into objects of special curiosity as mental health professionals meticulously probed behind the presenting symptoms of their crime to bring to light the dark secrets of the unconscious mind. Indeed, diagnoses of criminal insanity remained at a minimal level in England: '5,158 cases were referred for psychiatric investigation, but 5,000 were considered unsuitable for treatment' (Report of the Commissioners of Prisons, 1945: 39); 'it is interesting to note that despite the great increase in the number of remands for medical reports, the numbers found insane and mentally defective have considerably decreased' (Report of the Commissioners of Prisons, 1951: 20).

In such ways, the much more extensive regulatory state powers with which the social democratic welfare sanction was associated were largely shut out of the liberal model. In the social democratic welfare sanction, these powers had allowed searches for psychological deficiencies in the individual, which were then were likely to be followed by the provision of state care – often indefinite institutionalization. In contrast, in the liberal model, a gradually widening category of special circumstances was allowed to mitigate the level of punishment that would otherwise have been imposed. Rather than the provision of more state care as a response to crime and deviance, there was to be less punishment and more assistance *within prescribed categories of acceptability*. From the late nineteenth century through to the 1960s, a series of measures were introduced to this effect. The introduction of probation orders was one of the first. As Howard Vincent MP thus explained, when proposing his First Offenders' Probation Bill in the British parliament, 'there were many offenders whose crimes did not arise from a criminal and habitually vicious mind – the means ought to be found of reforming the character without giving the prison taint' (Hansard [UK], HC Deb, 5 May 1886, col. 334). In the early twentieth century, further extensions of probation followed – it became available to most deserving offenders, not just first timers[37]– along with the introduction of 'time to pay' legislation for fines (imprisonment for non-payment declined from 85,000 in 1910, to 15,000 in 1920 (Bailey, 1997)).[38]Although, at that time, further ameliorations in the form of suspended sentences and parole were blocked (such measures seemed to contravene the strict principle then in place in these societies that only judges could determine the extent of punishment[39]), these measures were subsequently introduced in the post-war period, indicative, in themselves, of the stronger influence of welfare expertize on policy formation then.[40] By this time, there were also restrictions and prohibitions on sending first offenders and young adult offenders to prison.[41]

Furthermore, while the social democratic welfare sanction sought to extend the state's powers of regulation and correction, these were cut back during the operation of the liberal welfare sanction. One of the most striking illustrations of this difference can be seen in the respective approaches to alcohol-related conduct. There was a higher level of tolerance of this in the Anglophone societies. While these also had strong temperance movements in the early twentieth century, there was a much larger constituency for whom 'having a drink' carried little by way of any immoderate, licentious connotations. Indeed, in Australia and New Zealand especially, 'drinking, not abstinence [was] usually regarded as desirable behaviour' (Sargent, 1973: 2). Heavy drinking had acted as a form of male bonding, and had encouraged mutual reciprocities and obligations during their evolution from being frontier colonies in the early nineteenth century. As Ward (1958: 35) explained in relation to Australia, 'no people on the face of the earth ever absorbed more alcohol per head of population'. By the same token, 'the pub' had become the focal point of community interaction in these societies, rather than the church or the school-room, as in the Nordic.[42] These differences in tolerance led to imprisonment for drunkenness in England declining from 7,764 such receptions in 1905 to 1,933 in 1930. Post-1945, there were further declines in the prosecution of drunkenness, from 52,700 in 1938 to 23,700 in 1947. As Göransson (1949: 147) observed, during the course of a study tour to England, 'the social workers do not find the issue of alcohol a big problem [here]'. There were also markedly different approaches to alcohol-related driving offences. In the Anglophone societies, these were likely to be committed by all classes, rather than confined to the poor, and thereby carried much less moral turpitude than in the Nordic. Indeed, such conduct seemed to belong merely to that category of crime that was described by the New Zealand Department of Justice (1968: 11) as 'social welfare offences': 'those who commit them are not properly regarded as "criminals". A similar attitude certainly tends to apply to traffic offences including even serious breaches which result in death or injury to others. If these offences are not exactly condoned, they do not appear to carry serious moral blame. The offender is felt to be unfortunate rather than wicked.' In contrast to Sweden, where the prosecution of such offences was driven by a much stronger commitment to use criminal law to provide community safety, only 3.9 per cent of those convicted of driving under the influence of alcohol were sent to prison by magistrates courts in England in 1959, and 6.6 per cent of those so convicted by higher courts. The overwhelming majority were simply fined (Willett, 1964: 165).

The result was that, by the mid-twentieth century, while Anglophone prison populations were made up largely of serious/violent offenders serving long sentences, along with short-term prisoners who did not belong in the 'deserving categories', those of the Nordic societies – Sweden, especially – were made up of white collar criminals, drivers who had been drinking alcohol and 'mentally abnormal' offenders serving indefinite sentences. As a consequence, the operation of the liberal welfare sanction, in its focus on protecting individuals from over-use of the state's power to punish, had helped to bring about dramatic reductions in the Anglophone rates of imprisonment, to the extent that, in England in 1939, it

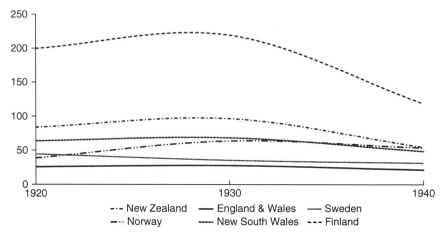

Figure 5.1 Imprisonment rates, 1920–1940 (all six societies).

Sources: New Zealand: New Zealand Yearbook (various). England and Wales: Home Office (2003). Sweden: Christie (1968). Norway: Statistics Norway (2012a). New South Wales Official Yearbook (various). Finland: Christie (1968).

was lower than that of all the Nordic countries in which the social democratic welfare sanction had been more active in the development of its elaborate networks of regulation and assistance (see Figure 5.1).

Thereafter, up to the mid-1950s, the prison rates of both clusters remained much the same (with the exception of Finland, still coming to terms with its extreme poverty, post-war repairs and the cultural legacy of its civil war).

The limitations and constraints of the liberal welfare sanction in reducing penal severity

Nonetheless, the inherent limitations and constraints of the liberal welfare sanction allowed these reductive possibilities, as well as any reformatory intents, to be surpassed and ultimately overwhelmed by the longstanding exclusionary penal characteristics of the Anglophone societies. This was subsequently reflected in (1) the increases in Anglophone imprisonment rates from the mid-1950s (see Figure 5.2); and (2) deteriorating prison conditions brought about by the continuing stamp of less eligibility on prison policy, which undermined the reformist intentions of the liberal welfare sanction.

The increases in the Anglophone imprisonment rates from the mid-1950s

The shift from pre war prison reductionism to post-war inflation in these Anglophone societies was caused *first*, by the parameters that had been set for the operation of the liberal welfare state itself. There were firm limits to the degree of equalization and inclusion it could achieve. In effect, it was unable to redress the much more

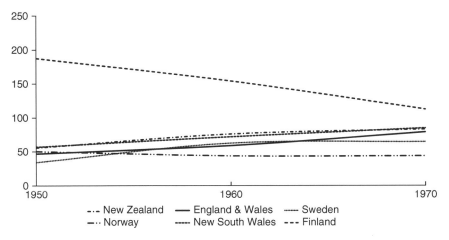

Figure 5.2 Imprisonment rates, 1950–1970 (all six societies).

Sources: New Zealand: New Zealand Yearbook (various). England and Wales: Home Office (2003). Sweden: Falck, von Hofer and Storgaard (2003).

Norway: Statistics Norway (2012a). New South Wales Official Yearbook (various). Finland: Falck, von Hofer and Storgaard (2003).

extended criminogenic social distances and inequalities that were still in place in these societies. While the Nordic countries not only maintained high levels of homogeneity but also a much more entrenched commitment to egalitarianism that their model of welfare cemented firmly in, the Anglophone divisions and disparities became more obvious from the mid-1950s with the growth of affluence and consumerism. In England, class divisions and barriers remained largely in place. In Australia, there were concerns about the criminal behaviour of new Eastern and Southern European migrants, now that the immigration laws had been liberalized (Mukherjee, 1999). In New Zealand, these disparities were ethnic rather than class-based. Maori urban migration at this time led to suspicion and alarm, among the white urban communities, at this sudden intrusion of 'difference' to the idealized world they had come to this country to create, or had expected to find. The New Zealand Department of Justice (1968: 398) thus warned that 'theft and car conversion are not regarded as seriously in a Maori community as in a European . . . sexual *mores* amongst Maori also have a slightly different basis . . . the traditional Maori attitude towards common assault is that it is a matter for the community to deal with . . . A relatively low income, together with high city rents, makes it difficult for [the Maori] to obtain reasonable accommodation. Loneliness and the anonymity of city life are especially difficult for [them] when used to a full community life. Crime is often a product of temptation.' The point is that each of these societies had their increasingly visible and prominent underclasses, with very loose social bonds, that were then held largely responsible for the increases in violent crime and property crime that began to occur in these societies in the 1950s and 1960s.[43] At the same time, the prevailing social distances and barriers restricted the formation of interdependencies and reciprocities that might have been able to put restraints on immoderate conduct, whether this related to committing crime or punishing it.

And *second*, by the parameters that had been set for the operation of the liberal welfare sanction. The limits that were to be placed on the exercise of the state's power to punish in these societies, the limits to which it would be allowed to assume responsibility for the behaviour of its own citizens, also meant that most offenders were still likely to be held fully responsible for their actions. As such, there were very clear limits to tolerance in the operation of the liberal welfare sanction. It was not the case that assistance would be extended to all – this was not, after all, the 'the people's home' model of welfare. The emphasis on individual responsibility, family responsibility, *but not that of the state*, is seen in the comments of the Report on the [New Zealand] Department of Justice (1968: 400): 'insufficient parental care and affection, an unacceptable code of behaviour derived from parents or peers, difficulties in learning . . . and lack of training for work and leisure combine to produce a sense of inadequacy, frustration and resentment. This either turned inward in self-destructiveness, or outward in aggressive, defiant behaviour that flouts the laws of society.' When they came to the attention of the courts, inadequates and incapables could be helped, as could juveniles and the inexperienced, and even those who had 'responded to treatment', with the introduction of parole in these societies in the 1960s. *However*, outside of these special 'deserving' categories, the vast majority of offenders were still understood as wilfully challenging the authority of the state. *They would continue to remain outsiders: the liberal welfare sanction did not change this.* Thus, in the pre war period, while there had been none of the internment provisions of the social democratic welfare sanction for vagrants, nor any compulsory despatches of them to work colonies, they would periodically have to spend a few days in prison if caught without any means to support themselves. In between, they were left to beg or seek assistance from charities.[44] In 'public assistance institutions' in Britain in the 1930s, still run on workhouse principles, they were allowed to stay one night only, in the most spartan conditions, before being moved on.[45] In contrast to the inclusionary intents of the social democratic welfare sanction, the liberal welfare sanction wanted to be rid of them – their fate was in their own hands, given that they did not fit the criteria for assistance that was given to 'the deserving'. It did not wish to go about the business of trying to normalize their conduct, nor did it have the resources to do so. Indeed, throughout the era of the liberal welfare sanction, the vast majority of adult offenders were thought to have no special features: they were entirely forgettable, mundane, criminals, nothing more, nothing less – even the prison psychologists denied them otherwise. Accordingly, without being thought worthy of any mitigation, they would still be met with punishment and exclusion. Thus, while crime rose across Western society as a whole, post-1945, the way of understanding and responding to it in the two clusters of societies came to be very different. In the Nordic countries, the emphasis was on the gravity of white collar crime and the dangers of alcohol. In the Anglophone, the emphasis was much more on penalizing the crimes of all the 'undeserving' criminals; this, in practice, meant the crimes of the poor and the powerless[46] who then began to populate the Anglophone prisons in increasing numbers.

Deteriorating prison conditions brought about by the continuing
stamp of less eligibility on prison policy, which undermined the
reformist intentions of the liberal welfare sanction

From the late nineteenth century through to the 1960s, the authorities attempted to ameliorate prison conditions, thereby reducing the severity of punishment in line with the broad expectations of the liberal welfare sanction. In England, the Gladstone Committee's report (Gladstone, 1895: 16) now specified that prison policy should pursue both deterrence *and* reform: 'so much can be done by recognition of the plain fact that the great majority of prisoners are ordinary men and women, amenable more or less to all those influences which affect persons outside'. From that point, more attention was, indeed, given to social and educational training. The Report of the Prisoners' Education Committee (1896: 6) thus wished to 'double the amount of time given to teaching: the present limit of 15 minutes per week is by no means sufficient'. Reflecting the increased priority given to education in New South Wales, the Report of the Comptroller-General of Prisons (1911: 17) noted that, at Darlinghurst, 'a schoolroom is now being used for education, instead of a shed'. In New Zealand, the Report on the Prisons Department (1928: 11) later observed that 'education classes supplemented by lectures are provided by the Workers Education Association'. Similarly, prison labour changed from being afflictive to productive in purpose. In England, the treadwheels and cranks were phased out in 1898. By 1920, only 'one in 33 [English prisoners] were employed on picking, teasing and soaking oakum, cotton etc' (Report of the Commissioners of Prisons, 1920: 25). In New South Wales it was claimed that 'no capable able-bodied prisoner is engaged at labour that condemns him. He is encouraged to do good work and take a pride in it' (Report of the Comptroller-General of Prisons, 1916: 43). In New Zealand, it was reported that 'the days are over when, until comparatively recently, it was by no means uncommon in our local prisons to see prisoners using wheelbarrows to convey soil backwards and forwards in profitless and pointless task fulfilment' (Report on the Prisons Department, 1934: 2). Indeed, some innovations, such as tree planting camps and farms, were introduced to the prison systems of New South Wales and New Zealand in the early twentieth century.

Furthermore, living conditions became more relaxed. In England, conversation was to be allowed for good conduct and 'convicts were allowed to retain the photographs of their respectable friends and relatives' (Report of the Commissioners of Prisons, 1900: 27). At the same time, more emphasis was placed on elevating prisoners' self-respect and dignity ('shaving has made a great difference to self-respect . . . the hang-dog look so characteristic of many prisoners in former days tends to disappear' (Report of the Commissioners of Prisons, 1923–1924: 19)). Uniforms that had been deliberately designed to humiliate were replaced by workmen's overalls. There was also more freedom of association: 'most prisoners are no longer locked up for the day at 4.40 pm. They either come out again after the evening meal and resume associated work, or in some cases, the evening meal is postponed to a later hour' (ibid.: 23). In New South Wales it was claimed that 'prisoners are now treated as human beings' (Report of the Comptroller-General of Prisons, 1917: 4). This allowed 'wires and bars [to be] removed as far as possible from compartments in which visits paid by relatives and friends and governors are asked to exercise freely the option of allowing visits to take place in a room, if no risks are to be apprehended. The prisoner and his friends in such cases merely sit on opposite sides of the table . . . the general object of enabling prisoners to see friends under ordinary conditions . . . is being pushed forward' (Report of the Comptroller-General of Prisons, 1927: 8). And there was to be less austerity and more opportunities for socialization. Thus, in New Zealand, there were 'facilities for team sports; sheets are provided for all prisoners; there are shelves for books; a cell chair replaces the stool; flowers and pictures are allowed in the cells' (Report on the Prisons Department, 1939: 3). Dietary arrangements also improved: 'there is now no penal element in the diet . . . each ration is weighed out after cooking, and no reasonable fault could be found with the food, its cooking or distribution' (Report on the Prisons Department, 1928: 5); 'the nutrition of the prisoners has been kept well up to standard, and the majority of both men and women are found to put on weight' (Report of the Comptroller-General of Prisons, 1937: 6).

As these changes occurred, relationships between prison staff and some prisoners began to be conducted on the basis of trust, rather than command. 'Red collars' were thus introduced for trustworthy prisoners in England in 1912. The first open prison was established in this country in 1933, receiving 'star' prisoners (New Zealand and New South Wales followed suit in the 1950s): 'there were no walls nor fence, the men sleeping in wooden huts and the boundaries designated, if at all, by whitewash marks on the trees' (Fox, 1952: 152). At the tree planting camps and farms, it was reported that 'a considerable amount of trust is necessarily placed in the young men and while there is a reasonable measure of disciplinary control, there is little of the prison characteristics about the treatment' (Report of the Comptroller-General of Prisons, 1927–1928: 8). The authorities were also insistent that the underlying purpose of these new possibilities of imprisonment should not be compromised by security concerns.

Post-1945, it was intended that imprisonment should further throw off its exclusionary effects and become more productive in purpose. The 1948 English Prison Rules thus stated that the purpose of imprisonment was to help inmates 'to lead a good and useful life on release.' Similarly, in New Zealand and New South Wales, 'the primary aim of the [Prisons] Department is the ultimate satisfactory rehabilitation of every prisoner' (Report on the Prisons Department, 1949: 1); and 'a prisoner's punishment consists of being sent to prison, with its ensuing loss of freedom. If an effort is to be made to rehabilitate, it is essential that, so far as is reasonable and consistent, conditions within the prison should constitute a social life that is approximately that of the community' (Report of the Comptroller-General of Prisons, 1949–1950: 10). To help them bring about these possibilities, educational services were to be increased – there was a reported 45 per cent attendance of the prison population at evening classes in England, for example (Report of the Commissioners of Prisons, 1948: 27). Nor would these continue to be restricted to illiterates: '240 prisoners in New South Wales have enrolled in tertiary education since 1960' (Report of the Comptroller-General of Prisons, 1965–1966: 3). Similarly, there were improvements to hygiene and other aspects of everyday living arrangements. As regards diet, 'the traditional breakfast of porridge' was supplemented by 'sausage and gravy' or 'bacon and fried bread' with 'a reduction in the amount of oatmeal and bread being balanced by an additional item of food suitable for providing an extra dish, [giving] a welcome break in the breakfast monotony' (Report of the Commissioners of Prisons, 1956: 126). In relation to personal appearance, uniforms were redesigned with a view to further reducing the prisoner's sense of shame and difference from the rest of society: 'new dresses for women prisoners have been completed. These are non-institutional in appearance and offer a choice of colour to meet, to some degree, the personal taste of the women' (Report of the Commissioners of Prisons, 1950: 4). Thereafter, 'a start was made on a programme that aimed at improving practically every article of prison wear and at bringing scales of issue up to modern standards of living and hygiene. Outer wear has already been radically altered with a smarter jacket to replace the outmoded battle dress style blouse. More and better shirts, socks and sets of underwear were issued' (Report on the Work of the Prison Department, 1968: 11). The authorities also wished to further relax prison security, with Sir John Simon, Under-Secretary of State at the Home Office, explaining that 'the public should accept something less than 100 per cent security. Protection of this standard . . . could no doubt be brought about by the strategic confinement of prisoners by loading them with fetters and manacles and irons and so on. [But] no-one today would countenance such a thing . . . if society wants to develop the positive and redemptive side of prison work, it must face the fact that the occasional prisoner may escape and do damage' (quoted in the Report of the Director of Penal Services, 1957: 8).

However, running alongside these ameliorative developments, less eligibility insisted throughout that prisoners had to be disadvantaged, rather than advantaged, by their crimes. Thus, the improvements in prison conditions had to be carefully tailored to demonstrate that the prison would remain a place to which its former inmates would never wish to return: 'it is, we hope, quite unnecessary to refute the idle statements which obtain currency among those unacquainted with the system, that prisons are made "comfortable"; they are only "comfortable" so far as the laws of hygiene compel cleanliness and wholesome food and decent clothing' (Report of the Commissioners of Prisons, 1912: 27); 'before discussing the progress of education and other measures, it is worthwhile to make their object clear . . . *this is not to make prisons pleasant*' (Report of the Commissioners of Prisons, 1923: 17, our italics). Furthermore, prisoners still had to internalize the indissoluble taint of being imprisoned – the state was not going to absorb it for them, in these societies, and allow them to escape the consequences of their crimes. It thus remained that 'the penalty is in the dishonorary circumstances which must accompany loss of liberty, in the deprivation of what liberty permits in the way of indulgence and self-gratification; in compulsory labour; in the loss of self-respect. Nothing can add to the *fletrissure* [humiliation] which these things involve' (Report of the Commissioners of Prisons, 1925: 14). Prisoners had to recognize the distance that they, *of their own volition*, had placed between themselves and the rest of society: 'a prisoner must be made to realize that he must first discipline himself by learning to adopt himself to the institutional regime before he can conform to more exacting standards in civil life. It is fundamental that he should appreciate that offending against society involves deprivation of liberty and the denial of certain privileges that law-abiding men enjoy' (Report on the [New Zealand] Prisons Department, 1936: 5).

And, while some prisoners might indeed now be considered more trustworthy, the vast majority were still seen as utterly worthless. Formally, at least,[47] they were no longer compelled to perform afflictive labour; however, there seemed little point in trying to organize more productive work for them: '[the prison population] is of a low order of physical and mental development, it is constantly changing, and in short presents no favourable feature whatsoever for the development of industrial work' (Gladstone, 1895: 22). The Report of the Departmental Committee on the Employment of Prisoners (1933: 17, our italics) later noted that 'the Prison Commissioners make no claim that a prisoner is taught a trade that he can follow on release, *as they have reached the conclusion that the poor quality of labour [and] the conditions of an institutional life . . . make this impossible for all but a minority of prisoners.*' At the same time, employment prospects in prison were limited by stringent opposition from trade unions to any possibility of prison-made products competing with those of free labour.[48] In these societies, solidarity between workers was not extended to prisoners. Nor was there any tradition of corporate governance, whereby the unions would have some involvement in the development of prison labour, as in Sweden.

Furthermore, notwithstanding the more inclusionary emphasis in post-1945 policy, *prisoners remained at the bottom of the hierarchy of acceptability and worthiness that directed the operation of the liberal welfare state.* They were still unwanted outsiders, rather than just another group of welfare clients, as in the Nordic countries. All other state organizations had priority on the welfare state's resources, and the prison authorities themselves accepted this: 'with pressing social need for houses, hospitals, and schools, we very well know where we stand in order of priority for capital works' (Report on the [New Zealand] Department of Justice, 1954: 6); 'the erection of prisons is a slow and costly business and it would have been completely wrong for the department to have sought to build prisons which may or may not have been needed, particularly at a time when the erection of schools, hospitals and houses could have had a high priority' (Report of the [New South Wales] Comptroller-General of Prisons, 1956–1957: 5). This kind of public recognition – prison was the home of the dregs of society and it thus could not expect any embellishment that would change its standing – added to the difficulties of recruiting uniformed staff. There was no possibility of this employment becoming a more attractive vocation, as was beginning to occur in the Nordic countries. Instead, as the Report on the Prisons Department (1951: 4) noted, in New Zealand 'the vocation of prison officer is not popular'. In England, it was acknowledged that 'the staff situation is serious and discouraging. Recruiting is worse than ever' (Report of the Commissioners of Prisons, 1955: 32). Thereafter, following 'an extensive recruiting campaign, on television and in the press, the result is most disappointing. Of 378 inquiries, only 35 were appointed' (Report on the Department of Justice, 1966: 15). In these countries, inducements to join the prison service consisted of trying to improve the material rewards of this employment – providing housing subsidies, overtime and triple-time payments for weekend work and so on. There was very little to try and raise the status or educational background of the applicants, as if such skills would be wasted in this low status occupation. As it was, standards had had to be further reduced to facilitate recruitment, while enhanced training opportunities were periodically cut because of economic stringencies.[49] At the same time, officers were largely excluded from participating in the much higher status treatment work that did begin to be developed in some English prisons in the 1950s.[50] Roper (1955: 99, our italics) thus distinguished the role of 'discipline staff' in the following way: 'whilst [these] officers are mainly in a supervisory and custodial position, it is perfectly natural that benign authoritarianism should be the ideal *because simple obedience is the chief requirement from the prisoners who are in their charge.*' While there were, from time to time, plans to make the work of the prison officer more challenging and demanding,[51] it remained that 'much of the time of the general prison officer is spent on custodial duties, including court and escort work' (Home Office, 1969: 94).

Even so, deteriorating conditions in the Anglophone prisons in the 1950s and 1960s further widened the gulf between these and the Nordic prisons that less eligibility had already put in place. These deteriorations were caused by, *first, a combination of under-investment and over-use* (itself the reaction to increasing crime in these societies). References to overcrowding – the confinement of three prisoners in a cell built for one – began in England in 1947 (Report of the Commissioners of Prisons, 1949). By 1950, there were 2,000 inmates living in such conditions. By 1961, the figure was 8,000, or around one third of the total prison population. In New Zealand it was acknowledged that 'prison accommodation is on the verge of crisis. Overcrowding is always a source of trouble and we must strive to avoid the expedient of holding more than one to a cell' (Report on the Department of Justice, 1954: 6). In New South Wales, it was recognized that 'one has a penal system operating largely in walled prisons which are too small, built 50 to 120 years ago, with inadequate facilities' (Report of the Comptroller-General of Prisons, 1965/6: 3). Although major prison building programmes began to be put in place in the early 1960s, the design of the new prisons gave little recognition to the importance of personal space and freedom of movement that had become such an important feature in Swedish prison building. Indeed, cell sizes were actually *reduced* from the standard measurements of the Victorian era.[52] This was justified on the assumption that '[the cell] is no longer a place in which the prisoner will eat his meals and do his work; nor will he be occupied [there] during the day. [It] is primarily a place in which he sleeps and need not therefore be as large as the cells of earlier prisons . . . The new cell is designed for occupation by one prisoner only, and could not be used to house three prisoners . . . careful consideration was given to the possibility of providing washbasins and waterclosets in individual cells, but it was decided that the considerable expense involved would not be justified in this type of prison' (Paterson, 1961: 309).

Sir Alexander Paterson's assumptions were unfounded. Work, education and association – the main activities that took prisoners out of their cells – were all restricted, anyway, by the very nature of the less eligibility determined prison policies of these societies. Now, though, they were to become more so. Prisons remained largely separated off from the rest of society – still a place to send those who were different, who did not belong; those, in fact, who would never be able to hold on to a legitimate place in these societies and who were thus not worthy of any attempt to assist them to do so: 'the government recognizes it is right to provide facilities for the comparatively small proportion of offenders who are capable of learning and benefitting from a skilled trade . . . *it is, however, neither practicable nor indeed necessary to provide for most offenders exactly the same work in custody as they might obtain after release*' (Home Office, 1969: 26, our italics). Indeed, in contrast to Eriksson's *dictum*, 'first we build the factory', the Report of the Commissioners of Prisons (1956: 26, our italics) insisted that '*prison is not a factory*'. Here, then, the demands and rules of the prison determined the employment opportunities of its inmates. The result was that most prisoners who did have work in England found themselves sewing mailbags: 'nobody likes it . . . it fits a man for no form of work he is likely to do outside, and few are likely to feel anything but dislike for doing it inside. And you do not even train men "in orderly and industrial habits" by setting them to work in which they do not take and can scarcely be expected to take any intelligent interest' (Fox, 1952: 181). Prison labour was no longer tortuous and backbreaking in these societies; instead, it had become tedious and pointless. Work thus remained a punishment, something to be avoided if possible. In the Nordic countries, however, it was not only intended to assist in prisoner reintegration but was also to be something that gave pleasure and enjoyment: 'all prisoners have a duty to undertake work in prison. The aim for such work is that it should be of interest to the inmate, that he should enjoy it and gain something from it' (Report of the Director of the [Norwegian] Prison Board, 1973: 91).

Similarly, education services remained limited and generally of a low standard: 'we may now say that any educable prisoner whose sentence gives him or her enough time to learn and is willing to, need not leave prison as an illiterate' (Report of the Commissioners of Prisons, 1951: 51). In addition, these services remained a *privilege*, not a right, available only after working hours. Even though, as the prison population rose, employment prospects within the prison declined further,[53] education was not allowed to become a substitute for work. If this happened, prisoners would be provided with opportunities to better themselves without having done anything to earn them.

Second, by a new emphasis on security during the 1960s. This was the reaction to a series of high profile escapes.[54] While the Nordic authorities had been able to handle their own escapes – with some of these also being high profile[55] – with equanimity, the greater social divisions, and the more threatening nature of imprisonment itself and the inmates it housed, had begun to create a more heightened sense of alarm and drama over prison escapes in the Anglophone societies. Its media then exacerbated these concerns in its more melodramatic and sensationalist reporting style.[56] For example, after two armed robbery prisoners murdered a guard during the course of their escape from a New South Wales prison, *The Sydney Morning Herald* (10 October 1959: 1), in episodic detail, reported 'Dangerous Escapees Holed Up in Dramatic Hunt'. Thereafter, 'One Thousand Pound Government Reward for Recapture of Long Bay Fugitives' (*The Sydney Morning Herald*, 12 October 1959: 1); 'Police Told Escapees "Must Be Caught At Any Cost"' (*The Sydney Morning Herald*, 13 October 1959: 1); 'Milkman Says [Escaper] Spoke to Him: Police Defied' (*The Sydney Morning Herald*, 20 October 1959: 1); 'Alarm Over [Escaper]. People Lock Homes' (*The Sydney Morning Herald*, 15 November 1959: 4) – and so on, until their eventual recapture some five weeks later. Furthermore, without the degree of autonomy and the respect that, as civil servants, their Nordic counterparts enjoyed, the Anglophone authorities could only acquiesce to government insistence that security was to become the first priority of prison policy. By the same token, the authorities were also hemmed in and constrained in their attempts to modernize, make improvements or construct alternatives to the prison estate. The intended expansion of open prisons in England was halted for these reasons (Report of the Commissioners of Prisons, 1957: 23). Despite Simon's expectations to the contrary, the public were *not* prepared to accept 'something less than 100 per cent security' (indicative of the gulf that existed here between penal elites and the public at large). While education services were further cut,[57] investment increased in floodlighting, CCTV and 'electronic devices that were introduced at selective prisons . . . even though the number of escapes [had not] been appreciably higher' (Report on the Work of the Prison Department, 1966: 2). Freedom of movement and association within the institution was also curtailed and restricted: 'educational and hobby groups were among the first to suffer. The allotment gardens . . . organized for lifers at Wormwood Scrubs [London] disappeared under the "dog track" of the steel-mesh inner perimeter fence' (Morris, 1989: 134–5).

'Prison is not a pleasant place'

By the end of the 1960s, the differences in the way in which it was possible to think about punishment in these two types of societies were now manifested in both their rates of imprisonment (or the direction of these rates in respect of Finland and the Anglophone countries) and their prison arrangements (the different approaches taken to prison size and location, the different approaches to staff recruitment, the different status and standing of the prison authorities, the different conditions in which prisoners lived and so on). The Nordic prison reports had begun to contain references to 'prison hotels'; to prisoners and students studying together; to prisons that were intended to painlessly restore their 'interns' to citizenship rather than impose further disqualifications on this section of the population. But there were no such references in the Anglophone reports. Even the earlier references to trust, and to a readiness to reduce security, had gone. Instead, with increasing regularity from the mid-1950s, it was noted, in England, that 'disturbances at two prisons attracted public attention' (Report of the Commissioners of Prisons, 1954: 4); 'morbid incidents [that is, riots] occurred at three more institutions' (Report of the Commissioners of Prisons, 1957: 32); 'mass indiscipline occurred at a number of prisons and included a work standstill' (Report of the Commissioners of Prisons, 1961: 13); there was 'a riot' at Dartmoor in 1962 (Report of the Commissioners of Prisons, 1962: 2); and 'major disturbances in Durham and Leicester' (Report on the Work of the Prison Department, 1968: 5). In New Zealand, there were 'riots in two prisons' (Report on the Department of Justice, 1961: 12); an 'insurrection' at New Plymouth Prison (Report on the Department of Justice, 1963: 12). In New South Wales, there was a 'disturbance' at Bathurst and also at the State Penitentiary (Report of the Comptroller-General of Prisons, 19561–1957: 5). There were 'demonstrations and fires' at Long Bay Prison (Report of the Comptroller-General of Prisons, 1965–1966: 3); and 'three arson attempts at Bathurst Prison' (Report of the Comptroller-General of Prisons, 1967–1968). As the New Zealand authorities themselves recognized, 'by any standards, save the very lowest, prison remains an unpleasant place' (Report on the Department of Justice, 1961: 6).

In contrast to the shining icon of Western tolerance and humanity that the social democratic welfare sanction had come to be understood as, at this juncture, the liberal welfare sanction was turning into a crumbling ruin, neither able to arrest the growth of imprisonment nor the declining standards of its prisons. It was in the process of being destroyed by its own limitations, those of the liberal welfare state itself, and the exclusionary values of these societies that it had ultimately been unable to scale back or hold in check. Just as there had been two lines of development in penal policy within the social democratic welfare sanction (more extensive social control in conjunction with a reduction of penal pain), so there were two within the liberal welfare sanction. In the former, however, these were complementary to each other, running consensually out of its structural arrangements; in the latter, these were contradictory, competing against each other for power, influence and resources. One was a reflection of the emphasis given to alleviating levels of punishment and reducing the rigours of prison life; the other, altogether more forceful, insistent and ultimately dominant, emphasized that, save for specific categories of deserving offender, those who broke the law would continue to face disqualificatory, exclusionary punishments, exemplified by restrictive and deteriorating prison conditions.

6 Punishment in the age of anxiety

From the 1970s, we then see the emergence of the 'age of anxiety', with all its uncertainties and insecurities brought on by the social and economic restructuring that has taken place across modern society as a whole. Its development in these ways has had important consequences for the expectations and understandings of punishment. When social cohesion breaks down to such an extent, then punishment, as Tyler and Boekmann (1997) have argued, is likely to be called upon to play a much more central role in governance. This is because of its ability to unite the general public against common-sensically obvious enemies, while sending out messages of reassurance that social order and the authority of the state are being restored in visible and demonstrative ways. However, as we have seen, the intensity and effects of this restructuring have been experienced differently in the Nordic and Anglophone societies.[1] In the former, although *likhet* and *lagom* have weakened somewhat, these values still inform and contribute to much of the conduct and understandings of everyday life; at the same time, the social democratic welfare state, despite some narrowing and paring back, remains very much in place. The result has been that cohesion and solidarity remain relatively strong, without the need for punishment to stabilize and bolster them with dramatic excesses. Instead, although there have been some detours and checks along the way, much the same penal route – one that reflects the values of moderation, restraint and inclusion – has continued to be followed. However, in the latter, the much deeper and more intense restructuring of already more divided and unequal societies has led to a further erosion of the liberal welfare state itself. In the absence of more inclusionary social mechanisms, punishment comes to play a much larger role in providing stability and cohesion. In so doing, its powers have become more exaggerated, enhanced and exclusionary, its signs and symbols more shrill, unequivocal and uncompromising. This has been the route that has taken these Anglophone societies to their penal excesses of the early twenty-first century, while the Nordic societies have demonstrated their exceptionalism to these trends.

The Anglophone route to penal excess

What was it that made this journey possible? Two features that propelled these societies along this route from the 1970s stand out: *first*, the removal of the penal restraints that the liberal welfare sanction had previously been able to put in place; *second*, in their absence, the emergence of a more emotive and more exclusionary brand of punishment.

Exit the liberal welfare sanction and the limits it had placed on punishment

This was the product of five separate but interconnected social forces. *First*, increasing opposition to the liberal welfare sanction from criminal justice elites. It had never had the level of acceptance from academics, intellectuals, senior judges and civil servants that the social democratic welfare sanction had enjoyed from their Nordic counterparts. Now, amidst its ruins at the end of the 1960s, there were few voices from this quarter that were prepared to speak for it, particularly after new revelations of its ineffectiveness and expense.[2] Instead, what faith there had been in the 'treatment' for crime that it offered evaporated altogether – 'the rhetoric of treatment and training has had its day' (May Committee, 1979: para 426). In addition, the injustices it had made possible by its insidious assumptions should be brought to an end: 'imprisonment must be justified as punishment and not be based on false claims of "rehabilitation"' (Report of the Director of the [New South Wales] Corrective Services Commission, 1979: 1). Similarly, there was disapproval of its insistence that welfare experts knew what was best for the individual: 'it is probably a mistake to suppose criminal tendencies can be "cured". In any event, *paternalism – doing something to a person for his own good – cannot by itself justify measures that would not otherwise be appropriate for the offence*' ([New Zealand] Penal Policy Review Committee, 1981: 32).

What should replace it? It was the intent of these elites that there should be less use of punishment altogether, particularly imprisonment. There would then be less scope for the abuses of the power to punish that were now associated with the welfare sanction. In England, Lord Lane, Chief Justice, issued a Court of Appeal guideline judgment that prison sentences should be 'as short as possible, consistent only with the duty to protect the interests of the public and to punish and to deter the criminal' (*R* v *Bibi*, 1980[3]). Some prominent Conservative politicians even shared these views at that time. William Whitelaw, the first Home Secretary in the three Thatcher governments, was of the opinion that 'building new prisons cannot by itself be a solution [to crime] . . . there could be a substantial fall in our use of imprisonment without any significant rise in the threat to individual safety' (Home Affairs Committee, 1981: 221). Thereafter, the Home Office Green Paper (1988: 2) *Punishment, Custody and the Community* took the view that 'imprisonment is not the most effective punishment for most crime'. In New South Wales, the Corrective Services Commission, throughout the 1980s, reiterated the view that prison should be a 'last resort' sanction.[4] In New Zealand, one of the explicit aims of the Penal Policy Review Committee (1981: 39) was 'to consider the means by which the incidence of imprisonment can be reduced'. By the late 1980s, these aspirations for less punishment, rather than more, had found a philosophical home in the ideas of the 'Justice Model' (von Hirsch, 1985; Ashworth,

1989). With invocations of Beccaria and Kant, Justice Model theorists argued that punishment should be proportionate to the offence rather than exceed its gravity; it should be certain, finite and limited, rather than uncertain and indefinite; and it should respect the rights and responsibilities of those on whom it was to be inflicted, rather than view them as 'sick' or 'deficient', in need of state-provided care and 'assistance'.

Further restrictions, indicative of the grip on penal power that these elites still held, had been put in the way of imprisonment, including presumptions against incarcerating property offenders;[5] and more liberal parole legislation (largely detached, now, from any connection with an applicant's response to 'treatment'). As a consequence, Anglophone imprisonment rates stabilized and declined somewhat in the late 1980s. In addition, to allow greater public scrutiny of prison life, an independent prison inspectorate was established in England in 1980 (following the recommendations of the May Committee). The English Criminal Justice Act 1991 was intended to further advance these reductionist trends. Under its provisions, an offender's past convictions would not be allowed to increase their punishment. In accordance with Justice Model thinking, this should fit the immediate crime they had committed, rather than be determined by any short-comings in their life that came to light as a consequence. The legislation also provided for 'day fines' to ensure that the pain of this sanction would be equally distributed, whatever an offender's income (and introduced, of course, in all the Nordic countries by the 1930s). At the same time though, the idea of welfare assistance as a response to crime, along with the welfare language of punishment – 'needs', 'insights', 'support', 'rehabilitation' – and the curbs and blocks that it had offered by its willingness to reduce penal severity for some offenders at least, had been largely removed from the penal thinking of these elites.

Second, the insistence from the political right wing that punishment needed to play a more dramatic role in these societies. The liberal welfare sanction was also under attack from the political Right, for whom punishment – more demonstrative punishment, free from moderation and restraints – was needed, rather than less, if social order was to be maintained. From this quarter, the operation of the liberal welfare sanction and, more generally, the liberal welfare state itself, had put this at risk. The cry that welfarism would only encourage feckless dependency and irresponsibility was nothing new in these societies, of course. However, rising crime from the beginning of the post-war period, amidst a range of other graphically documented scenes of turbulence, disaffection and disorder in the 1970s (strikes, high taxes but seemingly generous benefits, creaking and collapsing public services[6]), was hailed as irrefutable proof of these predictions of catastrophe. The right wing British ideologue Patricia Morgan (1978: 12–3) thus claimed that '[crime] has now ceased to be merely a symptom of urban breakdown in this country . . . and has become a major contributor to it'. In effect, it was as if the liberal welfare state had only brought social disintegration, rather than the improvements in social cohesion that had once been the expectations of some of its leading proponents. The implications were, as Margaret Thatcher (1993: 626, our italics) later explained, that 'the root cause of our contemporary social problems – to the extent that these did not reflect the timeless influence and bottomless resources of old fashioned human wickedness – was that *the state had been doing too much.*' Accordingly, while the post-1970s social and economic restructuring of the Anglophone societies was justified as being necessary to free individuals from the constraints that the welfare state was thought to have placed on their aspirations and horizons, *these same individuals would also have to be ready to accept much greater responsibility for their conduct.* Rather than excusing them from this if they fell into one of the 'deserving' categories of the liberal welfare sanction, punishment should act as a constant reminder of the consequences of lawbreaking through the more identifiable and understandable signs and symbols that it sent out.

One of the first intimations of the possibilities of this enhanced role for punishment was set out in the Conservative Party election manifesto that brought Margaret Thatcher to power in 1979. It carried a section on 'Deterring the Criminal' (rehabilitation received no mention at all), signposted by the promise of the reintroduction of 'short, sharp shock' detention centres[7] for young offenders, and a free vote in the House of Commons on whether the death penalty should be restored (a sanction that still had a nostalgic place in the hearts of most of the British public[8]). The resurrection of these two particularly expressive penalties from the past conjured a return to mythically untroubled days of order and certainty, of fixed and certain social hierarchies, where what threats that did emerge to social stability could simply be beaten down or expelled, without any recourse to troubling social questions or investigations into an offender's background. The detention centres, modelled on the British army's own disciplinary institutions, resonated with past glories of militarism and imperialism, and stood in contrast to the apparent national decline and degeneracy that had coincided with the development of the post-war welfare state. Initial incomprehension from critics[9] that detention centres could be reintroduced in contravention of the vast body of research demonstrating that such deterrent policies failed to reduce crime, were simply ignored. But criticisms of this nature had anyway missed the point. For the Thatcher government, and others in its wake, policies that brought about measures such as the reactivated detention centres were not to be judged by the reconviction rates they produced. Instead, they were to be judged by the power they possessed to bring unity and political support for the undisguised, unequivocal expressions of authority that these measures symbolized. This was the way forward for penal policy: not with reference to the statistics of reconviction rates or even economic costings; but, instead, the ability of a particular sanction and the imagery associated with it to galvanize public support and unite it as it despatched those who brought the most obvious kinds of instability and disorder to these societies. The sanctions themselves, of symbolic, rather than real, importance, could then be simply tossed away at quieter moments, as was the fate of the detention centres,[10] or when further innovations were needed to reaffirm the cohesive role that punishment was now expected to perform.

Similarly, the death penalty was presented by its supporters as some majestic, magical power, the very threat of which would be able, once again, to sear its way through the social fabric, reasserting an authority that welfarism had eroded. As one Conservative MP explained in the ensuing House of Commons debate in 1982,

'I believe that the death penalty would act as a deterrent. The elderly and the young are worried about going out at night, using subways or opening their doors after dark . . . I believe that [the death penalty] would also provide added incentive for parents to accept more responsibility for correcting their children during their formative years. It might also, in time, lead to more discipline in our schools. The young must be taught the difference between right and wrong and it is in youth that the problems first begin. If the problems can be resolved at a far earlier stage, so much the better' (Hansard [UK], HC Deb, 11 May 1982, col. 612). While, in fact, the restoration of the death penalty itself was voted down on this and on further occasions in 1983 and 1987 by the UK parliament, the power of punishment to unite communities through its expressive signs and symbols continued to be invoked – at the expense of those criminals held responsible not just for their crimes, but for the way in which the world was losing its familiarity and security. These were worthless outsiders anyway, deserving of the expulsion a reinvigorated and strengthened penal system would now bring to them. In New South Wales, a commitment to 'Truth in Sentencing' – putting an end to remission and early parole – was to reassert the authority of the courts over Corrections bureaucrats and ensure that those sent to prison would serve a sentence more in line with public expectations of what this meant (NSW Department of Corrective Services, 1987–1988). In England again, Conservative Home Secretary Michael Howard proclaimed in 1993 that 'prison works', and that there were to be 'no more half-time sentences for full-time criminals'. Not only would prisons be used more often, but the early exit door that parole had offered would now be closed to many more inmates. Furthermore, such a deliberate rejection of the penal conventions and restraints that had been built up over most of the twentieth century, in favour of the deliberate embrace of the pain that punishment now promised, was to be celebrated and championed, as if this was a sign of strong government rather than weak, strong government that would maintain the authority of the state, rather than allow it to be dissipated as had happened under more welfare-oriented government administrations.[11] In New Zealand, a 1999 citizens-initiated 'law and order' referendum, which included a proposal for 'hard labour for prisoners', received a 91.75 per cent vote in favour.[12] Here again, outmoded remnants from the penal past were brought back to life, as if in affirmation that, in that mythical time, such penalties had been sufficient to hold societies together and to quell those who threatened this into obedience.

Third, the subsequent formation of a political consensus that disavowed the liberal welfare sanction and the penal restraints previously associated with it. Conservative governments in the Anglophone societies had always been circumspect, at the most, in their support for such welfare-based initiatives. From the 1980s, however, this turned into outright hostility as the liberal welfare sanction began to be pulled to pieces after being overwhelmed by their new approaches to punishment and the language in which these were couched. Thus, in England, restrictions on the imprisonment of young offenders, introduced in 1961, were removed in 1980; those serving life sentences would remain in prison until the Home Secretary, rather than the Parole Board, decided otherwise; at the same time as parole was being liberalized in the 1980s, its availability for sexual and violent offenders was retrospectively tightened (see Sim, 2009: 35–52). But, rather than try to repair the damage to the welfare sanction, successive Labour governments (in New Zealand and New South Wales, as well) then abandoned what previous commitments they had given it and joined – and then began to outbid – Conservatives in arguing for more, rather than less, punishment. Here again, then, any alternative way of thinking about punishment that welfarism had made possible disappeared.

In England, the murder of 2-year-old James Bulger in 1993 by two 9-year-old Liverpool boys was pivotal in bringing about this shift in Labour thinking. The case became a signifier of the fragility of cohesion and order in these societies – the hatred expressed for the two juveniles by local crowds at their court hearings, egged on by a frenzied media (Green, 2008), was evidence enough of this. However, it was not *the limitations* of the liberal welfare state – that it was not sufficiently equipped to secure the level of cohesion and order, with bonds and reciprocities, that might otherwise have prevented the child's murder – that were understood as its cause; rather, it was *the liberal welfare state itself*, in relation to which the Bulger case became one of the most vivid illustrations of the disorder and moral decline it was thought to have engineered. The reaction of Tony Blair, then Shadow Labour Home Secretary, was that 'a solution to this disintegration doesn't simply lie in legislation. It must come from the rediscovery of a sense of direction as a country . . . We cannot exist in a moral vacuum. If we do not learn and then teach the value of what is right and wrong, then the result is simply moral chaos that engulfs us all' (quoted by Sim, 2009: 55). As with the Thatcherite view of the world, the implication was that the state had previously been too eager to absorb responsibility and guilt for the wrongdoing of individuals: they should have to make their own moral choices instead, and be held accountable for them. In this way, a mainstream political consensus was established for which the only legitimate response to crime was in the form of more dramatic, exclusionary punishment. This was the solution to it, rather than any more discredited welfare-type responses – there had been a surfeit of welfare thinking already. Thereafter, for both left and right governments in these societies, the duty of the state would not be to alleviate the burdens of the unfortunates who appeared in court, but instead to punish and exclude them for challenging its authority. As Blair later explained: 'crime, anti-social behaviour, racial intolerance, drug abuse, destroy families and communities. They destroy the very respect on which society is founded . . . Fail to confront this evil and we will never build a Britain where everyone can succeed . . . by acknowledging the duty to care, we earn the right to be tough on crime . . . it is time for zero tolerance of yob culture' (*The Guardian*, 27 September 2006: 6).

Fourth, silencing opposition. As punishment became increasingly suffused with melodramatic symbolism, so the policy making and advisory role of the expert – likely to recoil in revulsion at such distasteful representations (Loader, 2006) – was undermined and reduced. It was such experts whom Morgan (1978: 48) had referred to as 'the new establishment' – the cadre of civil servants, officials and academics whose powers had been aggrandized during the welfare era but who, simultaneously, she claimed, had undermined the traditional structures of authority: 'the procedures of social control and socialisation . . . have been largely taken away from lay experience and practice, and exchanged for a body of socio-psychological theory, whose special recipes only special practitioners are competent to apply.' Here, then, was the opportunity for the longstanding suspicions of the expert in these societies to reassert themselves. One of the first actions of the newly elected Thatcher government was thus to abolish ACTO in 1979: the development of penal policy would not, any longer, be the exclusive prerogative of its elite membership; instead, it came to be forged out of a partnership between governments and the public at large or, more specifically, those who claimed to speak on their behalf, notably the tabloid media and law and order lobbyists. Meanwhile, as in other areas of the social body, the authority of the civil service was gradually emasculated, as it was made more directly accountable to the political interests of successive governing parties. Rock (1995: 2) subsequently reported on the consequences of this: 'Home Office policy no longer follows once standard processes of informal consultation . . . portions of criminal justice policy making have become somewhat less cohesive, coherent, controlled and centralized as they come under the sway of devolution, "contracting out" and external consultants.' In New South Wales, the Corrective Services Commission, established in 1979, with a professor of behavioural sciences as its first chair, was abolished in 1989 on the basis that it was 'inefficient *and not sufficiently responsive to Ministerial Direction*' (NSW Department of Corrective Services, 1988–1989: 15, our italics). In New Zealand, the Department of Justice (2002: 1) demonstrated its own acquiescence to the shifting balance of penal power by acknowledging 'the need to respond to the 1999 referendum which revealed public concern over the sentencing of serious violent offenders', notwithstanding the 'hard labour' proposal in its content and the other contradictions and uncertainties in its phrasing.

Furthermore, those criminal justice elites who still had the temerity to place themselves in opposition to the removal of the restraints and moderation that was occurring were likely to become the subject of attack and vilification themselves if they now spoke out. In these anxious, more insecure societies, in which simple, magical, solutions promised deliverance from social problems, in contrast to their more measured equivocations, there were few reservations about removing what tenuous grip they still had on penal power: what grudging respect that there had been for their pedigrees was not sufficient to protect them. In New Zealand, the response of the organizer of the 1999 law and order referendum to those who were sceptical of its validity was to say that these were typically 'upper class individuals and a few trendies . . . [are] they saying the public is thick? You can't twist the result around and start shanghai-ing it . . . what we have before us is a document that has gone through the whole process . . . as far as I'm concerned, the question was plain English' (*The Dominion*, 17 February 2000: 1). More vituperative insults and criticisms from MPs came the way of the New Zealand Governor-General who, when opening the Crime and Justice Research Centre at Victoria University of Wellington, in 2002, dared to suggest that 'prison does not work' (see Pratt and

Clarke, 2005). Similarly, the subsequent reactions to the New Zealand Chief Justice, for expressing her reservations, in 2009, about the direction of criminal justice policy from politicians.[13]

Fifth, the reporting style of the Anglophone media. The nature of this – sensation, scandal, hostility towards the most worthless members of these societies (whether these were criminals, or the bureaucrats who seemed to shed tears for them), amidst demands for more protection for law-abiding members of the public – had the effect of making the kind of restraint associated with the liberal welfare sanction politically untenable. The way in which it was possible to think about crime and punishment in this setting was no longer directed by criminal justice elites. Instead, new media outlets – 24 hour news channels on satellite television and talk back radio – provided the opportunities for loquacious law and order lobbyists to simply drown out any opposition to their views, usually based on anecdote or one-off cases, that maximum use of punishment would bring an end to insecurity and fear: and here, also, was the way to provide headlines that would guarantee viewers, listeners and advertizers for this section of the media.[14] Furthermore, the size and popularity of the tabloid press, especially, created a framework of understanding outside of which it became very difficult to stand. One of the clearest illustrations of this occurred in the campaign waged against 'paedophiles' by the now defunct, but then the most popular, British Sunday newspaper, the *News of the World* (owned by Rupert Murdoch) in 2000. Widespread vigilante attacks against suspected paedophiles by local citizens' groups took place across the United Kingdom after it ran a 'naming and shaming' campaign.[15] That is, it published the names and photographs of 49 convicted sex offenders (it went on to publish similar details of 200 more, notwithstanding that they had all served their punishments, almost always imprisonment). This, though, was no longer sufficient to mollify the hostilities of the public that had been aroused to them. The 'naming and shaming' was prompted by the rape and murder of a child by a previously convicted sex offender. The newspaper demanded that the government establish a sex offender registry to which the public would have access, in order to check on suspicious neighbours, strangers in the locality and so on, rather than giving authorized welfare professionals alone the right to do so, as was then the policy. As the Labour government prevaricated, the paper ran a series of exposés on convicted paedophiles, beginning with the headline: 'Does a Monster Live Near You?' It then claimed that 'everyone in Britain has a child sex offender living within one mile of their home' (*News of the World*, 23 July 2000: 2). The feature sparked vigilante attacks on convicted paedophiles, suspected paedophiles, people who were 'different' and even paediatricians – any connection with the prefix 'paedo' was sufficient evidence of guilt.

The very fact that such attacks did occur on this occasion, and have subsequently occurred on numerous others in these three societies,[16] is a reflection of the way in which, with the unravelling of social cohesion, fantastic fears that the media stimulates, rather than rational deliberation, can come to inform the conduct of everyday life; and a reflection of the shallow interdependencies that undermine levels of trust, civic duties and responsibilities in these societies. Popular social movements in the Nordic countries had always been brought within the orbit of the state, thereby strengthening its authority. Here, though, these *ad hoc* vigilante groups operated outside of it, directly challenging and undermining its authority. They were indicative of its weakness, a weakness that was further reflected in the absence of any formal inquiry into the attacks (these led to a number of suicides, physical assaults and verbal abuse, as well as property destruction and harassment); or into the power and morality of the media in provoking these incidents (any such inquiry would have run into conflict with the ability of the media barons to not only single out 'monsters' and feed them to an outraged public but, also, to direct the flow of political preferences).

Enter a new brand of punishment, thick on emotion and exclusion

In these ways, then, welfare thinking about punishment came to be largely erased from public and political discourse in these societies, *while, at the same time,* the carefully calibrated moderation offered by the Justice Model was also jettisoned: the elites that favoured it were, themselves, just as remote from the public at large as the welfare experts had been. As this occurred, so a new brand of punishment with three central features emerged. *First,* a determination to make victims' experiences pivotal in the criminal justice process. Their experiences, or those claiming to speak for them, came to be recognized as the new authority for directing the course of penal development. As Tony Blair (2004: 5) subsequently put the matter, 'the law-abiding citizen must be at the heart of our criminal justice system. For too long it was far from the case . . . the system seemed only to think about the rights of the accused. The interests of victims appeared to be an afterthought, if considered at all.' Here was the real injustice of the welfare sanction, rather than the way in which it had cloaked state coercion, as the criminal justice elites had previously maintained. The subsequent 'rebalancing' that has taken place has thus been marked by a series of measures restricting the rights of defendants (to jury trials, legal aid entitlements, to silence during questioning, to the principle of *autrefois* acquit), while boosting and enhancing those of their victims. They have been given the right to read out impact statements describing the extent of their suffering and loss; the right to receive legal aid; the right to pursue redress, themselves, against those who have harmed them, rather than simply hand over their conflict to the state; the right to give their own views about the level of punishment to be imposed; the right to challenge the judiciary's ownership of courtroom practices and previous etiquettes and protocols that might stifle or censor their outpourings of emotion;[17] and the right to haunt, thereafter, successive stages of the penal process, confronting all in attendance with the baleful stare of Banquo's ghost, as if to say, 'now you will never forget that I am why you are here': attending and making submissions to parole hearings, disputing prisoner applications, proclaiming the presence, still, of unwarranted pain and suffering, as they are provided with the opportunity to re-live their experiences over and over again.

Rather than hastening the departure of victims from a process with which they never expected to be involved, and allowing them to peacefully rebuild their lives, they have been enthusiastically propelled to the centre of the criminal justice system, with their stays often prolonged, further undermining state authority, as the criminal justice process continues to produce turbulence, animosity and disappointment instead of healing and closure. In New Zealand, the mother of one murder victim – attacked by a gang of six – appeared at 28 separate parole hearings for his assailants between 2006 and 2010 (*New Zealand Herald*, 30 August 2010: A3). At the same time, any departures from their expectations of the process of justice after the rights that, with much political acclaim, they have been awarded, any departures from the level of punishment they think is warranted – in many cases, some sort of exactitude between this and the level of pain they have had to endure, which is beyond the capability of modern criminal justice systems to provide – are seen as another betrayal of them by the state and its representatives. Their anguish at such moments can then be projected onto a national canvas by the media, ensuring that punishment and its supposed inadequacies – lack of commonsense, lack of transparency, lack of ability to punish enough and to keep on punishing until such victims and their supporters are satiated – remain a central issue of everyday discourse in these societies,[18] requiring further rounds of legislation to rectify, and then rectify again when more dissatisfaction inevitably comes to light.

Second, a direction that punishment should be a more differentiating and extensive experience. If it is to act as a symbol of deterrence to offenders, and as a symbol of assurance to the general public, then punishment should take on more theatrical, spectacular, understandable forms, to ensure that those being punished are made to stand apart from the rest of society with their criminal identity and outsider status proclaimed for all to see. Hence the transformation of the British community service order. Introduced to that penal system in the 1972 Criminal Justice Act, it was intended to allow offenders to expiate their crimes through the longstanding tradition of voluntary work. It would provide them with the opportunity of working alongside others – they would be at one with them, rather than standing out as different from the rest of society. Its purpose was to utilize 'the positive attributes of the offender' (Young, 1979: 40). In 2008, however, this sanction became *the community payback order*. Now offenders so sentenced are made deliberately identifiable as such as they perform their tasks. They are no longer one anonymous member of a company of volunteers. To ensure that they *are* known as criminals, they have to wear orange fluorescent jackets with 'Community Payback' on the back – the then 'Victims' Commissioner', Louise Casey, had suggested this, along with 'conviction posters' that would be displayed in public places, showing the identity of those convicted of crime: 'criminals must wear their badges of shame', she reported to the Labour government.[19]

At the same time, to make punishment more central to the ordering of everyday life, *it has become more extensive*. At one end of the penal spectrum, punishment involving a prison term may no longer be punishment enough. On completion of sentence, the post prison conduct of sex offenders can be regulated by stipulating how far they are to keep away from parks, schools, swimming pools and so on – any venue, in effect, where young people gather. Or the end of a prison term can be ignored altogether: in New South Wales, post sentence detention provisions for some sex offenders, who would otherwise have been released on completion of a finite sentence, have been introduced. In New Zealand, there are similar plans for 'civil detention orders' for 'high risk sexual offenders' that will allow for their continued incarceration, in a 'secure civil detention centre'. At the other end of the penal spectrum, there are opportunities to punish and control the most minor deviance, in ways in which the liberal welfare sanction had never been inclined, nor given the power to do. The then Shadow British Home Secretary, Jack Straw, thus promised that New Labour would 'wage war on aggressive beggars, winos and squeegee merchants . . . we have literally to reclaim the streets for the law-abiding public citizen, to make street life everywhere an innocent pleasure again' (*The Independent*, 5 September 1995: 2). When social cohesion is not strong enough to absorb such irritants in these societies, the state only seems capable of reacting negatively to them with injunctions and threats, promising that they will be expelled altogether if these are not heeded. The subsequent anti-social behaviour legislation of 1998 took the rare form of a hybrid measure that imposed a civil penalty (the kinds of behaviours it was to regulate were not crimes), backed by criminal sanctions of up to five years imprisonment for non-compliance.

Third, a strengthening and enhancement of punishment's exclusionary capabilities. To this end, it is not only the restraints of the liberal welfare sanction that have been removed; those from the brief and tenuous Justice Model interregnum of the 1980s and early 1990s also disappeared. This was marked in the subsequent reversal of two of its cardinal features. *First*, indefinite sentences of imprisonment have been revitalized and have pushed aside the importance it had given to fixed and certain punishments. Previous restrictions and stipulations on the use of such measures, in relation to mental health, age and recidivist criteria, have been relaxed, bringing these sanctions much more into sentencing mainstream, rather than leaving them as a largely unused reserve power. In England, the Butler Committee's report (1975), with its suggestion that a 'reviewable sentence should be introduced for offenders who are dangerous [*and*] who present a history of mental disorder which cannot be dealt with under the Mental Health Act, and for whom the life sentence is not appropriate', had encouraged reviving such measures (Bottoms, 1977). However, at that time, 'dangerous behaviour' was still linked to mental disorder – it was not to be determined only on the basis of crimes committed or likely to be committed. Twenty years later, however, the Home Office (1996: 48) White Paper, *Protecting the Public*, demonstrated the important changes that had since occurred in conceptualizing dangerousness: 'too often in the past, those who have shown a propensity to commit serious or violent sexual offences have served their sentences and been released only to offend again . . . the government is determined that the public should receive proper protection [from such criminals].' Now, removing the previous connections between dangerous offending and mental disorder, dangerous offending per se would be sufficient justification for indefinite detention. The Home Office (2001: 32) thus recommended the introduction of a new 'special sentence' for dangerous offenders, those who had 'a high risk of committing a further offence that would cause serious harm to the public'. Such offenders would only be released at the discretion of the Parole Board when 'their risks are considered manageable in the community' (Home Office, 2002: 95). The courts were then given powers under the Criminal Justice Act (2003) to impose 'indeterminate sentences for public protection' [IPPS] on all offenders – no longer just recidivists – who were likely to cause 'serious harm' in the future (Harrison, 2011). After only six years of its existence, this had led to more than 6,000 IPPS prisoners in 2010 (that, along with another 10,000 serving life terms, meant that around one fifth of the prison population had no certain date of release). Parole has thus become an all-important means of getting out. But, to gain this, prisoners are likely to have to successfully complete various 'programmes', demand for which dramatically exceeds supply, while ensuring that release dates become ever more uncertain.

The situation is similar in New Zealand, where the Penal Policy Review Committee (1981) had counselled that there was a strong case *for the abolition of preventive detention* (it was then restricted to persistent sexual offenders aged over 25 years). However, this sanction was then *extended* in the Criminal Justice Act 1985 to include recidivist violent offenders, and further extended in 1993 when it was made available for first time sexual offenders. Furthermore, the minimum length of preventive detention increased from seven to 10 years, while the age of eligibility was reduced from 25 to 21 – then reduced again in the 2002 Sentencing Act to 18. From having only 12 preventive detention prisoners in 1986, there were 250 in 2010. Meanwhile, the previous judicial resistance to such measures seems to have largely evaporated, or has been bypassed by mandatory sentencing legislation (Baldry, *et al.*, 2011), or has simply been worn down by heavily publicized oversight of sentencing by governments eager to prove their own virility. They seize on this chance to put themselves on the side of victims and against judges still harbouring suspicions over such dramatic uses of the state's power to punish. When setting new lengths for non-parole periods of imprisonment, the New Zealand courts have thus justified them on the grounds that 'society's attitude to very serious crime has hardened' (*R v Lundy*, 2002[20]) and that 'society's attitude to violent crime has moved on since [a 1995 case], as have sentencing levels' (*R v Bell*, 2003[21]).

Second, the introduction of punishments that are disproportionate, rather than proportionate, to the crime that has been committed. In a reversal of the intents of the Criminal Justice Act 1991, repetition of crime, as well as the gravity of a particular crime, became a trigger for penal severity in England (day fines were also abandoned in 1993, after much public outcry, orchestrated by the tabloid press, against this 'injustice' that allowed the levels of fines to penalize the rich as much as the poor,[22] and the presumptions against the imprisonment of property offenders have gone). The Crime (Sentences) Act 1997 then required the imposition of a life sentence after an offender was convicted of a second serious violent or sexual offence; a minimum term of seven years' imprisonment on those convicted for a third time of drug trafficking; and a minimum sentence of at least three years for those convicted of domestic burglary for the third time (Cavadino and Dignan, 2002: 106).[23] In New Zealand, a 'three strikes law' was introduced in 2010: those convicted for a third time of one of 40 qualifying offences (that carried with them prison terms of five years or more) would automatically receive the maximum penalty with no possibility of parole. In proposing this legislation, the government chose to ignore the submission of its own Ministry of Justice to the Parliamentary

Law and Order Select Committee that 'three strikes' would not deter criminals. It also ignored a warning from its Attorney-General that this legislation might contravene the New Zealand Bill of Rights. Instead, the legislation was another symbolic gesture – one that promised an immediate solution to violent crime, even though the law change would not begin to take effect for another 10 years or so – the earliest time when those on their third strike would be likely to come up for sentence: 'if offenders are going to do the crime, they need to do the time. They need to think more about their behaviours' (Hansard [NZ], 4 May 2010: 10679); 'deterring criminals who are rational enough to see that their repeat violent offending will be met with an escalating level of punishment. Those who are not rational will be locked away, which is as it should be' (ibid., 10684); 'this Bill assures me that violent offenders will think twice before deciding to become recidivist offenders' (ibid., 10694).

Punishment has thus been able to celebrate its unrestrained freedom in these ways. And it has an unequivocal purpose again, to single out, differentiate, and exclude – there is to be no more welfare-ridden hesitation about this – in the hope of bringing about security and cohesion: social cohesion through exclusion, then. To perform these tasks, old powers have been rekindled and new ones placed on its agenda. Indeed, so much faith has been placed in punishment's supposedly magical qualities that the more elusive these effects become, the more the resources that are thrown to it and devoured in these already punishment–saturated societies.

Prison and the normalization of security

The development of prison policy has followed much the same course. Continuing attempts to make imprisonment a more reintegrative experience by liberal prison authorities have been overwhelmed by government policies that have had the effect of enhancing and extending its disqualificatory, exclusionary impact. Certainly, during the 1970s and 1980s, improvements continued to be made in relation to visiting arrangements, more regular changes of clothing, and personal hygiene. Censorship was reduced; radios, then televisions, were allowed in cells. There were also attempts to engineer more harmonious, co-operative working relationships between prisoners and officers: 'inmates cook and eat in units. This style of accommodation creates a more relaxed and informal atmosphere and encourages closer relationships among inmates and between inmates and staff' (Report of the Director of the Corrective Services Commission, 1983: 15). But, even as these ameliorations were being put in place, conditions were also becoming more intolerable, because governments chose to ignore the fundamental problems of under-investment and over-use of the prison in these societies. Prisons remained not worth investing in – they were merely useful dumping grounds for increasing numbers of those judged to be unwanted or unacceptable in free society: what did the squalor inside them matter for those who probably knew no better, and certainly deserved no better, anyway?

As a consequence, in England, the Report on the Work of the Prison Department (1971: 3) acknowledged that 'more than one third of those in custody sleep two or three in a cell designed for one, usually in prisons built 100 years ago'. In addition, 'there are not enough places [in open prisons] because of the lack of resources. Category C makes up 41 per cent of prisoners, but only one quarter are in C [open] accommodation' (Report on the Work of the Prison Department, 1976: 10). In New Zealand, the Report on the Department of Justice (1971: 12) noted that 'there is a need for restraint in staff numbers and expenditure . . . we are forced to restrict staff overtime and abandon most staff training . . . we continue to have a relatively high rate of imprisonment.' In New South Wales, the Department of Corrective Services (1977: 1) acknowledged that 'there is no relief in accommodation problems or progress towards fully implementing the policy of "one man, one cell"'. In addition, the more productive features of prison life – education, for example – became further restricted,[24] while resources continued to be made available for security. Although the number of escapes declined in the 1970s, the *continued possibilities* of escape in these increasingly anxious and insecure societies represented a danger and hazard that now demanded foolproof solutions from the authorities.[25] 'Special units' were thus introduced, and specialist security squads within the prison officer corps were formed, along with changes in the physical design of prisons to more efficiently bring about 'lockdown'.

In these ways, the causes of the 1960s disturbances were not only ignored but were exacerbated, ensuring that the disturbances themselves continued unabated through the 1970s and 1980s. They were also sometimes provoked by the officers themselves, feeling empowered, it would seem, by the new importance given to them as security enforcers: cells might be ransacked under the guise of searches for contraband or security checks; prisoner demonstrations might be met by retaliatory punishments in the form of beatings or other abuses – the insistence that there should be 'no retaliation' became a regular demand of prisoners attempting to 'surrender' after rioting or trying to bring mass demonstrations to an end (see Fitzgerald, 1977; Brown and Zdenkowski, 1982). The physical and geographical isolation of most prisons in these societies – from the late nineteenth century, public antipathy to them for what they represented had forced them away from urban locations to remote rural areas (Pratt, 2002) – allowed the officers to act more or less with impunity in these ways. Indeed, it was as if they were simply passing a secondary judgment on those who had already been judged to be unfit to live amongst the rest of society and, in so doing, distancing themselves from the inmates who shared the same prison space within them.

At the same time, the authorities and the inmates stood so far apart that it was difficult to de-escalate the conflicts. Any attempt to resolve them through dialogue and discussion was impossible for this reason. For the authorities to have acted in this way would have meant that they were prepared to acknowledge a degree of legitimacy to prisoners and their representatives. In these societies, though, the very fact of being a prisoner meant the forfeiture of rights of negotiation, or representation, or of being able to dispute in any way their conditions of confinement. Although a prisoners' rights group was formed in England, and played a leading role in coordinating and organizing demonstrations and strikes in the prisons in the 1970s, 'the Home Office refused to publicly acknowledge its influence or even

[its] existence' (Fitzgerald, 1977: 150). Indeed, the very idea of any such prisoners' organization in England provoked derision.[26] Thus, with no possibilities of compromise, or of resolution other than through force and intimidation, the rioting became so inflamed that both Bathurst Prison in New South Wales, in 1974, and Strangeways Prison in England, in 1990, were virtually razed to the ground. In the immediate aftermath of these very visible,[27] symbolic events, which seemed to signal the futility of existing prison policy – how was it possible to expect ever increasing numbers of human beings to live peacefully in such debasing surrounds that continued to deteriorate still further? – a Royal Commission into New South Wales Prisons (Nagle, 1978) and a Public Inquiry, headed by Lord Justice Woolf (Woolf, 1991) were established. In New Zealand, after regular, if less spectacular, disturbances during the 1980s, a Committee of Inquiry into the Prison System was set up in 1987 (Roper, 1989).

These settings now provided the opportunity for criminal justice elites to reassert themselves. Amidst some measure of respect and acknowledgement that they were prepared to show prisoners, the reality of the prison experience that precipitated the demonstrations and the destruction – and the response of the authorities to this – could be revealed. Nagle's report, in particular, provided graphic accounts of the ferocity of the violence that had occurred *throughout the prison system of this state* – Bathurst was simply the most visible manifestation of it. After previous disturbances and protestations had achieved nothing, those of 1974 that culminated in the prison being destroyed were met by 'floggings and bashings' from the officers: '[prisoners'] heads were cut open. Some were left lying unconscious or semi-conscious on the prison floor. One was seen huddled and whimpering in the corner of his cell. Another lay naked on the floor surrounded by seven or eight officers who beat him with batons. These are a few sordid examples of what occurred' (Nagle, 1978: 16). Other systemic abuses emerged: revelations of longstanding practices that were indicative of what could happen when prisons, as shameful stains on the fabric of these societies, were shut out of public life. Thus Grafton, 650 kilometres to the north of Sydney, had served as an institution for 'intractables' – those inmates designated as troublemakers – from the 1940s, and 'over a 33 year period, brutal, savage and sometimes sadistic physical violence was inflicted on prisoners sent there' (ibid.: 108).[28]

Gestures of reconciliation, prompted by these revelations, then followed. For example, after Woolf, there was to be no more reading of prisoners' letters (except those in high security prisons); and pilot projects were introduced, whereby prisoners would be allowed to wear their own clothes (Report on the Work of the Prison Service, 1990–1991: 15). After Roper, 'traditional antagonisms . . . declined and at Wellington Prison, staff and inmates even played together on the same football team in the local competition' (Newbold, 2007: 56). After Nagle, censorship, including that of newspapers, was removed; inmates could now have 'contact visits' (that is, they could sit together round a table, rather than being separated by a glass partition); prisoners were to be called by their names, rather than their numbers; and communal dining facilities were introduced. Furthermore, both Nagle and Woolf attempted to systematize strategies that were intended to make the prison experience more inclusionary. For the former, 'the deprivation of liberty is an essential punishment but prisoners should retain other rights, except those necessarily limited or curtailed by the maintenance of security . . . prison officers must possess the necessary training and means of containing disturbances quickly and with the minimum of danger to people and property; there must be grievance channels for prisoners; *the daily management of* prison must depend on a system of initiatives, rather than physical coercion' (as noted in the Report of the Director of the Corrective Services Commission, 1980–81: 14, our italics). For the latter, there had to be a balance between 'security, control and justice': 'justice itself is compromised if prisoners are held in conditions that are "inhumane or degrading", or which are otherwise wholly inappropriate' (Woolf, 1990: 241).

But, in just the same way that the 1991 Criminal Justice Act represented the high-water mark of the possibilities for moderation and restraint in the penal arena in general, so these inquiries came to have the same significance in relation to prisons. Their proposals for change were offset and overtaken by government demands for further intensifications of security and control – immediately so, in relation to Woolf. The day after its publication, the Home Secretary stated that 'the country will not tolerate the kind of disgraceful behaviour witnessed [by prisoners at Strangeways]. We must make clear our utter condemnation of it by introducing a new deterrent. We shall, therefore, bring before [parliament] proposals to create a new offence of prison mutiny, which will carry a maximum penalty of ten extra years in prison . . . Dangerous criminals have to be detained to protect the public' (Hansard [UK], HC Deb, 25 February 1991, col. 659). There would be a high price to pay for any further insurrections. Prisoners could now wear their own clothes and even be allowed more regular changes of underwear but, fundamentally, there could be no compromises on intensified levels of security that greatly restricted freedom of association, time out of cell, access to visitors and so on.

Furthermore, having set so much store by the way in which dramatic, exclusionary punishment would now be central to the governance of these societies, escapes from, and disturbances within, the prison now represented something more than the inefficiency of prison staff, something more than the innate cunning and duplicity of prisoners: in addition, these were an intolerable affront to the authority and credibility of the government itself. Therefore, after more high profile escapes in England – soon after Howard's claim that 'prison works' – new inquiries, one headed by a former Chief Inspector of Police, the other an army general, rather than judges, were established.[29] Now, there were to be no gestures of reconciliation emanating from these much more narrow enquiries – security, and how best to police it. Instead, there was a reaffirmation that the purpose of prison was as a *deterrent* in the first instance; in the second, a means of incapacitation. The way to prevent further escapes and future rioting was not to relax conditions but to further limit the movements of prisoners, as well as putting new limits on the quality of prison life. Moreover, it was no longer sufficient to affirm that there would be more people sent to prison to demonstrate governmental authority; in addition, prison should also become more demonstratively associated with misery and deprivation, a reassurance to the public that these were indeed the unhappy consequences of crime. Prison regimes should thus be constructed in such a way as to remind those who were sent to prison that their rightful place was at the very bottom of society. As Cavadino and Dignan (2002: 196) observed, improvements in conditions beyond this then came in the form of privileges to be earned, rather than allowances that were available to all. In England, this meant, as Howard explained, that 'prisoners who behave responsibly, work hard and participate fully in the regime could qualify for extra visits and wages . . . those who fail to conform and refuse to make positive use of their time in prison will find themselves on a basic regime without privileges' (*The Independent*, 30 June 1995: 7).

To ensure that the authorities did not depart from or dilute such expectations, private sector ownership and private sector management practices were now introduced to these prison systems. The prison did not escape from the more general restructuring of public services in these societies. Indeed, its inadequacies and inhumanities that had been revealed in Woolf, Nagle and all the other reports became another illustration of the inevitable failure of *publicly provided state services*, rather than the failure of the culture of exclusion that had put so much emphasis on the use of prison and the character of life that could be experienced in it. Private prisons, it was thought, would bring competition and efficiency (the power to punish could be offloaded like any other state responsibility in these societies where employment in the private sector was held in so much higher regard than the public), while also making those it employed more *compliant* with government demands and expectations. This would be the opportunity, for example, to weaken the power base of the prison officers' unions, who were held responsible for a remuneration system heavily weighted with double and triple payments for overtime, extra shifts and so on. This had been the only way, of course, to entice recruits to the public prisons, so stigmatic had any association with them become, but unions remained an enemy to be kept at a distance from governance, rather than brought within it. Meanwhile, the introduction of private sector management practices would ensure that the prisons advertized their successes rather than their failings. Accordingly, while, in England, the Report on the Work of the Prison Department (1977: 1) had referred to 'the continued problems of overcrowding [and] the growing numbers of difficult and subversive prisoners', from the 1990s the reports contained only references to the excellence of the service that was being provided: 'our vision is to provide a service . . . of which the public can be proud and which will be regarded as a standard of excellence around the world' (HM Prison Service Annual Report, 1994–1995: 1).[30]

What such services might be was then set out in a series of 'Visions', 'Mission Statements' and 'Goals' that reveal the shift that has taken place in the priorities of the Anglophone prison services from the 1990s: from services that had aspirations (however unlikely in reality) of turning their inmates into better people, to services that had to provide more cast-iron guarantees of public protection. The first English Mission Statement had maintained that 'the task of the prison service is to use with maximum efficiency its resources to keep prisoners in custody with such degree of security as appropriate. [And to] provide for prisoners as full a life as possible as is consistent with the facts of custody' (Report on the Work of the Prison Service,

1986–1987: 3). However, in the HM Prison Service Annual Report (1992–1993: ii) this had become 'the prison service serves the public by keeping in custody those committed by the courts. Our duty is to look after them with humanity and help them lead law-abiding and useful lives in custody and after release.' In New South Wales, the Mission of its prisons became one of 'protect[ing] the community by managing inmates in an environment which is safe, secure, fair and humane and to actively encourage personal development through correctional programmes' (NSW Department of Corrective Services, 1991–1992: 1). In New Zealand, the first Mission of the Penal Division was 'to contribute to the protection of society [and] reduce the likelihood of reoffending by providing the secure, fair, safe and humane containment of persons committed to custody' (Report of the Department of Justice, 1991: 67). However, the Report of the Department of Justice (1994: 60) then stated that this was 'to promote safety and social cohesion in society; contribute to a reduction in reoffending; and promote public confidence and support for public corrections. [It is] charged with providing a secure, fair, safe and humane corrections system.' Thereafter, its vision is 'to have the New Zealand public's understanding and confidence' (Report of the Department of Corrections, 1996: 11). In these ways, what level of autonomy the authorities once had had been stripped away: their first duty is to give satisfaction to their 'stakeholders' – the public at large, rather than their inmates; the security of the former rather than the well-being of the latter was to be paramount. This, rather than present them with details of treatment programmes and the statistics of reconviction, was the way to ensure 'public understanding and confidence'.

Moreover, although both Woolf and Nagle had spoken of the need to open up the prisons to public scrutiny (as May had also done), the effects of the new management practices have been to neutralize the potential for criticism from within the prison service. This has then meant that the reality of prison life has become more opaque, rather than transparent. The Report on the Work of the Prison Department (1980: 4, our italics) had argued that '*a reduction in the prison population is the only way of achieving any improvement in [prison] conditions*'. However, the Report of HM Prison Service (2001–2002: 12, our italics) simply stated that '*the prison service has no control over the numbers of prisoners sentenced*'. Indeed, the annual reports have turned into a self-congratulatory paean of praise, reciting the various KPIs that have been achieved. In England, although the aim was to have 36 per cent of prisoners unlocked on weekdays for at least twelve hours, '40 per cent was achieved' (HM Prison Service Annual Report, 2001–2002: 12). In 2003–2004, the prison service met nine out of its 14 KPIs, and 'its excellent record on security was maintained' (HM Prison Service Annual Report, 2003–2004: 6). And the HM Prison Service Annual Report (2006–2007: 6; 30) states that it 'is delighted to report how well the prison service performed . . . the service met 9 out of 12 annual delivery targets agreed with Ministers . . . escapes fell from 238 in 1992–1993 to just one in 2006–2007'.

There is very little publicly accessible knowledge to counter these testimonies of untroubled excellence. In these countries, members of the prison service cannot make any public representations – letters to newspapers, for example – about their work. In England, the annual report by the Inspector of Prisons makes headlines in the broadsheet press, but seems to carry little weight or influence elsewhere[31] (New Zealand and New South Wales do not have an independent inspector). As a consequence, public understandings of an institution that has come to have so large a symbolic and material presence in these societies has continued to be shaped by the morbid curiosity that the popular media demonstrates in it. This both reaffirms these understandings and also exacerbates public antagonism to those who live and work in the prison. News features on New Zealand prisons, for example, are likely to take the form of 'scandals' that expose the supposed luxuries of prison life, along with the incompetence of prison officials: 'Inmates Fed Diet of Violent Flicks [movies]' (*The Dominion Post*, 27 February 2006: A1); 'Jail Lets Sex Crims Out to Pick Fruit' (*The Dominion Post*, 28 February 2006: A1); 'Good Inmates Get Steak and Lollies' (*The Dominion Post*, 18 March 2006: A5); 'Violent Crim in Chalet with TV' (*The Dominion Post*, 8 June 2006: A1). These representations of prison life, with very little alternative to them because of the structure of the news media in this society, then put more public pressure on the authorities to demonstrate their acquiescence to popular expectations of what it should be.

As this has occurred, rights that might previously have given prisoners a stake in the world have been removed or denied them in a series of 'gestures of nullification' (Garland, 2005: 814). Although the courts had shown a willingness to protect the rights of prison inmates in the 1970s and 1980s (Brown, 2002; van Zyl Smit, 2007), such matters have since tended to be brushed aside (as also with some of the more punitive legislation of this period, such as the New Zealand three strikes law), as if of no consequence in relation to the more utilitarian intent of making public safety a priority. Indeed, the division between prisoners and the rest of society is so entrenched, and the expectation that going to prison involves substantial loss, rather than mere detention, is so acute, that any attempt to reduce these divisions and losses is likely to be met with derision and disbelief (see p. 25). In New Zealand (where, as with New South Wales, there is no equivalent oversight of the ECHR), the justification for removing the right to vote under the provisions of the Electoral (Disqualification of Prisoners) Act 2010 was that possession of this right implied that prisoners were being treated as if they were 'normal people': 'if people do a crime, they do the time and give up the electoral right that normal citizens have. The legislation gives supremacy to a person's moral obligation not to commit a crime, rather than to the moral obligation of that person to vote' (Hansard [NZ], 21 April 2010: 10345). Equally, the right of prisoners to receive compensation for wrongful treatment was removed (retrospectively) by the 2005 Prisoners and Victims Claims Act. The legislation prescribed that any such 'windfalls' must go to their victims instead. It had been prompted by five prisoners being awarded \$NZ136,000 damages by the New Zealand High Court [32] after they were subjected to 'inhumane treatment' in a 'behaviour management regime' – something similar to conditions in a US supermax prison, and for which there was no lawful authority. In the ensuing parliamentary debate on the bill,[33] it was variously claimed that 'criminals have won awards for things like hurt feelings. It is pathetic!' (Hansard [NZ], 14 December 2004: 17998); 'these prisoners – who may be feeling a sense of grievance because they have not had fresh towels, or because they have been forced to clean out their own cells – are claiming for breaches of standards that are not extended to law-abiding innocent citizens' (ibid.: 17997); 'in prison it is very simple; in prison are the greatest thugs – the most brutal people – in our society . . . those poor, darling prisoners will work out for themselves that if they make life very hard for the prison guards, who, ultimately, will retaliate, they will get some compensation because their human rights have been breached' (Hansard [NZ], 1 June 2005: 21021).

At the same time, further deteriorations in the conditions of prison life have reversed much of the improvements that the authorities had been able to put in place from the 1970s to the 1990s. Despite new prison building programmes, the provision of places has been unable to keep up with the numbers being sentenced: in England, double-bunking increased from 17 per cent of the prison population in 2001–2002 to 24.7 per cent in 2006–2007. Similarly, in New Zealand, four new prisons, optimistically built on the expectation of single cell accommodation in the early twenty-first century, became double-bunked within three or four years of opening. If the prison diet has become more varied, and there is more careful adherence to nutritional science, virtually all provisions for communal dining in closed prisons have disappeared. Meals have to be eaten in cell, while food is prepared from a central kitchen, which means that its quality is likely to have deteriorated by the time it arrives. Here, then, are some of the aspects of that 'tighter and deeper', 'more intense' experience that imprisonment has come to be in these societies. [34]

The Nagle Committee (1978: 270) had been shocked to find that, 'in some prisons, inmates are locked in their cell for up to 15 hours a day'. This is now routine for the vast majority of prisoners in closed institutions in these countries – indeed, it is often exceeded. That this has become so is emblematic of the dramatic changes in values in relation to what are tolerable and intolerable conditions of prison life since Nagle, as the prison itself has come to assume a much larger role than a mere receptacle, unwanted and ignored, for society's undesirables. As restraints on punishment have been stripped away, it has become, for many, a necessary symbol of security in an age of insecurity and anxiety, the point of division between respectable, worthy members of society and all those thought to pose a danger to them; a point of division that has become much sharper as public fears demand that security within the prisons be intensified to keep them safe from those inside, while public hostilities demand that those being sent to prison should know only disadvantage and misery from this experience.

The Nordic route to penal exceptionalism

While there have certainly been modifications to the social democratic welfare sanction over the same period, these have not been sufficient to undermine its foundations. The familiar Nordic dualism of extensive forms of control and regulation, on the one hand, and the simultaneous depenalization of punishment, on the other, remains largely in place.

The social democratic welfare sanction under threat

As in the Anglophone societies, so too, in the 1970s, there was recognition in the Nordic that welfare-sponsored 'treatment' was little more than a sham. Norman Bishop (1974: 97), head of the Research Group of the Prison and Probation Services in Sweden, argued that 'evidence for successful penal treatment [in Sweden] is both meagre and unreliable'. Moreover, it was also recognized that its benign language could be a mask for unnecessary and unjust levels of coercion – *especially so* in these countries where legal traditions generally upheld the procedures and practices of state organizations, rather than the rights of prison inmates (the pioneering work of Nils Christie (1960) and Thomas Mathiesen (1965) had helped to ignite this awareness). In the light of this, the Finnish Prison Administration Decree of 1971 stipulated that 'the enforcement of punishment must be arranged so that it does not needlessly complicate, but if possible promotes the prisoner's relocation in the free community'. In Norway, the Ministry of Justice (1977–1978: 25, our italics) took the view that 'the treatment optimism underlying many penal sanctions earlier in the century is difficult to maintain today . . . *the use of imprisonment can never be justified as a measure of rehabilitation.* There is an inherent contradiction in the fact that as society implements penal sanctions on groups in need of help, this only serves to exacerbate their problems.' As a consequence, crimes were no longer so readily seen as symptoms of some sort of illness. And, similar to the moves to restrict some of the more extensive powers of the social democratic welfare state (along with the abolition of the sterilization laws by the mid-1970s, a few hesitant steps had been taken towards the liberalization of alcohol policy[35]), the social democratic welfare sanction's powers of control and coercion began to be scaled back, sometimes rescinded altogether. Preventive detention was thus allowed to fall into disuse in Norway, and internment for alcoholics was abolished in 1970. In addition, the vague concept of 'mental abnormality' that had provided a prescription for indefinite detention was removed in 1974, with separate sanctions available for 'sane' and 'insane' offenders. In Finland, from 1971, from being an extensively used penal sanction in the 1960s,[36] preventive detention became available only for those 'who actually presented a danger to society – that is, who were in certain ways a danger to the life or health of other people' (Lahti, 1977: 145). In 1974, the term 'recidivist' was to be applied only to offenders who had previously been found guilty of an offence involving serious violence: 'the result has been that in a five year period the number of individuals sentenced as dangerous recidivists has fallen from 389 to seven' (Zagaris, 1977: 457). In Sweden, public drunkenness was decriminalized in 1977, indefinite youth prison terms were abolished in 1980 and other forms of indefinite detention in 1981.

To further prevent the kinds of injustices that the welfare sanction had allowed, Justice Model principles of proportionality, certainty and rights began to be written into the penal codes of these societies. Hence, the Finnish Sentencing Act (1976, s.1, our italics): 'in measuring a punishment, all the relevant grounds increasing and decreasing the punishment, as well as the uniformity of sentencing practice, shall be taken into consideration. *The punishment shall be measured so that it is in just proportion to the harm and risk involved in the offence and to the culpability of the offender manifested in the offence.'* In Norway, the Ministry of Justice (1977–1978: 2) proclaimed that 'the demand for justice is a more secure penal foundation than theories that are grounded in the view that punishments are meant to achieve other goals'. In Sweden, the Report of the Council for Crime Prevention (1977: 12) argued that sanctions should be determined not by the kind of person an offender was thought to be but by the penal value (*straffvärde*) of the offence they had committed: 'with special regard to the harm, offence, or risk which the conduct involved, what the accused realized or should have realized about it, and [their] attention and motivation.' This principle finally became law in 1989: 'punishment shall be decided with regard to the desirability of uniform and consistent adjudication and set within the scale of punishment applicable to the culpability of the offence or the offences taken as a whole' (Jareborg, 1995: 110). In effect, the individualization of treatment, one of the foundation stones of the social democratic welfare sanction, had been removed.

With such curbs on its powers, it was thought that the place of punishment in these societies could be further reduced. Indeed, the consensus to this effect between politicians, civil servants and academic critics of the welfare sanction led to a sense of penal optimism at this juncture, rather than the despair that then permeated Anglophone discourse, where there was much greater division over the role and place of punishment.[37] Lennart Geijer, the Swedish Minister of Justice, thus predicted that the Swedish prison population could be reduced from its existing daily average of 2,808 to 500 (Ministry of Justice, 1974: 2). Finland, now free from its highly repressive social defence legislation, had begun its decarceration programme: 'there is no reason to toughen imprisonment penalties. Prison sentences nowadays have anyway led to problems in the prison administration, which cannot be aggravated any further. This is why the general prevention effect of the penal system must be otherwise improved: by enhancing the risk of getting caught, expanding the range of punishments, and using other sanctions besides imprisonment, with the same general preventive value as short-term incarceration would have' (Government Bill 110/1975: 6). Fines began to be used in place of short prison sentences, while the latter were also reduced in length: the average length of imprisonment for theft came down from 7.4 months in 1971 to 2.6 in 1991 (Lappi-Seppälä, 2000: 31). Following 'driving under the influence' reforms in 1976, more use was made of conditional prison sentences. As a consequence, while 70 per cent of those charged with this offence were imprisoned in 1971, by 1981 the number had been reduced to 12 per cent. In Norway, there were also plans to scale back the level of punishment. From 1973, the time in remand was to be included in a prison sentence. Life sentences were abolished in 1981 and replaced by a maximum finite term of 21 years. In addition, a prison 'waiting list' was introduced for those sentenced to prison for non-violent or non-drug related crimes, to limit the size of the prison estate: they would have to wait until a 'vacancy' occurred in their local prisons before commencing their term – something that could only be conceived of in a society with high levels of cohesion and stability, trust and tolerance. In further revisions to the Swedish penal code, imprisonment was designated as a 'last resort' penal option: 'wherever possible, preference is to be given to measures that avoid the deprivation of liberty' (Report of the Prison and Probation Board 1980, 1981: 2). The 1986 Commission on Prison Sentences then argued for more fines and less use of imprisonment, particularly for alcohol related driving offences. Parole, more or less automatic, became available on completion of 50 per cent of sentence in Norway and Sweden, and two thirds of sentence in Finland, in the 1980s.

However, Geijer's predictions did not come to fruition, and the optimism proved somewhat unfounded. In 1974, the prison rates of these societies had stood at 50 per 100,000 of population in Norway and Sweden, 112 in Finland. By 1992, these had increased to 58 in Norway and 63 in Sweden, but had declined to 70 in Finland. By 2010, though, while the Finnish imprisonment rate had declined further to 59, that for Norway had increased to 72, and that for Sweden to 78. Moreover, instead of looking forward to reducing the level of imprisonment, the website of *Kriminalvården* announced in 2006 that Sweden was undertaking 'the biggest prison building programme in Europe'. Similarly, in Norway, *VG* (11 May 2006: 3) reported that 'the government is establishing 150 new prison places this year . . . [overall] the government will establish 500 new prison places over four years'. In addition, the prison 'waiting list' (although not the possibility of deferment of the prison sentence) was to be terminated. These steady increases in imprisonment in Norway and Sweden point to some weakening of the restraints that had previously been placed on punishment in these societies. Indeed, the increases coincided with declines in their homogeneity (it is surely no coincidence that, in Finland, where homogeneity has been least threatened by immigration, prison rates continued to decline) and the arrival of economic uncertainties in Sweden and disparities in Norway. New risks and dangers had emerged – exemplified by drug use and violent crime – that seemed to have the power to corrupt and destroy the fundamental qualities of stability, cohesion and solidarity with which these societies had come to be associated.

These concerns have been most prominent in Sweden, the Nordic country where the social and economic changes have probably been greatest, and where welfare retractions are likely to provoke the deepest angst – the commitment to welfare had been so firmly embedded and so emblematic a characteristic of this society that *any* retractions of it would be likely to be given an exaggerated significance. In these respects, the concerns about drugs and violence have a symbolism that go beyond their particular threats to the well-being of individual Swedes. Although both drug use and levels of violence are actually *very low* in these Nordic countries (see, for example, Tham, 1995; Estrada, 2001; Lenke and Olsen, 2003; von Hofer, 2011), *the way in which these crimes are understood* conjures up age old anxieties that this former standard bearer of the West is under threat, once again, from 'the East' (Tham, 1995). This no longer comes, of course, from Mongol hordes, Tsarist Cossacks or even the Red Army but, instead, from drug trafficking and organized crime and corruption. These activities are thought to be endemic in this mythologized but geographically proximate region, and, so these fears go, have been allowed to make their way into Sweden because of its liberal immigration policies.

When having to carry such highly charged, emotional burdens, the punishment for drug crimes is going to assume dramatic, excessive dimensions. Prison terms for trafficking were thus increased from a maximum of four years imprisonment in 1968 to 10 in 1972. Penalization of consumption became law in 1988. The Ministry of Justice (1993: 1) later confirmed that 'punishment for minor drug offending has been increased'. Thereafter, no mainstream political party could afford to be seen as being 'soft on drugs', in just the same way that being thought to be 'soft on crime' became a precursor for political disaster in the Anglophone countries. As a consequence, the constituency of the Swedish prison population has been transformed. Eight per cent of inmates were drug offenders in 1980; by 2010 this had increased to 24. In much the same way, drug smuggling in Norway is one of the two crimes (the other being murder) that can lead to the 21-year maximum prison sentence – here, too, drug crime has become linked to broader anxieties about immigration and its effects on social cohesion and solidarity.

Equally, concerns about violence, which also began to gather momentum in the 1980s, can be traced back to the same source: the worrying threat of national decline and identity that was being brought about by 'Eastern' influences and immigration, as Åkertström (1998: 323, our italics) inferred: 'violence [in the 1980s in Sweden] seemed to be regarded as something more than violent behaviour: *it was seen as a foreign social force with a life of its own.*' In a country where there had been no involvement in war for nearly 200 years, and where there were stringent prohibitions on violence in the home, on television, in sport, in the penal system and in schools,[38] then the growing appearance of violent crime in the media was inevitably shocking and threatening and has since helped to change public sensibilities: the values of moderation, restraint and high levels of self-control are no longer such prominent features of everyday life. Frederik Fleisher (1967: 170), in *The New Sweden*, had written that 'the appreciation of restraint, a certain aloofness, and the disapproval of displays of emotion play a vital part in forming the general outlook toward violence'. Since the 1980s, however, 'new ceremonies to commemorate the memories of those who had fallen victim to violence occurred. People lit candles and put flowers in the streets on the spot where someone had been killed; torchlight processions and demonstrations opposing violence were held in the streets, and support groups organized in the name of murder victims' (Åkertström, 1998: 325). These public outpourings of grief reached a crescendo at the funeral of 10-year-old Engla Höglund in 2008, murdered by a man with a history of violent crime. State television broadcast the funeral in full, the first time for any such event, and a special funeral song was composed – 'Living without You'. Furthermore, new reports of violence can seem all the more alarming and 'foreign' because of the strong associations that have been made between ethnic minorities and violent crime (although Engla Höglund's murderer was a local truck driver), pointing again to the way in which immigration was jeopardizing one of the strongest pillars of support – homogeneity – on which the values of moderation and restraint had been built. As Brown (2008: 203) observed, 'immigration is certainly not the only threat to [Swedish values and conventions] which are understood and enforced by almost everyone in the community. But it is the most visible. The behaviour of the immigrants need not be destructive. The belief in foreign scroungers can be destructive even when they don't exist.'

For the right wing populist parties in Sweden and the other Nordic countries, social problems of this nature are seen, and have been exploited by them, as being both the creation of the social democratic welfare state and, at the same time, beyond its capacity to remedy because of its willingness to assist refugees, illegal immigrants and so on. Moreover, dissent from 'the social democratic image of society' has periodically surfaced in the political mainstream as well, with the accompaniment of promises that there would be more emphasis on penal exclusion, rather than inclusion. One of the slogans *Moderaterna* used to win the 1991 Swedish election was 'Keep them locked in, so we can go out!' (Leander, 1995: 169). Thereafter, the Ministry of Justice (1993: 5) White Paper, *To Restore a Degenerated Criminal Policy*, took the form of a repudiation of the social democratic welfare sanction: '[Under the Social Democrats], criminal policies were shaped from the perspective of the offender and the suffering of the victim was treated as a less important element. The offender was regarded as a victim of the forces of society . . . the new criminal policy is based on the idea that the most important task of the state is to protect its citizens from crime . . . by punishing the offender the state gives victims restitution.' Here, then, we have a way of thinking about punishment that does not differ greatly from similar pronouncements made during the course of Anglophone restructuring, amidst public displays of pain and emotion brought about by needless victimization that are likely to put pressure on governments to make more punitive, more authoritarian gestures in response, rather than stand back and allow its officials to pursue their policies of moderation and tolerance.

The reaffirmation of social democratic values and the social democratic welfare sanction

There is a strong sense of familiarity about this post-1970s Nordic sketch so far: the intentions of a liberal establishment to bring more leniency to the penal system, with recognition that the Justice Model, rather than the welfare sanction, was the means to achieve this, only for these elites to be undermined as 'the age of anxiety' began to change the social landscape and the prevailing Nordic mindset. Yet, it is from this point that the similarities in penal development between the Nordic and Anglophone societies cease. Indeed, while the restraints on punishment have been further eroded in the latter, these have remained largely in place in the former, while the values that are represented in the social democratic image of society have been reaffirmed rather than replaced.

How has this happened? *First*, the responses to drug related and violent crime can be seen as a continuation of social democratic thinking rather than some sort of dramatic right wing, repressive departure from it. If the reactions of the Swedish state to these crimes are indicative of the way in which *trygghet* has become more precarious, then these reactions are also indicative of the way in which social democracy, as we have seen, has *always* been preoccupied with protecting its communities from risk and danger, and *particularly from out of control, unpredictable behaviour.* While its tolerant and humane penal measures have become prominent internationally, this side of social democracy has always run in tandem with its less well known, more coercive and regulatory side. As such, it was always the state's duty to correct, to change, to 'cure' such propensities in the individuals concerned – the security of the community overrode the liberties of the individual, as we have already seen. This was in contrast to the Anglophone societies where it was thought that the liberty of the individual needed protection from over-excessive state regulation. From the late nineteenth century, alcohol consumption had borne the brunt of these concerns, followed by the sexual conduct of the mentally abnormal and so on. *During the late twentieth century, drugs and violence became their latest manifestations.* And just as, in the past, social movements had been instrumental in identifying and defining problematic behaviour, this also remains the case. In relation to violence, the women's movements in these societies have been able to draw public attention to the gendered nature of much of this crime. By the same token, the Social Democrats, as has always been the case, were prepared to support initiatives that protected the vulnerable from oppressors and exploiters: here, women and children from male abusers. Accordingly, as well as increasing penalties for assaults and sexual attacks, the 'Violence against Women' proposal (Department of Justice, 1990) urged the new crime of 'violence against women's integrity' – repeated crimes of violence by men against female partners – which became law in 1995. The motivation was the same for the subsequent criminalization of the purchase of sexual services – aimed at the male clients of prostitutes – which became law in 1999 (and was then replicated in Norwegian legislation that took effect in 2009[39]). As Ekberg (2004: 1189) explained, 'in Sweden, it is understood that any society that claims to defend principles of legal, political, economic, and social equality for women and girls must reject the idea that women and children, mostly girls, are commodities that can be bought, sold, and sexually exploited by men. To do otherwise is to allow that a separate class of female human beings, especially women and girls who are economically and racially marginalized, is excluded from these measures.'

Having once identified problem behaviour in this way, a familiar pattern of development then takes place: a series of commissions are established to examine it, eventually followed by the introduction of sweeping regulatory measures based on the commissions' recommendations. The Swedish anti-drugs campaign had begun around 1970. Geijer himself, when proclaiming that prison numbers could be reduced to 500, had also acknowledged that 'there is a small group of lawbreakers who[se] dangerousness for all of us leaves us with no other option than to place them in prison' (Ministry of Justice, 1974: 3). Thereafter, the ideal of Sweden becoming a 'drug free society' was *first* approved by the *Social Democrat* Congress in 1978. This would drive out drug crime and rid Swedish society from the impurities, real and symbolic, associated with it. Commissions were set up during the 1980s for further investigations of the problem. These were staffed by representatives from all the main political parties to ensure consensus, and also narcotics experts. In these respects, it is not the case that the previous importance given to expert knowledge in policy making has been abandoned. Instead, rather as had been the case with the medical professionals during their earlier dominance in the development of criminal justice policy, experts are invited to participate in examining a problem they have a vested interest in enlarging. The commissions and other official inquiries have thus continued to highlight the urgency of the drugs issue ('worrying deterioration' (Department of Justice, 2000: 126); 'the research on the pernicious effects of cannabis is not conclusive [but] it appears to have far more wide ranging and far more malicious effects than previously thought' (Swedish National Drug Policy Coordinator, 2003: 4); 'cannabis is more harmful than previously thought' (*Statens Folkhälsoinstitut*, 2011: 143)). At the same time, they have broadcast the 'success story' of Sweden becoming a drug free society to the rest of the world in ways that are redolent of its past presentations of social and penal policy (Nilsson, 2011): 'there are hardly any countries comparable to Sweden where the attitude to drugs is so repudiating, new recruitment of drug abusers so limited and mortality among drug abusers so low' (Government Bill 91, 2001–2002: 1–10). The point is, then, that, while concerns about drugs and violence may be indicative of the social tensions that have emerged in these societies since the 1970s, *the reaction to them* represents the continuation of a long tradition of state activity to protect *trygghet* from perceived dangers to it. The introduction of extensive state powers of regulation and control to bring this about is not something new to the Nordic region.

Second, while the social democratic welfare sanction has been restructured, it has not been dismantled. Although its psychodynamic 'treatment' aspects have been greatly scaled back, *faith in rehabilitation and inclusion has been maintained*. In the criticisms of the social democratic welfare sanction, treatment and rehabilitation were not conflated, as happened in the Anglophone societies: there was no full scale repudiation of the welfare sanction itself, nor the broader welfare programme of these societies. Instead, the deficiencies in the existing practices of the social democratic welfare sanction were seen as reaffirming the need for *stronger welfare policies*, rather than any kind of reversal of them – the exact opposite, then, of what happened in the Anglophone societies. In this regard, there was not so much a 'collapse of the faith in the rehabilitative ideal' (Allen, 1981) but *a lack of faith in the ability of punishment to produce any productive solution to crime*. As the Finnish Criminal Law Committee (1976, 2: 41, our italics) acknowledged, in one of its briefing documents around this time, 'the penal system is not the only system or even the main device to manage behaviour so that it is in accordance with socio-political goals . . . *it is the nature of penal provisions and punishments to be subsidiary*: cultural changes cannot be led by them'. Rather than being abandoned, rehabilitation remained central to social democratic thinking. The manifesto of the Finnish Social Democratic Party (1969: 2, our italics) had thus stated that 'crime forms a major part of social policy. Hence the solving of the problems of social policy and the achieving of the goals set for it may affect the problems of crime policy a great deal. *This is why crime policy must strive for the same economic, educational values and values of fairness that are strived for in other solutions related to social policy.*' Similarly, the Norwegian White Paper *On Criminal Policy*, although rejecting treatment ideology, insisted that '*we should*

however maintain the humanisation of the penal system, as was introduced with
the welfare model . . . responsibility for the convicted person's rehabilitation and
return to society is not vested in the Ministry of Justice alone . . . the convicted
person should not be deprived of their civil rights, and [state organizations] should
be responsible for offering their services also to convicted persons and inmates'
(Ministry of Justice, 1977–8: 26, our italics).

In effect then, there was no Kantian insistence in these countries that offenders
were responsible citizens who had *the right* to be punished for their misdeeds, as
if their term of exclusion from society would then annul their offence. Instead,
they were still seen as the victims of disadvantage for whom the state had the
responsibility to ensure more effective inclusion into society at large. As Geijer
had observed, '[offenders] come from deprived backgrounds, their schooling and
vocational education has been neglected. Society carries a larger responsibility
when it comes to alleviating these scarcities' (Ministry of Justice, 1974: 2). Even
drug criminals were not to be written off as 'evil'. A former Minister of Health
and Social Affairs confirmed that 'Sweden's drug policy is part of our general social
policy, which aims at giving everyone in Sweden social security via a system of
common welfare. The restrictive form taken by Sweden's drug policy is part of
the general perspective. Everyone has the right to a dignified life, and no groups
may be ostracized from the collective agreements of society' (Westerberg, 1994:
94). Similarly, 'a restrictive drug policy has to be combined with measures
characterized by humanity, dignity and care' (*Socialdepartementet*, 2003: 12).
Again, then, social democracy was prepared to take extensive measures to protect
all its citizens from the drugs menace with its high penalties for using, selling and
trafficking; but, at the same time, it was not prepared to simply expel those who
constituted such a threat. Instead, *it took upon itself the task of integrating them*
back into society. Similarly, in relation to violent crime, '*[the violent male] is*
often a socially marginalised person with drug and alcohol problems and a difficult
psychological background. Hence actions to reduce violence against women must
consist of both efforts that reduce the general oppression of women and
interventions aimed particularly against men who abuse women' (Department of
Justice, 1990: 14, our italics).

And, while it is no longer the case that Social Democrats have political hegemony
in this region, *the social democratic way of thinking about crime and punishment*
remains the dominant one. In Sweden, the attempt by *Moderaterna* to break away
from social democracy when in government from 1991 to 1994 led to electoral
disaster and their subsequent rebranding. Returned to government, the Social
Democrats then reaffirmed a more familiar penal policy in the subsequent White
Paper, *A Reformed System of Punishment* (Department of Justice, 1995): the
emphasis was on the need to *restrict* the prison population because of its negative
effects on offenders, rather than increase it in the name of public protection, as in
the Anglophone countries: 'in general, prison has negative consequences for those
who are subjected to it. To be locked up means that the sentenced person is isolated,
institutionalized and in many cases finds it difficult to return to a normal life in
society. Prison is also very expensive from a social cost perspective . . . there is no

evidence to suggest that prison would have a greater general deterrence effect than other types of punishment.' In Norway, the Labour Party was elected to government in 2006 and 2010 with a penal policy that emphasized the importance of inclusionary responses to crime. In contrast to the way in which Anglophone Labour parties reaffirmed the Conservative *weltanschauung* of those societies with their exuberant use of exclusionary punishments from the 1990s, the social democratic values of this region were reaffirmed: 'with good welfare services for everyone, crime can be prevented and many of the initial incentives for a life of crime can be removed. Given that 60 per cent of violent crime is committed under the influence of alcohol, it is important to adhere to a restrictive drug and alcohol policy. Good psychiatric health care services and an active labour market policy are important for comprehensive crime fighting' (Norwegian Labour Party, 2006: 1).

Third, the social democratic welfare sanction has been largely able to contain the emotions provoked by crime victimization. Crime victims feature very little in the Nordic criminal justice process. In contrast to the Anglophone societies, they are treated as welfare rather than juridical subjects, the purpose being to expedite their release from victimhood with therapeutic and financial assistance, rather than providing them with legal rights of representation that prolong it. Nor has it been the case that the social democratic welfare sanction gave thought only to rehabilitating offenders[40] – the Social Democrats extended welfare responsibilities to victims as well: 'a system for damages caused by offences should be developed in such a way that it would not depend solely on the solvency of the offender. This could be partly achieved by developing the [state] insurance system so that all property owners could share the damages caused to risky property. There has to be research done on how to compensate all bodily injury and loss of earnings by social insurance provisions. The securing of the family's livelihood is especially important when the breadwinner has been victim of an offence' (Finnish Social Democratic Party, 1969: 2). Thereafter, under the provisions of the Finnish Victim Compensation Act 1973, crime victims have been given the right to receive compensation from the state, initially for personal injuries suffered, but then extended on a discretionary basis in the 1980s to cover property crime. The victims' claims are dealt with at the same time as conviction is secured. In unproblematic cases, they need not appear in court at all – the prosecutor claims damages on their behalf. In effect, the 'victim's rights are associated, not with the right to exercise personal vendetta in the court, but with the victim's possibilities of getting his/her damages and losses compensated' (Lappi-Seppälä, 2007: 284). Victim impact statements – and their inflammatory capabilities – are thus unknown: 'a search from the Finnish supreme court case register covering the years 1980–2004 did not find a single case with the words 'public opinion' or 'general sense of justice' cited in the decision' (ibid.: 272).

Of course, with the undeniable changes that have taken place in public sensibilities, there may well be occasions when inconsolable crime victims and their supporters come more to the forefront of these societies. However, by taking care of most prior to the court, the overall effect has been to ensure that they are not left confused and helpless within it, and then vulnerable to political exploitation after it. Without the politicization of victimhood that has allowed raw emotions to be injected into the Anglophone criminal justice system, the dispensation of punishment is more likely to remain determined by calm, objective deliberation. It also ensures that crime continues to be understood *as a problem that must be solved by society as a whole*: victims have not been granted 'ownership' of the solutions to it. In Norway, the *Punishment that Works* White Paper (Ministry of Justice, 2008: 4, our italics) insisted that 'the government desires corrective services based on knowledge – *policy must not be based on individual incidents. National and international research is therefore of great significance for the government's choice of measures.*' Preparation for this document had involved discussions with 'former Justice Ministers . . . [then] a think-tank of professors and artists . . . two big professional conferences were held . . . in six prisons dialogue conferences were held in which both inmates and staff participated and discussed what a good day in prison would be like for them . . . Victims and the family and friends of inmates also had the opportunity to have their say . . . At a "grand conference" in May 2007, the relevant partners were invited to discuss the work of returning prisoners to society. Both public agencies and voluntary organizations took part.' Here, then, instead of being shrouded with invocations of 'public opinion' and expressions of reverence for victims, primacy is given, first, to former Justice Ministers, demonstrating the relatively consensual nature of political life in this country. Thereafter, it was the views of professors and artists that were elicited, demonstrating the continuing respect for the intelligentsia. Victims were consulted at a later stage – as were all other 'stakeholders' in penal policy development, *including their offenders*.

Fourth, important sectors of the Nordic media have continued to demonstrate a commitment to the social democratic image of society. Because there is not the same preponderance of sensation and drama in the reporting as there is in the Anglophone, and because state broadcasting and the broadsheet press remain popular and influential, crime and punishment issues still seem to be reported more dispassionately and descriptively. As regards the media reaction to prison escapes, we see in a Swedish example that 'Escapee Stabbed Birthday Guests'. The wet [that is, alcohol had been consumed] birthday party in Hedemora went off the rails. Fighting started and two of the guests were stabbed by a 37-year-old man who was later identified as an escaped prisoner. The man, who was later arrested, had absconded from the prison in Uppsala' (*Dagens Nyheter*, 9 May 2006: 8). And, as regards its reaction to new crimes committed by ex-prisoners on parole, a Norwegian example is 'Raped Woman (62) While Going to Therapy'. As soon as the twenty-three year old had completed his sentence and was attending therapy, he is suspected to have brutally raped [the woman] . . . in 2002 he was sentenced to five years in prison for aggravated assaults and rapes in Kristianstad. The Prison Service released [him] on parole in May 2004. He then had one year and 255 days left to serve of his sentence . . . The Prison Service states that "we never comment on individual programs, not even when the people we are dealing with will be charged in new cases or the reasons for parole" said Signe Gunn Ropstad of Correctional Services, Western College' (*VG*, 11 May 2006: 6). It is evident from the latter that the prison service still controls the flow of information to the public, and the news item was content to leave the matter at this. There was no attempt to undermine or criticise the prison authorities for their parole decision. Again, then, it is not that there is no mention of prison escapes and so on in the media in these countries; rather, it is the restrained and factual nature of the reporting that stands in contrast to the emotive sensationalism of much of the Anglophone press. At the same time, the overall context of escapes remains in view, rather than the thrilling minutiae of each incident: 'Fewer Escaped From Prison: last year, 15 escaped from closed prisons. Never before have there been so few escapes. The number is the lowest since statistics began being collected and can be compared with 33 escapes in 2004' (*Svenska Dagbladet*, 10 January 2006: 8).

This style of reporting has also meant that some of the other dynamics that underlie the more uncontrolled and emotional outbursts to crime of the Anglophone societies are either much more muted, or missing altogether, in this region. Thus, notwithstanding the public grief that child murders can now provoke in Sweden, there have been no subsequent nationwide vigilante activities against suspected paedophiles, nor any agitations, led by the media, for publicly accessible registries of sex offenders. At the same time, there seems no desire to have their supervision by state employed social workers made more publicly transparent and accountable. Moreover, the values of moderation and restraint, along with the more respected authority of the central state itself, are still strong enough to prevent vigilante excess and the 'naming and shaming' practices that have become regular occurrences in the Anglophone countries. This is not to say that the barriers against punitiveness have been impenetrable in this region. However, while there have been increases in sentence lengths in all three societies from the 1990s, it remains that *most* offenders in the Nordic countries are sent to prison for significantly shorter periods than in the Anglophone. In New South Wales, the average prison sentence length in 2009 was 395 days; in New Zealand, it was 325 days; in England 300, compared with 100 in Norway, 220 in Sweden and 250 in Finland. Average prison sentences in England are twice the length of those in Norway: 'only seven per cent of Norwegian prisoners serve more than 10 years whereas a full 17 per cent of prisoners in England are serving over 10 years' (Green, 2008: 67). Certainly, in Norway, dangerous offender legislation was reactivated in 2002 after decades of equivocation: under the new sentence of *forvaring* (literally, 'storing') for those so judged, the maximum twenty-one year finite prison term can be given, with the possibility of indefinite extensions to this. Sixty prisoners were serving indefinite sentences in 2009. In Finland, the number of preventive detention prisoners increased from 10 in 1992 to 33 in 2010 – but these developments have to be seen in contrast to the much more dramatic escalation in indeterminate sentencing that has taken place in England and New Zealand (see p. 176). If the time to be served before parole eligibility has increased in the Nordic countries (two thirds of sentence in Norway and Sweden, five sixths in Finland), then the *granting* of parole has become much more problematic for many in the Anglophone countries. Moreover, there are no vestiges of the highly symbolic three strikes laws or powers to extend prison sentences after the term set by the courts has finished in the Nordic countries, as is variously the case in the Anglophone.

When we return to our initial indicator of punishment – imprisonment rates – we find that this increased by 24 and 23 per cent, respectively, in Norway and Sweden between 1992 and 2010, *from a relatively low starting point*; and there was a 16 per cent *decrease* in Finland. However, in England, *from a relatively high starting point*, the increase in imprisonment was 73 per cent over the same period; New Zealand 67 per cent; and New South Wales, 35 per cent. This was the growing gulf in imprisonment rates that was observed in Chapter 1, and which positions the two clusters of societies at opposite ends of the Western imprisonment spectrum.

The normalization of prison life

In the Nordic prisons, the paternalistic authoritarianism – *uppfostran* – that was characteristic of the operation of the unreconstructed social democratic welfare sanction was also challenged. A series of strikes, demonstrations and sit-ins that began in Swedish prisons in 1966 spread across the other Nordic countries over the next few years. Initially, the prisoners demanded better food,[41] hygiene and improved access to 'treatment'. However, this quickly turned into a demand for *the greater democratization* of prison life. Thus, the aims of KROM (the Norwegian prisoners' rights group, with members consisting of prison inmates and ex-prisoners, academics and other supporters) were to 'work for measures towards offenders which are more worthy of human beings and more expedient . . . in particular, to reduce the damaging effects of incarceration, and which may make incarceration less burdensome for inmates' (Mathiesen, 1974: 68). Now, prison was understood as the product of the divisions brought about by 'class society', rather than a necessary institution for rectifying the assumed personality deficiencies of those offenders sent to it. On this basis, the need for the prison itself would cease when such social divisions were healed, rather than any quality of treatment that it was able to provide for individual inmates. Prisoner demands thus changed from simply wanting more treatment to wanting more *influence* over their treatment and a range of other aspects of prison life.

However, the subsequent conflicts in the Nordic prisons took on a very different form and were resolved in a very different way from those in the Anglophone. In the former, inmate participation was on a much wider scale, at one point involving 60 per cent of the Swedish prison population, whereas the demonstrations in England never exceeded 25 per cent (Fitzgerald, 1977). At the same time, the disturbances and protests were conducted without any violence from the prisoners or prison staff. Indicative of the higher levels of trust in these institutions and these societies at large, there was no insistence from Nordic prisoners that there should be 'no retaliation' at the end of their demonstrations. There was certainly obfuscation on the part of the prison authorities when dealing with prisoners and their representatives, and various prison officers voiced disapproval at the legitimacy given to the prisoners and their organizations, but there was no violence, no destruction (see Mathiesen, 1974[42]). Moreover, in contrast to their reception in the Anglophone countries, prisoners' rights organizations were accorded much greater legitimacy. Mathiesen (1974: 171) thus wrote that, in Sweden, the influential and social democrat leaning *Dagens Nyheter* 'faithfully supported the prisoners'; there were also expressions of support for them from some prison officials, including Director of Finnish Prisons K.J. Lång, in Finland, as well as prison psychologists and prison teachers (Marnell, 1974).

The much shorter social distances between prisoners and the rest of society in Sweden also made it possible for the prison authorities to negotiate with inmates and their representatives over extensive reforms, something impossible, as we have seen, in the Anglophone countries. A Director of Prisons' press release in 1971 (our italics) thus stated that 'negotiations at Österåker prison are unique in history. *They placed on an equal footing* the delegates of the country's 5,000 prisoners on one side and representatives of the correctional authorities and the personnel organizations on the other' (quoted by Mathiesen, 1974: 174). Of course, the extent to which both parties to these negotiations really were on an 'equal footing' is highly contestable. However, what is so different from the approach to such matters in the Anglophone countries is that the authorities were not only prepared to enter into negotiations with prison inmates about reform *but were formally prepared to acknowledge that they were doing this*. At the same time, the social movement and 'organizing from the bottom of society' Nordic tradition[43] also helps to explain the more conciliatory attitudes and approaches of the authorities and mass media to prisoners' rights movements than in the Anglophone countries. Marnell (1974: 17) explained that 'it should be kept in mind when speaking of democracy within prisons that similar trends have existed for years in Sweden's universities and schools, hospitals, factories and armed services. The general public has thus been accustomed to think in terms of democracy, democratization and the cooperative influence of clients in different organizations.' Accordingly: 'for many years KRUM [the Swedish prisoners' rights group] has had a government grant, on the decision of the Swedish parliament after a government proposal. It has also been accepted as an official body to which proposed legislative measures concerning the treatment of prisoners and other questions of prison policy are referred for comment' (idem).

The ability of these new social movements to highlight the injustices of another oppressed group – prisoners – also rekindled the interest of Social Democrats in prison reform. In Finland, a Penal Code Reform Committee was constituted in 1972, consisting exclusively of academics and civil servants, most of whom had been active in 'the November Movement' formed in 1967 and the precursor to KRIM (the Finnish prisoners' rights group). Tham (1995: 92) wrote, of Sweden, that 'Social Democrat Party congresses up to 1975 were clearly influenced by the criticism voiced by KRUM . . . a number of motions demanded equality under the law, humanization of the correctional system and more effective aftercare for released prisoners'. Indeed, Geijer had referred to the presence of 'a small but vocal group [the prisoners' rights organization] that demands complete abolition of the prison system. *This opinion cannot be ignored. It has to be observed that well-established criminological researchers form part of that group*' (Ministry of Justice,

1974: 2, our italics). These comments provide another illustration of the continuing respect for expert knowledge in these countries at that time, and the importance given to allowing this knowledge to inform policy development, even if it now came from abolitionists, rather than those skilled in psychodynamic theory. In addition, the integrated and still largely homogeneous nature of Nordic society meant that there were 'close personal and professional contacts with senior politicians and academic research', further consolidating the influence of expert knowledge on policy development (Lappi-Seppälä, 2000: 37). In Finland for example, K. J. Lång was thus not only the Director of Prisons but also the Chairman of the Council for Mass Media, from which he was able to criticize any over-sensational reporting of crime and punishment issues, while at the same time playing a leading role in the development of prison policy.

In these respects, the Nordic prison disturbances contributed to *the further normalization of prison life* (as we saw in Chapter 5, this progression was already taking place) rather than the normalization of security. The Swedish Correctional Treatment in Institutions Act 1974 thus stipulated that 'inmates shall be treated with respect for their human dignity . . . they shall be treated with understanding for the special difficulties connected with a stay at any institution'. To this end, 'prison conditions in penal institutions have to be arranged as well as possible to resemble the common living conditions in society' (Prison Administration Decree, 1975). In Finland, 'the prison sentence should be carried out in such a way that punishment involves only the loss of freedom'. As such, prison conditions were to correspond 'as close as possible to living conditions in a society' (Ministry of Justice, 1975). Such developments would go some way to meeting the inmates' demands for improved material conditions and greater democratization within the institutions; at the same time, they would be in line with Social Democrat thinking that the negative, stigmatic consequences of punishment should be further reduced. Geijer thus confirmed that 'this year a reform is being introduced that will result in improvements for normal prisoners – they will be given expanded rights to parole, improvements in visitation rights, the right to use the phone and so on' (Ministry of Justice, 1974: 2). Inmate councils were set up, along with the introduction of minimum standards of payment for prison labour, the abolition of censorship, and more liberal visiting rules, including provisions for unsupervised visits and more home leaves.

Prison design and refurbishment also followed these attempts to further depenalize the Nordic prison experience. In Norway, *VG* (6 March 1976: 17) reported on the refurbishment of Oslo *Botsfengslet*: 'the cells now resemble little *hybler* [bed-sitting rooms] with hot and cold running water, a radio and a desk. There is also an intercom in each room so that the prisoner can contact staff any time of the day or night. There are also new bathrooms and toilets in each *avdelning* [wing, literally 'department'] and a living room with television, a kitchen for making snacks, and in the fridge prisoners can keep some milk and sandwich fillings . . . since lockdown is at 9.00 pm, TV programmes after this time are taped, so that prisoners can watch them the next day.' Bishop (1991: 136–8) described conditions in a Swedish medium security institution: 'there is little to suggest to the passerby that this is a prison. It could well be a factory or office similar to those around it. All buildings are inter-connected and reached by corridors painted and decorated in light colours . . . each unit of five has its own set of showers and a small well-equipped kitchen-cum-pantry combined with a breakfast room . . . Each room has its own toilet separated from the living space in the same way as in most modern hotels. There are no bars on the windows; strengthened laminated glass is used instead. Recreation rooms and a sauna are provided for common use in four of the residential blocks. Coin-operated telephones are installed in the inmate's living quarters . . . between 06.30 and 07.30 prisoners are expected to wake up (a clock radio is in each room) prepare and eat breakfast in the living units . . . staff and inmates share the same dining room and food . . . the evening meal is served in the cafeteria at 17.00. Locking-up time for the living units is at 19.45 but organized leisure activities can continue until 21.30.'

At the same time, plans to build any more large, impersonal institutions were abandoned. Thus, in Sweden, 'no more prisons like Kumla will be erected . . . the local [prison] community is intended to be as much as possible integrated with its neighbourhood. This has a twofold objective: to counteract the negative effects of institutions and to encourage citizens living close by to play an important part in preparing for the after care stage' (Marnell, 1974: 11). To this end, new, smaller institutions continued to be built in or near urban centres, with 40 places per institution: 'the local institutions have open, flexible regimes that will permit inmates to have intensive contact with normal society and especially with families, employers, education facilities and leisure time associations (Report of the [Swedish] Prison and Probation Board, 1981: 4). In addition, 'inmates are increasingly able to improve general education and to take vocational training. Some institutions now offer full courses at the secondary level. A few institutions cooperate with nearby folk high schools. The teachers from these schools hold daily classes . . . for the inmates interested in studying' (ibid.: 3). In these countries, the authorities emphasised *the importance of the similarities* – not the differences – that there should be between prison conditions and those in everyday life outside the prison. It was thus claimed that 'industrial workshops in the new institutions are comparable in every respect with their [non-prison] counterparts' (idem). In Finland, 'the normal working [prison] day lasts eight hours, with a 40 hour week, and accelerated payments for overtime work. A four week vacation from work is afforded inmates' (Zagaris, 1977: 45). Rather than having rights stripped away from them simply because they were prisoners, inmates continued to have the same rights of access to healthcare and other social services as non-inmates: 'it has been decided that health services in prison should be dealt with in the same manner as for all other people – through the social services. That department is taking over responsibility for all health services in prisons, and each local community is responsible for that particular area' (Prison Administration/Department of Justice, 1986: 73).

Again, rehabilitation (but not psychodynamic treatment) remained central to Nordic prison administration. There seem to have been no references to 'humane containment' – the concept that began to feature strongly in the administration of

Anglophone prisons over this period,[44] a negative value based on recognition of how little the prisons were expected to achieve, other than containment itself. Instead, the productive possibilities of the prison, and the way to bring these about by normalizing prison life, continued to be emphasised. In Finland, the Prison Administration Decree of 1971 stated that, 'while the objective of incapacitation was previously defined as curing the prisoner[,] it was now set to be the reducing of harm imposed on the prisoner by the punishment *and promoting the prisoners' relocation in society*' (our italics). And a Norwegian advert for those wanting to join the prison service specified that 'in this job it is important that you are a responsible person and that you have the desire and ability to solve human problems in a difficult but rewarding environment. You need to be able to deal with a two-sided task: first, to undertake the deprivation of freedom that has been given by society; and secondly, *to help the inmates to solve a range of problems that occur as a result of their stay in prison*' (*VG*, 20 June 1986: 40, our italics).

Moreover, continuing high levels of prison escapes and disturbances were not allowed to interrupt this pattern of development. There were more than 1,000 escapes in Sweden in 1973, while, in Norway, escapes doubled from 86 in 1980 to 170 in 1982. Prison disturbances had also become more dramatic, with hostage-taking incidents in Norway and rioting in Sweden in the 1980s. The escalation of these incidents, involving property destruction and personal violence, is perhaps a reflection of the transformation of the prison populations of these societies then taking place, with considerably more drug and organized crime inmates serving longer sentences. It is also likely to be a reflection of how the broader social changes – the erosion of trust and interdependencies that homogeneity and guarantees of security had made possible – now make such conduct more of a likelihood than in the past. However, in just the same way that the solution to social problems outside the prison was seen as more welfare, rather than less, so problems within the prison were seen as demanding more rehabilitation and less security: 'instead of giving up on tough prisoners, further efforts at reintegration are made. The staff are trying to reduce the harmful effects of prison by extended use of furloughs, increase probation staff and the education of prison officers to ensure a service delivery marked by knowledge and compassion' (Report of the [Swedish] Prison and Probation Board, 1977: 9). In Norway, the response to escapes from the Ministry of Justice (Prison Administration/Department of Justice, 1986: 71, our italics) was that 'society shies away from methods that would completely incapacitate those people who have committed the most serious and heinous acts. These people will be released after a certain number of years. *This we must live with in a society that strives for a humane criminal justice policy.*'

Meanwhile, the Nordic press not only put little pressure on the authorities to intensify security after escapes, but its reports on other features of prison life also continued to demonstrate the very different way of thinking about punishment in these societies. For example, there was a meeting between 15 *Moderaterna* politicians and 70 prisoners at Österåker Prison: '[they] met over coffee and cakes. The aim of the visit was to show that *Moderaterna* were not advocates for a harsh criminal justice policy' (*Svenska Dagbladet*, 26 January 1976: 6). Despite the way in which the prison has become such a central feature of political discourse in the Anglophone societies, very few of their politicians would ever consider visiting one, let alone try to explain their policies to inmates.[45] On another occasion, at the end of a rooftop demonstration, prisoners were allowed to give a press conference – something unimaginable in the Anglophone societies, where prisoners, as non-citizens, have no access to such self-promotion: 'prisoners were pleased with the opportunity to address the press and voice their complaints' (*Svenska Dagbladet*, 21 May 1976: 8). The much greater freedom of movement that inmates were allowed was also in stark contrast to the Anglophone prisons. Thus, in Norway, under the headline 'Jogging Robber at Seminar', *VG* (18 January 1986: 14) reported that 'he will attend a KROM seminar . . . and talk about his experiences of being in prison, without yet having a right to furlough. The former policeman had been sentenced to seven years in prison for four armed robberies in 1984 . . . the Associate Prison Director at Ila prison will accompany him. He says that "I trust him and do not rate him as an escape risk. The purpose of a prison sentence is also to rehabilitate the inmate and give them social training so they can return to society".' And, while Anglophone prison officials are not allowed to write to the press, it had become permissible for Nordic prison inmates to do so: under the headline 'Letter From Despairing Inmate', a prisoner writes to ask, 'Can someone get me a job?' (*VG*, 30 June 1976: 14).[46]

It has only been in the early twenty-first century that there has been any significant interruption to this pattern of normalization – specifically, the sudden intensification of security in Swedish closed prisons following the escapes of 2004 (see p. 22). The reaction to them was dramatically different from what it had been to previous escapes and violent incidents. In 1996, after riots at Tidaholm, the Director of Prisons presented the familiar argument that '*the recipe for increased security is not tougher measures – but a rather more humane and flexible system*' (*Svenska Dagbladet*, 23 May 1996: 6, our italics). Accordingly, 'common wake up calls, showering times, and strictly scheduled days will disappear. Recreation activities such as sport will be allowed during the day. Visitors are allowed during weekdays and relatives who have a long way to travel are offered stay overs in special visitation flats' (idem). The different reaction in 2004, however, demonstratively indicates that escapes of this magnitude can no longer be ignored, nor will they provide the opportunity for further liberalizations of prison life. Instead, they now constitute risks that can no longer be tolerated and the authorities will be held to account for endangering public safety.[47] The social fabric of 'the new Sweden' is more taut and fragile than the previous one, less able to absorb disorder and disharmony, more likely to provoke it, instead, and needing to respond to it with more overt demonstrations of state authority. Indeed, in the aftermath of these escapes, there was an attack on the erstwhile 'exceptional' Swedish prison conditions in *A Safer Sweden*, a policy document authored by *Moderaterna* and their political allies (Alliance for Sweden Political Group, 2006). However, rather than this marking the beginning of some great retreat from the prison regimes that these societies have become known for, these proposals came to nothing. Facilities, 'benefits' and rights are still distributed across the vast majority of the prison population, irrespective of the prisoner's status. Furthermore, the report, written by an alliance of right of centre parties in the highly charged aftermath of the 2004 escapes and murders, had, anyway, argued for more self-care arrangements in the prisons, thereby giving inmates more autonomy, along with improved visiting facilities for their families. There was no mention of the need for 'austerity' or 'spartan conditions'.

These differences are also reflected in the 'Mission Statements' of the Nordic prison systems. Rather than the attention given to 'public protection' in the corresponding Anglophone documents, the emphasis continues to be on the rehabilitation and reintegration of the prisoner. That for Sweden states that 'the purpose of prison is to prepare prisoners for a return to society *and to counteract any adverse effects of imprisonment*' ([Report of the] Prison and Probation Board, 2010: 3, our italics); that for Norway notes that 'punishment shall be served in a manner which secures society *and gives the sentenced prisoner the best possible opportunities for a life without* crime' (Report of the Prison Administration Board, 2006: 1, our italics); that for Finland is 'to take care of security in society by maintaining a legal and safe system of enforcement of sentences [and] to contribute to the reducing of recidivism and to the breaking of the cycle of social exclusion which is known to reproduce crime' (Annual Report of the Finnish Prison and Probation Services, 2002: 4). Nonetheless, the implications of the changes taking place in the closed Swedish prisons should not be underestimated. The new emphasis on security, along with the high numbers of non-Swedish prisoners (27.6 per cent in 2011), many of whom will be deported on completion of their sentence, and the normalization of body searches and urine samples to check for drugs (Hörnqvist, 2010), may eventually undermine the 'exceptional qualities' of this part of its prison estate.

This, though, does not mean an end to the exceptional prison conditions – by comparison with those in the Anglophone countries – in the Nordic region as a whole. These qualities are still firmly embedded in the Finnish and Norwegian prisons. In Finland, after eight escapes from closed institutions in 2008, the Report of the Criminal Sanctions Field (2008: 14) merely noted that 'this means that 1.4 prisoners per 100,000 prison days escaped from prison in 2008. At the end of the year, three prisoners were at large. There is no single reason for the . . . escapes. In most cases, the prisoner had just taken advantage of the situation.' Here, then, the authorities were still sufficiently powerful to be able to define down such events – this is prison, its inmates try to escape, this is what happens here, there is nothing unusual or untoward about this. Meanwhile, although the designs for a new prison in Finland had a high security unit, those for the routine wings in this closed institution included 'an open kitchen area, a common room and a sauna. All in all, 85 of the 263 cells are designed for two prisoners and the rest are single cells . . . the size of the cells is 12 square meters. In general, these are equipped with a toilet, shower, television, radio, DVD player, and speech connection to the ward control room' (idem: 5). In Norway, there are clearly defined limits to the extent that security will be allowed to dominate prison policy: 'public safety is a paramount objective of the government's crime policy . . . *security work in the Norwegian*

Correctional Services shall not, however, mean an unnecessary high level of security for all inmates and convicted persons. It is only a minority that constitute a threat to public or individual safety' (Ministry of Justice and the Police, 2008: 4, our italics).

Indeed, it is as if Norway has become the new standard bearer in the development of prisons that represent the furthest departures from the way in which it has been possible to think about imprisonment in the Anglophone societies. Halden prison thus received a number of awards for interior design and innovation. The jury nomination for the innovation award stated that '[this] is the first prison in Norway that does not have bars in front of the windows, but rooms with lots of light, space and good views out over green areas. There are different colours for different areas in the buildings . . . Emphasis has been placed on the movement between different buildings and functions, so to reflect the difference between home, school, and work place . . . The project touches very important aspects of how we design our society. The way this has been resolved touches us and makes us reflect on our common values' (Norwegian Design Council, 2011: 1).

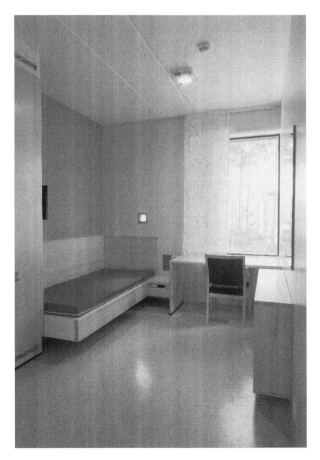

Figure 6.1
Cell in Halden prison, Norway. Photograph: Statsbygg, Norway.

Figure 6.2 Cell in one of New Zealand's newest prisons. Photograph: John Pratt.

Figure 6.3 Visiting room in New Zealand's newest prison. Note that the tables and chairs are bolted to the floor for 'security reasons'. Prisoners wearing red Guantanomo Bay-style clothing, have to sit in the light-coloured chairs where they are observed at all times by prison officers in attendance. Photograph: John Pratt.

Figure 6.4
Visitation house inside prison grounds, Halden prison, Norway.
Photograph: Statsbygg, Norway.

Rather than have them hidden away in disgust and built with the insistence that inmates will find no luxuries and enjoy no privileges when sent there, here was a society in which it was thought that penal institutions should neither be shameful buildings, nor should they be buildings intended to emphasize deprivation and misery – leave all that to the Anglophone countries saturated as they already are with punishment: let them advertize themselves to the world about the kinds of societies they have become, with their prisons made out of shipping containers and the latest initiatives they have conjured in the hope of locking up more people for less money.

Instead, there is pride in the very fact that prisons are not built in this fashion, amidst recognition that the Halden design is a signifier of Norwegian society as a whole, not just that particular institution; it is a signifier of its longstanding inclusionary values and the way in which these have made it possible to think about punishment in this country and in this region.

***

When punishment is spoken about, it is usually by reference to crime rates and which are then the most 'effective' types of sanction – matters such as these, it is thought, control its level and intensity. This is mistaken. Instead, deeply embedded cultural values that have come into existence over the last 200 years or so have provided the Nordic and the Anglophone societies with ways of thinking about punishment that are now represented in the penal exceptionalism of the former and the penal excesses of the latter. The Nordic values emerged out of their particular early nineteenth century social arrangements, whereby the state was able to assume a 'saviour' role in this region. It provided longed-for guarantees of security, thereby generating high levels of trust and prestige in its own organizations of government. These arrangements also necessitated strong and extensive interdependencies and reciprocities between individuals, then also facilitated by the extreme homogeneity of these societies that encouraged mutual identification and solidarity. In addition, without being prepared to aid and assist their neighbours, each individual's well-being would be put at risk. In this way, the strength and vitality of the community at large assumed a greater importance than those of the particular individuals living within it. At the same time, Lutheranism gave a necessity to educational achievement, and educational qualifications became emblems of success in these otherwise egalitarian societies. The end product was the values of moderation, restraint and inclusion that shaped both everyday interaction and the state's programmes of governance, presided over by civil servants and directed by experts. As regards punishment, this meant that corporeal sanctions could be very quickly dispensed within the modern period; and prison was intended to bring about the reintegration of its inmates – initially through the provision of 'soul care', then psycho-therapeutic treatment followed by the normalization of prison life itself – in a bid to reduce, as much as possible, the distinctions and divisions between prisoners and the rest of society.

There was a price to be paid, though, for these values. Indeed, the informal controls that policed and regulated moderation and conformity became too high a price for many: poverty was not the only reason for mass emigration from these societies during the nineteenth and early twentieth centuries (Barton, 1976); and the extensive formal controls that allowed the state to correct and cure departures from the norm, as well as the most serious law-breaking, produced their own injustices. Nonetheless, what has ultimately been purchased are the low rates of imprisonment of this region and, by comparison with Anglophone countries at least, remarkably humane and liberal prison conditions. In contrast, the values of the Anglophone countries came from England, of course, in the first instance. Great store was set on individual success – personal wealth, land and property ownership – rather than community vitality and strength. In this society, the state was seen more as an enemy than a saviour, as if it only impeded the route to success, providing unfair props for those who would never have been able to complete this journey anyway, while simultaneously blocking the route of potential champions. In a society with such extensive social divisions and exclusionary barriers, there could be little of the interdependencies and reciprocities, little of the solidarity and trust that marked the Nordic countries. Accordingly, rather than endowing the state with the positive, preventative, powers of normalization it came to exercise in the Nordic countries, it was thought that it should have mainly reactive, negative powers of punishment – powers that should be used almost exclusively on those kept behind these divisions and barriers.

Much the same set of values came to be adapted in Australia and New Zealand, albeit mediated through their own particular colonial histories. Thus, while these gave much more emphasis to egalitarianism, this came to mean equality of opportunity that would then allow those who made the most of this to enjoy the same kinds of successes as in England; it did not mean everyone receiving very similar rewards, as in the Nordic countries. Furthermore, the 'fair go' reputation that Australia and New Zealand did come to be known for has, since the post-1970s restructuring, been overwhelmed by a much more aggressive individualism on the one hand, and an increasing fear and intolerance of outsiders, of those who are different due to race or social background, on the other. In addition, while the state had a more legitimate place in infrastructural development in these two societies, there was still a suspicion of anything more than this, and a lack of trust in its officials. And, in all three Anglophone societies, there has been a strong anti-intellectualism running through their histories to the present day. Thus, in New Zealand, the British broadcaster and scientist Lord Robert Winston observed that 'the culture of New Zealanders undervalues thinkers and idolizes sports stars . . . In New Zealand, being an intellectual is slightly disadvantageous and is often seen by the press as being something . . . not to be celebrated' (as reported in the *New Zealand Herald*, 14 December 2009: A6).

The end product of these particular arrangements has been a set of values where division, intolerance and exclusion have been stronger than moderation, restraint and inclusion – with its own costs, in terms of countless thousands of lives unfulfilled and burdens unfairly shared. In terms of punishment, then great symbolism was attached to the death penalty, amidst fears of social collapse should it be abolished. Alongside this, there was the particularly repressive nature of nineteenth century imprisonment. There were also the limitations of the liberal welfare sanction in bringing about more fundamental changes to prison life, then followed by the outlandish growth in prison numbers, and the new intensity of the prison experience in these societies, as policy was influenced more and more by 'public opinion' and sensational one-off cases rather than research. Of course, though, these values are not set in stone and individual differences in punishment will occur in these clusters depending on their 'local centrifugal forces' (Elias, 1939/1979) – that is, the extent and intensity of their fundamental cultural characteristics and the social arrangements underpinning them.

Nonetheless, the ability of these values to shape the way in which it is possible to think about punishment in these different types of modern society was seen in the responses to two major crime incidents that occurred in 2011 in England and Norway. In August, in the former, mass rioting, involving property destruction to the value of around £100,000,000, assaults and murder took place across the country. Indeed, such scenes have taken place on a fairly regular basis since the early 1980s when the consequences of the restructuring being engineered by the first Thatcher government began to take effect, deindustrializing and making redundant large sections of British society. At that time, the rioters were met with punishment, but also with gestures of reconciliation and government aid.[48] Such gestures, though, have been long since abandoned as the divisions, distances and distrust in this society have become still more firmly set in place. On this latest occasion, the government decided that there was no need for any further formal enquiries (what happened should no longer come as a shock or even a surprise, here, anyway): the rioting was caused by 'sheer criminality' claimed the Home Secretary (*London Evening Standard*, 8 August 2011: 1). For Prime Minister David Cameron, the riots were a sign of a 'broken society' in 'moral collapse' (*BBC News*, 15 August, 2011). The way his government chose to restore this broken society, though, was to continue to withdraw the already limited forms of welfare assistance and other social measures. In so doing, the weakness of the authority of the central state, which was reflected in both the riots themselves and in the formation of disparate vigilante groups during them, some to protect property, others to make racial attacks, was further weakened by the government's own responses. Evidence that the rioting was caused by extensive social deprivation was ignored.[49] Instead, it was to be met with a 'war on gangs' (idem), amidst proposals that those involved in the rioting should lose social security benefits as well as face penal sanctions; and that the families of looters should be evicted from state housing properties.[50] Once again, it is as if the state in this society only knows how to use its powers negatively: more divisions, more punishment, more exclusions. Six months after the riots, almost 1,000 people had been sent to prison as a result of their involvement in these incidents, with the average prison sentence of 14.2 months being four times the average for similar offences in 2010.[51] One received a six-month sentence for theft of a case of water (£3 in value) from a supermarket. In another case, a Blackberry message was sent, inviting its recipients to 'kick off' in another northern city: nobody did so, there was no riot, and the sender was sentenced to 39 months for inciting the riot that never happened.[52]

However, the Norwegian reaction to the mass murders (77)[53] committed by Anders Breivik in Oslo and on the island of Utøya in July was very different. When apprehended, Breivik claimed to be 'saving Norway' from the perils of mass immigration. Three days afterwards, there was a march and memorial meeting outside the City Hall in Oslo, with around 150,000 to 200,000 of the city's population of 600,000 in attendance. This, though, was not a meeting where speakers demanded savage recrimination from the state, on peril of vigilantism if this was not forthcoming. There were no demands for the death penalty nor, at that time, that 'life should mean life'. Instead, the emphasis was on reaffirming solidarity, democracy and unity. The citizens held hands and carried roses. Speaking to the crowds, Crown Prince Haakon declared that 'tonight the streets are filled with love'. Prime Minister Jens Stoltenberg, at the same event, reaffirmed Norway's unwavering commitment to social democratic values: 'by taking part [in the march], you are saying a resounding "yes" to democracy . . . a march for democracy, a march for tolerance, a march for unity . . . Evil can kill a person but never conquer a people' (*BBC News*, 26 July 2011). Similarly, Nils Christie (2011, our italics) has since written that '*what has happened is a catastrophe that can only be met by holding on to the foundational values of Norwegian society*. If we abandon those, then Breivik has achieved something . . . Of course a society has to react, otherwise there would be no society. But with most terrible crimes, we also see the help-lessness of punishment clearer than at other times.'

These 'foundational values' of Norwegian society, similar to the foundational values of the other Nordic countries, had become weaker since the 1970s. Now, though, when subjected to such a profound test, they reasserted themselves. They may even have been strengthened by this catastrophe.[54] And what they show in such a stark light are the differences in reacting to crime and to thinking about punishment that exist between these two types of societies.

Notes

Introduction

1 Australia has both commonwealth and state jurisdictions. Each state develops its own penal policy independently of the federal government. This means that there is no penal policy for Australia *as a whole*. We thus decided that the best way to present this was to use its largest and oldest state (New South Wales, population 6,890,000) for fieldwork and data collection purposes.

2 Even though those Finns whose mother tongue is Swedish have declined from around 12 per cent of the population at the end of the nineteenth century to 5.5 per cent in 2011.

3 It was not ratified in Australia until 1942 (wartime exigencies necessitated that Australia develop its own defence policy rather than allow Britain to dictate what this should be), and in New Zealand not until 1947.

4 Dostoyevsky, quoted by Pisciotta (1994: 150), claimed that 'the standards of a nation's civilization can be judged by opening the doors of its prisons'. In a House of Commons speech, Churchill declared that 'the mood and temper of the public in regard to the treatment of crime and criminals is one of the most unfailing tests of the civilization of any country' (Hansard [UK], HC Deb, 20 July 1910, col. 1354). For Mandela (1994: 201), 'it is said that no-one truly knows a nation until one has been inside its jails. A nation should not be judged by how it treats its highest citizens, but its lowest ones.'

Chapter 1

1 Of the other *Western* countries (that is, not including former Eastern bloc countries, such as Hungary), apart from the USA at 752 per 100,000 of population, only Spain, at 152 in 2012, comes close to the rate of imprisonment of New South Wales and England and Wales. New Zealand (obviously behind the USA) is the second highest imprisoning Western society. At the other end of the spectrum, only Switzerland (76) and Japan (55) are within the parameters of the Nordic cluster.

2 The fieldwork was conducted by John Pratt between 2006 and 2010. It also involved visits to aftercare hostels and to probation offices, as well as interviews/discussions with 80 penal policy 'stakeholders' across the six societies (politicians, representatives of pressure groups and prisoners rights groups, civil servants, prison managers, academics and senior criminal justice officials). In addition, between 500 and 600 annual prison reports from the early nineteenth century to the early twenty-first were examined (this also involved, after Anna Eriksson joined the project in 2009, the translation of the Nordic reports), as well as other official documents (government reports, papers and propositions covering all six countries). Those from the Nordic countries were again translated from their original Swedish, Norwegian, Danish and Finnish. A wide range of other primary and secondary sources was also consulted – see the comments on Elias

in the text at p. 31. There was also a systematic attempt to contrast press coverage of prison issues. We were told at the outset by a respected Finnish colleague that we should not bother to include Finland in this part of the research simply because 'prison' featured so rarely as a news item in that country. For the other five societies, however, we reviewed the way prison was reported as 'news' in the first six months of the year at ten-yearly intervals from 1956. These selections were very much determined by time and resources, and, in particular, which of the Anglophone newspapers were available online, since this part of the project was undertaken by a research assistant in New Zealand. Those selected were: *The Times*, one of the world's oldest newspapers and still an authoritative broadsheet in England; *The Dominion* (now *The Dominion Post*), one of the largest selling regional broadsheets in New Zealand; *The Sydney Morning Herald*, one of the most important broadsheets in New South Wales; *Svenska Dagbladet*, a broadsheet newspaper that has the second largest circulation in Sweden; and *Verdens Gang* (*VG*), a Norwegian tabloid that is the largest selling and most widely read newspaper there. All five profess to be politically independent. While these selections were made on a pragmatic, rather than a scientific, basis, each reveals commonalities with the other selection(s) in the cluster in which they are located and, at the same time, very different values and reporting practices between the two clusters.

3   This was then abandoned by the New Labour government in favour of five 1,500 bed prisons – which, in turn, was abandoned by the incoming Conservative-Liberal coalition government in 2010.

4   There are three private prisons in New South Wales and one in New Zealand, with another one planned.

5   That is, the daily ritual of emptying chamber pots in the morning after their use for ablution purposes during the night.

6   Sugar is not available in Norwegian prisons because of the possibility of it being used to make alcohol, see Ugelvik (2011).

7   <http://www.ilsengfengsel.no> The reality of Swedish practice, in this respect, is illustrated in *The Girl with the Dragon Tattoo* (Larsson, 2005: 386–8) in which Mikael Blomkvist's prison sentence is deferred in this way. When he does arrive to serve his two month term, he finds 41 fellow inmates. 'On the first day [he] was invited to the Director's office and was offered therapy, adult education courses or possibilities for other studies and vocational guidance . . . he asked for permission to keep his laptop in his cell so as to be able to continue work on the book he was authoring. His request was granted without hesitation.'

8   As occurred in reforms to the New Zealand prison service during 1991 and 1992. Similar reforms were introduced to the English prison service in the Home Office's *Fresh Start* proposals in 1986.

9   With some qualifications. It seems to have been a longstanding feature in New South Wales that prisoners have no voting rights. In New Zealand, prisoners serving under three years *had been* allowed the vote, but this has now been removed under 2010 legislation (see p. 183). In England, prisoners (from 1872) were not allowed to vote, a decision overturned by the ECHR in 2004, but which, in 2011, was still only in the process, most reluctantly, of being put into effect by the British government, see p. 25.

10 The Australian structure of government means that no national crime data set is readily available. We have thus relied on the crime rate and crime patterns in New South Wales. However, for reasons we do not understand, statistics for crimes reported to the police – the most usual measurement on which crime rates are calculated – are not available in this state until the 1980s. Prior to this, only 'convictions in higher courts' were available for this calculation. We have chosen not to use this measure because of the obvious inconsistencies with the rest of the crime data from this and the other societies.

11 Nor, anyway, is there some simple correlation between welfare provision and imprisonment rates. As is discussed in more detail in Chapter 5, as Sweden became the most advanced welfare state in the world between 1950 and 1965, its rate of imprisonment *increased*.

12 In post-war Norway, 37 out of 45 death sentences passed on war criminals, those convicted of treason and so on, were carried out. Our focus, though, is on punishment under *peace time* conditions. Clearly, when a country undergoes occupation in time of war, as in Norway by Nazi Germany, then the aftermath of this is likely to lead to reactions that transcend existing values and understandings about appropriate levels of punishment. Similarly, during the Finnish civil war and its aftermath, there were 9,700 executions, usually ordered by court martial and carried out by firing squad; 250 were sentenced to death in the courts. During WWII, there were 500 more executions, around half for spying. Again, then, in times of civil war or invasion, restraint and prohibitions are likely to be suspended.

Chapter 2

1 The usual translation of this term is 'peasant', but this is misleading because it implies landlessness, which is clearly not the case here. Travers (1911: 36) thus observed, in Finland, that 'what I have carelessly called "peasants" are most often yeomen, like the Cumberland Dales folk, farming their own lands . . . they live in the changeless way of small farmers under a simple civilization . . . the family and some two servants live all together beneath the same roof'.
2 At the beginning of the twentieth century, 62 per cent of its population then lived in cities.
3 See, variously, Belich (1996, 2001), Eldred-Grigg (1980), Hatch (1992), Miller (1958), Nicholls (1990), Sherington (1980) and Selzer (2002).
4 They had been given rights of Australian citizenship in 1948. They were given Commonwealth voting rights in 1962 and final state restrictions on the right to vote were removed in 1965.
5 'Mateship' was very nearly inserted in the 1999 Australian Constitution, at the wish of then Prime Minister John Howard (Page, 2002).
6 Accordingly, in Norway in 1900, 99.4 per cent were registered as 'Professing Christians' and Protestants; in Finland, it was 100 per cent and 98.3 respectively; in Sweden, 98.3, of the population were Protestants, with no other religious beliefs recorded at all.
7 In Britain, 97.4 per cent of the population were professing Christians in 1900, with 64.4 per cent being Anglicans, 24 per cent Protestants and 6.4 Roman Catholics. In Australia, the figures were 96.8, of whom 36 per cent were Anglicans, 27 per cent Protestants, 22.3 Roman Catholics. In New Zealand, it was 98.3, of whom 39.2 per cent were Anglicans, 37.9 Protestants, and 13.5 Roman Catholics.
8 In addition to the role played by religion in the seventeenth-century civil war in Britain, on Protestant and Catholic conflicts in Australia in the nineteenth and early twentieth century, see Hughes (1987) and O'Farrell (2001). For New Zealand, see Belich (2001).
9 This is a derogatory term in the Anglophone countries, directed at intellectuals (with seemingly larger than usual brain power, and craniums to match) who are thought to be remote and detached from the concerns of ordinary people.
10 These are references to membership of the school cricket (First XI) and rugby (First XV) teams, bringing with it very high status and prestige amongst peers.
11 A 'fag' was a term given to a junior student at a British public school who was assigned to a senior student and was required to perform menial tasks for them (for example, making breakfast and afternoon tea, cleaning shoes, fetching shopping). Fagging was finally abolished in England's most exclusive public school, Eton, in 1980.
12 After Thomas Arnold, Headmaster of Rugby School between 1828 and1841 (Tom Brown 'attended' the school during his headship). He emphasized the importance of classical scholarship rather than the physical sciences, and also developed the prefect system to maintain order at all levels of school life.
13 See, for example, Adam Smith (1776), *The Wealth of Nations*; Jeremy Bentham (1796), *Essays*; Herbert Spencer (1842/1981), *The Proper Sphere of Government*; John Stuart

Mill (1859), *On Liberty;* and A. V. Dicey (1919), *Lectures on the Relation between Law and Public Opinion in England during the Nineteenth Century.*

Chapter 3

1 Thus in England, the 'job seekers' allowance (that is, unemployment benefit) in January 2012 was £65 per week, irrespective of previous earnings and financial commitments. In the Australian means tested 'newstart' allowances, the maximum benefit a single person with no children would be able to receive, in May 2012, was $A489.70 every two weeks. In New Zealand, the means tested nature of unemployment benefits leads to the position that if one person loses their job in a two income household, they are not then eligible for unemployment benefit even though they have been paying national insurance contributions to this end.

2 There is no reference to Finland at this time because the welfare state did not really begin to form in that country until the 1960s – again, for much of the first half of the twentieth century, its social development had been arrested and put on hold in the aftermath of the civil war. Kuusi's (1964) *Social Policy for the Sixties* then became the Finnish equivalent of the *Beveridge Report.*

3 In 1900, the workhouses held 188,000 inmates, or 0.59 per cent of the total population of England and Wales (Peter Higginbotham, 'The Workhouse Website', personal communication). USA prisons in 2012 hold about one per cent of that country's total population. However, the much shorter periods of workhouse confinement meant that many thousands more would have had experience of admission. On this basis, the workhouse probably had a larger cultural and material significance than the prison currently does in the USA.

4 For example, well-behaved elderly couples were no longer separated, and were allowed such privileges as newspapers and their own teapot.

5 See, for example, Walter Greenwood's (1933) *Love on the Dole.*

6 The reaction of OPEC to Western support for Israel in the Yom Kippur war of 1973.

7 Thus, in Selma Lagerlöf's (1918) *Gösta Berling's Saga*, set in Sweden in the early nineteenth century, the hero is an unfrocked clergyman, turned beggar, who is given refuge by the Lady of the Manor in an annex on her country estate. She finds a place for him with twelve similar 'cavaliers' (sic), or tramps. Thereafter, 'the Lady gave him a cottage and strip of land . . . and he tried to live the life of a workman. It answered for a time, but he grew weary of the loneliness and of the daily round of small duties . . . Later he became tutor to [a Count]. While there he fell in love with the Count's sister, but she died just when he thought to win her, and after that he gave up all thought of being anything but a cavalier' (ibid.: 31–2). Here, then, Berling experiences no loss of status, no suffering imposed by the local or central state and no disqualifications as he chooses the 'cavalier's' life.

8 Such events are described in the Nobel Prize winning Finnish novelist F. E. Sillanpää's (1938: 47) *Meek Heritage*: after the family farm had been sold due to unpaid bills, 'Maja had to leave the stripped house, taking her son with her. She did not elect to stay on in her birthplace, where her little life ever since her childhood days had been so full of disappointments, but after drying her eyes decided to try her luck with her brother, who was rumored to be fairly well off . . . the first part of the journey they were alone. Soon, however, Jussi (her son) and Maja had company. When they came to the main road they saw, wherever the land lay open, long, unbroken lines of tramps.'

9 See, for example, Golding and Middleton (1982).

10 The Norwegian Progress Party emerged in the 1970s, originally as an anti-tax social movement. It later became associated with anti-immigration and more severe law and order policies. At the time of writing (June 2012), it is the second largest party in the Norwegian parliament with 41 seats, gaining its highest share of votes in national elections at 22.9 per cent in 2008. Similarly, the Swedish Democrats were founded in

1988, and gained parliamentary representation for the first time in 2010 by polling 5.7 per cent of the vote and winning 20 seats. The True Finns party came into existence in 1995 and won 19.1 per cent of the votes in the national elections of 2011, making it the third largest party in the Finnish parliament.

11 Cf. Kuhnle (2000: 211): 'international winds of welfare state criticism and warning quickly reached Scandinavian shores, but hardly seemed to rock the solid historical position of the state . . . economic rather than ideological factors drove reform'; Lindbom (2001: 171): 'although the Swedish welfare state was reformed in many ways in the 1990s and some cutbacks were made, the welfare state has not been dismantled. Its major attributes when compared to other countries – e.g. its generosity, universality and developed welfare services – are almost as prominent as before the crisis.'

12 For example, *Time* (15 April 1966: 7) reported that 'resource rich, welfare-loving Sweden has long enjoyed the highest living standard in Europe . . . after 32 years of unbroken and rising prosperity, Sweden's workers have grown so affluent that about all the tiny Communist Party could find to demand in the last election was "two houses for every family". Swedish families already own 375,000 vacation homes and 300,000 pleasure boats . . . domestic tranquillity is rarely ruffled by labour trouble: the last strike of consequence took place in 1945.'

13 Literally, 'awkward/difficult Sweden'. In Norway, *supperådet* ('The Soup Council'), based on a 1969 television programme, has become a term that refers to unnecessary, wasteful government bodies (Thomas Ugelvik, personal communication).

14 There were taxation levels of 85 per cent on some income levels amongst the self-employed at this time.

15 In the 1990s, unemployment rates reached 10 per cent in Sweden and 18 per cent in Finland.

16 The Beveridge Report intended to rid British society of five 'Giant Evils': 'squalor, ignorance, want, idleness and disease' (Beveridge, 1942: 6).

17 Although, as we have seen, social planning was an integral feature of the social democratic welfare state. *The Economist* (10 February 1951: 329) reported that 'the economic and social policy that has been pursued in recent years was to some extent mapped out in the "post-war Programme of the Labour Movement", published in 1944 . . . the authors were much more interested in planning than in nationalisation measures, the latter being largely rejected to a dim and distant future.'

18 The phrase of the Conservative Minister for Work and Pensions (*Daily Telegraph*, 11 November 2010: 1).

19 Prime Minister David Cameron thus referred to civil servants as 'the enemies of enterprise', and attacked the 'mad bureaucracy that holds back entrepreneurs' (*The Guardian*, 7 February 2011: A2).

20 The British Conservative Party was in government from 1951 to 1964. The National Party was in government in New Zealand from 1949 to 1957 and from 1960 to 1971. Although, in New South Wales, the Labour Party was in power from 1940 to 1965, more importantly, the Liberal-Country Alliance was the federal government from 1949 to 1972 (after 1942 the Commonwealth government assumed much greater powers, including the collection of income tax which had previously been left to state governments to determine, thereby ensuring the Commonwealth's domination).

21 As well as New Labour in England, renamed in 1994 to avoid its previous associations with 'extremism', Labour was in power in New Zealand from 1984 to 1990 and 1999 to 2008, and in Australia from 1983 to 1995 and 2007 to 2012.

22 Most notably, in New Zealand, the watersiders' strikes of 1913 and 1971, and the general strike of 1979; in Australia, the general strike of 1911 and the watersiders' strike in New South Wales in 1909.

23 In Norway, 'the 'Main Bargain' (*Hovedavtalen*), 1935; Sweden, the 'Saltsjöbaden Agreement' 1938; Finland, the 'January Agreement', 1940.

24 Although the Danish People's Party has been an exception to this. It supported Liberal-Conservative coalition governments from 2001 to 2011, although it has never been in cabinet.

25 Sweden had the largest circulation of newspapers in the world in the 1960s per capita of population (Tomasson, 1970).

26 See, for example, Åkerström (1998); Pollack (2001); Makipää (2004); Rossland (2007); and Smolej and Kivivuori (2008).

27 This is an inquiry set up by the British government in 2011 to inquire into the culture, practices and ethics of the press in the aftermath of the phone hacking scandal at the Murdoch owned *News of the World* (at the time of writing it has yet to report).

28 As the British demographer David Glass (1938: 317) wrote, their book 'dropped a bombshell on the thinking public of Sweden. And apparently the thinking public of Sweden is much larger, proportionately, than in England, for so far the book has sold 16,000 copies, equivalent to a sale of over 100,000 here – a figure rarely reached even by popular books.'

29 Trust in the two main political parties in this country had declined to 11 per cent for Labour and 13 per cent for National in a 1993 opinion poll (see Pratt, 2007).

30 A *Google* search for 'flats for sale in Thailand' in Swedish revealed 330,000 hits on this website; the same search in Norwegian revealed 2,500,000 hits.

31 http://crystalfromsweden.com/swedish-glassware/

32 This tradition probably begins with Sir Arthur Conan-Doyle's (1887) *A Study in Scarlet*, the first of the Sherlock Holmes short stories. Two of the latest British invocations of the detective-as-outsider genre are Ian Rankin's Inspector Rebus novels, beginning in 1987 with *Knots and Crosses*; and Peter Robinson's Chief Inspector Banks, also beginning in 1987 with *Gallows View*. In contrast, J. J. Maric's (1964) *Inspector Gideon* series was one of the much smaller genre in which the emphasis was on the success of the police as a crime fighting organization, rather than the capabilities of its individual officers, and was written at the peak of authority of the liberal welfare state.

33 http://oecd-ilibrary.org/sites/soc_glance-2011 (last accessed 29 January 2012).

34 As translated by Nils Christie.

Chapter 4

1 Unlike these other societies, New South Wales kept the death penalty for murder and rape until abolition, even though it had been abolished for the latter offence in England in 1841. The most celebrated occasion when it was used for this offence was in 1886: after a gang rape, four of the nine defendants were hanged. The last occasion on which it was used to punish rape in this state seems to have been in 1932.

2 Public executions were abolished in New South Wales in 1855, in New Zealand in 1858, in England in 1868, in Norway in 1876 and Sweden in 1877.

3 William Crawford (1834), the English prison inspector, went to the USA to observe and report back on the merits of both prison systems. The Governor of New South Wales, Sir George Gipps, noted in 1840 that the cells in Sydney and Paramatta gaols were designed on 'the plan of the American separate system, or, which is nearly the same thing, the plan approved by the English Inspectors of Prisons' (quoted by Kerr, 1988: 45). The Swedish novelist Fredrika Bremer visited the penitentiaries in the USA during her sojourn there from 1849 to 1851 (Bremer, 1853), as did the leading Norwegian physician Dr Fredrick Holst in the 1830s (see Schaaning, 2007).

4 Bentham's plans for the panopticon were produced in 1787 (Bozovic, 1995). The idea was that prison inmates, separated from each other at all times, would also be seen at all times by prison staff from a central inspection house. While, in reality, exact replicas of the panopticon were never built, and Bentham's subsequent influence on nineteenth-

century prison development should not be overstated (*pace* Foucault, 1977), the importance he gave to separation – along with other pioneering prison reformers in the late eighteenth century, such as Sir George Onisipherous Paul (see Whiting, 1975) – and surveillance was clearly of landmark importance.

5 The death penalty, *for all intents and purposes* (it was retained for some time thereafter in these societies for treason and arson in Her Majesty's shipyards but no such cases were brought post-1945) was abolished in New South Wales in 1955, New Zealand 1961 and England in 1965.

6 Responsible government was granted to New Zealand in 1853 and New South Wales in 1855, with executive authority vested in their respective Governor-Generals. Prior to this, as Crown colonies, English law automatically applied in these societies.

7 See Palmer (1990), *Bernadotte: Napoleon's Marshal, Sweden's King.* It seems that the European connections of King Charles John (formerly Jean-Baptiste Bernadotte) who, as a Marshal of France, had served under Napoleon, made him popular in Sweden and Norway.

8 The Swedish Law Commission of 1811 contained 'some of the finest lawyers and civil servants of their time' (Seth, 1984: 34), but the first report was written by Professor Lars Rabenius; the second by the prominent jurist Johan Gabriel Richert. The Norwegian Penal Law Commission of 1841 had, as its members, a general (representing the King), the Christiania city planner and architect, a senior magistrate and lawyer, the governor of the then Akershus Fortress (or local prison in Oslo) and Professor Frederik Holst, the Christiania 'Town Physician', also involved in treating prisoners and mental patients. There were three Finnish Law Commissions. That of 1862 was chaired by a prominent philanthropist and had two civil servants, but its leading member was Professor Karl Gustav Ehrström. The latter was also the most prominent figure of the 1865 Commission, the membership of which, in addition to Ehrström, was made up of a judge and four civil servants. That of 1880 had Professor of Law Jaakko Forsman, another professor (Emeritus) and four civil servants.

9 See Tate (1975) and Zander (2004).

10 See Stephen (1895), Bresler (1977), Devlin (1979) and Heward (1990).

11 The Court of Exchequer was an Appeal Court, dealing with matters of equity and common law. It was replaced by the Supreme Court of Judicature in 1873.

12 In England, between 1837 and 1868, there were around twelve per year. In New South Wales there were around five per year between 1840 and 1859, although between 1830 and 1839 there were around 30 per year. In New Zealand, there had been seven between 1840 and 1858. Between 1800 and 1850, there were around ten executions per year in Sweden, dwindling away to hardly any by 1870. In Norway, there were 44 executions between 1815 and 1876.

13 The pastors often voted in favour of retaining the death penalty and, in the 1867 debates in the *riksdag*, several speakers from the clergy estate also favoured public executions: the condemned should be able to repent their crimes before God and society, the vote being 27:11 in favour of retaining public executions.

14 See Seth (1984).

15 The last execution in Norway in 1876 was in private, the last four in Sweden.

16 *Karlstad Tidningen*, although Seth (1984) does not provide the date of publication.

17 See Collins (1962: 248) regarding the support of Dickens and Carlyle for capital punishment per se. Mill, as a Liberal MP, spoke against a motion to abolish the death penalty (Hansard [UK], HC Deb, 21 April 1868, col. 1047–55) – although on the grounds that execution was a more *humane* punishment than the alternative of life imprisonment.

18 See Pratt (1992) and McGuire (1988).

19 The last execution in New South Wales was in 1940.

20 In Australia, especially, it was thought that the death penalty offered a cloak of protection against the transient nature of its population: 'the time is not opportune, with the present

conditions of development and introduction of vast numbers of people from other countries' (Hansard [NSW], 23 March 1955: 3259).

21 Public opinion polling in England in 1939 was 55–45 in favour of abolition (see Potter, 1993).

22 Although in England there was an average of 13 executions per year between 1900 and 1949, the number had fallen to eight between 1930 and 1939, but was then inflated between 1940 and 145 with an average of 14.5 per year during this wartime period. Between 1950 and 1964, there were around four per year. In New Zealand, there had only been 28 between 1898 and 1957. In New South Wales, there were only 12 between 1910 and 1940.

23 For some Australians and New Zealanders, the very fact that it had been retained in England was, in itself, good enough reason for its retention in the colonies: 'if there is one thing a British community can pride itself upon it is that punishment follows more swiftly upon wrongdoing than it does any other civilised community in the world. That has been the effect of bringing into existence a very law abiding community', (Hansard [NSW], 10 Sept 1925: 739).

24 This is particularly ironic, given that Salisbury was, himself, a hereditary peer, and thereby allowed to automatically assume his seat in the House of Lords.

25 See, for example, Hansard [NZ], 1 May 1956: 531–572.

26 Dickens (1842: 123) was one of the fiercest critics of the separate system – 'a rigid, strict, and hopeless solitary confinement.'

27 Thus the Revd John Field (1848: 146), Chaplain of Reading prison, explained that, in the separate system, 'an appeal is made to the moral sense and understanding of the prisoner as he is led through . . . a contemplation of past actions and an acknowledgement of their wickedness'. And William Clay (1861/1969: 142), Chaplain of Preston gaol, affirmed that, under the separate system, 'the prisoners, in many cases, have shown that softening of the heart which is evinced by tears'.

28 Austin Bidwell (1895:187), serving a fifteen-year sentence for bank robbery, observed the consequences of this kind of prison regime: 'the first part of the [prisoner's] body to be visibly affected by the effects on them of hunger and torment of the mind is the neck. The flesh shrinks, disappears, and leaves what look like two artificial props to support the head. As time goes on, the erect posture grows bent; instead of standing up straight the knees bulge outwards as though unable to support the body's weight, and the convict drags himself along in a kind of despondent shuffle. Another year or two and his shoulders are bent forward . . . The projecting head, the sunken eye, the fixed expressionless features are the outward exponents of the hopeless, sullen brooding within.'

29 Hume trained under Du Cane before coming to New Zealand as that country's first Inspector of Prisons. Harold Maclean, New South Wales' first Inspector of Prisons in 1864, travelled to England and met Du Cane during 1869–70, and then remained in correspondence with him (Kerr, 1988: 101).

30 It was calculated that the treadwheel required the prisoner to raise the lower half of their bodies 11,000 feet (over 3,000 metres per day). The prisoner turned the crank in his cell, which paddled sand through a drum. The norm was for it to be turned through 10,000 revolutions per day. Reade's (1856) *It is Never too Late to Mend* is a novel based on a scandal at Birmingham prison where, after being made to perform labour on a crank that weighed four times more than was recommended, a prisoner was then subjected to further privations and dietary restrictions that led to his suicide (Anderson, 2005: 191). Although treadwheels had been used in New South Wales prisons up to the 1850s, Maclean banned their use in 1864, and male prisoners, at least, were involved in productive labour; women prisoners, however, might be engaged in oakum picking (Ramsland, 1996: 41). The Report of the Comptroller-General of Prisons (1908: 6) later stated that 'no afflictive labour is performed in New South Wales prisons'. There were never the resources for 'hard labour machines' in New Zealand.

31 One gramme is roughly equal to one small paper clip.

32 Up to the 1830s, transportees on arrival in New South Wales might be assigned to work as a servant, often to those who had been transported themselves, before being emancipated; or to work on road gangs or other forms of public works. They would receive tickets of leave on completion of their term and might even be granted settlements of land, where they could then assume something like full citizenship.

33 The Royal Commission on Brutality in Berrima Prison (1875) found that officers had been involved in the widespread use of 'spread-eagling' and the use of wooden 'gags', for up to 10 hours at a time on recalcitrant prisoners, practices which were then prohibited. Spread-eagling involved 'the tricing up of a man by the wrists, with his feet not quite on the ground' (Ramsland, 1996: 98). The prison doctors had approved of the gag, described by the 1875 Commissioners as 'made of hard wood. . . [with] a base about three inches long, 3/4 of an inch thick, and about 1¾ inches broad. From this base projects a thick, conical turned tube . . . for insertion into the mouth. A strap is tacked to the back of the base of the gag and buckles at the back of the head of the prisoner upon whom it is used' (ibid.: 99). The Report of the Comptroller-General of Prisons (1894: 2) then stated that, 'in consequence of very gross misconduct of a certain incorrigible class of prisoners in the use of blasphemous and frequently vile and filthy language, it was decided by the Minister of Justice that the use of a gag should again be sanctioned in gaols'. The last whipping in a New South Wales prison was in 1905 (Finnane 1997: 114). In England, flogging remained as a sanction for prison indiscipline until 1967, and was used as late as 1966. The last flogging in New Zealand prisons was in 1935 (Newbold, 2007).

34 Shorthand for 'cat of nine tails', that is, a multi-tailed whip.

35 Roddy Nilsson, personal communication.

36 'A bell rings and my door is unlocked. No word is spoken because I know exactly what to do. I leave my cell and fall into single file, three paces in the rear of my nearest fellow convict. All of us are alike in knowing what we have to do and we march away silently to Divine Service. We are criminals under punishment and our keepers march us like dumb cattle to the worship of God' (Maybrick, 1905: 67).

37 Other critics included, in Sweden, Clas Livijn, first Director of the Prisons Board in the 1840s – largely on the grounds of its costs and inefficiency (see Nilsson, 1999).

38 On the growing importance and influence of the 'professional classes' towards the end of the nineteenth century, see Ibsen (1882), *An Enemy of the People*; and Strindberg (1890), *By the Open Sea*.

39 See also Rossa (1882) and Lee (1885).

40 See Report of the Commissioners of Prisons (1899: 21).

41 But not in Finland where, until 1979, variations of striped uniforms, albeit with decreasing ostentation over time, were worn (at least in the closed prisons).

42 In the Nordic countries, remands in custody – in isolation – had, by this time, also become a routine administrative convenience. This practice can be traced back to the mid-nineteenth-century concerns about hygiene and fear of moral contagion. The Swedish Penal Code 1864 prescribed that 'detention shall be of such a nature that it is not dangerous to the health of the person detained, nor shall several people be placed in one room when it can be avoided. If private rooms are not available, all those arrested shall not be detained in company with those arrested for more serious crimes . . . a person arrested must not be detained in company with one who is serving a prison sentence' (quoted by Almquist, 1931: 198).

Chapter 5

1 For helpful overviews, see, for example, Mannheim's (1960) *Pioneers in Criminology*; and Bierne's (1994) *The Origins and Growth of Criminology*.

2 *Élimination* is the French term that was used in the texts of these scholars to convey the intent of punishment, most usually, 'to set apart the most dangerous individuals so as to deprive them of the opportunity of causing harm' (Ancel, 1965: 55).

3 Although Garofalo (1914) was of the view that habitual criminals should be executed.

4 The other two were Adolph Prins of Belgium and G. A. van Hamel of the Netherlands.

5 von Liszt (1851–1919) receives virtually no mention in English language overviews of the history of criminology – see, for example, Mannheim (1960), Beirne (1993, 1994), and Becker and Wetzell (2006). Radzinowitz (1991) is one of the very few English texts to acknowledge his significance. He was a pivotal figure, though, in the development of both German and Nordic criminology (see Landecker, 1941; Stang Dahl, 1985).

6 In addition, 'the distinction between the detention of incorrigible criminals and the institutionalization of dangerous insane persons is not only impracticable but also to be dismissed as a matter of principle': von Liszt (1897: 74).

7 That is, fines that were proportionate to the daily income of the particular offender.

8 On the subsequent impact of von Liszt in Sweden, see Simson (1949: 32): 'despite things being different from how von Liszt envisaged, there is a common goal: to protect society. "Mutual" is the keyword. The crime is important, but the offender is more important. The goal and the keyword are what rules modern criminal law and what will rule it in the future.'

9 In Finland, the high prison population of the inter war period was the product of severe sentences for theft at a time of great financial hardship, and increases in murder and violence in general which, to a degree, were the legacy of the civil war (Lehti, 2001). At the same time, this also meant that psychiatric and other welfare services were off limits for financial reasons, let alone for other reasons; see Soine (1958).

10 The 1956 Penal Code Commission then noted that 80 per cent of murderers had been found to be insane in 1953.

11 Developed in England in 1843, following the acquittal of Daniel M'Naghten for attempting to murder Queen Victoria. In its aftermath, a panel of judges narrowed the existing insanity laws to the effect that the insanity defence would only be applicable in those cases where the accused 'did not know the nature and quality of the act he was doing, or, if he did, did not know it was wrong' (M'Naghten's Case, (1843) 10 C & F 200).

12 The other three contributors included Torsten Eriksson, then a senior civil servant at the Ministry of Social Welfare (the other two were a historian and a doctor).

13 Kleen co-authored, with Bruno Poukka, one of the few that were written: Poukka and Kleen (1939), *Gröna Ön* [The Green Island].

14 See, for example, Nordin (2005), although membership of the Lutheran Church has always remained high, since not only are all members of these societies automatically born into it, but they can only leave by resigning from it.

15 It would seem that, from the late nineteenth century to around 1970, Finland remained largely to true to the von Liszt outline of prison administration, if not the numbers being sent to prison, particularly in relation to the division of conditions in the closed and open prisons. In relation to the former, Uusitalo (1970: 324) wrote that 'the main aim of the Finnish prison is to guard the interns. Great emphasis is placed on security, a strict and authoritarian discipline, and constant control over inmates. These institutions have as their task the prevention of attempts to escape and to maintain internal order through the use of walls, steel reinforced doors, barred windows and constant presence of armed guards. The regulations inmates are expected to follow are many and detailed. The restrictions regarding visits are strict, and all mail, all books and magazines censured. The intention with the strict rules and restrictions is to achieve a total control over inmates.' See also Granfelt (1949) and Soine (1958).

16 Magnus Hörnqvist, personal communication, and derived from Per Albin Hansson's famous 'people's home' speech in the *riksdag* in 1928 (see p. 73).

17 There were 1,214 in Sweden in 1961, from an average prison population of 4,909 ([Report of the] Prison and Probation Board, 1962: 9).

18 In part, this was brought about by increasing Nordic cooperation in policy development. For example, the establishment of the Nordic Council in 1962, as an inter-parliamentary body that could give recommendations on all political matters to its member states, solidified the unity between these societies and insulated them from other modes of economic, social and penal governance. In the same year, the Scandinavian Research Council for Criminology [NSFK] was established 'to further criminological research within the member countries and advise the [Nordic] governments and the Nordic Council on issues related to criminology' (http://www.nsfk.org/ABOUTTHE COUNCIL/tabid/64/Default.aspx). Furthermore, with the need to repress and freeze out civil war experiences gradually fading out of that country's collective memories, the Finnish Social Democrats in 1968 recognized that 'crime policy forms a major part of social policy . . . crime policy must strive for the same economic and educational values of fairness that are strived for in other solutions related to social policy' (quoted by Miikkulainen and Suominen, 1981: 303). Now armed with these values, its own aberrant prison population began its dramatic decline, along with liberalization of conditions within its closed prisons: 'the prisoner's connections to the outside world have to be arranged so that they are not totally isolated from the community', Report of the State Imprisonment Commission (1969: 35).

19 Indeed, it was not until the Geneva Congress of Criminal Anthropology in 1896 that England sent its first official delegate (Garland, 1997: 34).

20 In New Zealand and New South Wales, Kayll, in the former, and Frederick Neitenstein, Comptroller-General of New South Wales in the late nineteenth century, and others, were in correspondence with Lombroso. See Pratt (1992) and Finnane (1997).

21 See Report of the Inter-Departmental Committee on Physical Deterioration (1904). To counter these differences in breeding habits, Leonard Darwin stated that the aim of the eugenics programme was 'to promote the fertility of the better types which the nation contains, while diminishing the birth rate amongst those which are inferior' (quoted by Garland, 1985: 147).

22 In particular, through the development of multiple correlation, by which it now became possible to test the relationship between any number of variables; and the tetrachoric coefficient which, Pearson (1903) claimed, made it possible to measure the strength of heredity in determining nominal human characteristics such as eye colour and intelligence.

23 See Pember Reeves (1902) regarding Australia and New Zealand; also Fraser (2009) for documentation regarding Liberal governments in England in the early twentieth century and the development of welfare legislation.

24 Similarly, in New Zealand, the Liberal Justice Minister Dr John Findlay took the view that 'the idea of putting a man in gaol simply to punish him for his offence . . . was rapidly passing from the public mind. We are beginning to recognize that we not only owe a duty of society in punishing the criminal, but we owe a duty to the criminal himself in endeavouring to reform him' (Hansard [NZ] 1909: 294).

25 Hobhouse and Brockway's (1922) *English Prisons Today* was the product of these inter-relations. Both the authors had been imprisoned as conscientious objectors during the 1914–1918 war, and their research was subsequently sponsored by the Labour Research Committee.

26 It was reduced to three months for recidivists and one month for first offenders in 1910, before being abolished altogether in 1922.

27 Camp Hill, on the Isle of Wight, was one such prison in England. As if to note the transfer of the inmates from penal detention to, in effect, civil detention, in the second stage of the preventive detention sentence, Morris (1950: 397) later commented that 'it was

intended to secure the detainee's safe custody with a minimum of hardship for the individual inmate'; hence the reference (p. 144) to 'bland neutralization'.

28 Other categories of mental deficiency included 'idiocy', 'imbecility' and 'feeble-mindedness'.

29 Cr App R 201 (at 204).

30 7 Cr App R 283 (at 285).

31 14 Cr App R 118.

32 19 Cr App R 1.

33 Although the Royal Commission on the Care and Control of the Feeble-Minded (1908) had estimated that were some 150,000 'mental defectives' in Britain, in the first year of the 1913 legislation, 'only 6,612 were in mental deficiency institutions, and the vast majority of these were simply transferees from lunatic asylums, workhouses etc.' (Simmons, 1978: 400). In a study of the application of this law in one English county, Walmsley (2000: 66–7) writes that four young men were detained in institutions under the provisions of the legislation between 1916 and 1918 and 'out of the 15 girls and young women [so detained], 11 were described as displaying inappropriate sexual behaviour. The other four were institutionalized because their families . . . could not manage them.'

34 As well as the lingering presence of the death penalty in these societies, flogging, as a judicial penalty in England, was not abolished until 1948. And it continued to be available for offences against prison discipline until 1967, see note 33, Chapter 4.

35 That is, those who, on the face of it, were most likely to be suffering from some sort of mental disorder.

36 Thereafter, the British Conservative government – illustrating the extent of the political recognition and respect for these elites at that time – established a Royal Commission on the Penal System in 1964, which became the Advisory Council to the Home Office on the Penal System in 1966.

37 By 1938, probation orders were being awarded to 15 per cent of adults convicted of indictable offences in England (Bottoms, 1983). However, probation was little used in Australia and New Zealand until the 1950s. Thus, in New Zealand, the first full time probation officers were not appointed until 1927 (four in number). Thereafter, the number of orders *declined* from 658 made in 1925 to 605 in 1935. In England, over the same period, the number of persons placed on probation increased from 15,094 to 18,934. This difference may explain why the fall in the prison population in England was significantly greater at this time than in New South Wales and New Zealand. It may be that the lack of a bureaucratic infrastructure in the thinly populated colonies was one reason for this difference. At the same time, however, the liberal thinking behind such developments seems to have been much more diluted and treated with caution, at least in New Zealand. Here, the *Report of the Chief Probation Officer* (1926: 1) stated that 'probation should not be used for confirmed habitual offenders, drug addicts, dipsomaniacs, the feeble-minded, the psychopathics [sic], the mentally unstable and sex perverts . . . and that premeditated assaults for revenge or gain, criminal assaults on females, and crimes resulting in the corruption of children, are altogether outside the scope of the probation system. Probation is also discountenanced in the cases of habitual drunkenness and professional prostitution long continued. The crimes for which probation is most extensively used are for offences against property such as theft and embezzlement.'

38 For example, in England, under the provisions of the 1914 Criminal Justice Administration Act.

39 Home Secretary Churchill's proposals for suspended sentences were rejected because this would 'quickly bring the administration of justice into ridicule', his Abatement of Imprisonment Committee informed him: see Radzinowicz and Hood (1986: 651–2).

40 As well as arguing for compulsory prison aftercare (ACTO 1958) – this was now regarded as a legitimate extension of state responsibilities – ACTO (1965) justified

parole on the basis that it should be available for those prisoners who had arrived at 'the peak of their treatment'.

41 For example, following the recommendations of ACTO (1959), the Criminal Justice Act 1961 prohibited 'courts from sending young offenders under 21 to imprisonment unless they considered that a sentence of at least three years would be appropriate' (Hall Williams, 1970: 308). In New Zealand, the Minister of Justice, in a speech to the House of Representatives, stated that 'there are certain offenders who should not be in prison. The first and most obvious of these offenders are alcoholics . . . the second can be classified as borderline mental defectives . . . I am also concerned at the number of young people and first offenders who are detained in prison pending trial or who are remanded for sentence' (Marshall, 1957, 12).

42 Dingle (1980) provides an overview of Australian drinking habits (see Fairburn (1989) in relation to New Zealand in the late nineteenth and early twentieth century). While, in fact, some scholarship now disputes the affinity for heavy drinking in these former colonies, Australia especially (see Kirkby, 2006), there seems little doubt that there was a much higher level of tolerance towards alcohol consumption in these societies than the Nordic. On the pub as a focal point of community life, see Freeland (1966) *The Australian Pub* and Jennings (2007) *The Local: A History of the British Pub.*

43 As Morris (1989: 96) shows, in relation to England, violence against the person offences increased from 7,884 in 1955 to 25,549 in 1965 and offences against property from 399,924 in 1955 to 1,064602 in 1965. Regarding New South Wales, Grabosky (1977: 143) wrote that, 'beginning in 1963, rates of burglary, larceny, armed robbery, and robbery with assault showed sharp increases . . . to 1970'. Regarding New Zealand, 'estimates of offending by race indicate that [Pacific] Islanders and Maoris [sic] offend against the person at a much greater rate than does the European population . . . in 1964, the rate of sexual offending by Islanders was twice and other assaults about 13 times the statistical expectancy . . . the rate of sexual offending involving Maoris [sic] was almost four times, and of assaults over six times the statistical expectancy . . . members of racial minorities may have fewer and less effective controls than more sophisticated persons belonging to the numerically dominant race' (Report on the Department of Justice, 1968: 209).

44 In relation to tramps or 'swaggers' in New Zealand around the turn of the twentieth century, see Fairburn's (1995) *Nearly Out of Heart and Hope.*

45 See Orwell's (1933) *Down and Out in Paris and London.*

46 The Home Office (1959: 1) referred to 'the startling increase in convictions of young men aged, roughly, from 16 to 21. These men are responsible for more than their share of the increase in offences of violence; but the increased rate of crime at these ages extends to offences of all kinds.'

47 Although, in practice, this still occurred up to the 1970s. See Nagle (1978).

48 See Report of the Departmental Committee on the Employment of Prisoners (1933). In New Zealand, there had been opposition from the 1890s to any kind of factory production in the prisons. See Lingard (1936).

49 For example: 'unfortunately it has been necessary to suspend central training courses and to place full responsibility for training on Prison Superintendents. This results from the need to use Wellington prison, formerly used as a training school, for normal institutional purposes' (Report on the Department of Justice, 1958: 4).

50 Seventeen out of 78 prisons in England had some form of psychotherapeutic programme, according to the Home Office (1959), in *Penal Practise in a Changing Society.*

51 The Report of the Commissioners of Prisons (1956: 31) thus refers to 'the experiment at Norwich prison, designed to establish a new prison officer/prisoner relationship by allocating groups of prisoners to specific officers. [Furthermore,] dining in association has been introduced for all convicted prisoners; [and] prisoner working hours have been increased from 26 to 35 hours per week.'

52 Hall Williams (1970: 91) thus wrote that '[the] new type of prison cell . . . is actually smaller than the traditional cell, which was 13 feet by 7 feet by 9 feet, and the bars are built into the window frame which incorporate manganese steel bars. There is a table built into the wall and the general impression is of more space. There is still no W. C. [toilet] provided to avoid the daily "slopping out" procedure which is the bane of prison reformers.'

53 '[T]he working week is restricted to 20 to 30 hours, but a number of prisoners in recent years have been unemployed': Report of the Commissioners of Prisons (1955: 10).

54 Particularly in the aftermath of the Mountbatten Report of the Inquiry into Prison Escapes and Security (Mountbatten, 1966) and the report from the Advisory Council on the Penal System (1968). The Prison Officers' Association also took this opportunity to criticize 'the liberal regimes' put in place by the authorities and reemphasized their own importance in enforcing security – at the expense, again, of any more productive aspects of their work (*The Times*, 7 June 1966: 10; see also Report on the Work of the Prison Department, 1967: 5).

55 For example, the Swedish spy Karl-Axel Gustafsson 'escaped by using a ladder he had himself constructed in the [prison] carpentry shop, and he climbed the wall having made his way through a window . . . the public have raised questions about how easy it is to construct large tools such as a ladder to be used for escape, but Prison Director Rudstedt said that it was not that difficult, since many prisoners had considerable freedom while working in various shops inside the walls' (*Svenska Dagbladet*, 4 August 1951: 1).

56 *The Times* (3 February 1966: 12), claimed, in relation to an *anticipated* escape, that 'Tanks Expected in Gaol Rescue Attempt. Why Army Guards Were Used. The friends of [prospective escaper], one of three mail train robbers in Durham Prison, would be prepared to launch a full scale military attack to free him, "even to the extent of using tanks, bombs and what I believe are known as limited atomic weapons", it was stated tonight by the Durham Chief Constable.'

57 For example, 'there has been a need to restrict expenditure on education in the interests of economy' (Report of the Commissioners of Prisons, 1962: 18); but at the same time: 'there are signs of an increase in the number of prisoners for whom backwardness in basic subjects is a problem' (Report on the Work of the Prison Department, 1967: 8).

Chapter 6

1 Symptomatic of these differences, fear of crime, as indicated in surveys from 1989 to 2009, has remained much lower in the Nordic countries than the Anglophone.

Table 6.1 Fear of burglary, 1898–2009 (all six societies). Percentage of public who consider a burglary in their houses in the coming year to be "likely" or "very likely"

Country	1989	1992	1996	2000	2001	2004–05	2006	2009
Australia	44	47	27[#]	36		36		
New Zealand		53			57*	36	59^	58^
England & Wales	35	45	41	33		35		
Finland	9	14	11	13				
Norway	21					21		
Sweden		34	16	16		17		

Sources: van Dijk, van Kesteren and Smit (2007), unless otherwise indicated.
[#] Weatherburn, Matka and Lind (1996).
* Morris and Reilly (2003).
^ New Zealand Ministry of Justice (2010).

Table 6.2 Feeling unsafe on the streets, 1992–2005. Percentage of population feeling "unsafe" or "very unsafe" on the street after dark.

Country	1992	1996	2000	2004–05
Australia	31		34	27
New Zealand	38			30
England & Wales	33	32	26	32
Finland	17	17	18	14
Norway				14
Sweden	14	11	15	19

Source: van Dijk, van Kesteren and Smit (2007).

Furthermore, while levels of punitivity over the same period do not show such clear differences, the same surveys indicate that there is still a greater tolerance, a greater willingness, to consider leniency in punishment in the Nordic countries than the Anglophone.

Table 6.3 Levels of punitivity, 1989–2009. Percentage of the public opting for imprisonment as punishment for a recidivist burglar

	1989	1992	1996	2000	2003	2004–05
Australia	36	34	34*	37		33
New Zealand		26	25*		50+^#	40
England & Wales	38	37	49	51		51
Finland	15	14	18	19		15
Norway	14					29
Sweden		26	22	31		33

Source: van Dijk, van Kesteren and Smit (2007), unless otherwise indicated.
  *Figures taken from Mayhew and White (1997).
  ^Figure taken from New Zealand Ministry of Justice (2003).
  #Participants in this survey were given slightly different scenarios than those in van Dijk, van Kesteren and Smit (2007). However, for five out of the six scenarios in this New Zealand survey, at least half of the respondents said that they would sentence the 'offender' to prison.

2 See, for example, in addition to the general criticisms made by Martinson (1974), Bottoms and McClintock (1973).
3 [1980] 1WLR 1193.
4 See, for example, Report of the Corrective Services Commission (1983: 9).
5 As, for example, in the provisions of the New Zealand Criminal Justice Act 1985.
6 For a more detailed examination of the run up to the 1979 British general election, see Taylor (1982).
7 Detention centres, based on army-style 'glasshouses', or punishment blocks, had been introduced to the English penal system in 1948, after much agitation for them from the Magistrates' Association. The first was not opened until the early 1950s, however, but the 'short sharp shock' aspects of these centres came to very little at that time. They were reintroduced in 1980 in two pilot centres.
8 Public opinion support for the death penalty ranged from 81 per cent in 1977 to 76 in 1995: http://www.ipsos-mori.com/researchpublications/researcharchive/2582/Support-for-the-Death-Penalty-19772009.aspx?view=wide

9 See NACRO (1984). Cavadino and Dignan (2002: 291, our italics) also write that, 'to few people's surprise, monitoring found that the modified regimes appeared to be no more effective than the previous ones at deterring [offenders]. *However, the government's response to the failure of its 'experiment' was not to abandon it but, remarkably, to extend the tougher regime to all detention centres.*'

10 The detention centres 'disappeared' in 1988 when they became 'youth custody institutions': see Muncie (1990).

11 The irony being, of course, as Garland (1996) astutely observed, that this is in reality a sign of weak government: it can only bring about unity by expelling some of its own citizens.

12 The full referendum question was: 'should there be a reform of our justice system placing greater emphasis on the needs of victims, providing restitution and compensation for them and imposing minimum sentences and hard labour for all serious violent offences?'

13 After raising critical questions about New Zealand's high level of imprisonment, the New Zealand Chief Justice was herself criticized by the Minister of Justice 'for speaking publicly on policy matters' (*New Zealand Herald*, 17 July: A3).

14 Bartlett (2009: 49) shows how, in New Zealand, the 'Sensible Sentencing Trust', a law and order lobby group, dominated news reporting of crime and punishment in 2004, despite their claims that the voice of 'ordinary people' was never heard on these matters.

15 'Naming and shaming' practices are widespread in these Anglophone countries. They can refer to activities by the media against particular groups or individuals, as with the *News of the World* in this case. But they can also refer to local police practices in circulating neighbourhoods about particular individuals; shopkeepers who display photographs in their windows of those who have stolen from them; and local citizens' groups that distribute posters or other forms of information about suspected criminals.

16 See Pratt (2000) for further examples. More recently, in New South Wales, Dennis Ferguson, convicted of sexual offences against children, was released from prison in 2004. Since then, he has been driven out of his accommodation on several occasions in Queensland and New South Wales by angry neighbours groups. For example, in 2009, he moved into a public housing apartment in the Sydney suburb of Ryde where he was given a five-year lease. Some residents of the area were outraged at Ferguson's presence, after news organizations revealed where he was living – near a primary school and playgrounds. The police then obtained an order banning him from public pools and parks and the New South Wales government introduced legislation to evict child sex offenders from public housing (*Daily Telegraph*, 19 September 2009: 4; *Daily Telegraph*, 22 October 2009: 2).

17 A judge's deletion of some of the content of a victim impact statement – in New Zealand, these are meant to refrain from criticisms of the offender and the criminal justice system but speak only to their sufferings – was described by its writer, the father of a murdered young woman, as 'just another way the justice system puts victims down' (*Otago Daily Times*, 13 November 2009: 1).

18 Thus, 'angry family members have denounced as a joke the seventeen-year prison sentence imposed on a multiple sex offender yesterday' (*The Dominion*, 4 April 1996: 3).

19 *Daily Telegraph* (16 June 2008: 3), although the proposals for 'conviction posters' seem to have come to nothing.

20 (2002) CA106/02, CA137/02, 19 CRNZ 574.

21 [2003] HC Auckland, T020505, BCL 360.

22 See Cavadino, Crow and Dignan (1999). The fines legislation was repealed by the Criminal Justice (Amendment) Act 1993.

23 Although these provisions have now been overturned by the IPPS legislation.

24 '[C]uts in public expenditure will delay the completion of plans for . . . providing every establishment with suitable and sufficient educational accommodation; for ensuring that all people in custody who need remedial education (not simply the most backward) receive it' (*Report on the Work of the Prison Department*, 1975: 17).

25 Thus, in New South Wales, the *Report of the Department of Corrective Services* (1976–1978: 4) noted the 'increased press publicity on escapes in spite of the lack of change in the overall escape rate'. For example, 'Nine of the Most Wanted Criminals Are Prison Escapers', the *Sydney Morning Herald* (26 February 1986: 2) gratuitously proclaimed, complete with photographs of each and details of their *modus operandi*.

26 The situation was similar in Australia: see Brown and Zdenkowski (1982).

27 For a detailed review of press coverage of Bathurst, see Brown and Zdenkowski (1982), and, for Strangeways, see Carrabine (2004).

28 In addition, '[the Grafton "intractables"] would be kept for 16 hours per day in cellular separation and whose exercise was to consist of "formal marching in single file for 20 minutes each day"' (Ramsland, 1996: 228).

29 Respectively, the Woodcock Report (Woodcock, 1994) and the Learmont Report (Learmont, 1995).

30 In New South Wales, this was 'to provide a correctional system that is internationally recognized for excellence' (NSW Department of Corrective Services Annual Report, 1998–9: 1); in New Zealand, 'to be recognised for our expertise in contributing to community safety and reducing reoffending' (Report of the Department of Corrections, 1999–2000: 1).

31 On retiring from his position as Chief Inspector of Prisons after five years in the post, Sir David Ramsbotham commented that 'I have never received ministerial acknowledgement of, or response to, any of these reports or their contents, or their recommendations' (*The Weekly Telegraph*, 27 July–31 July: 10, 2001).

32 *Taunoa and others* v *Attorney-General* (2006) SC 67/2006. After the Court of Appeal ruled in favour of the prisoners, the decision was reported in the *New Zealand Herald* (9 December 2005: A1) as 'Inmates in Line for Millions After Appeal Court Decision'.

33 In fact, the vote in favour of this legislation was only 62–56. However, this disguises the fact that the vast majority of the opponents of the legislation did not want to allow prisoners *any right to compensation at all*. Under the legislation itself they still had a nominal right, but would now receive none of the proceeds if successful in their claim.

34 Uncertainties over release because of indeterminate sentencing could 'trigger repeat of Strangeways' a former Chairman of the Parole Board is quoted as saying in the *Daily Telegraph* (14 May 2012: 3).

35 Increasing foreign travel during the 1960s and 1970s seems to have created public pressure for more liberalization. Indeed, from 1965, mid-strength beer was allowed to be sold in Swedish grocery stores, although this was in the hope that it would divert consumers from hard liquor, rather than any enthusiasm from the state for greater freedom of choice. Indeed, when this was found to be illusory, the grocery sales were prohibited; further legislation banning alcohol advertising was introduced in 1978; in 1981, *Systembolaget* was no longer allowed to open on Saturdays (Sundin, *et al.*, 2008).

36 Six per cent of the total prison population of 6,284 in 1966.

37 For example, see Bottoms and Preston (eds.) (1980), *The Coming Penal Crisis*.

38 Corporal punishment had been banned in senior elementary Swedish schools in 1918 and in all schools in 1962. Sweden was also the first country to prohibit parents from chastising their children with corporal punishment, in 1978. Professional boxing was banned in 1969, in part on the grounds of its brutalizing effects on the audience (Anderson, 2007: 127).

39 Prostitution remains legal in Finland except, from 2006, the buying of sexual services that are linked to human trafficking.

40 In Sweden, the Report of the Penal Code Commission no. 55 (1956: 30) noted that 'it is of great importance that the person who commits the crime is made to restore the damage done from it . . . when ordering compensation, the offender's personal circumstances have to be taken into account [but] the courts can use pressure to insist

the offender makes up for the damage done'. It goes on to note that money for these purposes can be deducted from their welfare payments or wages.

41 A hunger strike at the Oslo *Botsfengslet* 6–9 March, 1965, had been over poor quality food. In particular, the inmates 'complained that the food was not warm enough. A Committee looked into this and changed the way the food was delivered, and introduced heated food cabinets that could be loaded up in the kitchens and then taken to each wing' (Report of the Director of the Prison Board, 1965–1966, 1973: 72).

42 Ward (1972: 241) subsequently interviewed inmates who had been involved in disruption at Österåker and reported that 'even when they were engaged in hunger or work strikes, they said they had never felt pressed to the point where they considered taking staff members hostage, let alone injuring them. Neither guards nor inmates carry weapons in Swedish prisons. Perhaps for these reasons the Swedish inmates were not concerned about protection from "physical punishment by the staff", being held "incommunicado" or being "kept in isolation".'

43 As we were informed by a member of KROM during an interview with them.

44 'Humane containment' first appeared in the Home Office (1969: 7) document *People in Prison*. It was then proposed by King and Morgan (1980), following their submission to the May Committee (1979). While rejected then, the phrase has become part of the parlance of Anglophone prisons. For example, in 2009, the Department of Corrections website in New Zealand advertized positions for prison officers who would be 'responsible for the safe, secure and humane containment of prisoners within or outside the institution' (http://www.corrections.govt.nz/careers/opportunities-at-corrections/prison-services-jobs/corrections-officer/job-description.html, last accessed 20 March 2012).

45 Tony Blair's visit to Pentonville in 2001 'to announce a 10 year crackdown on crime' (rather than engage in a meaningful dialogue with inmates) was the first such visit by a serving Prime Minister (*ITV Lunchtime News*, 26 February 2001). We were informed by one of the New Zealand interviewees that, between 1999 and 2002, when 'prison' had become a particularly highly charged topic of public and political debate, only four MPs visited a such an institution.

46 There was also a report of a prisoner who had written a book about while in prison (*VG*, 15 April 1986: 23).

47 The Director of Prisons thus resigned after the Hall escapes in 2004.

48 See the Scarman report, *The Brixton Disorders 10–12 April 1981* (Scarman, 1981). Furthermore, after disturbances in Liverpool in 1981, the charismatic Conservative MP, Michael Heseltine, took a leading role in the redevelopment of that city, for which he was honoured with the 'Freedom of Liverpool' in 2011.

49 See, for example, Newburn (2011).

50 'Government Plans to Withdraw Benefits From Convicted Rioters Criticised' (*The Guardian*, 19 August 2011: 1), 'Westminster Vows to Evict Social Tenants Involved in Riots' (*The Guardian*, 10 August 2011: 1).

51 <www.guardian.co.uk/uk/2012/feb/23/almost-1000-jailed-riot-related-offences> (last accessed 22 May 2012).

52 <www.telegraph.co.uk/news/uknews/crime/8695988/London-riots-Lidl-water-thief-jailed-for-six-months.html>; <www.guardian.co/uk/2012/feb3/. . ./riot-inciter-jailed-message-disorder> (last accessed 22 May 2012).

53 In terms of victims per head of population, it was greater in magnitude than 9/11 in the USA: 77 deaths in Norway in a population of 4.9 million in 2011; in the USA there were 2,752 deaths from a population of over 300,000,000 in 2001. With the equivalent populations, the number of Norwegian deaths would have been over 4,600.

54 An opinion poll in October 2011 found that support for the Norwegian Progress Party had declined by more than half in two years, to 11.1 per cent of the electorate: <www.newsinenglish.no/2011/10/13> (last accessed 22 May 2012).

Bibliography

Aase, A. (2005) 'In search of Norwegian values', in E. Maagerø and B. Simonsen (eds) *Norway: Society and Culture*, Kristiansand: Portal

Abel Smith, B. and Townsend, P. (1965) *The Poor and the Poorest: A New Analysis of the Ministry of Labour's Family Expenditure Surveys of 1953–54 and 1960*, London: Bell.

Adams, S. and Adams, S. (1825) *The Complete Servant*, London: Knight and Lacey.

Adler-Karlsson, G. (1969) *Functional Socialism: A Swedish Theory for Democratic Socialization*, Stockholm: Prisma.

Advisory Council on the Penal System (1968) *Regime for Long-Term Prisoners in Conditions of Maximum Security – Report of the Advisory Council on the Penal System*, London: HMSO.

Advisory Council on the Treatment of Offenders (ACTO) (1958) *The After-Care and Supervision of Discharged Prisoners*, London: HMSO.

—— (1959) *The Treatment of Young Offenders*, London: HMSO.

—— (1965) *The Organisation of After-Care*, London: HMSO.

Åkertström, M. (1998) 'The moral crusade on violence in Sweden', in V. Ruggerio, N. South and I. Taylor (eds) *The New European Criminology: Crime and Social Order in Europe*, London: Routledge.

Alestalo, M. and Kuhnle, S. (1987) 'The Scandinavian route: Economic, social, and political developments in Denmark, Finland, Norway, and Sweden', in R. Eriksson, E. J. Hansen, S. Ringen and H. Uusitalo (eds) *The Scandinavian Model. Welfare States and Welfare Research*. New York: M. E. Sharpe.

Allen, F. (1981) *The Decline of the Rehabilitative Ideal: Penal Policy and Social Purpose*, New Haven: Yale University Press.

Alliance for Sweden Political Group (2006) *A Safer Sweden*, Stockholm: Government Printer.

Almquist, V. (1924) 'Stafflagstiftningens och straffverställningens utveckling i Sverige' [The development of the penal code and practice in Sweden], *Nordisk Tidsskrift for Strafferet*, 12: 40–61.

—— (1927) 'Svensk lagstiftning om förvaring av förminskat tillräkneliga och internering av återfallsförbrytare' [Swedish legislation on the internment of mentally irresponsible offenders and recidivists], *Nordisk Tidsskrift for Strafferet*, 15: 322–331.

—— (1931) 'Scandinavian Prisons', *The Annals of the American Academy of Political and Social Science*, 157: 197–207.

Alper, B. S. and Boren, J. F. (1972) *Crime: An International Agenda: Concern and Action in the Prevention of Crime and Treatment of Offenders, 1846–1972*, Lexington: Heath.

'An Old Bushman' (1865) *Ten Years in Sweden*, London: Groombridge and Sons.

Ancel, M. (1965) *Social Defence: A Modern Approach to Criminal Problems*, London: Routledge and Kegan Paul.

Andenaes, J. (1959) 'Strafferett, kriminologi og kriminalpolitikk [Criminal law, criminology and criminal justice]', *Nordisk Tidsskrift for Kriminalvidenskab*, 47: 107–117.

Anderson, J. (2007) *The Legality of Boxing: A Punch Drunk Love?*, New York: Routledge.

Anderson, R. (1907) Crime and Criminals, London: James Nisbet and Co.

Anderson, R. (1908) 'Criminals and crime: A rejoinder', *The Nineteenth Century and After*, 63: 199–208.

Anderson, S. (2005) 'Imagining the prison: Literary representations and the development of modern penality in England', unpublished PhD thesis, Victoria University of Wellington.

Andrews, C. (1877) *On Pauperism and Poor Laws in Sweden and Norway*, New York: John S. Levey.

Annan, N. (1955) 'The intellectual aristocracy', in J. H. Plumb (ed.) *Studies in Social History: A Tribute to G. M. Trevelyan*, London: Books for Libraries Press.

Annual Report of the Finnish Prison and Probation Services (2002) Helsinki: Criminal Sanctions Agency.

Annual Report of the Finnish Prison and Probation Services (2004) Helsinki: Criminal Sanctions Agency.

Anononymous (1871) *Modern Etiquette in Private and Public*, London: F. Warne.

Arnold, H. (2005) 'The effects of prison work', in A. Liebling and S. Maruna (eds) *The Effects of Imprisonment*, Cullompton: Willan Publishing.

Ashby, W. (1889) *New Zealand, the Land of Health, Wealth and Prosperity: Its Present Position and Future Prospects*, London: S. Riorden.

Ashworth, A. (1989) 'Criminal justice and deserved sentences', *The Criminal Law Review*, 36: 340–355.

Aubert, V. (1956) 'The housemaid: An occupational role in crisis', *Acta Sociologica*, 1 (3): 149–158.

Aughterson, V. W. (1953) *Taking Stock: Aspects of Mid-Century Life in Australia*, Melbourne: F.W. Chesire.

Austin, P. B. (1970) *The Swedes: How They Live and Work*, New York: Praeger Publishers.

Australian Bureau of Statistics (1982) *Year Book Australia no. 66*, Canberra: Australian Bureau of Statistics.

——— (2000) *Prisoners in Australia 2000*, Sydney: Australian Bureau of Statistics. [cat. 4517.0].

Baden Powell, G. (1872) *New Homes for the Old Country*, London: Richard Bentley and Son.

Bailey, V. (1997) 'Penal culture and the abatement of imprisonment 1895–1922', *Journal of British Studies*, 36 (3): 285–324.

Baldry, E., Brown, D., Brown, M., Cunneen, C., Schwartz, M. and Steel, A. (2011) 'Imprisoning Rationalities', *Australian and New Zealand Journal of Criminology*, 44 (1): 24–40.

Balfour, J. (1901) *My Prison Life*, London: Chapman and Hall.

Barker, M. E. (1947) *The Character of England*, Oxford: Clarendon Press.

Bartlett, T. (2009) 'The power of penal populism', unpublished MA thesis, Victoria University of Wellington.

Barton, H. A. (1976) *Letters from the Promised Land: Swedes in America, 1840–1914*, Minneapolis: University of Minnesota Press.

——— (2003) *Sweden and Visions of Norway: Politics and Culture, 1814–1905*, Carbondale, IL: Southern Illinois University Press.

Bauman, Z. (2001) *Liquid Modernity*, Cambridge: Polity Press.

Beccaria, C. (1764/1995) *On Crimes and Punishments*, Cambridge: Cambridge University Press.

Becker, P. and Wetzell, R. F. (2006) *Criminals and their Scientists: The History of Criminology in International Perspective*, Cambridge: Cambridge University Press.

Beckett, S. J. (1936) *A Wayfarer in Norway*, 2nd edn, New York: McBride.

Belich, J. (1996) *Making Peoples: A History of New Zealand, from Polynesian Settlement to the End of the Nineteenth Century*, Auckland, NZ: Allen Lane/Penguin Press.

—— (2001) *Paradise Reforged: A History of the New Zealanders from the 1880s to the year 2000*, Auckland, NZ: Allen Lane/Penguin Press.

Bentham, J. (1796) *Essays 1796*, London: Bentham MSS, British Museum. [Box CLIIIa].

Berry, J. (1879) *New Zealand as a Field for Emigration*, London: James Clarke.

Beveridge, W. (1942) *Report of the Inter-Departmental Committee on Social Insurance and Allied Services [The Beveridge Report]*, London: HMSO. [Cmd. 6404].

—— (1943) *The Pillars of Security: And other War-Time Essays and Addresses*, London: Allen & Unwin.

Bidwell, A. (1895) *From Wall Street to Newgate*, Hartford, CT: Bidwell Publishing Co.

Bierne, P. (1993) *Inventing Criminology: Essays on the Rise of Homo Criminalis*, Albany: State University of New York Press.

—— (1994) *The Origins and Growth of Criminology: Essays on Intellectual History, 1760–1945*, Aldershot: Dartmouth Publishing.

Binney, T. (1853) *Formation of Character: A Book for Young Men*, London: J. Nisbet & Co.

Bishop, N. (1974) 'Aspects of European penal systems', in L. Blom-Cooper (ed.) *Progress in Penal Reform*, Oxford: Clarendon Press.

Bishop, N. (1991) 'Nyköping Closed Neighbourhood Prison, Sweden', in R. G. Whitfield (ed.) *The State of the Prisons – 200 Years On*, London: Routledge.

Bjørnson, B. (1857) *Synnøve Solbakken*, Christiania: Johan Dahls.

—— (1882) *The Happy Lad: A Story of Peasant Life in Norway and other Tales*, London: Blackie and Son.

—— (1898) *Absalom's Hair & A Painful Memory*, London: W. Heinemann.

Blainey, G. (1966) *The Tyranny of Distance: How Distance Shaped Australia's History*, Melbourne: Sun Books.

Blair, Tony (2002) 'My vision for Britain', *The Guardian*. Online, available at <http://www.guardian.co.uk/politics/2002/nov/10/queensspeech2002.tonyblair> (last accessed 10 February 2012).

—— (2004) 'Foreword' in Office for Criminal Justice Reform (OCJR) *Cutting Crime, Delivering Justice: A Strategic Plan for Criminal Justice 2004–08*, London: HMSO. [Cm. 6288].

Blinder, S. (2011) *UK Public Opinion toward Immigration: Overall Attitudes and Level of Concern*, Oxford: The Migration Observatory.

Blomstedt, M. and Book, F. (eds) (1930) *Sweden of To-Day: A Survey of its Intellectual and Material Culture*, Stockholm: A. -B. H. W. Tullberg.

Blomstedt, Y. (1964) *Rikoslakireformin Ensimmäiset Vaiheet Vuoden 1866 Osittaisuudistuksiin Saakka* [Reform of the Penal Code. The first steps to 1866], Helsinki, Historiallinen Arkisto.

Blumenberg, H. (1884) *Om Fattiggårdar* [On Poor-Farms], Linköping: H. W. Tullberg.

Bolton, I. M. (1938) 'Social services', in M. Cole and C. Smith (eds) *Democratic Sweden: A Volume of Studies Prepared by Members of the New Fabian Research Bureau*, London: Routledge.

Booth, C. (1894) *The Aged Poor in England and Wales*, London: Macmillan.

Bottoms, A. E. (1977) 'Reflections on the renaissance of dangerousness', *Howard Journal of Criminal Justice*, 16: 70–96.

—— (1983) 'Neglected features of contemporary penal systems', in D. Garland and P. Young (eds) *The Power to Punish*, London: Heinemann.

Bottoms, A. E. and McClintock, F. H. (1973) *Criminals Coming of Age: A Study of Institutional Adaptation in the Treatment of Adolescent Offenders*, London: Heinemann Educational Books.

Bottoms, A. E. and Preston, R. H. (eds) (1980) *The Coming Penal Crisis: A Criminological and Theological Exploration*, Edinburgh: Scottish Academic Press.

Bowden, J. (1867) *Norway: Its People, Products and Institutions*, London: Chapman and Hall.

Bowlby, J. (1947) *Forty-Four Juvenile Thieves: Their Character and Home Life*, London: Bailliere Tindall & Cox.

—— (1951) *Maternal Care and Mental Health*, Geneva: World Health Organization.

Bozovic, M. (ed.) (1995) *The Panopticon Writings,* London: Verso.

Braithwaite, J. (2001) 'Crime in a convict republic', *The Modern Law Review*, 64 (1): 11–50.

Bremer, F. (1853) *The Homes of the New World: Impressions of America*, trans. M. Howitt, New York: Harper.

Bresler, F. (1977) *Lord Goddard: A Biography of Rayner Goddard, Lord Chief Justice of England*, London: Harrap.

Broberg, G. and Roll-Hanssen, N. (eds) (1996) *Eugenics and the Welfare State: Sterilization Policy in Denmark, Sweden, Norway and Finland*, East Lansing, MI: Michigan University Press.

Brodeur, J-P. (2007) 'Comparative Penology in Perspective', Crime and Justice, 36 (1): 49–91.

Brown, A. (2008) *Fishing in Utopia: Sweden and the Future that Disappeared*, London: Grant Books.

Brown, D. (2002) 'Prisoners as citizens', in D. Brown and M. Wilkie (eds) *Prisoners as Citizens: Human Rights in Australian Prisons*, Annandale, NSW: Federation Press.

Brown, D. and Zdenkowski, G. (1982) *The Prison Struggle: Changing Australia's Penal System*, Harmondsworth: Penguin Books.

Bruhn, A., Nylander, P-Å. and Lindberg, O. (2010) 'The prison officer's dilemma: Professional representations among Swedish prison officers', *Les Dossiers des sciences de l'education*, 23 (1): 77–93.

Buller, J. (1880) *New Zealand: A Short History*, London: Allen and Unwin.

Bumsted, J. (1992) *The Peoples of Canada*, Toronto: Oxford University Press.

Burnett, J. (1966) *Plenty and Want: A Social History of Diet in England from 1815 to the Present Day*, London: Nelson.

Butler Committee (1979) *Report of the Committee on Mentally Abnormal Offenders*, London: HMSO. [Cmnd. 6244].

Cameron, D. (2009) 'The Big Society', Hugo Young Memorial Lecture, Kings Place, London, November 2009.

Capek, K. (1925) *Letters from England*, trans. P. Selver, London: Geoffrey Bles.

Carey, J. (2007) '"Not only a white race, but a race of best whites": The woman's movement, white Australia and eugenics between the wars', in L. Boucher, J. Carey and K. Ellinghaus (eds) *Historicising Whiteness: Transnational Perspectives on the Emergence of an Identity*, Melbourne: RMIT Publishing.

Carlyle, T. (ed.) (1850) *Latter-day Pamphlets*, London: Chapman and Hall.

Carrabine E. (2004) *Power, Discourse and Resistance: A Genealogy of the Strangeways Prison Riot*, Aldershot: Ashgate Publishing.

Castberg, F. (1954) *The Norwegian Way of Life*, London: Heinemann.

Castles, F. (1978) *The Social Democratic Image of Society: A Study of the Achievements and Origins of Scandinavian Social Democracy in Comparative Perspective*, London: Routledge and Keegan Paul.

Cavadino, M. and Dignan, J. (2002) *The Penal System: An Introduction*, 3rd edn, London: Sage.

—— (2006) *Penal Systems: A Comparative Approach*, London: Sage.

—— (2007) *The Penal System: An Introduction*, 4th edn, London: Sage.

Cavadino, M., Crow, I., and Dignan, J. (1999) *Criminal Justice 2000: Strategies for a New Century*, Winchester: Waterside Press.

Chadwick, E. (1843) *Report on the Sanitary Conditions of the Labouring Population of Great Britain*, London: W. Clowes and Sons, HMSO.

Chapple, W. A. (1903) *The Fertility of the Unfit*, Melbourne: Whitcombe and Tombs.

Chibnall, S. (1977) *Law and Order News: An Analysis of Crime Reporting in the British Press*, London: Tavistock Publications.

Childs, M. W. (1936) *Sweden: The Middle Way*, New Haven, CT: Yale University Press.

Christie, N. (1960) *Tvangsarbeid og Alkoholbruk* [Forced Labour and the Use of Alcohol], Oslo: Universitetsforlaget.

—— (1968) 'Changes in penal values', *Scandinavian Studies on Criminology*, 2: 161–172.

—— (2011) 'Han er en av oss' [He is one of us], Online, available at <http://www.aftenposten.no/meninger/article4226375.ece#.T77yU7A7htV> (last accessed 22 May 2012).

Christoph, J. B. (1962) *Capital Punishment and British Politics: The British Movement to Abolish the Death Penalty, 1945–57*, Chicago: University of Chicago Press.

Clarke, E. D. (1823) *Travels in Various Countries of Europe, Asia and Africa*, London: R. Watts Crown Court Temple Bar.

Clay, W. (1861/1969) *The Prison Chaplain: A Memoir of the Reverend John Clay, B. D., Late Chaplain of Preston Gaol*, Montclair: Patterson Smith.

Coghlan, T. A. (1888) *The Wealth and Progress of New South Wales*, Sydney: C. Potter, Government Printer.

Cole, M. and Smith, C. (eds) (1938) *Democratic Sweden: A Volume of Studies Prepared by Members of the New Fabian Research Bureau*, London: Routledge & Sons.

Collier, P. (1909) *England and the English from and American Point of View*, New York: Charles Scribner's Sons.

Collins, P. (1962) *Dickens and Crime*, London: Macmillan.

Conan-Doyle, A. (1887) *A Study in Scarlet*, New York: American Publishers Corporation.

Connery, D. S. (1966) *The Scandinavians*, London: Eyre & Spottiswoode.

Conservative Party (1979) *Conservative General Election Manifesto 1979*, London: Conservative Party.

Conway, D. (1829) *A Personal Narrative of a Journey through Norway, Part of Sweden and the Islands and States of Denmark*, Edinburgh: Constable and Co.

Cooper, I. R. (1857) *The New Zealand Settlers' Guide*, London: E. Stanford.

Council for Crime Prevention (1977) *Nytt Straffsystem. Ideer och Förslag. Arbetsgruppen rörande Kriminalpolitiken* [New Penal System. Ideas and Suggestions], Stockholm: Brottsförebyggande Rådet.

Cowie, G. (1937) *New Zealand from Within*, London: George Routledge and Sons Ltd.

Crawford, W. (1834) *Report of William Crawford, Esq., on the Penitentiaries of the United States, addressed to His Majesty's Principal Secretary of State for the Home Department*, Sessional Paper 593, London: HMSO.

Crichton, A. (1842) *Scandinavia, Ancient and Modern*, New York: Harper.

Criminal Law Committee (1976) *Report*, Helsinki: Ministry of Justice.

Crosland, A. (1962) *The Conservative Enemy: A Programme of Radical Reform for the 1960s*, London: Jonathan Cape.

Crowe, J. R. (1875) 'Norway' in Great Britain Foreign Office (ed.) *Poor Laws in Foreign Countries: Reports Communicated to the Local Government Board by Her Majesty's Secretary of State for Foreign Affairs*, London: HMSO. [C. 1255].

Crown Prince Oscar of Sweden (1840) *Om Straff och Straffanstalter* [On Punishment and Punishment Institutions], Stockholm: P. A. Norstedt and Söner.

Davitt, M. (1886) *The Prison Life of Michael Davitt*, Dublin: Lalor.

De Mare, E. (1952) *Scandinavia. Sweden, Denmark and Norway*, London: Batsford.

De Windt, H. (1901) *Finland As It Is*, London: John Murray.

Deacon, A. (1978) 'The scrounging controversy: Public attitudes towards the unemployed in contemporary Britain', *Social Policy and Administration*, 12 (2): 120–135.

Department of Justice (1956) *55 Skyddslag* [Report of the Penal Code Commission], Stockholm: Department of Justice.

—— (1990) *92 Våld och Byrottsoffer* [Violence and Victims of Crime], Stockholm: Department of Justice.

—— (1995) *91 Ett Reformerat Straffsystem* [A Reformed System of Punishment], Stockholm: Department of Justice.

—— (2000) *126 Vägvalet: Den Narkotikapolitiska Utmaningen* [The Crossroads: The Drug Policy Challenge], Stockholm: Department of Justice.

Derry, T. K. (1979) *History of Scandinavia: Norway, Sweden, Denmark, Finland, and Iceland*, Minneapolis: University of Minnesota Press.

Devlin, P. (1979) *The Judge*, Oxford: Oxford University Press.

Dicey, A. V. (1919) *Lectures on the Relation between Law and Public Opinion in England during the 19th Century*, 2nd edn, London: Macmillan.

Dickens, C. (1838/1992) *Oliver Twist*, Ware: Wordsworth.

—— (1842) *American Notes for General Circulation*, Paris: Baudry's European Library.

—— (1849–50/1992) *David Copperfield*, Ware: Wordsworth.

—— (1850) 'Pet prisoners', *Household Words*, 1 (5): 97–103.

—— (1854/1992) *Hard Times*, London: David Campbell.

—— (1857) *Little Dorrit*, London: Bradbury and Evans.

—— (1860–61/1996). *Great Expectations*, Ware: Wordsworth.

—— (1865) *Our Mutual Friend*, Leipzig: Tauchnitz.

Dingle, A. (1980) 'The truly magnificent thirst: An historical survey of Australian drinking habits', *Australian Historical Studies*, 19: 227–249.

Dixon, H. (1850) *The London Prisons*, London: Jackson and Walford.

Du Cane, E. (1875) 'Address on the repression of crime', *Transactions of the National Association for the Promotion of Social Science*, London: Longmans, Green and Co.

—— (1885) *The Punishment and Prevention of Crime*, London: Macmillan.

Durkheim, E. (1893/1933) *The Division of Labour in Society*, trans. G. Simpson, New York: The Free Press.

East, W. N. (1923) 'The incidence of crime and mental deficiency' *British Medical Journal*, 3267: 228–229.

East, W. N. and Hubert, W. H. de B. (1939) *Report on the Psychological Treatment of Crime*, London: HMSO.

Eckstein, H. (1966) *Division and Cohesion in Democracy: A Study of Norway*, Princeton, NJ: Princeton University Press.

Ekberg, G. (2004) 'The Swedish law that prohibits the purchase of sexual services: Best practices for prevention of prostitution and trafficking in human beings', *Violence Against Women*, 10 (10): 1187–1218.

Eldred-Grigg, S. (1980) *A Southern Gentry: New Zealanders who Inherited the Earth*, Wellington, NZ: A.H. & A.W. Reed.

Elias, N. (1939/1979) *The Civilizing Process*, London: Blackwells.

Eliot, G. (1859, 1980) *Adam Bede*, Harmondsworth: Penguin.

Ellis, H. (1890) *The Criminal*, London: Walter Scott.

Elwin, G. (1977) 'Swedish anti-terrorist legislation', *Contemporary Crises*, 1 (3): 289–301.

Emerson, R. W. (1857) *English Traits*, London: G. Routledge & Co.

Eriksson, T. (1954) 'Postwar prison reform in Sweden', *Annals of the American Academy of Political and Social Science*, 293: 152–162.

—— (1967) *Kriminalvård: Ideer och Experiment* [Corrections: Ideas and Experiments], Stockholm: P. A. Nordstedt & Söners Förlag.

—— (1977) *Politik och Kriminalpolitik* [Politics and Criminal Justice Policy], Stockholm: P. A. Nordstedt & Söners Förlag.

Ericsson, T. (2004) 'A silent class: The lower middle class in Sweden', in T. Ericsson, J. Fink, and J. E. Myhre (eds) *The Scandinavian Middle Classes, 1840–1940*, Oslo: Oslo Academic Press.

Ericsson, T., Fink, J. and Myhre, J.E. (eds) (2004) *Scandinavian Middle Classes 1840–1940*, Oslo: Unipub forlag – Oslo Academic Press.

Escott, T. H. S. (1885) *England: Her People, Polity and Pursuits*, London: Chapman and Hall.

Esping-Andersen, G. (1990) *The Three Worlds of Welfare Capitalism*, Princeton, NJ: Princeton University Press.

Estrada, F. (2001) 'Juvenile violence as a social problem: Trends, media attention and societal response', *British Journal of Criminology*, 41 (4): 639–655.

Eurobarometer 71: National Report, United Kingdom (2009) London: European Commission.

Evang, K. (1957) *Health Services in Norway*, Oslo: Norwegian Joint Committee on International Social Policy.

Fairburn, M. (1989) *The Ideal Society and its Enemies: The Foundations of Modern New Zealand Society, 1850–1900*, Auckland, NZ: Auckland University Press.

—— (1995) *Nearly out of Heart and Hope*, Auckland, NZ: Auckland University Press.

Falck, S., von Hofer, H., and Storgaard, A. (2003) *Nordic Criminal Statistics 1950–2000*, Stockholm: Department of Criminology, Stockholm University.

Falsen, C. (1930) 'Fengselmannens utdannelse' [The training/education of prison staff], *Nordisk Tidsskrift for Strafferet*, 18: 58–68.

—— (1933) Straff, sikring og tvangsarbeide' [Punishment, incapacitation and forced labour] *Nordisk Tidsskrift for Strafferet*, 21: 81–102.

Faucher, L. (1844) *Manchester in 1844: Its Present Condition and Future Prospect*, London: Cass.

Fennell, S. (2001) 'Psychiatry and Seacliff 1912–1948', in B. Brooken and J. Thomson (eds) *Unfortunate Folk. Essays on Mental Health Treatment*, Dunedin, NZ: Otago University Press.

Ferri, E. (1928) *Principles of Criminal Law: Criminal and Crime Science, Legislation and Jurisprudence*, Madrid: Editorial Reus.

Field, Rev. J. (1848) *Prison Discipline: And the Advantages of the Separate System of Imprisonment, with Detailed Account of the Discipline Now Pursued in the New County at Reading*, London: Longman, Brown, Green and Longmans.

Finlay, A. M. (1943) *Social Security in New Zealand: A Simple Guide for the People*, Christchurch, N.Z: Whitcombe and Tombs Ltd.

Finnane, M. (1997) *Punishment in Australian Society*, Melbourne: Oxford University Press.

Finnish Criminalist Society (1951) *Annual Journal of the Finnish Criminalist Society*, Helsinki: National Research Institute of Legal Policy.

Finnish Social Democratic Party (1969) *Criminal Justice Policy in a Changing Society*, Online, available at < http://www.fsd.uta.fi/pohtiva/ohjelma?tunniste=sdpkriminaali 1969>. (last accessed 15 April 2012).

Fitzgerald, M. (1977) *Prisoners in Revolt*. New York: Penguin.

Fleisher, F. (1967) *The New Sweden: The Challenge of a Disciplined Democracy*, New York: David McKay.

Fleisher, W. (1956) *Sweden: The Welfare State*, Michigan: J. Day and Co.

Ford, F. M. (1907) *England and the English: An Interpretation*. New York: McClure, Phillips & Co.

Forsell, C. af (1835) *Anteckningar i anledning af en resa till England i slutet af sommaren år 1834* [Notes on a Trip to England at the end of Summer in 1834], Stockholm: John Hörberg.

Foucault, M. (1977) *Discipline and Punish: The Birth of the Prison*, London: Allen Lane.

Fouche, G. (2009) 'In Norway, prisoners take part in TV debates', *The Guardian*, 10 September 2009.

—— (2010) 'Is small government best for society?' *The Guardian: Society Guardian*, 3 February, p. 1.

Fowler, S. (2008) *Workhouse: The People, the Places, the Life behind Doors*, Kew: National Archives.

Fox, L. (1952) *The English Prison and Borstal Systems: An Account of the English Prison and Borstal Systems after the Criminal Justice Act 1948, with a Historical Introduction and an Examination of the Principles of Imprisonments as a Legal Punishment*, London: Routledge and Kegan Paul.

Fraser, D. (2009) *The Evolution of the British Welfare State*, 4th edn, Basingstoke: Palgrave Macmillan.

Freeland, J. M. (1966) *The Australian Pub*, London: Cambridge University Press.

Fukuyama, F. (1995) *Trust: The Social Virtues and the Creation of Prosperity*, New York: Free Press.

Galsworthy, J. (1910) *Justice: A Tragedy in Four Acts*, New York: C. Scribner's Sons.

—— (1922) *The Forsyte Saga*, London: Heinemann.

Garland, D. (1985) *Punishment and Welfare: A History of Penal Strategies*, London: Gower.

—— (1990) *Punishment and Modern Society: A Study in Social Theory*, Oxford: Oxford University Press.

—— (1996) 'The limits of the sovereign state', *British Journal of Criminology*, 36: 445–471.

—— (1997) 'Of crimes and criminals: The development of criminology in Britain', in M. Maguire, R. Morgan and R. Reiner (eds) *The Oxford Handbook of Criminology*, 2nd edn, Oxford: Clarendon Press.

—— (2001) *The Culture of Control*, New York: Oxford University Press.

—— (2005) 'Penal excess and surplus meaning: Public torture lynchings in twentieth-century America', *Law & Society Review*, 39: 793–834.

Garofalo, R. (1914) *Criminology*, Boston: Little, Brown and Co.

Gaskell, E. (1848/1996) *Mary Barton: A Tale of Manchester Life*, London: Everyman.

Gatrell, V. (1994) *The Hanging Tree: Execution and the English People, 1770–1868*, Oxford: Oxford University Press.

Gerhardsen, E. (1971) *Samarbeid og Strid: Erindringar 1945–55* [Cooperation and Combat: Recollections], Oslo: Tiden Norsk Forlag.

Gibbs, P. (1935) *England Speaks*, London: William Heinemann Ltd.

Gladstone Committee (1895) *Report from the Departmental Committee on Prisons*, London: HMSO. [C. 7702].

Glass, D. V. (1938) 'Population policy', in M. Cole and C. Smith (eds) *Democratic Sweden: A Volume of Studies Prepared by Members of the New Fabian Research Bureau*, London: Routledge & Sons.

Glover, E. (1922) 'The roots of crime', in E. Glover (1960) *The Roots of Crime. Selected Papers on Psycho-Analysis*, vol. 2, London: Imago.

Golding, P. and Middleton, S. (1982) *Images of Welfare: Press and Public; Attitudes to Poverty*, Oxford: Robertson.

Goldthorpe, J. (1968) *The Affluent Worker: Industrial Attitudes and Behaviour*, Cambridge: Cambridge University Press.

Göransson, H. (1938) 'Treatment of criminals and other asocial individuals', in *Annals of the American Academy of Political and Social Science, vol. 197* ('Social problems and policies in Sweden'.

—— (1949) 'Engelsk fångvård och svensk [English and Swedish prisoner care]', in K. Schlyter (ed.) *Festskrift Tillägnad f.d. Presidenten, Förutvarande Statsrådet juris Doktor Karl Schlyter den 21 December 1949*, [Festschrift for Karl Schlyter] Stockholm: Svensk Juristtidning.

Gorer, G. (1955) *Exploring English Character*, London: Cresset Press.

Goring, C. (1913) *The English Convict, a Statistical Study*, London: HMSO.

Government bill 110/1975 Governmental proposal on the revision on provisions on drunk driving (HE 1975 II 110: Hallituksen esitys Eduskunnalle laiksi rikoslain täydentämisestä liikennejuopumusta koskevilla säännöksillä sekä eräiksi siihen liittyviksi laeiksi.), Helsinki: Government Printer.

Government bill 2001/02: 91 Nationell Narkotikahandlingsplan [National drug action plan], Stockholm: Government Printer.

Grabosky, P. (1977) *Sydney in Ferment: Crime, Dissent and Official Reaction 1788 to 1973*, Canberra: Australian National University Press.

Granfelt, O. H. (1949) 'Några straffrättsliga reformer och reformplaner i Finland efter allmänna strafflagens tillkomst. Skisserad översikt [Some penal reforms and reform plans in Finland after the introduction of the penal code. An overview]', in K. Schlyter (ed.) *Festskrift Tillägnad f.d. Presidenten, Förutvarande Statsrådet juris Doktor Karl Schlyter den 21 December 1949* [Festschrift for Karl Schlyter], Stockholm: Svensk Juristtidning.

Green, D. A. (2008) *When Children Kill Children: Penal Populism and Political Culture*, Oxford: Oxford University Press.

Green, T. H. (1883) *Prologemena to Ethics*, Oxford: Clarendon Press.

Greenwood, W. (1933) *Love on the Dole: A Tale of the Two Cities*, London: Cape.

Grimley, O. (1937) *The New Norway*, Oslo: Griff-Forlanget.

Gruchy, A. G. (1966) *Comparative Economic Systems: Competing Ways to Stability and Growth*, Boston: Houghton Mifflin.

Gullenstad, M. (2002) 'Invisible fences: Egalitarianism, nationalism and racism', *The Journal of the Royal Anthropological Institute*, 8 (1): 45–63.

Hall Williams, J. E. (1970) *The English Penal System in Transition*, London: Butterworths.

Hancock, K. (1930) *Australia*, London: Ernest Benn.

Harris, A. (1847) *Settlers and Convicts: Recollections of Sixteen Years' Labour in the Australian Backwoods*, London: C. Cox.

Harrison, K. (2011) *Dangerousness, Risk and the Governance of Serious Sexual and Violent Offenders*, Abingdon: Routledge.

Harrop, A. (1935) *Touring in New Zealand*, London: Allen and Unwin.

Hartz, L. (1964) *The Founding of New Societies: Studies in the History of the United States, Latin America, South Africa, Canada, and Australia*, New York: Harcourt, Brace & World.

Hatch, E. (1992) *Respectable Lives: Social Standing in Rural New Zealand*, Berkley, CA: University of California Press.

Hay, W. D. (1882) *Brighter Britain! or, Settler and Maori in Northern New Zealand*, London: Richard Bentley.

Heathcote, D. (1927) *Sweden*, London: A & C Black.

Heward, E. (1990) *Lord Denning: A Biography*, London: Weidenfeld and Nicolson.

Hietala, M. (1996) 'From race hygiene to sterilization: The eugenics movement in Finland', in G. Broberg and N. Roll-Hansen (eds) *Eugenics and the Welfare State: Sterilization Policy in Denmark, Sweden, Norway, and Finland*, East Lansing, MI: Michigan State University Press.

HM Prison Service Annual Report (1992–3) London: HMSO. [Cm. 2385]

—— (1994–5) London: HMSO. [HC. 447]

—— (2001–2) London: HMSO. [HC. 957]

—— (2003–4) London: HMSO. [HC. 718].

—— (2006–7) London: HMSO. [HC. 717].

Hobhouse, S. and Brockway, F. (1922) *English Prisons Today*, London: Macmillan.

Hodson, J. L. (1948) *The Way Things Are*, London: Victor Gollancz.

Hogben, L. T. (ed.) (1938) *Political Arithmetic: A Symposium of Population Studies*, London: Allen and Unwin.

Höjer, K. (1938) 'The care of the indigent in Sweden', *The Annals of the American Academy of Political and Social Science*, 197: 72–79.

Holloway, W. and Jefferson, T. (1997) 'The risk society in an age of anxiety: Situating fear of crime', *British Journal of Sociology*, 48 (2): 255–266.

Holmberg, C. (1953) 'Brott och publicitet'[Crime and publicity], *Nordisk Tidsskrift for Kriminalvidenskab*, 41: 61–64.

Holst, F. (1828) 'Disciplinmøllen eller Traemøllen' [Discipline mill or treadmill], *Eyr*, 3: 24–37.

Home Affairs Committee (1981) *Administration of the Prison Service, Minutes of Evidence, Monday 16 March 1981*, London HMSO. [HC 39-ix].

Home Office (1959) *Penal Practice in a Changing Society: Aspects of Future Development*, London: HMSO. [Cmnd. 645]

Home Office (1969) *People in Prison (England and Wales)*, London: HMSO. [Cmnd. 4214].

—— (1988) *Punishment, Custody and the Community*, London: HMSO. [Cm. 424].

—— (1996) *Protecting the Public: The Government's Strategy on Crime in England and Wales*, London: HMSO. [Cm. 3190].

—— (2001) *Criminal Justice: The Way Ahead*, London: HMSO. [Cm. 5074].

—— (2002) *Justice for All*, London: HMSO. [Cm. 5563]

—— (2003) *Prison Statistics England and Wales 2002*, London: HMSO. [Cm. 5996].

—— (2012a) 'A summary of recorded crime data from 1898 to 2001/02', Online, available at < http://webarchive.nationalarchives.gov.uk/20110218135832/http://rds.homeoffice. gov.uk/rds/recordedcrime1.html> (last accessed 8 June 2012).

—— (2012b) 'Recorded crime statistics 2002/03–2009/10', Online, available at <http://www.homeoffice.gov.uk/publications/science-research-statistics/research-statistics/crime-research/crime-stats-2002–2010> (last accessed 8 June 2012).

Horne, D. (1965) *The Lucky Country*, Richmond, Vic: Penguin Books.

Hornqvist, M. (2010) *Risk, Power and the State: After Foucault*, Oxford: Routledge.

Hough, M. (1996) 'People talking about punishment', *Howard Journal of Criminal Justice*, 35: 191–214.

Hovde, B. J. (1943) *The Scandinavian Countries, 1720–1865: The Rise of the Middle Class*, Boston, MA: Chapman & Grimes.

Howard, J. (1792) *The State of the Prisons in England and Wales, with Preliminary Observations, and an Account of Some Foreign Prisons and Hospitals*, 4th edn, London: J. Johnson, C. Dilly, T. Cadell.

—— (1777/1929) *The State of the Prisons in England and Wales*, London: J. M. Dent and Sons.

Howitt, W. (1838) *The Rural Life of England*, London: Longman, Orme, Brown, Green and Longmans.

Hughes, R. (1987) *The Fatal Shore: A History of the Transportation of Convicts to Australia*, 1787–1868, London: Collins Harvill.

Hughes, T. (1857) *Tom Brown's School Days*, Cambridge: Macmillan & Co.

Huizinga. J. H. (1958) *Confessions of a European in England*, London: Heinemann.

Huntford, R. (1971) *The New Totalitarians*, London: Allen Lane.

Huxley, T. H. (1880) *Science and Education: Collected Essays*, vol. 3, New York, D. Appleton and Co.

Ibsen, H. (1882) *An Enemy of the People*, Auckland: Floating Press.

Inge, W. R. (1926) *England*, London: Ernest Benn.

Jareborg, N. (1995) 'The Swedish sentencing reform', in C. M. V. Clarkson and R. Morgan (eds) *The Politics of Sentencing Reform*, Oxford: Oxford University Press.

Jevons, W. S. (1878) *Political Economy*, New York: D. Appleton and Company.

Jenkins, D. (1968) *Sweden and the Price of Progress*, New York: Coward-McCann.

Jennings, P. (2007) *The Local. A History of the English Pub*, Stroud: Tempus.

Jupp, J. (2004) *The English in Australia*, Melbourne: Cambridge University Press.

Jutila, M. (2011) 'Narrowing of public responsibility in Finland, 1990–2010', *Social Policy and Administration*, 45 (2): 194–205.

Kayll, J. (1905) *A Plea for the Criminal. Being a Reply to Dr. Chapple's Work: 'The Fertility of the Unfit', and an Attempt to Explain the Leading Principles of Criminological and Reformatory Science*, Invercargill, NZ: W. Smith.

Kekkonen, J. (1999) 'Judicial repression after the civil wars in Finland (1918) and Spain (1936–1939), in M. Lappalainen and P. Hirvonen (eds) *Crime and Control in Europe from the Past to the Present.* Helsinki: Academy of Finland.

Kelsey, J. (1995) *The New Zealand Experiment: A World Model for Structural Adjustment?*, Auckland, NZ: Auckland University Press.

Kerr, J. S. (1988) *Out of Sight, Out of Mind: Australia's Places of Confinement 1788–1988*, Sydney: S. H. Ervin Gallery in association with the Australian Bicentennial Authority.

Kerr, R. (1865) *The Gentlemen's House*, London: J. Murray.

Keun, O. (1935) *I Discover the English*, Leipzig: Bernhard Tauchnitz.

Kinberg, O. (1930) *Aktuella Kriminalitets Problem i Psykologisk Belysning* [Current Problems of Criminality from a Psychological Perspective], Stockholm: Natur och Kultur.

King, M. (2003) *The Penguin History of New Zealand*, Auckland: Penguin Books.

King, R. and Morgan, R. (1980) *The Future of the Prison System*, Aldershot: Gower.

Kingsley, C. (1849) *Yeast*, New York: Harper and Brothers.

—— (1850) *Alton Locke*, New York: Harper and Brothers.

—— (1877) *Charles Kingsley: His Letters and Memories of his Life. Edited by his Wife [F. E. Kingsley]*, vol. 2, New York: Schribner.

Kirkby, D. E. (2006) 'Drinking the good life: Australia c. 1880–1980', in M. P. Holt (ed.) *Alcohol: A Social and Cultural History*, Oxford: Berg.

Kleen, E., Eriksson, T., Jonsson, G. and Nyström, P. (1944) *Fången, Människan och Straffet* [Prisoner, Person, Punishment], Stockholm: Kooperative Förbundets Bokförlag.

Kuhnle, S. (2000) *Survival of the European Welfare State*, London: Routledge.

Kuusi, P. (1964) *Social Policy for the Sixties: A Plan for Finland*, Helsinki: Finnish Social Policy Association.

Kvist, J. (1999) 'Welfare reform in the Nordic countries in the 1990s: Using fuzzy-set theory to assess conformity to ideal types', *Journal of European Social Policy*, 9 (3): 231–252.

Kynaston, D. (2010) *Family Britain, 1951–1957*, New York: Walker and Co.

Labour Party (1946) *Women's place in the sun: A message to all the women of New Zealand from M. Moohan, National Secretary of the N.Z. Labour Party*, Wellington: Standard Press.

Lacey, N. (2006) 'Historicizing contrasts in tolerance', in T. Newburn and P. Rock (eds) *The Politics of Crime Control: Essays in the Honour of David Downes*, Oxford: Oxford University Press.

—— (2008) *The Prisoners' Dilemma: Political Economy and Punishment in Contemporary Democracies*, Cambridge: Cambridge University Press.

Lagerlöf, S. (1918) *Gösta Berling's Saga*, New York: The American-Scandinavian Foundation.

Lahti, R. (1977) 'Criminal sanctions in Finland: A system in transition', *Scandinavian Studies in Law*, 21: 119–157.

Laing, S. (1837) *Journal of a Residence in Norway during the Years 1834, 1835 and 1836*, London: Longmans.

Lammers, A. (1875) 'Sweden and Norway' in A. Emminghaus (ed.) *Poor Relief in Different Parts of Europe; Being a Selection of Essays*, trans. E. Eastwick, London: E. Stanford.

Landecker, W. S. (1941) 'Criminology in Germany', *Journal of Criminal Law and Criminology*, 31: 551–575.

Lappi-Seppälä, T. (2000) 'The fall of the Finnish prison population', *Journal of Scandinavian Studies in Criminology and Crime Prevention*, 1 (1): 27–40.

—— (2007) 'Penal policy in Scandinavia', *Crime and Justice: An Annual Review of Research*, 34: 1–81.

—— (2008) 'Trust, welfare and political economy: Explaining the differences in national penal policy', *Crime and Justice: An Annual Review of Research*, 37: 313–387.

—— (2011) 'Changes in penal policy in Finland', in H. Kury and E. Shea (eds) *Punitivity. International Developments, vol. 1: Punitiveness – A Global Phenomenon?* Bochum: University Press Dr. N. Brockmeyer.

Larsson, S. (2005) *The Girl with the Dragon Tattoo*, Stockholm: Norstedt.

—— (2006) *The Girl Who Played with Fire*, Stockholm: Norstedt.

—— (2007) *The Girl Who Kicked the Hornets' Nest*, Stockholm: Norstedt.

League of Nations (1939) *Finland*, Geneva: League of Nations.

Leander, K. (1995) 'The normalization of Swedish prisons', in V. Ruggiero, M. Ryan and J. Sim (eds) *Western European Penal Systems. A Critical Anatomy*, London: Sage.

Learmont, J. (1995) *Review of Prison Service Security in England and Wales and the Escape from Parkhurst Prison on Tuesday 3rd January 1995*, London: HMSO. [Cm. 3020].

Lee, J. (1885) *The Man They Could Not Hang: The Life Story of John Lee*, London: Arthur Pearson.

Lehti, M. (2001) *The Homicide Wave in Finland from 1905 to 1932*, Helsinki, National Research Institute of Legal Policy.

Lenke, L. and Olsen, B. (2003) 'The drug policy relevance of drug related deaths', in H. Tham (ed.) *Review of Swedish Drug Policy*, Stockholm: Stockholm University Department of Criminology, The Senlis Council.

Lexbro, L. (2000) *Konflikt eller Konsensus? Kriminalpolitiken och Riksdagen 1946–1965* [Conflict or Consensus: Crime policy and government 1946–1965], Stockholm: Kriminologiska Institutionen.

Lindbeck, A. (1997) *The Swedish Experiment*, Stockholm: SNS Forlag.

Lindberg, O., Nylander, P-A. and Bruhn, A. (2011) 'Emotional labour and emotional strain among Swedish prison officers', *European Journal of Criminology*, 8: 469–483.

Lindbom, A. (2001) 'Dismantling the social democratic welfare model? Has the Swedish welfare state lost its defining characteristics?' *Scandinavian Political Studies*, 24 (3): 171–193.

Lindbom, A. and Rothstein, B. (2004) 'The Mysterious Survival of the Scandinavian Welfare States', paper presented at the annual meeting of the American Political Science Association, Chicago, September 2004.

Lindqvist, R. and Marklund, S. (1995) 'Forced to work and liberated from work – A historical perspective on work and welfare in Sweden', *Scandinavian Journal of Social Welfare*, 4(4): 224–237.

Lindvall, J. and Rothstein, B. (2006) 'Sweden: The fall of the strong state', *Scandinavian Political Studies*, 29: 47–63.

Lingard, J. (1936) *Prison Labour in New Zealand: A Historical, Statistical and Analytical Survey*, Wellington, NZ: Government Printer.

Lipset, S. M. (1990) 'The work ethic – then and now', *Public Interest*, 98: 61–69.

Lipson, L. (1948) *The Politics of Equality: New Zealand's Adventures in Democracy*, Chicago: Chicago University Press.

Loader, I. (2006) 'Fall of the "platonic guardians": Liberalism, criminology and political responses to crime in England and Wales', *British Journal of Criminology*, 46: 561–586.

—— (2010) 'For penal moderation: Notes towards a public philosophy of punishment', *Theoretical Criminology* 14, 349–367.

Lochhead, M. (1964) *The Victorian Household*, London: Murray.

Lombroso, C. (1876) *L' uomo Delinquente: Studiato in Rapporto alla Antropologia, alla Medicina Legale ed alle Discipline Carcerarie; con Incisioni*, Milano: Hoepli.

Lundberg, U. and Åmark, K. (2001) 'Social rights and social security: The Swedish welfare state, 1900–2000, *Scandinavian Journal of History*, 26 (3):157–176.

Luther, M. (1520/1915) 'A treatise on good works', in A. Spaeth, L. D. Reed, and H. E. Jacobs (eds) (1915) *The Works of Martin Luther*, Philadelphia: A. J. Holman Company.

—— (1521/1880) 'Let your sins be strong: A letter from Luther to Philip Melancthon', trans. E. Bullman, in J. G. Walch (ed) *Martin Luther's Saemmtliche Schriften*, St. Louis: Concordia Publishing House.

McGlone, F. (1990) 'Away from a dependency culture' in S. Savage and L. Robins (eds) *Public Policy Under Thatcher*, London: Macmillan.

McGowen, R. (1983) 'The image of justice and reform of the criminal law in early nineteenth-century England', *Buffalo Law Review*, 32 (1): 89–125.

McGuire, J. (1988) 'Judicial violence and the civilizing process', *Australian Historical Studies*, 23: 187–209.

Maillaud, P. (1945) *The English Way*, London: Oxford University Press.

Makipää, L. (2004) 'Taa lla niita psykoja riittaa' Ilta-Sanomien henkirikosuutisointi vuosina 1980, 1993 ja 2000 [Homicide Reporting in Ilta-Sanomat 1980, 1993 and 2000], unpublished MAThesis, University of Helsinki.

Mandela, N. (1994) *Long Walk to Freedom*, London: Little, Brown and Co.

Mandelson, P. (1997) *Labour's Next Steps: Tackling Social Exclusion*, London: Fabian Society.

Mankell, H. (2011) *The Troubled Man: A Kurt Wallander Mystery*, London: Vintage.

Mannheim, H. (1960) *Pioneers in Criminology*, London: Stevens.

Maric, J.J. (1964) *Gideon's Vote: A George Gideon Mystery*, New York: Harper.

Markström, U. (2003) *The Swedish Mental Health Reform among Bureaucrats, Users and Pioneers*, Doctoral Dissertation, Ulmea University.

Markus, A. (2011) *Mapping Social Cohesion: The Scanlon Foundation Surveys Summary Report 2011*, Caulfield East, Vic: Scanlon Foundation, Monash University.

Marnell, G. (1974) 'Penal Reform: A Swedish Viewpoint', *Howard Journal of Criminal Justice*, 14 (1): 8–21.

Marshall, J. (1957) *A Review of Penal Policy*, Wellington, NZ: Mount Crawford Prison.

Marshall, T. H. (1950) *Citizenship and Social Class*, Cambridge: Cambridge University Press.

Martin, A. (1952) *Norwegian Life and Landscape*, London: Elek Books.

Mathiesen, T. (1965) *The Defences of the Weak: A Sociological Study of Norwegian Correctional Institutions*, London: Tavistock.

—— (1974) *The Politics of Abolition*, New York: Wiley.

—— (1990) *Prison on Trial: A Critical Assessment*, London: Sage.

May Committee (1979) *Report of the Committee of Inquiry into the United Kingdom Prison Services*, London: HMSO. [Cmnd. 7673].

Maybrick, F. (1905) *Mrs. Maybrick's own Story: My Fifteen Lost Years*, New York: Funk & Wagnalls.

Mayhew, H. (1851) *London Labour and the London Poor*, London: G. Woodfall.

Mayhew, H. and Binny, J. (1862) *The Criminal Prisons of London and Scenes of Prison Life*. London: Griffin, Bohn and Co.

Mayhew, P. and White, P. (1997) *The 1996 International Crime Victimisation Survey*, Research Findings No. 57, London: Home Office Research and Statistics Directorate.

Maynard, M. (1994) *Fashioned from Penury: Dress as Cultural Practice in Colonial Australia*, Cambridge: Cambridge University Press.

Mead, W. (1968) *Finland*, London: Hurst.

Mendelsohn, R. (1954) *Social Security in the British Commonwealth: Great Britain, Canada, Australia, New Zealand*, London: University of London, Athlone Press.

Michanek, E. (1964) *For and Against the Welfare State*, Stockholm: Swedish Institute.

Miikkulainen, K. and Suominen, E. (1981) 'Vankeinhoito ja lehdistö 1946–78' [Correctional services and the press, 1946–1978], in E. Suominen (ed.) *Suomen Vankeinhoidon Historiaa, Osa 1: Katsauksia Vankeinhoidon Kehitykseen*, [A History of the Prison in Finland] Helsinki: Oikeusministeriön Vankeinhoito-Osasto.

Mill, J. S. (1859) *On Liberty*, London: Parker.

Miller, J. D. B. (1958) *The Commonwealth in the World*, London: Duckworth.

—— (1987) 'People to people', in J.D.B. Miller (ed.) *Australians and British: Social and Political Connections*, North Ryde, NSW: Methuen Australia.

Ministry of Justice (1974) 'Sweden's Minister for Justice speech', presentation at the Swedish and Finnish Social Workers' Union Conference, Turku, Finland, October 1974.

—— (1975) Statute on Prison Administration, Helsinki: Ministry of Justice.

—— (1977–78) *Om Kriminalpolitikken* [On Crime Policy], White Paper 104, Oslo: Justis-og Politidepartementet.

—— (1993) *To Restore a Degenerated Criminal Policy*, Stockholm: Justitiedepartementet.

Ministry of Justice and the Police (2008) *Punishment that Works: Less Crime – A Safer Society*. Oslo: Norwegian Government Administration Services.

Möller, G. (1952) 'Svensk socialpolitik' [Swedish social policy], *Tiden*, 44: 391–399.

Morgan, M. (2001) *National Identities and Travel in Victorian Britain*, New York: Palgrave.

Morgan, P. (1978) *Delinquent Fantasies*, London: Temple Smith.

Morris, A. and Reilly, J. (2003) *New Zealand National Survey of Crime Victims 2001*, Wellington, NZ: New Zealand Ministry of Justice.

Morris, N. (1950) *The Habitual Criminal*, London: School of Economics and Political Science.

Morris, T. (1989) *Crime and Criminal Justice since 1945*, Oxford: Blackwell.

Mountbatten, L. (1966) *Report of the Inquiry into Prison Escapes and Security*, London: HMSO. [Cmnd. 3175].

Moyer, L. K. (1974) 'The mentally abnormal offender in Sweden: An overview and comparisons with American law', *The American Journal of Comparative Law*, 22 (1): 71–106.

Mukherjee, S. (1999) 'Ethnicity and crime', *Trends and Issues in Crime and Criminal Justice*, No. 117, Canberra: Australian Institute of Criminology.

Mulgan, J. (1939) *Man Alone*, London: Selwyn & Blount.

Muncie, J. (1990) 'Failure never matters: Detention centres and the politics of deterrence', *Critical Social Policy*, 10 (28): 53–66.

Murphy, J. (2002) 'Shaping the cold war family: Politics, domesticity and policy interventions in the 1950s', *Australian Historical Studies*, 26: 544–567.

Murray, C. (1990) *The Emerging British Underclass*, London: Institute of Economic Affairs.

Myrdal, A. (1947) *Nation and Family: The Swedish Experiment in Democratic and Family Policy*, London: Kegan Paul, Trench, Trubner.

—— (1971) *Towards Equality: First Report of the Working Group on Equality set up by the Swedish Social Democratic Party and the Swedish Confederation of Trade Unions*, Stockholm, Prisma.

Myrdal, A. and Myrdal, G. (1934) *Kris i Befolkningsfrågan* [The Population Crisis], Stockholm: A. Bonnier.

Nadal, G.H. (1957) *Australia's Colonial Culture: Ideas, Men, and Institutions in Mid-Nineteenth Century Eastern Australia*, Cambridge: Harvard University Press.

Nagle, J. (1978) *Report of the Royal Commission into New South Wales Prisons*, Sydney: Government Printer.

National Association for the Care and Resettlement of Offenders (NACRO) (1984) *Tougher Regimes in Detention Centres*, London: HMSO.

Nellis, M. (1996) 'John Galsworthy's "Justice"', *British Journal of Criminology*, 36 (1): 61–84.

Nelson, G. (1953) *Social Welfare in Scandinavia*, Copenhagen: Danish Ministry of Labor and Social Affairs.

Nesbø, J. (2009) *The Leopard*, New York: Alfred A. Knopf.

Newbold, G. (2007) *The Problem of Prisons: Corrections Reform in New Zealand since 1840*, Wellington, NZ: Dunmore.

Newburn, T. (2011) 'A riot born in deprivation' *The Guardian*, Online, available at <http://www.guardian.co.uk/commentisfree/2011/oct/25/uk-riot-born-in-deprivation> (last accessed 23 May 2012).

New South Wales Official Yearbook (various) Sydney: Government Printer.

New Zealand Department of Justice (1968) *Crime in New Zealand*, Wellington, NZ: Government Printer.

—— (1981) *Annual Report Year Ended 31 March 1981*, Wellington, NZ: Government Printer.

—— (1991) *Conviction and Sentencing of Offenders in New Zealand 1981–1990*, Wellington, NZ: Department of Justice.

—— (2002) *Sentencing Act 2002, Parole Act 2002, Reforming the Criminal Justice System*, Wellington, NZ: Department of Justice.

—— (2003) *Attitudes to Crime and Punishment: A New Zealand Study*, Wellington, NZ: Department of Justice.

—— (2008) *Conviction and Sentencing of Offenders in New Zealand 1997 to 2006*, Wellington, NZ: Department of Justice.

—— (2010) *The New Zealand Crime and Safety Survey: 2009*, Wellington, NZ: Department of Justice.

New Zealand Police (2012) 'New Zealand crime statistics', Online, available at <http://www.police.govt.nz/service/statistics> (last accessed 8 June 2012).

New Zealand Yearbook (various) Wellington: Government Printer.

Nicholls, R. (1990) 'Elite society in Victorian and Edwardian Wellington', in D.A. Hamer and R. Nicholls (eds) *The Making of Wellington 1800–1914*, Wellington, NZ: Victoria University Press.

Nihill, D. (1839) *Prison Discipline in its Relations to Society and Individuals: As Deterring from Crime, and as Conducive to Personal Reformation*, London: J. Hatchard.

Nilson, U. (2007) *What Happened to Sweden? While America became the Only Superpower.* New York: Nordstjernan.

Nilsson, R. (1999) *En Välbyggd Maskin, en Mardröm för Själen: Det Svenska Fängelsesystemet under 1800-talet* [A Well-Built Machine, A Nightmare for the Soul: The Swedish Prison System during the Nineteenth Century], Lund: Lund University Press.

—— (2002) 'A well-built machine, a nightmare for the soul: The Swedish prison system in historical perspective', *Journal of the Institute of Justice and International Studies*, 1: 11–22.

—— (2003) 'Kontroll, makt och omsorg: Sociala problem och social politik i Sverige 1780–1940' [Control, power and care: Social problems and social policy in Sweden 1780–1940]. Studentlitterature: Lund, Sweden.

—— (2011) '"The most progressive, effective correctional system in the world": The Swedish prison system in the 1960s and 1970s', in J. Dullum and T. Ugelvik (eds) *Penal Exceptionalism*, Oxford: Routledge.

Nissen, H. (1935) 'Senare tiders fremskridt i norsk fengselveaesen: Framtids planer' [Recent developments in Norway's prison system, and plans for the future] *Nordisk Tidsskrift for Strafferet*, 23: 133–144.

Nolan, M. (2002) 'A subversive state? Domesticity in dispute in 1950s New Zealand', *Journal of Family History*, 27 (1): 60–81.

Nordin, D. S. (2005) *A Swedish Dilemma: A Liberal European Nation's Struggle with Racism and Xenophobia, 1990–2000*, Lanhom, MD: University Press of America.

Nordlund, A. (2000) 'Social policy in harsh times: Social security development in Denmark, Finland, Norway and Sweden during the 1980s and 1990s', *International Journal of Social Welfare*, 9: 31–42.

Northcott, C.H. (1918) *Australian Social Development*, New York: Columbia University.

Norwegian Design Council (2011) 'Honarable mention – Halden Prison', Online, available at <http://www.norskdesign.no/jurykjennelser/hederlig-omtale-halden-fengsel-article 19591–8815.html.> (last accessed 3 April 2012).

Norwegian Labour Party (2006) *Penal Policy*, Oslo: Norwegian Labour Party.

NSW Bureau of Crime Statistics and Research (1990) *New South Wales Recorded Crime Statistics 1989–90*, Sydney: NSW Bureau of Crime Statistics and Research.

—— (2012) 'Recorded crime statistics [various years]', Online, available at <http://www.lawlink.nsw.gov.au/lawlink/bocsar/ll_bocsar.nsf/pages/bocsar_pub_statistical> (last accessed 8 June 2012).

NSW Department of Corrective Services Annual Report (1976–8) Sydney: Government Printer.

—— (1987–8) Sydney: Government Printer.

—— (1988–9) Sydney: Government Printer.

—— (1991–2) Sydney: Government Printer.

—— (1998–9) Sydney: Government Printer.

O'Farrell, P. J. (2001) *The Irish in Australia: 1788 to the Present*, Notre Dame: University of Notre Dame Press.

Organisation for Economic Co-operation and Development [OECD] (2011) *Tackling Inequality, Growing Income Inequality in OECD Countries: What Drives it and How can Policy Tackle it?*, Paris: OECD.

Official Publication for the Paris Exhibition 1900, Kristiania: Aktie-bogtrykkeriet.

Olivecrona, K. (1866/1891) *Om dödsstraffet* [On the Death Penalty], Stockholm: Akademiska Boktryckeriet.

—— (1872) *Om orsakerna till återfall till brott och om medlen att minska dessa orsakers skadliga verkningar* [The Reasons for Recidivism and the Means to Reduce Its Harmful Consequences], Stockholm: P. A. Norstedt & Söner.

Orwell, G. (1933) *Down and out in Paris and London*, New York: Avon Publications.

—— (1941) *The Lion and the Unicorn: Socialism and the English Genius*, London: Secker & Warburg.

Page, J. S. (2002) 'Is mateship a virtue?' *Australian Journal of Social Issues*, 37 (2): 193–200.

Palmer, A (1990) *Bernadotte: Napoleon's Marshal, Sweden's King*, London: Murray.

Park, A., Clery, E., Curtice, J., Phillips, M. and Utting, D. (eds) (2012) *British Social Attitudes 28*, London: Sage.

Paterson, A. W. (1961) 'The prison building programme', *British Journal of Criminology*, 1 (4): 307–316.

Pearson, C. H. (1893) *National Life and Character: A Forecast*, London: Macmillan.

Pearson, K. (1903) 'Inheritance of psychical and physical characters in man', *Nature*, 68 (1773): 207–208.

—— (1907) 'The scope and importance to the state of the science of national eugenics', *The Popular Science Monthly*, 71: 385–412.

Pember Reeves, W. (1902) *State Experiments in Australia and New Zealand*, London: Allen and Unwin.

Penal Policy Review Committee (1981) *Report of the Penal Policy Review Committee* (1981) Wellington, NZ: Government Printer.

Perkin, H. (1969) *The Origins of Modern English Society 1780–1880*, London: Routledge and K. Paul.

Pisciotta, A. (1994) *Benevolent Repression: Social Control and the American Reformatory-Prison Movement*, New York: New York University Press.

Pollack, E. (2001) *Medier och Brott* [Media and Crime], Stockholm: J. M. K. Stockholms Universitet.

Poor Law Commissioners' Report of 1834 (1834) London: HMSO. [Cd. 2728].

Potter, H. (1993) *Hanging in Judgement: Religion and the Death Penalty in England from the Bloody Code to Abolition*, London: SCM Press.

Poukka, B. and Kleen, E. (1939) *Gröna Ön* [The Green Island], Stockholm, Bonnier.

Pratt, J. (1992) *Punishment in a Perfect Society: The New Zealand Penal System, 1840–1939*, Wellington: Victoria University Press.

—— (2000) 'Sex crimes and the new punitiveness', *Behavioural Sciences and the Law*, 18: 135–151.

—— (2002) *Punishment and Civilization*, London: Sage.

—— (2006) 'The dark side of paradise', *British Journal of Criminology*, 46 (4): 541–560.

—— (2007) *Penal Populism*, Oxford: Routledge.

Pratt, J. and Clarke, M. (2005) 'Penal populism in New Zealand', *Punishment and Society*, 7: 303–322.

Priestley, J. B. (1934) *English Journey*, New York: Harper and Brothers.

Prison Administration Decree 1971 (302/1971) Helsinki: Government Printer.

Prison Administration Decree 1975 (431/1975) Helsinki: Government Printer.

Prison Administration/Department of Justice [Fengselsstyrelsen / Justitiedepartementet] (1986) *Kriminalomsorgens Årbok 1980–1982*, Oslo: Norway.

[Swedish] Prison and Probation Board [Fångvårdsstyrelsen] (1962) *Report 1961*, Stockholm: Sveriges Officiella Statistik.

—— (1965) *Report 1964*, Stockholm: Sveriges Officiella Statistik.

—— (1969) *Report 1968*, Stockholm: Sveriges Officiella Statistik.

—— (1977) *Report 1976*, Stockholm: Sveriges Officiella Statistik.

—— (1980) *Report 1979*, Stockholm: Sveriges Officiella Statistik.

—— (1981) *Report 1980*, Stockholm: Sveriges Officiella Statistik.

—— (2010) *Report 2009*, Stockholm: Sveriges Officiella Statistik.

Purchas, H. T. (1903) *Bishop Harper and the Canterbury Settlement*, Christchurch, NZ: Whitcombe and Tombs.

Radzinowicz, L. (1948) *A History of English Criminal Law and its Administration: The Movement for Reform from 1750–1833*, 4 vols, London: Stevens and Sons.

Radzinowicz, L. (1991) *The Roots of the International Association of Criminal Law and their Significance: A Tribute and a Re-assessment on the Centenary of the IKV*, Freiburg: Max-Planck-Institut fu_r Ausa_ndisches und Internationales Strafrecht.

Radzinowicz, L. and Hood, R. (1986) *A History of English Criminal Law and its Administration from 1750: The Emergence of Penal Policy*, vol. 5, London: Stevens.

Rahikainen, M. (2002) 'Compulsory child labour: Parish paupers as indentured servants in Finland, c. 1810–1920', *Rural History*, 13(2): 163–178.

Ramsland, J. (1996) *With Just but Relentless Discipline: A Social History of Corrective Services in New South Wales*, Kenthurst, NSW: Kangaroo Press.

Rankin, I. (1987) *Knots and Crosses*, Garden City, NY: Doubleday.

Reade, C. (1856) *It is Never too Late to Mend*, Collins: London.

Reiner, R. (2007) *Law and Order: An Honest Citizen's Guide to Crime and Control*, Cambridge: Polity Press.

Report from the Select Committee of the House of Lords, appointed 'to take into consideration the present mode of carrying into effect capital punishments' (1856), London: HMSO. [366].

Report from the Select Committee of the House of Lords on Prison Discipline (1863) London: HMSO. [499].

Report from the Select Committee on the Public Prisons in Sydney and Cumberland (1861) Sydney: Government Printer.

Report of the Chief Probation Officer (1926) Wellington: Government Printer. [H. 20B].

Report of the Commissioners Appointed to Inquire into the Working of the Penal Servitude Acts (1879) London: HMSO. [C. 2368].

Report of the Commissioners of Prisons (1878) London: HMSO. [C. 2174].

—— (1879) London: HMSO. [C. 2442].

—— (1884) London: HMSO. [C. 4180].

—— (1888) London: HMSO. [C. 5552].

—— (1899) London: HMSO. [C. 9452].

—— (1900) London: HMSO. [Cd. 41].

—— (1912) London: HMSO. [Cd.6406].

—— (1918) London: HMSO. [Cd. 9174].

—— (1919) London: HMSO. [Cmd. 374].

—— (1920) London: HMSO. [Cmd. 972].

—— (1923–24) London: HMSO. [Cmd. 2307].

—— (1925) London: HMSO. [Cmd. 2827].

—— (1946) London: HMSO. [Cmd. 7271].

—— (1948) London: HMSO. [Cmd. 7777].

—— (1949) London: HMSO. [Cmd. 8080].

—— (1951) London: HMSO. [Cmd. 8692].

—— (1954) London: HMSO. [Cmd. 9547].

—— (1955) London: HMSO. [Cmnd. 10].

—— (1956) London: HMSO. [Cmnd. 322].

—— (1957) London: HMSO. [Cmnd. 496].

—— (1961) London: HMSO. [Cmnd. 1798].

—— (1962) London: HMSO. [Cmnd. 2030].

Report of the Committee of Inquiry on Prison Rules and Prison Dress (1889) London: HMSO. [C. 5759].

Report of the Comptroller-General of Prisons (1874) Sydney: New South Wales Department of Prisons

—— (1985) Sydney: New South Wales Department of Prisons.

—— (1892) Sydney: New South Wales Department of Prisons.

—— (1893) Sydney: New South Wales Department of Prisons.

—— (1896) Sydney: New South Wales Department of Prisons.

—— (1907) Sydney: New South Wales Department of Prisons.

—— (1908) Sydney: New South Wales Department of Prisons.

—— (1911) Sydney: New South Wales Department of Prisons.

—— (1916) Sydney: New South Wales Department of Prisons.

—— (1917) Sydney: New South Wales Department of Prisons.

—— (1927–29) Sydney: New South Wales Department of Prisons.

—— (1937) Sydney: New South Wales Department of Prisons.

—— (1949–50) Sydney: New South Wales Department of Prisons.

—— (1956–7) Sydney: New South Wales Department of Prisons.

—— (1965–6) Sydney: New South Wales Department of Prisons.

—— (1967–8) Sydney: New South Wales Department of Prisons.

Report of the Corrective Services Commission (1983) Sydney: Government Printer.

Report of the Criminal Sanctions Field (2008) Helsinki: Criminal Sanctions Agency.

Report of the Department of Corrections (1996) Wellington: Government Printer. [E. 61].

—— (1999–2000) Wellington: Government Printer.

Report of the Department of Justice (1971) Wellington, NZ: Government Printer. [H. 20]

—— (1991) Wellington: Government Printer. [E. 5].

—— (1994) Wellington: Government Printer. [E. 5].

Report of the Departmental Committee on Persistent Offenders (1932) London: HMSO. [Cmd. 4090].

Report of the Departmental Committee on Prisons (1895) London: HMSO. [C. 7702].

Report of the Departmental Committee on Sexual Offences Against Young Persons (1925) London: HMSO. [Cmd. 2561].

Report of the Departmental Committee on Sterilisation (1934) London: HMSO. [Cmd. 4485].

Report of the Departmental Committee on the Employment of Prisoners (1933) London: HMSO. [Cmd. 4462].

Report of the Director of Corrective Services (1979–1980), Sydney: Government Printer.

Report of the Director of the Corrective Services Commission (1979) Sydney: Government Printer.

—— (1980–1) Sydney: Government Printer.

—— (1983) Sydney: Government Printer.

Report of the Director of Penal Services (1957) in *Votes and Proceedings of the Legislative Assembly* 1958–1959, Melbourne: Government Printer.

Report of the Director of the [Norwegian] Prison Board 1901–1902 [Expeditionschefen for Fengselsvesenet] (1904) *Fængselsstyrelsens Aarbog 1904–1905*, vol. 86, Kristiania: Norges Officielle Statistikk.

Report of the Director of the [Norwegian] Prison Board 1903–1905 [Expeditionschefen for Fengselsvesenet] (1907) *Fængselsstyrelsens Aarbog 1903–1904*, vol. 29, Kristiania: Norges Officielle Statistikk.

Report of the Director of the [Norwegian] Prison Board 1904–1905 [Expeditionschefen for Fengselsvesenet] (1909) *Fængselsstyrelsens Aarbog 1904–1905*, vol. 80, Kristiania: Norges Officielle Statistikk.

Report of the Director of the [Norwegian] Prison Board 1965–1966 [Expeditionschefen for Fengselsvesenet] (1973) Oslo: Fengselsstyret.

Report of the Director of the [Norwegian] Prison Board [Expeditionschefen for Fengselsvesenet] (1973) *Fengselsstyrets Årbok 1950–1969*, Oslo: Fengselsstyret.

Report of the [Finnish] Prison Service for 1885 [Fångvården] (1887) *Fångvårdsstyrelsens berättelse för år 1885*, Bidrag till Finlands Officiela Statistik, vol. 4, Helsinki: Kejserliga Senatens Tryckeri.

Report of the [Finnish] Prison Service for 1886 (1888) *Fångvårdsstyrelsens berättelse för år 1886*, Bidrag till Finlands Officiela Statistik, vol. 3, Helsinki: Kejserliga Senatens Tryckeri.

Report of the [Finnish] Prison Service for 1890 (1892) *Fångvårdsstyrelsens berättelse för år 1890*, Bidrag till Finlands Officiela Statistik, vol. 5, Helsinki: Kejserliga Senatens Tryckeri.

—— (1925) *Vankeinhoitolaitoksen Kertomus Vuodelta 1922/Fångvårdsväsendets Berättelse för år 1922*, Suomen Virallinen Tilasto/Finlands Officiella Statistik , vol. 14, Helsinki: Valtioneuvoston Kirjapaino.

Report of the Inspector of Prisons (1881) Wellington: Government Printer. [H. 4].

—— (1895) Wellington: Government Printer.

—— (1899) Wellington: Government Printer.

Report of the Inter-Departmental Committee on Physical Deterioration (1904) London: HMSO [Cd. 2175].

Report of the [Norwegian] Penal Institutions Commission (1841) [Beretning om Beskaffenheden af Norges strafanstalter og Fangepleie m.v.] Christiania: Norway.

Report of the Prison Administration Board (2006), available at http://www.kriminalvarden. se/upload/statistik/kos/2006/KOSrapport_2006.pdf.

Report of the Prisoners' Education Committee (1896) London: HMSO. [C. 8154].

Report of the State Imprisonment Commission (1969) Helsinki: Ministry of Justice.

Report on the Department of Justice (1954) Wellington, NZ: Government Printer. [H. 20].

—— (1961) Wellington, NZ: Government Printer. [H. 20].

—— (1963) Wellington, NZ: Government Printer. [H. 20].

—— (1966) Wellington, NZ: Government Printer. [H. 20].

—— (1971) Wellington, NZ: Government Printer. [H. 20].

Report on the Prisons Department (1926) Wellington, NZ: Government Printer. [H. 20].

—— (1928) Wellington, NZ: Government Printer. [H. 20].

—— (1934) Wellington, NZ: Government Printer. [H. 20].

—— (1936) Wellington, NZ: Government Printer. [H. 20].

—— (1939) Wellington, NZ: Government Printer. [H. 20].

—— (1948) Wellington, NZ: Government Printer. [H. 20].

—— (1949) Wellington, NZ: Government Printer. [H. 20].

—— (1951) Wellington, NZ: Government Printer. [H. 20].

Report on the Work of the Prison Department (1966) London: HMSO. [Cmnd. 3408].

—— (1967) London: HMSO. [Cmnd. 3774].

—— (1968) London: HMSO. [Cmnd. 4186].

—— (1971) London: HMSO. [Cmnd. 4486].

—— (1975) London: HMSO. [Cmnd. 6523].

—— (1976) London: HMSO. [Cmnd. 6877].

—— (1977) London: HMSO. [Cmnd. 7290]

—— (1980) London: HMSO. [Cmnd. 8228].

Report on the Work of the Prison Service (1986–87) London: HMSO. [Cm. 246].

—— (1990–91) London: HMSO. [Cm. 1724].

Richardson, R. (2012) *Dickens and the Workhouse*, Oxford: Oxford University Press.

Rickards, C. (1920) *A Prison Chaplain on Dartmoor*, London: Edward Arnold.

Riley, D. (1983) *War in the Nursery: Theories of the Child and Mother*, London: Virago.

Roberts, H. (1850) *The Dwellings of the Labouring Classes*, London: Savill and Edwards.

Roberts, M. (1967) *Essays in Swedish History*, London: Weidenfeld and Nicolson.

Roberts, R. (1971) *The Classic Slum: Salford Life in the First Quarter of the Century*, Manchester: Manchester University Press.

Robinson, P. (1987) *Gallows View*, New York: Schribner.

Rock, P. (1995) *Helping Victims of Crime*, Oxford: Clarendon Press.

Rodnick, D. (1955) *The Norwegians: A Study in National Culture*, Washington: Public Affairs Press.

Roll-Hansen, N. (1996) 'Norwegian eugenics: Sterilization as social reform', in G. Broberg and N. Roll-Hansen (eds) *Eugenics and the Welfare State: Sterilization Policy in Denmark, Sweden, Norway and Finland*, East Lansing, MI: Michigan University Press.

Romilly, S. (1820) *The Speeches of Sir Samuel Romilly in the House of Commons*, vol. 1, London: J. Ridgway and Sons.

Roper, C. M. (1989) *Prison Review – Te Ara Hou: The New Way/Ministerial Committee of Inquiry into Prisons System*, Wellington, NZ: Government Printer.

Roper, W. F. (1955) 'Human relations in institutional treatment. Human relations in English prisons', *Howard Journal of Criminal Justice*, 9 (2): 91–100.

Rose, N. (1985) *The Psychological Complex*, London: Routledge and Kegan Paul.

Rossa, J. (1882) *Irish Rebels in English Prisons: A Record of Prison Life*, New York: P. J. Kennedy.

Rossland, L.A. (2007) 'The professionalization of the intolerable: Popular crime journalism in Norway', *Journalism Studies*, 8 (1): 137–152.

Rothery, A. (1939) *Norway: Changing and Changeless*, London: Faber & Faber.

Rothstein, B. (2001) 'Social capital in the social democratic welfare state', *Politics and Society*, 29: 207–241.

Rothstein, B. and Uslaner, E. M. (2005) 'All for all: Equality, corruption and social trust', *World Politics*, 50: 41–72.

Rowntree, B. S. (1902) *Poverty: A Study of Town Life*, London: Macmillan.

Royal Commission on Capital Punishment (1866) *Report of the Royal Commission on Capital Punishment*, London: HMSO. [3590].

Royal Commission on Capital Punishment (1953) *Report of the Royal Commission on Capital Punishment 1949–1953*, London: HMSO. [Cmd. 8932].

Royal Commission on Population Report (1949) London: HMSO. [Cmd. 7695].

Royal [Swedish] Prison Board [Kungliga Fångvårdsstyrelsen] (1912) *Report 1911*, Stockholm: Sveriges Officiella Statistik.

—— (1913) *Report 1912*, Stockholm: Sveriges Officiella Statistik.

—— (1928) *Report 1927*, Stockholm: Sveriges Officiella Statistik.

—— (1941) *Report 1938–1940*, Stockholm: Sveriges Officiella Statistik.

—— (1942) *Report 1941*, Stockholm: Sveriges Officiella Statistik.

—— (1943) *Report 1942*, Stockholm: Sveriges Officiella Statistik.

—— (1947) *Report 1946–1947*, Stockholm: Sveriges Officiella Statistik.

—— (1952) *Report 1951*, Stockholm: Sveriges Officiella Statistik.

—— (1954) *Report 1953*, Stockholm: Sveriges Officiella Statistik.

—— (1956–57) *Report 1956–1957*, Stockholm: Sveriges Officiella Statistik.

Rudstedt, G. (1972) *Långholmen: Spinnhuset och fängelset under två sekler* [Langholmen: From Spin House to Prison over Two Centuries], Stockholm: A.-B. Nordiska Bokhandeln.

Rudstedt, G. (1994) *I Fängelset: Den Svenska Fångvårdens Historia* [In Prison: The History of the Swedish Prison System], Stockholm: Tidens.

Ruggles-Brise, E. (1921) *The English Prison System*, New York: Garland.

Runciman, W. G. (1966) *Relative Deprivation and Social Justice: A Study of Attitudes to Social Inequality in Twentieth-Century England*, Berkeley: University of California Press.

Russell, P. (2002) 'The brash colonial: Class and comportment in nineteenth-century Australia', *Transactions of the Royal Historical Society*, 12: 431–453.

Rylander, G. (1954–55) 'Treatment of mentally abnormal offenders in Sweden', *British Journal of Delinquency*, 5: 262–268.

Sampson, A. (1962) *Anatomy of Britain*, New York: Harper and Row.

Sargent, M. (1973) *Alcoholism as a Social Problem*, St Lucia: University of Queensland Press.

Scarman, L. (1981) *The Brixton Disorders, 10–12 April 1981*, London: HMSO.

Schaaning, E. (2007) *Menneskelaboratoriet: Botsfengslets Historie* [The Human Laboratory: A History of Botsfengslet], Oslo: Scandinavian Academic Press.

Schlyter, K. (1934) *Depopulate the Prison!* [Avfolka Fangelserna!:Ttal a_ Auditorium den 5 December 1934], Stockholm: Tiden.

—— (1946) *Straffbalk eller Skyddsbalk? Tretton ars Strafflagsreformer* [Penal Code or Protection Code? Thirteen Years of Penal Law Reform], Stockholm: Nordiska Bokhandein.

Schmidt, F. and Strömholm, S. (1964) *Legal Values in Modern Sweden*, Stockholm: The Bedminster Press.

Scobie, I. (1972) *Sweden*, London: Ernest Benn.

Scott, F. D. (1988) *Sweden, the Nation's History*, Chicago: Southern Illinois University Press.

Second Report of the Royal Sanitary Commission (1871) London: HMSO. [C. 281].

Seip, A. -L. (1984) 'Motive forces behind the new social policy after 1870. Norway on the European scene', *Journal of Scandinavian History*, 9 (4): 329–341.

Sellin, T. (1948) *Recent Penal Legislation in Sweden*, Stockholm: Isaac Marcus Boktryckeri-Aktiebolag.

Selzer, A. (2002) *Governors' Wives in Colonial Australia*, Canberra: National Library of Australia.

Seth, I. (1984) *Överheten och svärdet – dödsstraffsdebatten i Sverige 1809–1974* [The Powers and the Sword: The Death Penalty Debate in Sweden 1809–1974], Stockholm: Stockholm Institute för Rättshistorisk Forskning.

Sherer, J. (1853) *The Gold-Finder of Australia*, London: Clarke, Beeton and Co.

Sherington, G. (1980) *Australia's Immigrants, 1788–1978*, Sydney: George Allen and Unwin.

Shirer, W. L. (1955) *The Challenge of Scandinavia: Norway, Denmark, Sweden and Finland in our Time*, Boston: Little, Brown.

Sidney, J and Sidney, S. (1848) *Sidney's Australian Handbook: How to Settle and Succeed in Australia*, London: Pelham Richardson.

Siegfried, A. (1914) *Democracy in New Zealand*, trans. E. V. Burns, London: Bell.

Sillanpää, F. E. (1938) *Meek Heritage*, London: Putnam.

Sim, J. (2009) *Punishment and Prisons: Power and the Carceral State*, London: Sage.

Simmons, H. G. (1978) 'Explaining social policy: The English Mental Deficiency Act of 1913', *Journal of Social History*, 11 (3): 387–403.

Simon, E. D. (1939) *The Smaller Democracies*, London: Victor Gollancz.

Simon, J. (2007) *Governing Through Crime: How the War on Crime Transformed American Democracy and Created a Culture of Fear*, New York: Oxford University Press.

Simson, G. (1949) 'Franz von Liszt und die schwedische kriminalpolitik' [Franz von Liszt and the Swedish Criminal Justice Policy] , in K. Schlyter (ed.) *Festskrift Tillägnad f.d. Presidenten, Förutvarande Statsrådet juris Doktor Karl Schlyter den 21 December 1949* [Festschrift for Karl Schlyter], Stockholm: Svensk Juristtidning.

Smiles, S. (1859) *Self-Help*, London: John Murray.

Smith, A. (1776) *An Enquiry into the Nature and Causes of the Wealth of Nations*, Dublin: Whitestone.

Smith, B. (2008) *Australia's Birthstain: The Startling Legacy of the Convict Era*, Crows Nest, NSW: Allen and Unwin.

Smith, T. (1915) *The Soul of Germany: A Twelve Years' Study of the People from Within, 1902–14*, New York: George H. Doran Co.

Smolej, M. and Kivivuori, J. (2008) 'Crime news trends in Finland: A review of recent research' *Journal of Scandinavian Studies in Criminology and Crime Prevention*, 9 (2): 202–219.

Socialdepartementet (2003) Sprutbyesprogram for Narkotikamissbrukare. Remissvar [Syringe Exchange Programme for Drug Abusers. Responses to Committee Report], Stockholm: Department of Social Affairs.

Soine, V. (1955) 'About the appropriateness of our penal system', *Against Crime*, 2: 1–36.

—— (1958) 'Finlands Fångvård [Finland's Prisoner Care]', *Nordisk Tidsskrift for Kriminalvidenskab*, 46: 238–256.

—— (1964) 'Open institutions in Finland', in M. Lopez-Ray (ed.) *Studies in Penology*, The Hague: Martin Nijhoff.

Sørnes, T. (2009) *Ondskap: De Henrettede i Norge 1815–1876* [Evil: The Executions in Norway 1815–1876], Oslo: Schibsted Forlag.

Spencer, H. (1842/1981) 'The proper sphere of government', in H. Spencer, *The Man Versus the State, With Six Essays on Government, Society and Freedom*, Indianapolis: Liberty Classics.

Stang Dahl, T. (1985) *Child Welfare and Social Defense*, Oslo: Norwegian University Press.

Statens Folkhälsoinstitut (2011) En samlad återredovisning av regeringens AND Tuppdrag till Statens folkhälsoinstitut 2010, Online, available at <http://www.fhi.se/Documents/Om-oss/redovisade-uppdrag/2011/En-samlad-aterraportering-ANTD-20110331.pdf>, (last accessed 8 May 2012).

Statistics Finland (2012a) 'Prisoners, 1974–2007', Online, available at <http://www.stat.fi/til/van/2007/van_2007_2008–06–27_tau_001.html> (last accessed 8 June 2012).

—— (2012b) 'Criminality' Online, available at <http://www.stat.fi/tup/suoluk/suoluk_oikeusolot_en.html> (last accessed 8 June 2012).

Statistics Norway (2012a) 'Population of penal institutions', Online, available at <http://www.ssb.no/histstat/tabeller/8–8-12t.txt> (last accessed 8 June 2012).

—— (2012b) 'Offences reported to the police, by group of offence and scene of crime (county) 2010', Online, available at < http://www.ssb.no/english/yearbook/tab/tab-148.html> (last accessed 8 June 2012).

Stenius, H. (1997) 'The good life is a life of conformity: The impact of Lutheran tradition on Nordic political culture', in B. Strath and O. Sorenson (eds) *The Cultural Construction of Norden*, Oslo: Scandinavian University Press.

—— (2003) 'How Finland has the most Nordic political culture', in W. Rothholz (ed.) *Political Culture in the Baltic Region and in Eastern Europe*, Berlin: Aland-Verlag.

Stephen, J. F. (1883) *A History of the Criminal Law of England, vol. 2*, London: Macmillan.

Stephen, L. (1895) *The Life of Sir James Fitzjames Stephen*, London: Smith, Elder & Co.

Stolt, R., Blomqvist, P. and Winblad, U. (2010) 'Privatization of social services: Quality differences in Swedish elderly care', *Social Science and Medicine*, 72: 560–567.

Stortinget (1896) *Udkast til Almindelig borgerlig Straffelov for Kongeriget Norge. II. Motiver* [Draft for Penal Code for the Kingdom of Norway. II. Motives], Kristiania: Det Steens Bogtrykkeri.

Stout, R. (1911) 'The Message of Eugenics', *Grey River Argus*, 12 July: 6.

Strindberg, A. (1890) *By the Open Sea*, Stockholm: Bonnier.

Strode, H. (1949) *Sweden, Model for a World*, New York: Harcourt, Brace.

Sundbärg, G. (1911a) *Det Svenska Folklynnet* [The Swedish Character], Stockholm: P. A. Norstedt & Soner.

—— (1911b) *Official Report on Emigration*, vol. 5, Stockholm: P.A. Norstedt.

Sundell, J.-O. (2000) 'Karl Schlyter – a Swedish lawyer and politician', *Scandinavian Studies in Law*, 40: 505–514.

Sundin, J., Hogstedt, C., Lindberg, J. and Moberg, H. (eds) (2005) *Svenska Folkets Hälsa i Historiskt Perspektiv* [Swedish People's Health in Historical Perspective], Stockholm: Statens folkhälsoinstitut.

Sutch, W. B. (1971) *The Responsible Society in New Zealand*, Christchurch, NZ: Whitcombe and Tombs.

Sutherland, J. M. (1908) *Recidivism: Habitual Criminality, and Habitual Petty Delinquency: A Problem in Sociology, Psycho-Pathology and Criminology*, Edinburgh: W. Green and Sons.

Svensson, C. (2009) *Culture Shock! Sweden: A Guide to Customs and Etiquette*, Tarrytown, NY: Marshall Cavendish Editions.

Swedish Law Commission (1815) *Betänkanda* [Proposition] Bihang till Riks-standens Protocoller, Stockholm: Marquardska Boktryckeriet.

—— (1826) *Betänkande* [Proposition] Bihang till Riks-standens Protocoller, Stockholm: Marquardska Boktryckeriet.

—— (1832) Stockholm: Marquardska Boktryckeriet.

Swedish National Council for Crime Prevention (2012) 'Reported offences, 1950–2011', Online, available at <http://www.bra.se/bra/bra-in-english/home/crime-and-statistics/crime-statistics/statistical-tables.html> (last accessed 8 June 2012).

Swedish National Drug Policy Co-ordinator (2003) *Is Cannabis a Harmless Drug?*, Stockholm: National Institute of Public Health.

Swedish Social Democrat Manifest (2006) [Valmanifest: Alla Ska Med. Social Demokratiskt Manifest], Online, available at <http://www.socialdemokraterna.se> (last accessed 15 April 2012).

Swedish Social Welfare Board (1952) *Social Sweden*, Stockholm: The Social Welfare Board.

Taine, H. (1874) *Notes on England*, trans. W. F. Rae, London: W. Isbister.

Tallack, W. (1889) *Penological and Preventative Principles.* London: Wertheimer, Lea & Co.

Tate, A. (1975) 'The justice function of the judge', *Southern University Law Review*, 1 (2): 250–265.

Taylor, I. (1982) *Law and Order: Arguments for Socialism*, London: Macmillan.

Temmes, M. (1998) 'Finland and new public management', *International Review of Administrative Sciences*, 64 (3): 441–456.

Thackeray, W. (1840) 'Going to see a man hanged', *Fraser's Magazine*, August 1840: 150–158.

Tham, H. (1995) 'Law and order as a leftist project? The case of Sweden', *Punishment and Society*, 3: 409–426.

—— (1998) Swedish drug policy: A successful model?, *European Journal of Criminal Policy and Research*, 6 (3): 395–414.

Thatcher, M. (1993) *The Downing Street Years*, New York: Harper Collins.

Therborn, G., Kjellberg, A., Marklund, S. and Ohlund, U. (1978) 'Sweden before and after social democracy: A first overview', *Acta Sociologica*, 21 (Suppl.): 37–58.

Thomas, W. W. (1892) *Sweden and the Swedes*, New York: Rand, McNally.

Thompson, F. M. L. (1988) *The Rise of Respectable Society: A Social History of Victorian Britain, 1830–1900*, Cambridge, MA: Harvard University Press.

Thompson, J. (2009) *Snow Angels,* New York: G. P. Putnam's Sons.

Tilton, T. (1990) *The Political Theory of Swedish Social Democracy*, New York: Oxford University Press.

Timonen, V. (2003) *Restructuring the Welfare State: Globalisation and Social Policy Reform in Finland and Sweden*, Cheltenham: Edward Elgar.

Titmuss, R. (1950) *Problems of Social Policy*, London: Longmans Green.

Tomasson, R. (1970) *Sweden: Prototype of Modern Society*, New York: Random House.

Townsend , P. (1957) *The Family Life of Old People*, London: Cox and Wyman.

Toynbee, P. (2012) 'Welfare cuts: Now they're slamming the door on the truly desperate', *The Guardian*, 24 January, p. 29.

Travers, R. (1911) *Letters from Finland, August, 1908–March, 1909*, London: K. Paul, Trench, Trubner and Co.

Trevelyan, G. M. (1942) *English Social History: A Survey of Six Centuries, Chaucer to Queen Victoria*, London: Longmans, Green and Co.

Trydegård, G. -B. (2000) 'From poorhouse overseer to production manager: One hundred years of old-age care in Sweden reflected in the development of an occupation', *Ageing and Society*, 20: 571–579.

Tsokhas, K. (2001) *Making a Nation State: Cultural Identity, Economic Nationalism and Sexuality in Australian History*, Carlton South: Melbourne University Press.

Tweedie, A. (1897) *Through Finland in Carts*, Macmillan: New York.

Tyler, T. and Boeckmann, R. (1997) 'Three strikes and you are out, but why? The psychology of public support for punishing rule breakers', *Law and Society Review*, 31: 237–265.

Ugelvik, T. (2013) 'Less eligibility resurrected? Immigration, exclusion and the Norwegian welfare state prison', in K. Franko Aaas and M. Bosworth (eds) *The Borders of Punishment*, Oxford: Oxford University Press.

Uusitalo, P. (1970) 'Reoffending after release from open and closed institutions', *Nordisk Tidskrift for Krimnalvidenskab*, 58: 324–347.

Vance, J. (2009) *A History of Canadian Culture*, Oxford: Oxford University Press.

van Dijk, J. van Kesteren, J. and Smit, P. (2007) *Criminal Victimisation in International Perspective: Key Findings from the 2004–2005 ICVS and EU ICS*, The Hague: Tilburg University; UNODC.

van Zyl Smit, D. (2007) 'Prisoners' rights', in Y. Jewkes (ed.) *Handbook on Prisons*, Cullompton, UK: Willan.

von Hayek, F. A. (1944) *The Road to Serfdom*, Chicago, IL: University of Chicago Press.

von Hirsch, A. (1985) *Past or Future Crimes: Deservedness and Dangerousness in the Sentencing of Criminals*, New Brunswick: Rutgers University Press.

von Hofer, H. (2011) 'Punishment and crime in Scandinavia, 1750–2008', *Crime and Justice*, 40 (1): 33–107.

von Liszt, F. (1882) 'Der Zweckgedanke im Strafrecht', in F. von Liszt (1905) *Strafrechtliche Aufsätze und Vorträge. Erster Band. 1875–1891* [The Idea of Purpose in Criminal Law. [In] Criminal Law Essays and Lectures, First Volume], Berlin: J. Guttentag.

—— (1897) 'Die strafrechtliche Zurechnungsfähigkeit' [Criminal Accountability], *Die Zeitschrift für die gesamte Strafrechtswissenschaft* , [Journal of Criminal Justice Research],17: 70–84.

Walmsley, J. (2000) 'Women and the Mental Deficiency Act of 1913, *British Journal of Learning Disabilities*, 28: 65–70.

Warbey, W., Palmer, A. M. F., Champion, A. J and Whyte, A. (1950) *Modern Norway: A Study in Social Democracy*, London: Fabian Publications.

Ward, D. (1972) 'Inmate rights and prison reform in Sweden and Denmark', *Journal of Criminal Law, Criminology and Police Science*, 63: 240–255.

Ward, R. (1958) *The Australian Legend*, Melbourne: Oxford University Press.

Ward, S. (2001) *Australia and the British Embrace: The Demise of the Imperial Ideal*, Melbourne: Melbourne University Publishing.

Weatherburn, D., Matka, E. and Lind, B. (1996) *Crime Perception and Reality: Public Perceptions of the Risk of Criminal Victimisation in Australia*, Crime and Justice Bulletin 28, Sydney: NSW Bureau of Crime Statistics and Research.

Webb, B. (1926) *My Apprenticeship*, London: Longmans, Green and Co.

Webb, B. and Webb, S. (1922) *English Prisons under Local Government*, London: Longmans.

—— (1959) *Visit to New Zealand in 1898: Beatrice Webb's Diary*, Wellington: Price, Milburn.

Webb, L. (1940) *Government in New Zealand*, Wellington, NZ: Department of Internal Affairs.

Webb, S. (1909) 'The decline in the birth rate', *Fabian Tract No. 131*, London: The Fabian Society.

Wells, H. G. (1904) 'Discussion of F. Galton's 'Eugenics: Its definition, scope and aims', *American Journal of Sociology*, 10 (1): 10–11.

Wessel, T. (2001) 'Losing control? Inequality and social dividions in Oslo', *European Planning Studies*, 9: 889–906.

Westerberg, B. (1994) 'Reply to Arthur Gould: "Pollution rituals in Sweden: The pursuit of a drug free society"', *International Journal of Social Welfare*, 3 (2): 94–96.

Whiting, J. (1975) *Prison Reform in Gloucestershire, 1776–1820: A Study of the Work of Sir George Onesiphorous Paul*, London: Phillimore and Co.

Whitman, J. (2003) *Harsh Justice: Criminal Punishment and the Widening Divide between America and Europe*, New York: Oxford University Press.

Wicker, T. (1975) 'Sweden: Almost the best of everything', *New York Times*, 28 September: 10.

Wieselgren, S. (1895) *Sveriges Fängelser och Fångvård från Äldre tider till Våra Dagar: Ett Bidrag till Svensk Kulturhistoria* [Swedish Prisons and Prison Care from Older Days to our Times: A Contribution to Swedish Cultural History], Stockholm: P. A. Norstedt & Söner.

Wilensky, H. (2002) *Rich Democracies: Political Economy, Public Policy, and Performance*, Berkeley: University of California Press.

Willett, T. C. (1964) *Criminal on the Road: A Study of Serious Motoring Offences and Those who Commit Them*, London: Tavistock Publications.

Wilson, R. (2003) 'Portrait of a profession revisited', *Public Administration*, 81: 365–378.

Wines, E. (1878) *The Actual State of Prison Reform throughout the Civilized World: A Discourse Pronounced at the Opening of the International Prison Congress of Stockholm, Aug. 20, 1878*, Stockhom: Central-Tryckeriet.

Winnicott, D. W. (1957) *Mother and Child: A Primer of First Relationships*, London: Tavistock.

Witte, J. (2002) *Law and Protestantism: The Legal Teachings of the Lutheran Reformation*, Cambridge: Cambridge University Press.

Wood, F. L. W. (1958) *This New Zealand*, London: Hammond, Hammond and Co. Ltd.

Woodcock, J. (1994) *Report of the Enquiry into the Escape of Six Prisoners from the Special Security Unit at Whitemoor Prison, Cambridgeshire, on Friday 9th September 1994*, London: HMSO. [Cm. 2741].

Woolf, Lord Justice (1991) *Prison Disturbances April 1990. Report of an Inquiry by the Rt Hon Lord Justice Woolf (parts I and II) and His Honour Judge Stephen Tumim (part II)*, London: HMSO. [Cm. 1456].

Wootton, B. (1959) *Social Science and Social Pathology*, London: Allen & Unwin.
Young, W. (1979) *Community Service Orders: The Development and Use of a New Penal Measure*, London: Heinemann Educational Books.
Zagaris, B. (1977) 'The Finnish penal system: Recent reforms', *New England Journal on Prison Law*, 3: 437–486.
Zander, M. (2004) *The Law-Making Process*, 6th edn, Cambridge: Cambridge University Press.
Zetterberg, H.L. (1995) *Before and Beyond the Welfare State: Three Lectures*, Stockholm: City University Press.

Cases cited

M'Naghten's Case (1843), 10 C and F, 200.
R v Sullivan [1913] 1 Cr App R 201.
R v Bell [2003] HC Auckland, T020505, BCL 360.
R v *Bibi* [1980] 1WLR, 1193.
R v Hammersly (1925) 14 Cr App R 118.
R v Lundy (2002) CA106/02, CA137/02, 19 CRNZ 574.
R v Mitchell (1912) 7 Cr App R 283.
R v Winn (1925) 19 Cr App R 1.
Taunoa and others v Attorney-General (2006) SC 6/2006, 40 VUWLR 613.

Index